HARDCORE ANXIETY

A Graphic Guide to Punk Rock and Mental Health

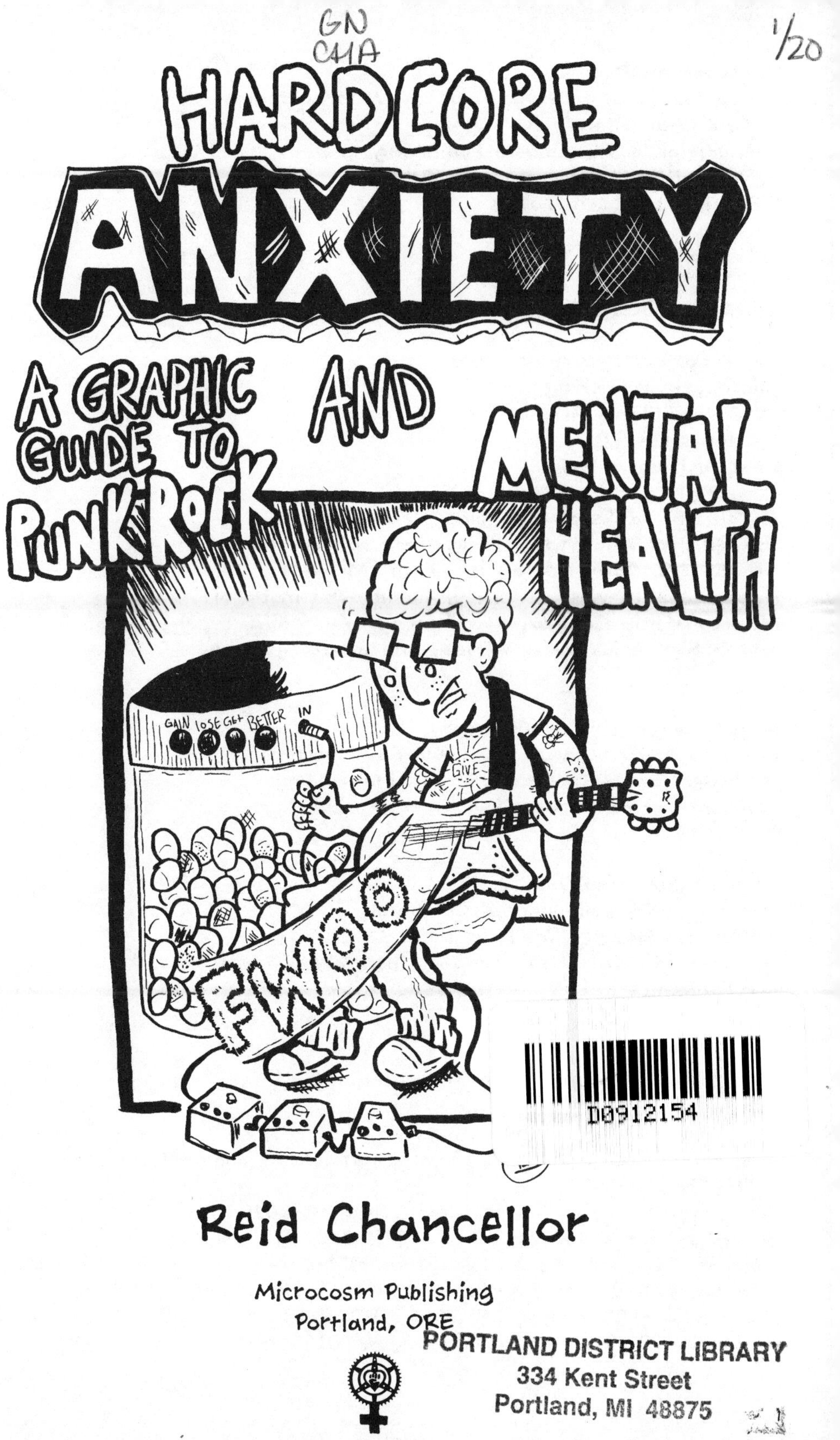
GAIN LOSE GET BETTER IN
GIVE
FWOOO

Reid Chancellor

Microcosm Publishing
Portland, ORE

Hardcore Anxiety
A Graphic Guide to Punk Rock and Mental Health
© Reid Chancellor
This edition © Microcosm Publishing
First published, September 10, 2019
ISBN 978-1-62106-767-2

This is Microcosm #345

Edited and designed by Joe Biel

For a catalog, write or visit:
Microcosm Publishing
2752 N Williams Ave.
Portland, OR 97227
www.Microcosm.Pub

To join the ranks of high-class stores
that feature Microcosm titles, talk to your rep:
In the U.S. Como (Atlantic), Fujii (Midwest),
Book Travelers West (Pacific), Turnaround in Europe,
Manda/UTP in Canada, New South in Australia,
and GPS in Asia, India, Africa, and South America.

If you bought this on Amazon,
we're so sorry because you could have gotten
it cheaper and supported a small, independent
 publisher at Microcosm.Pub

Global labor conditions are bad,
and our roots in industrial Cleveland
in the 70s and 80s made us appreciate
the need to treat workers right. Therefore,
our books are MADE IN THE USA.

T 123372

Library of Congress Cataloging-in-Publication Data

Names: Chancellor, Reid, author, illustrator.
Title: Hardcore anxiety : a graphic guide to punk rock and mental health /
    Reid Chancellor.
Description: Portland, OR : Microcosm Publishing, 2019.
Identifiers: LCCN 2019017912 I ISBN 9781621067672 (pbk.)
Subjects: LCSH: Punk rock musicians--Mental health--Comic books, strips, etc.
I Chancellor, Reid--Comic books, strips, etc. I LCGFT: Graphic novels.
Classification: LCC ML3838 .C45 2019 I DDC 781.66092--dc23
LC record available at https://lccn.loc.gov/2019017912

FOR KRISTAN:

Neither THIS Book NOR I Would exist Without your Support, CARE, AND LOVE. THANK you.

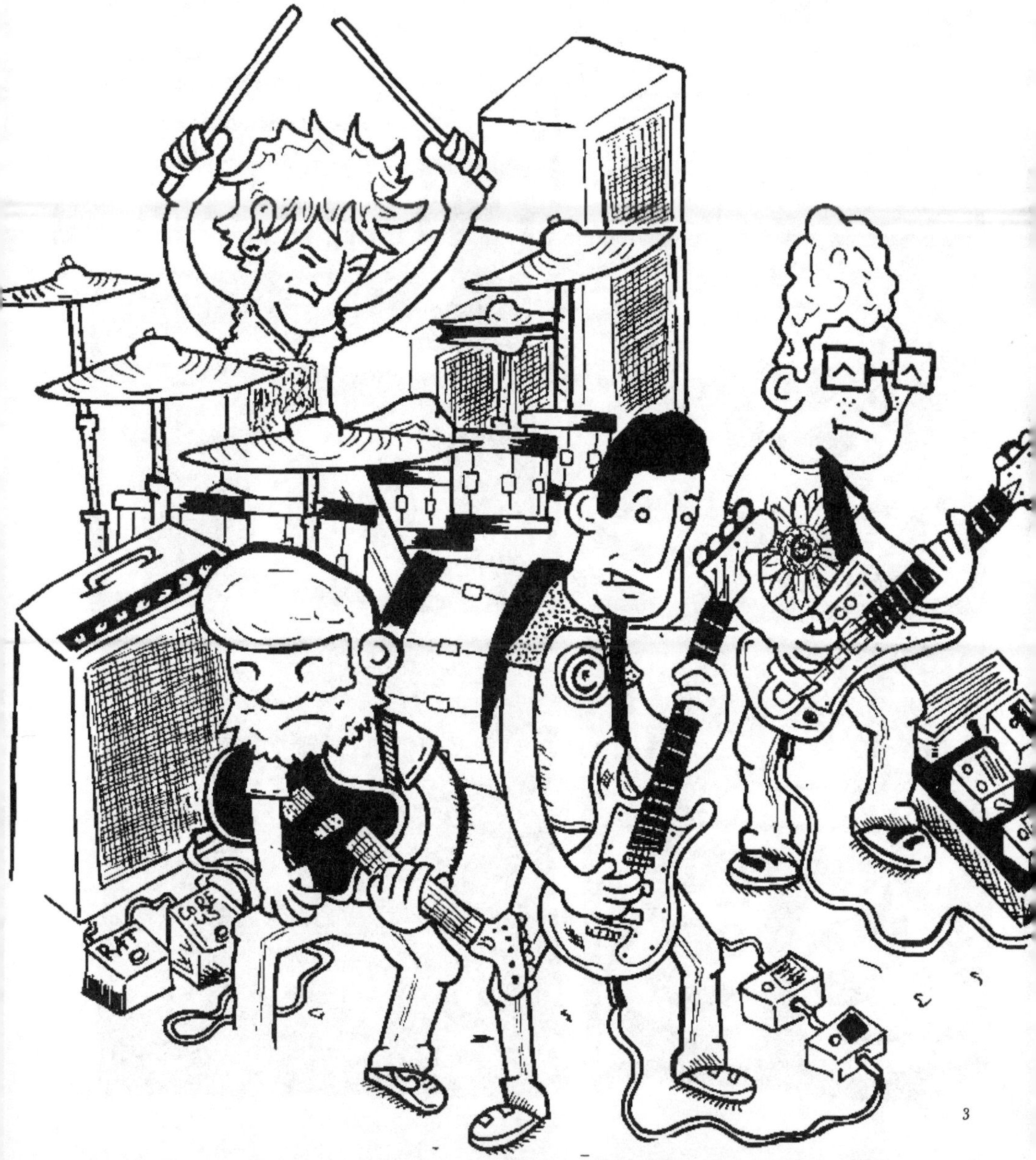
RAT

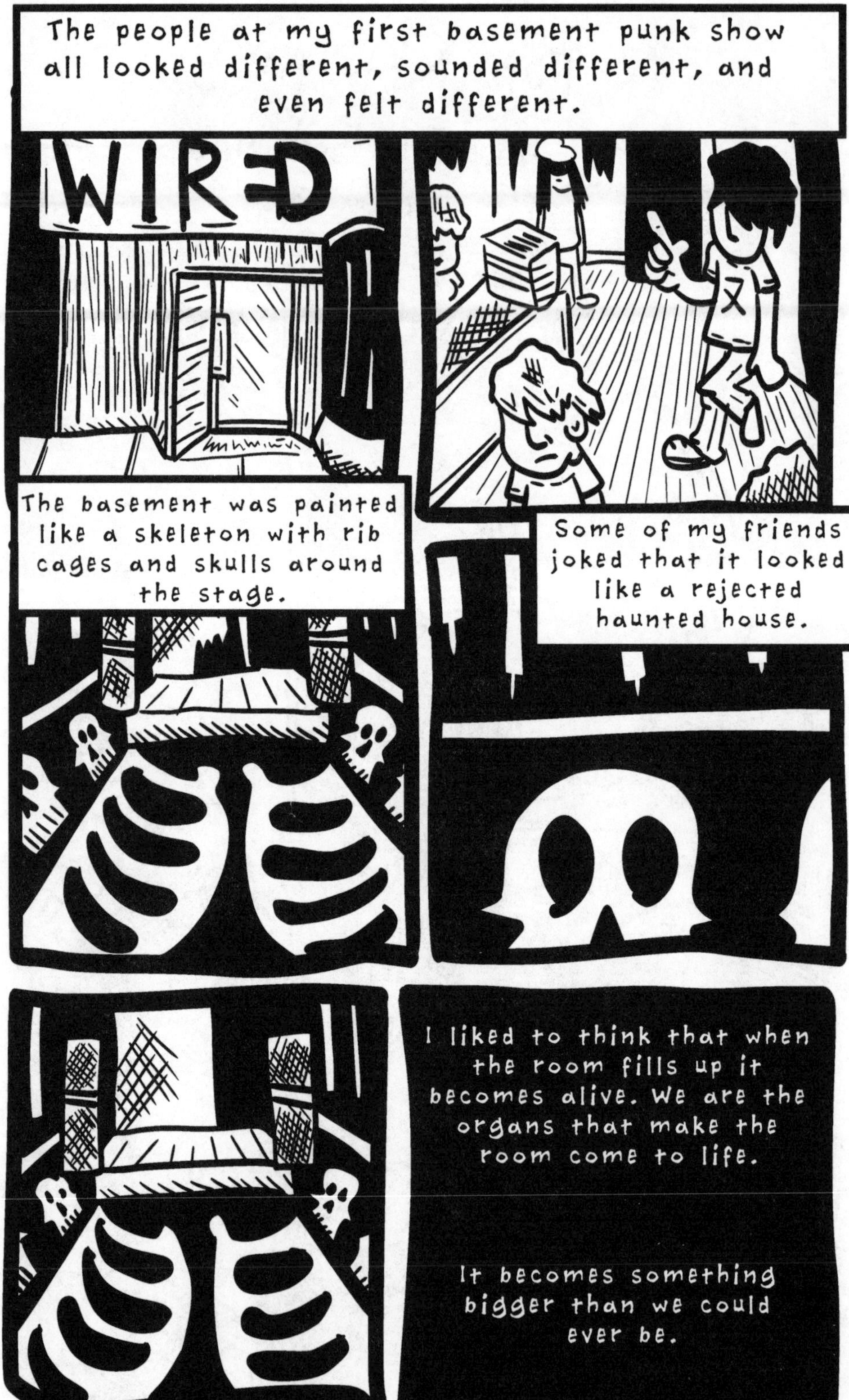

The people at my first basement punk show all looked different, sounded different, and even felt different.
WIRED
The basement was painted like a skeleton with rib cages and skulls around the stage.
Some of my friends joked that it looked like a rejected haunted house.
I liked to think that when the room fills up it becomes alive. We are the organs that make the room come to life.
It becomes something bigger than we could ever be.

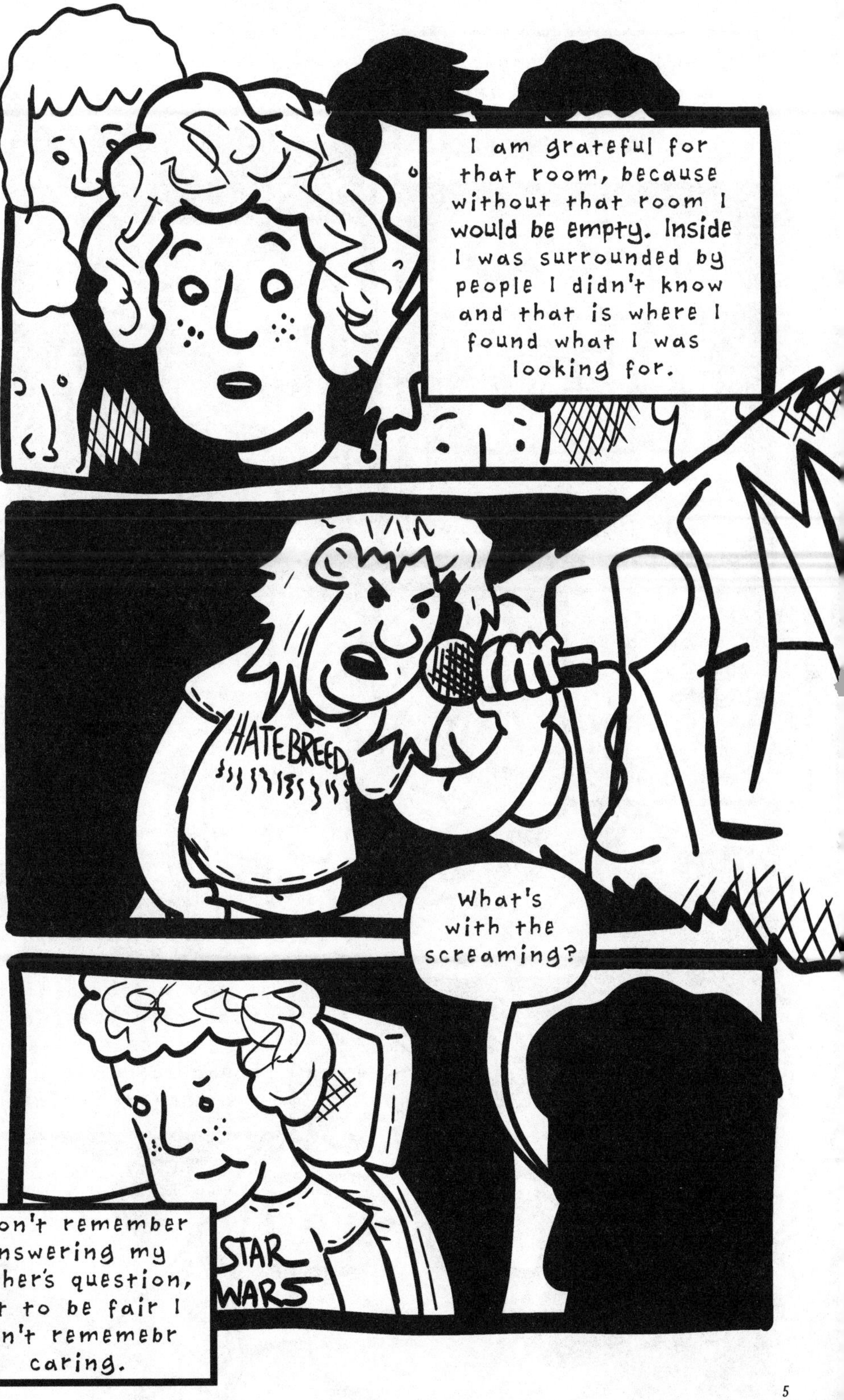
I am grateful for that room, because without that room I would be empty. Inside I was surrounded by people I didn't know and that is where I found what I was looking for.
HATEBREED
What's with the screaming?
STAR WARS
I don't remember answering my father's question, but to be fair I don't rememebr caring.

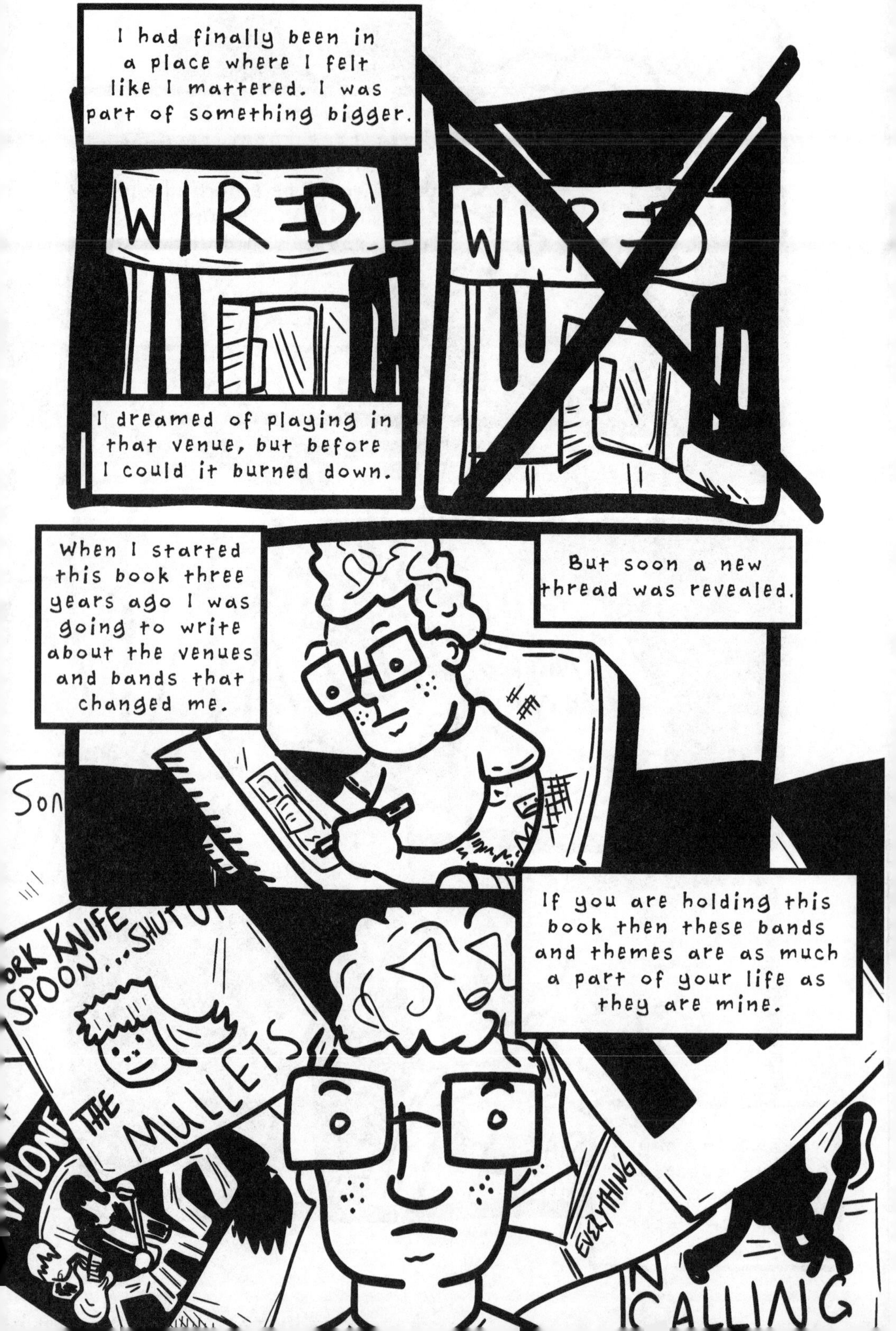
I had finally been in a place where I felt like I mattered. I was part of something bigger.
WIRED
I dreamed of playing in that venue, but before I could it burned down.
When I started this book three years ago I was going to write about the venues and bands that changed me.
But soon a new thread was revealed.
If you are holding this book then these bands and themes are as much a part of your life as they are mine.
FORK KNIFE SPOON...SHUT UP
THE MULLETS
EVERYTHING
CALLING

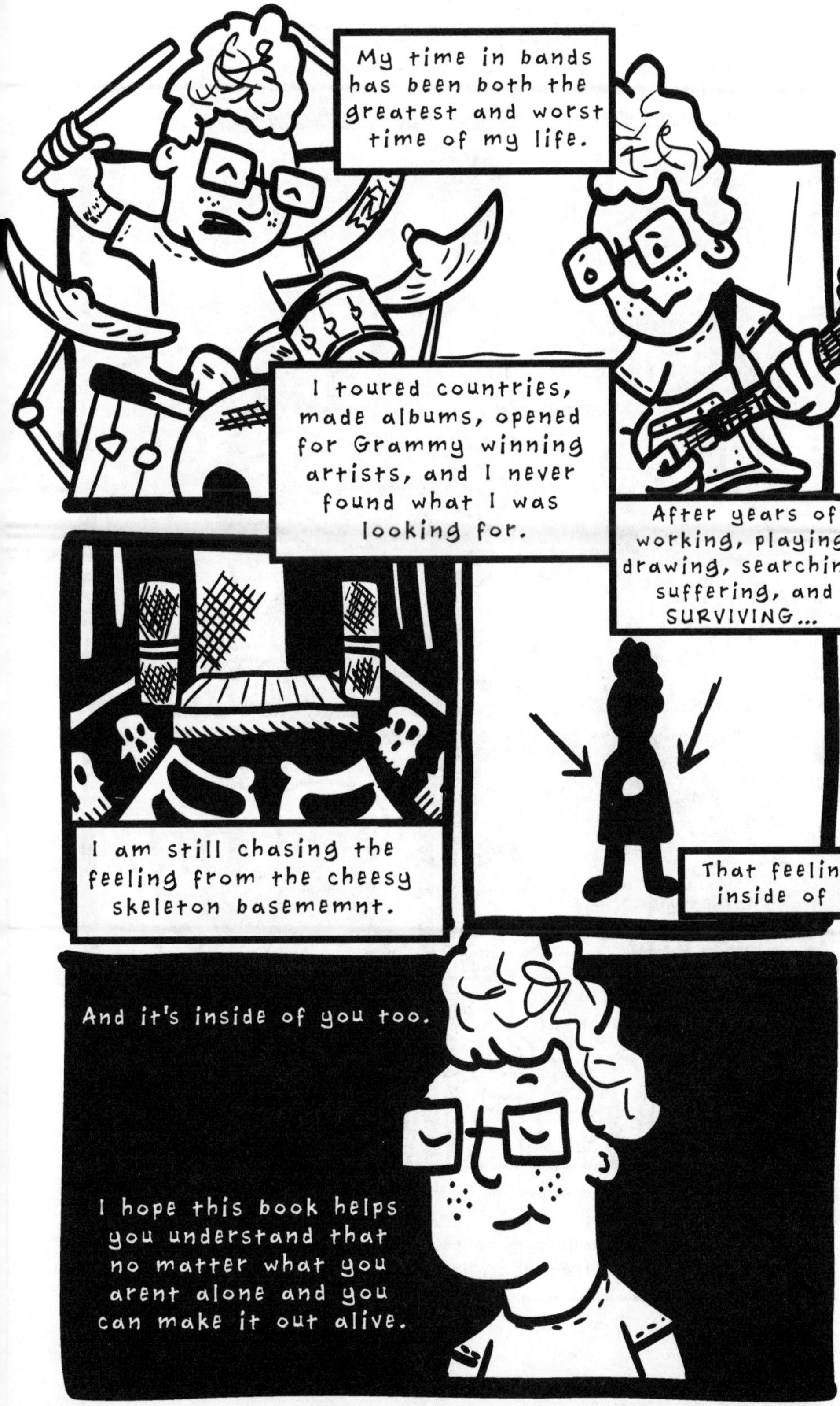
My time in bands has been both the greatest and worst time of my life.
I toured countries, made albums, opened for Grammy winning artists, and I never found what I was looking for.
After years of working, playing, drawing, searching, suffering, and SURVIVING...
I am still chasing the feeling from the cheesy skeleton basememnt.
That feeling is inside of me.
And it's inside of you too.
I hope this book helps you understand that no matter what you arent alone and you can make it out alive.

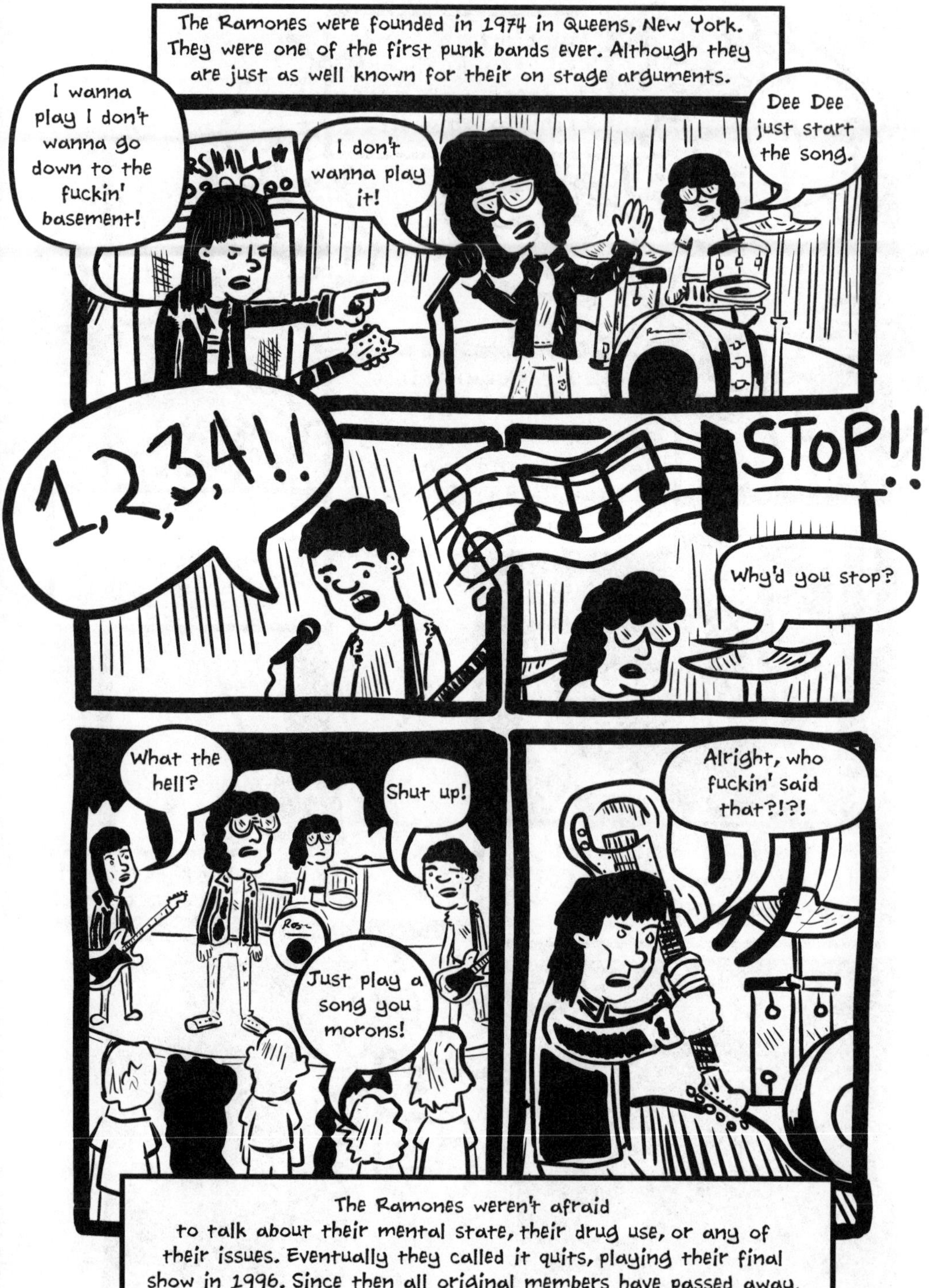
The Ramones were founded in 1974 in Queens, New York. They were one of the first punk bands ever. Although they are just as well known for their on stage arguments.
I wanna play I don't wanna go down to the fuckin' basement!
I don't wanna play it!
Dee Dee just start the song.
1,2,3,4!!
STOP!!
Why'd you stop?
What the hell?
Shut up!
Just play a song you morons!
Alright, who fuckin' said that?!?!
The Ramones weren't afraid to talk about their mental state, their drug use, or any of their issues. Eventually they called it quits, playing their final show in 1996. Since then all original members have passed away.

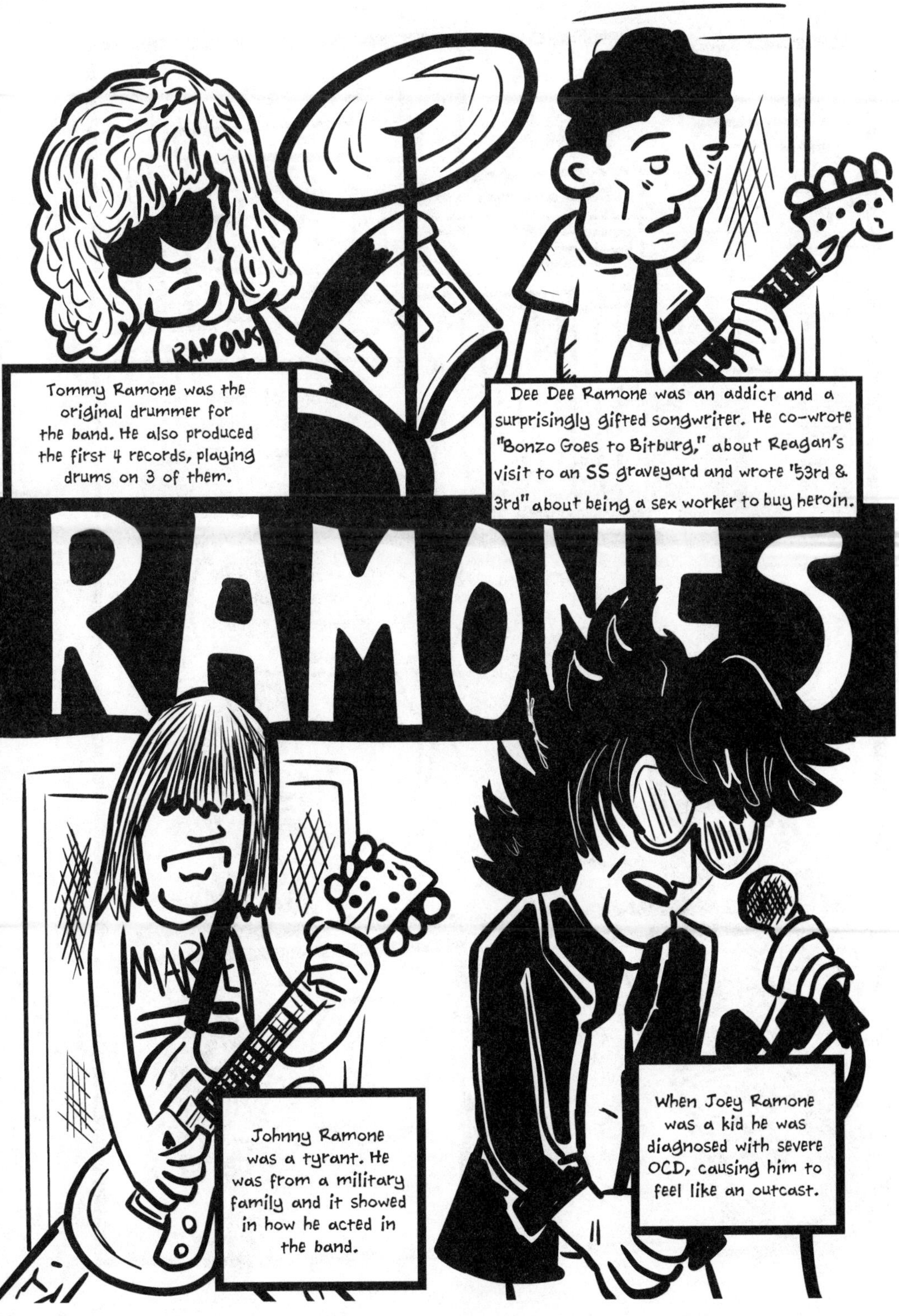
Tommy Ramone was the original drummer for the band. He also produced the first 4 records, playing drums on 3 of them.
Dee Dee Ramone was an addict and a surprisingly gifted songwriter. He co-wrote "Bonzo Goes to Bitburg," about Reagan's visit to an SS graveyard and wrote "53rd & 3rd" about being a sex worker to buy heroin.
RAMONES
Johnny Ramone was a tyrant. He was from a military family and it showed in how he acted in the band.
When Joey Ramone was a kid he was diagnosed with severe OCD, causing him to feel like an outcast.

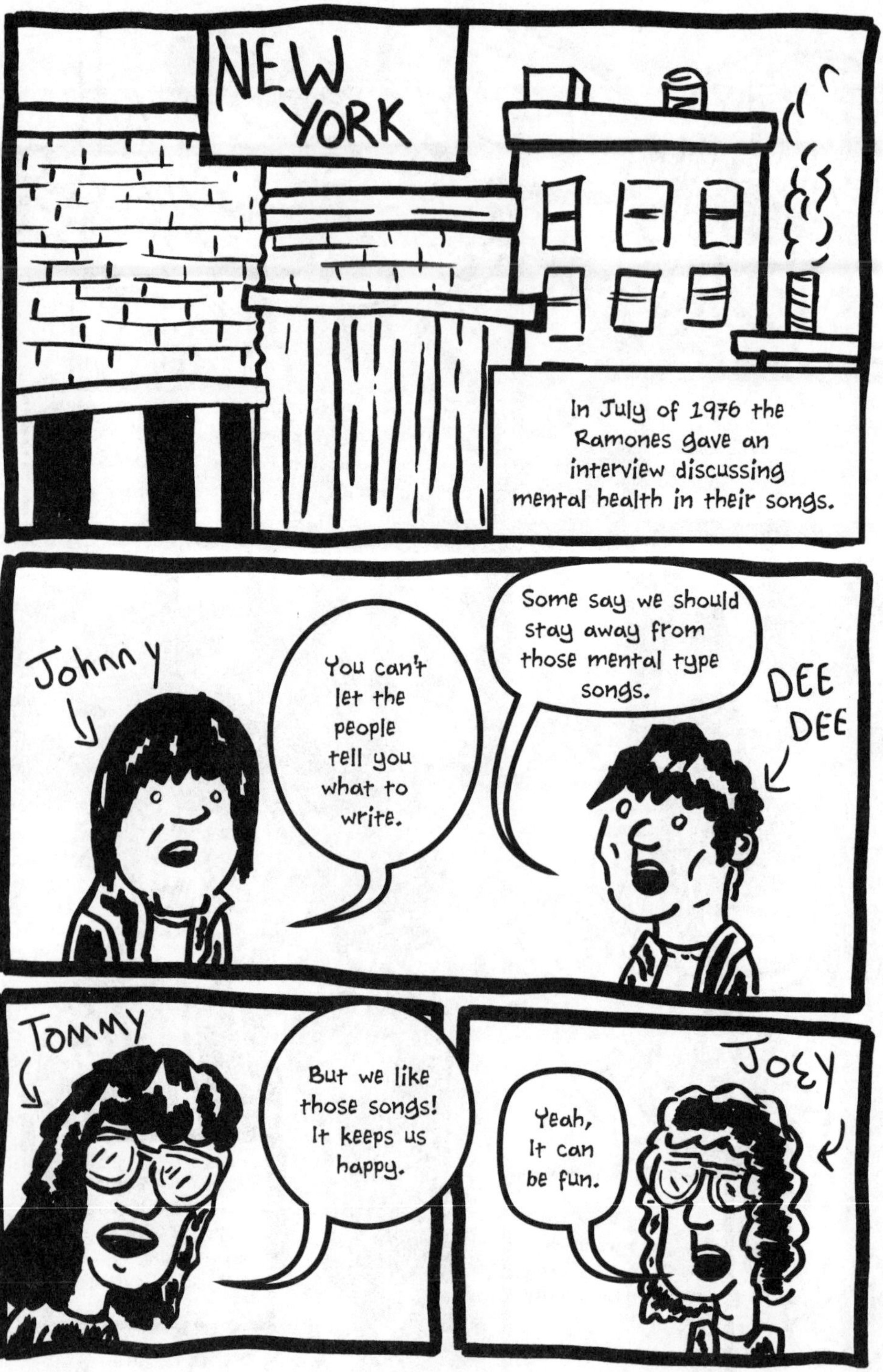

NEW YORK
In July of 1976 the Ramones gave an interview discussing mental health in their songs.
Johnny
You can't let the people tell you what to write.
Some say we should stay away from those mental type songs.
DEE DEE
TOMMY
But we like those songs! It keeps us happy.
JOEY
Yeah, It can be fun.

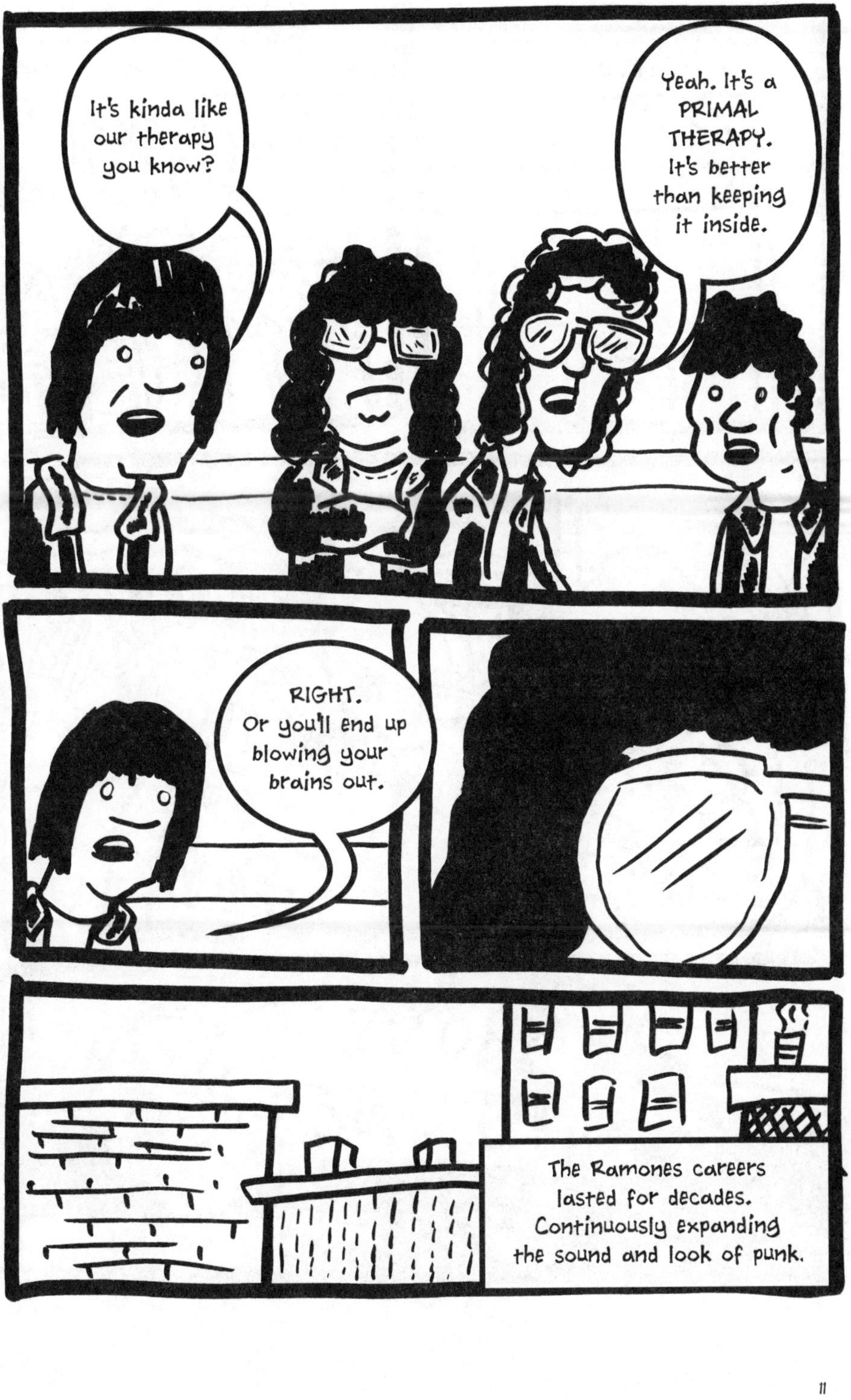
It's kinda like our therapy you know?
Yeah. It's a PRIMAL THERAPY. It's better than keeping it inside.
RIGHT. Or you'll end up blowing your brains out.
The Ramones careers lasted for decades. Continuously expanding the sound and look of punk.

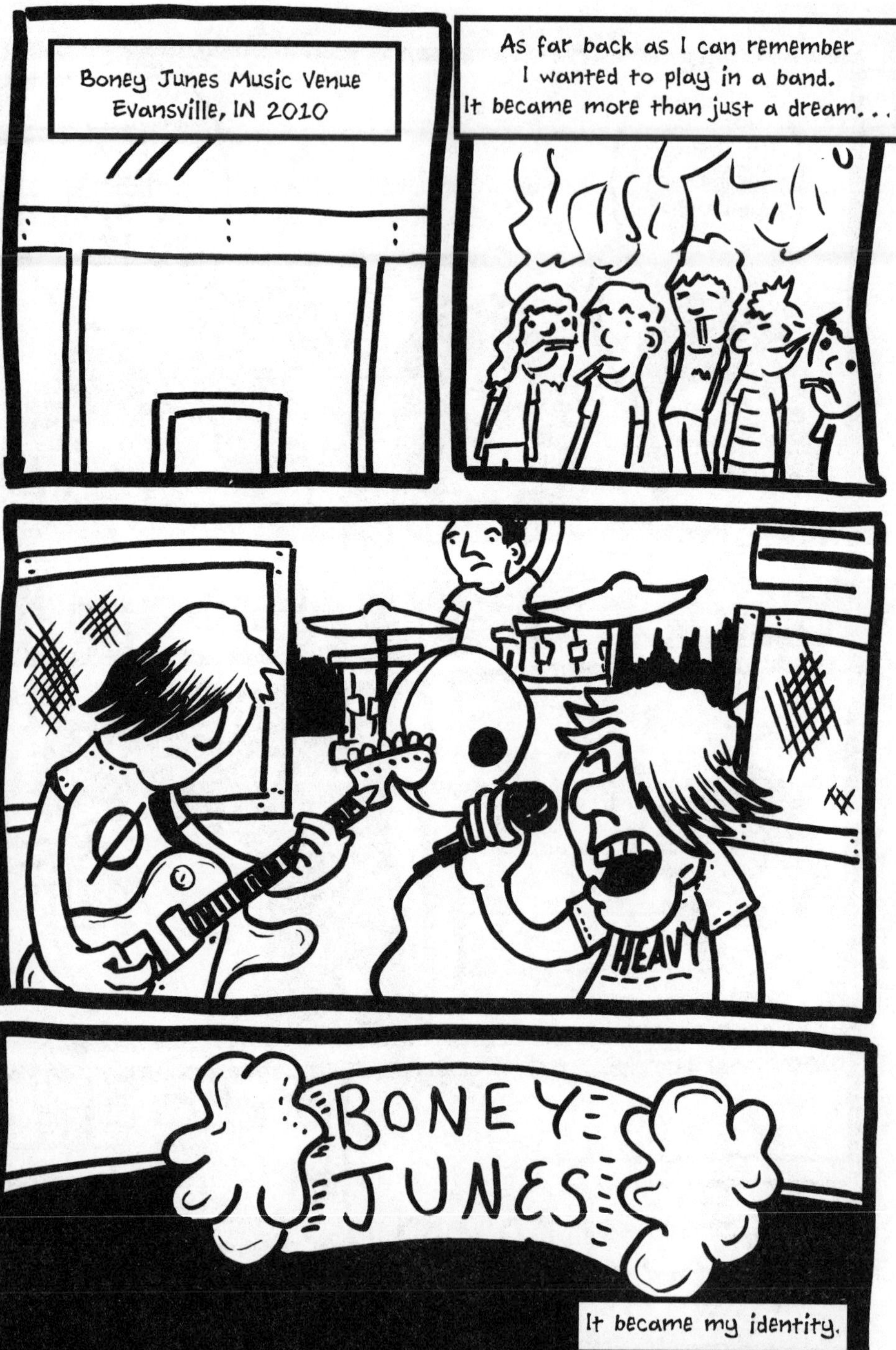
Boney Junes Music Venue
Evansville, IN 2010
As far back as I can remember
I wanted to play in a band.
It became more than just a dream...
HEAVY
BONEY JUNES
It became my identity.

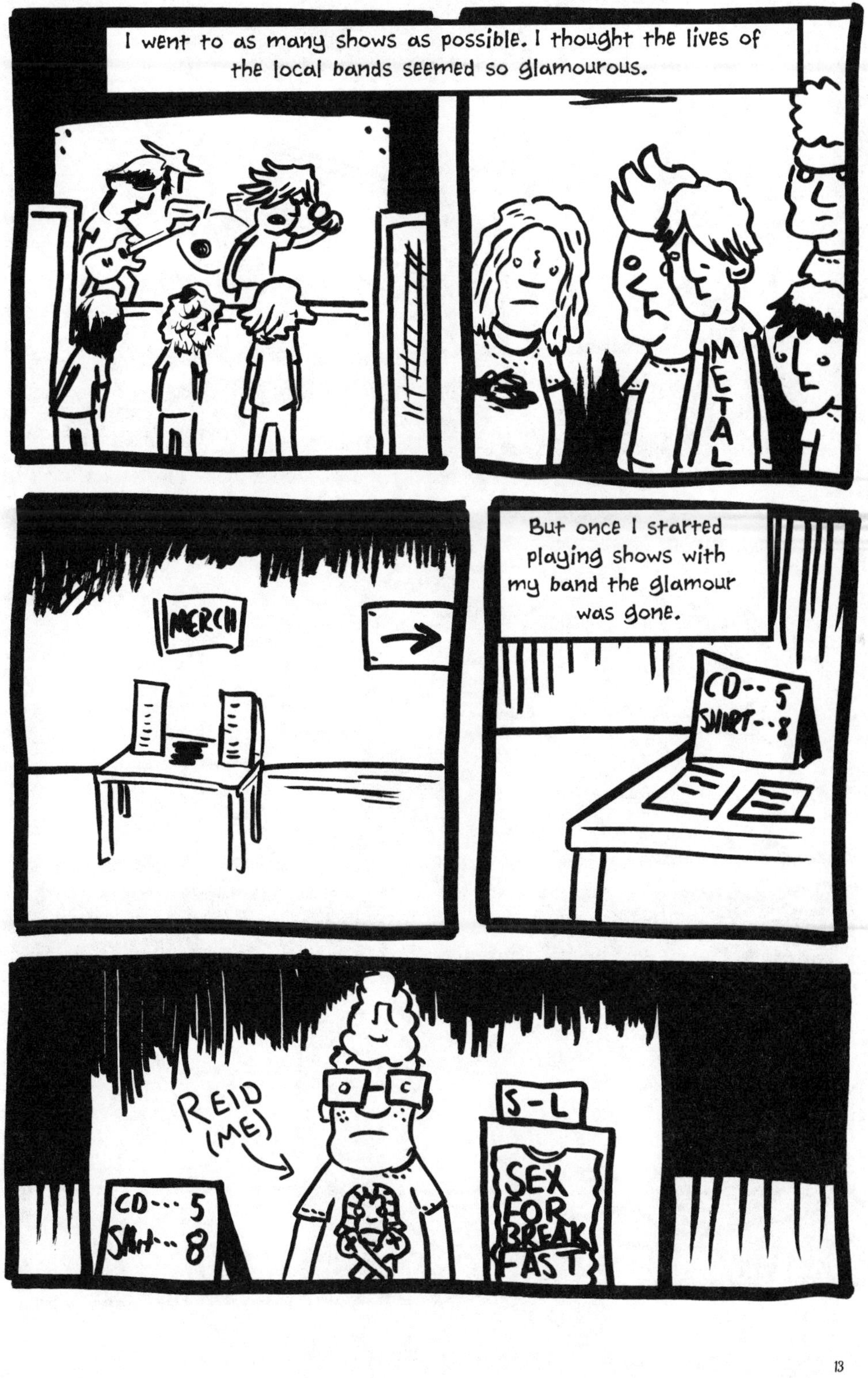
I went to as many shows as possible. I thought the lives of the local bands seemed so glamourous.
METAL
MERCH
But once I started playing shows with my band the glamour was gone.
CD--5
SHIRT--8
REID (ME)
CD--- 5
Shirt-- 8
S-L
SEX FOR BREAKFAST

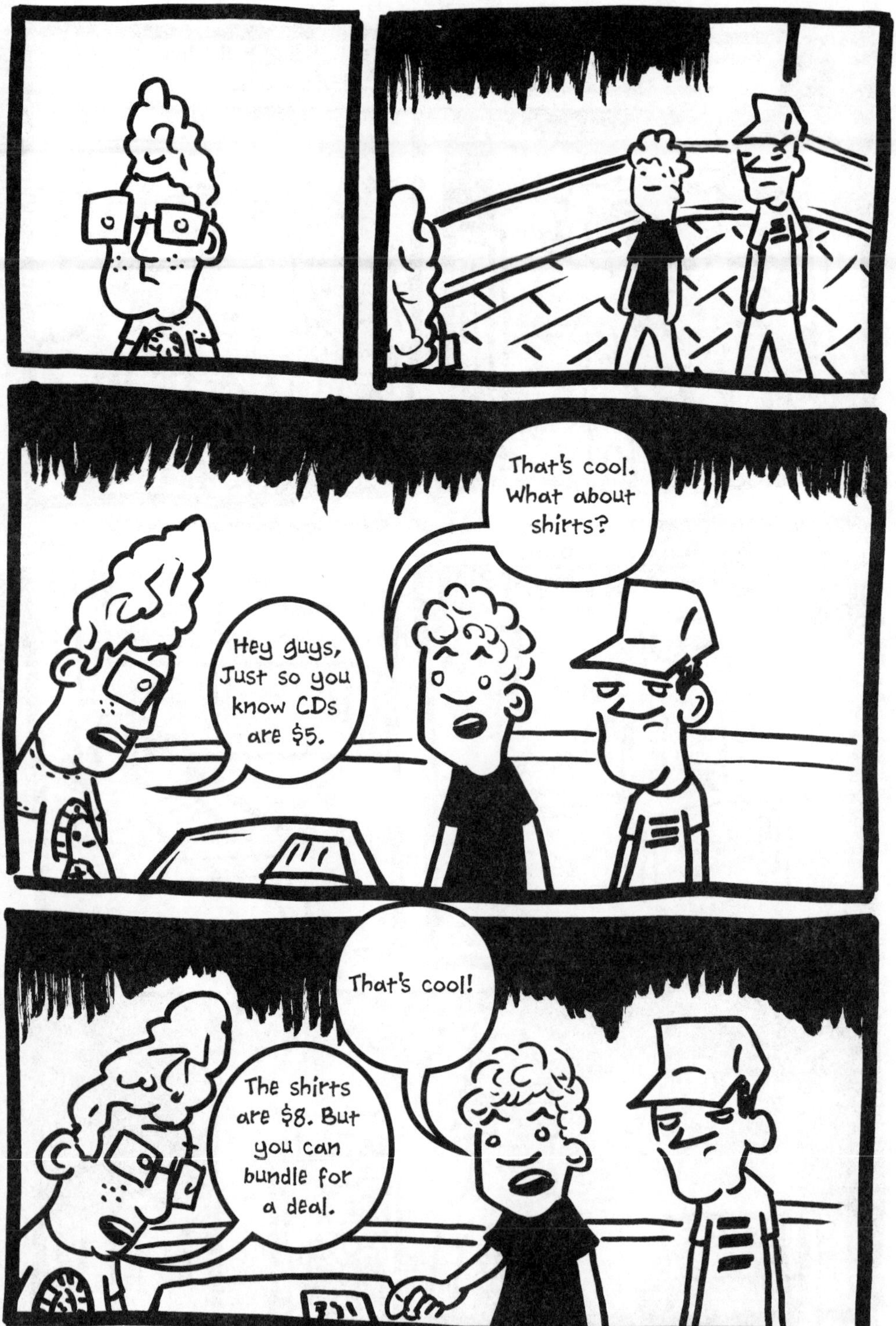
That's cool. What about shirts?
Hey guys, Just so you know CDs are $5.
That's cool!
The shirts are $8. But you can bundle for a deal.

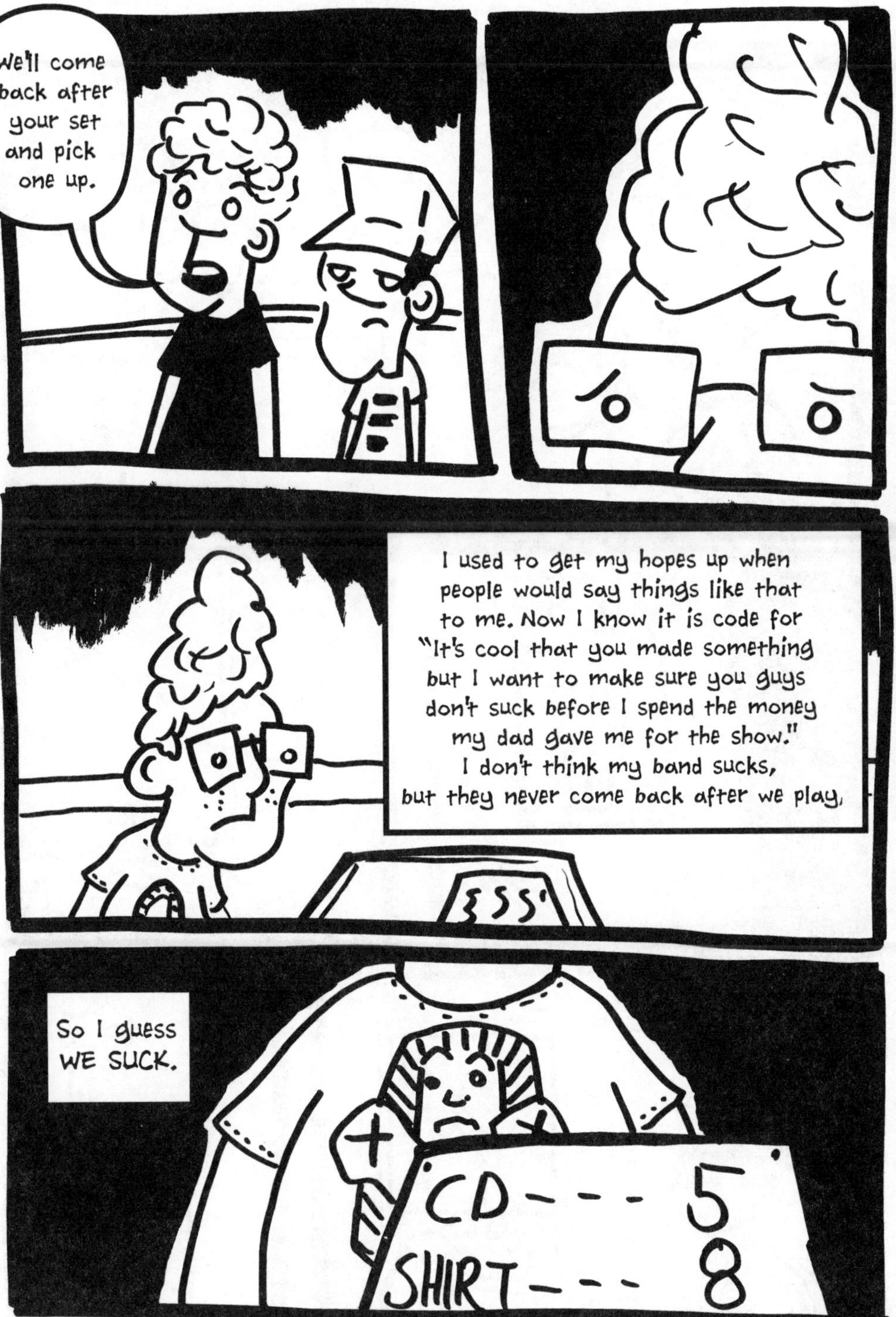

We'll come back after your set and pick one up.
I used to get my hopes up when people would say things like that to me. Now I know it is code for "It's cool that you made something but I want to make sure you guys don't suck before I spend the money my dad gave me for the show." I don't think my band sucks, but they never come back after we play,
So I guess WE SUCK.
CD - - - 5
SHIRT - - - 8

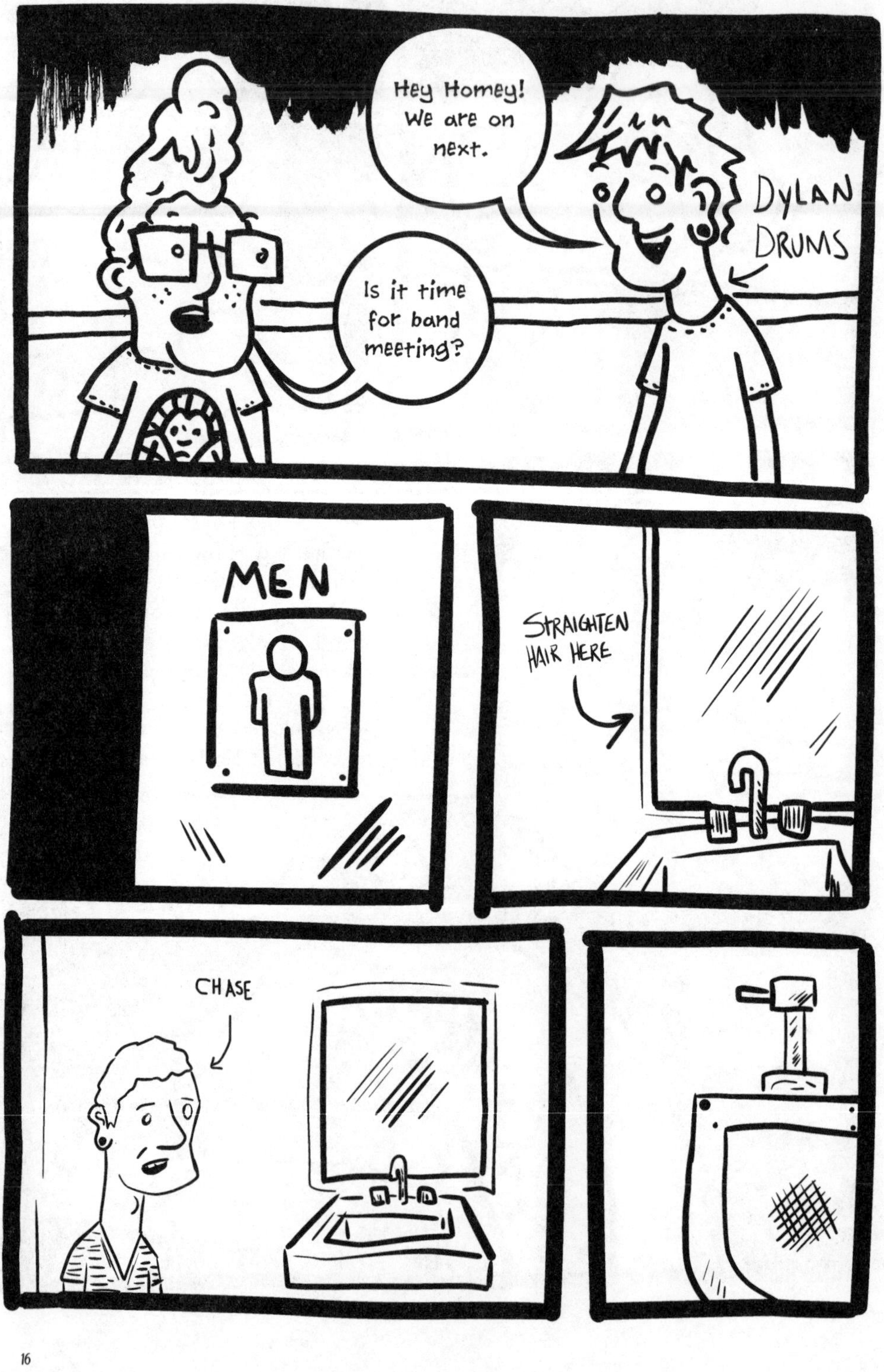
Hey Homey! We are on next.
Is it time for band meeting?
DYLAN DRUMS
MEN
STRAIGHTEN HAIR HERE
CHASE

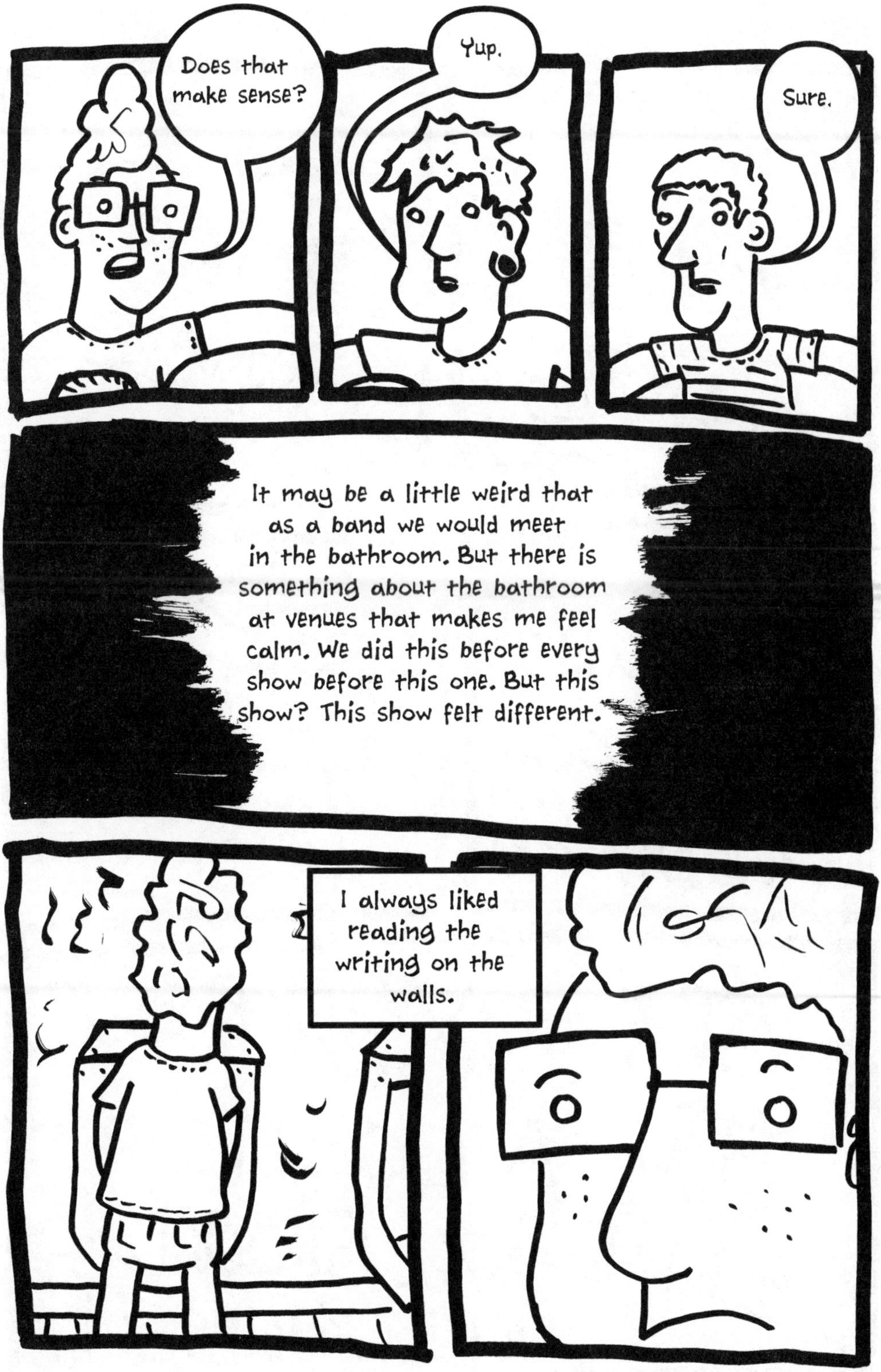
Does that make sense?
Yup.
Sure.
It may be a little weird that as a band we would meet in the bathroom. But there is something about the bathroom at venues that makes me feel calm. We did this before every show before this one. But this show? This show felt different.
I always liked reading the writing on the walls.

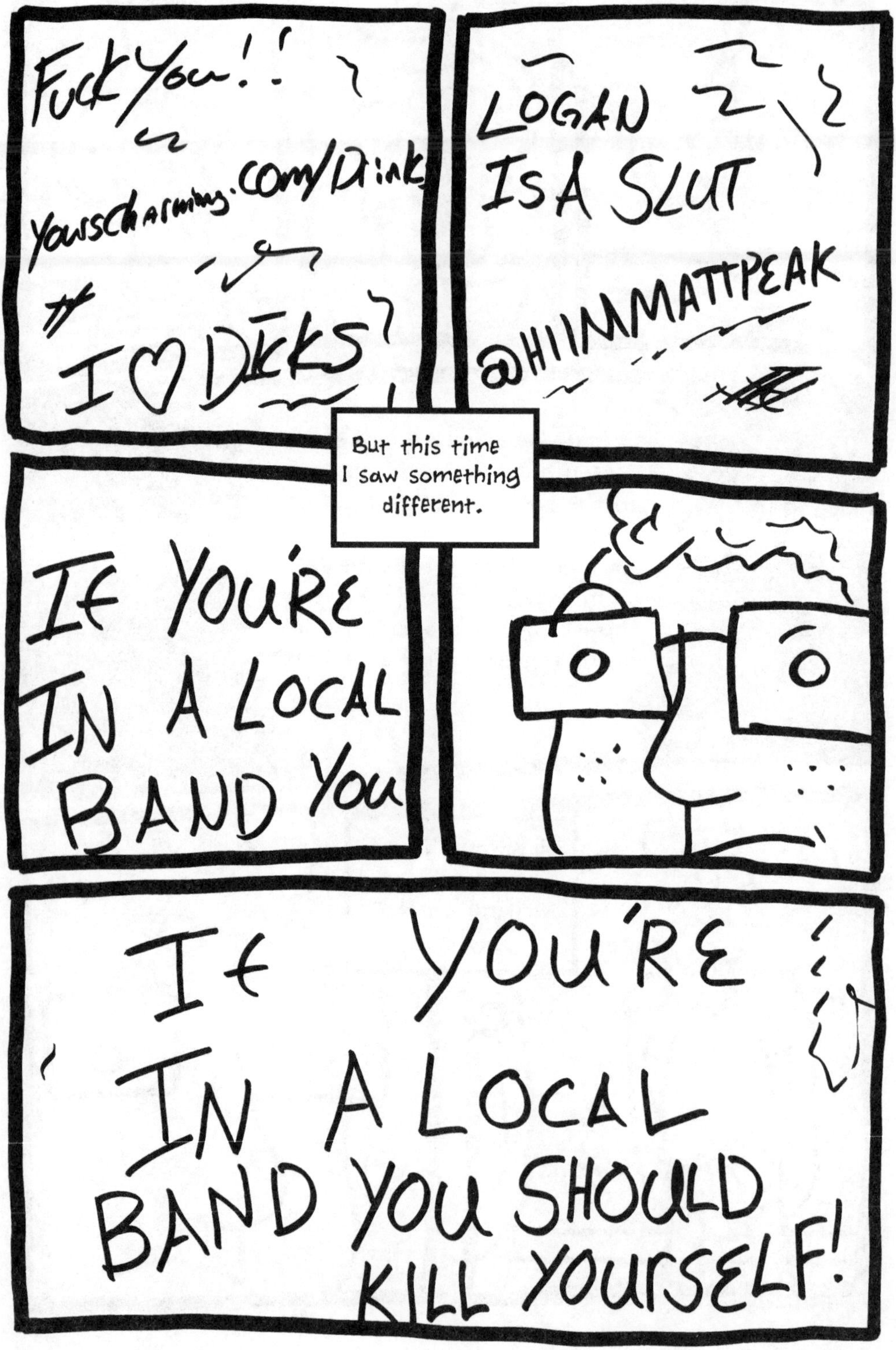

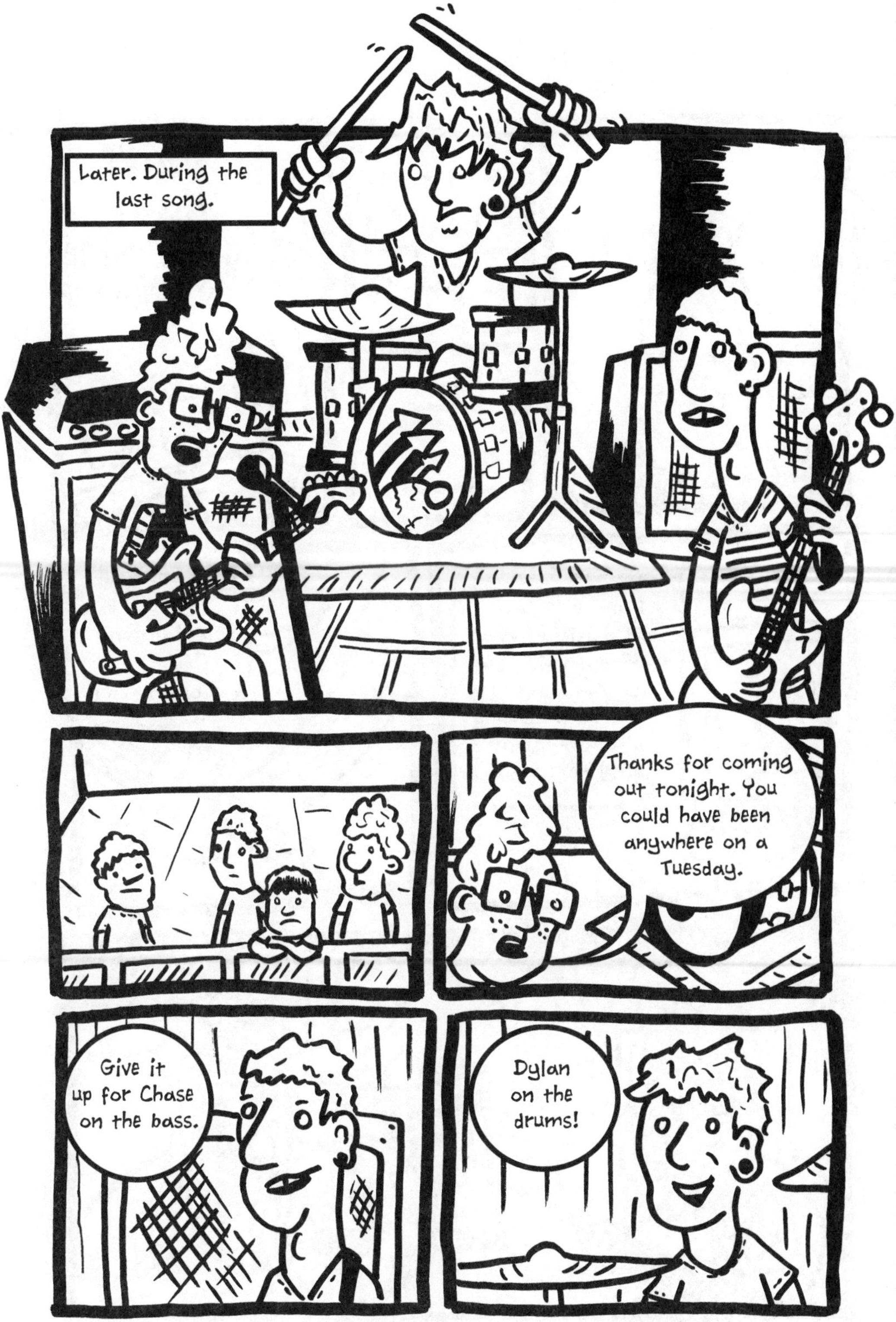
Later. During the last song.
Thanks for coming out tonight. You could have been anywhere on a Tuesday.
Give it up for Chase on the bass.
Dylan on the drums!

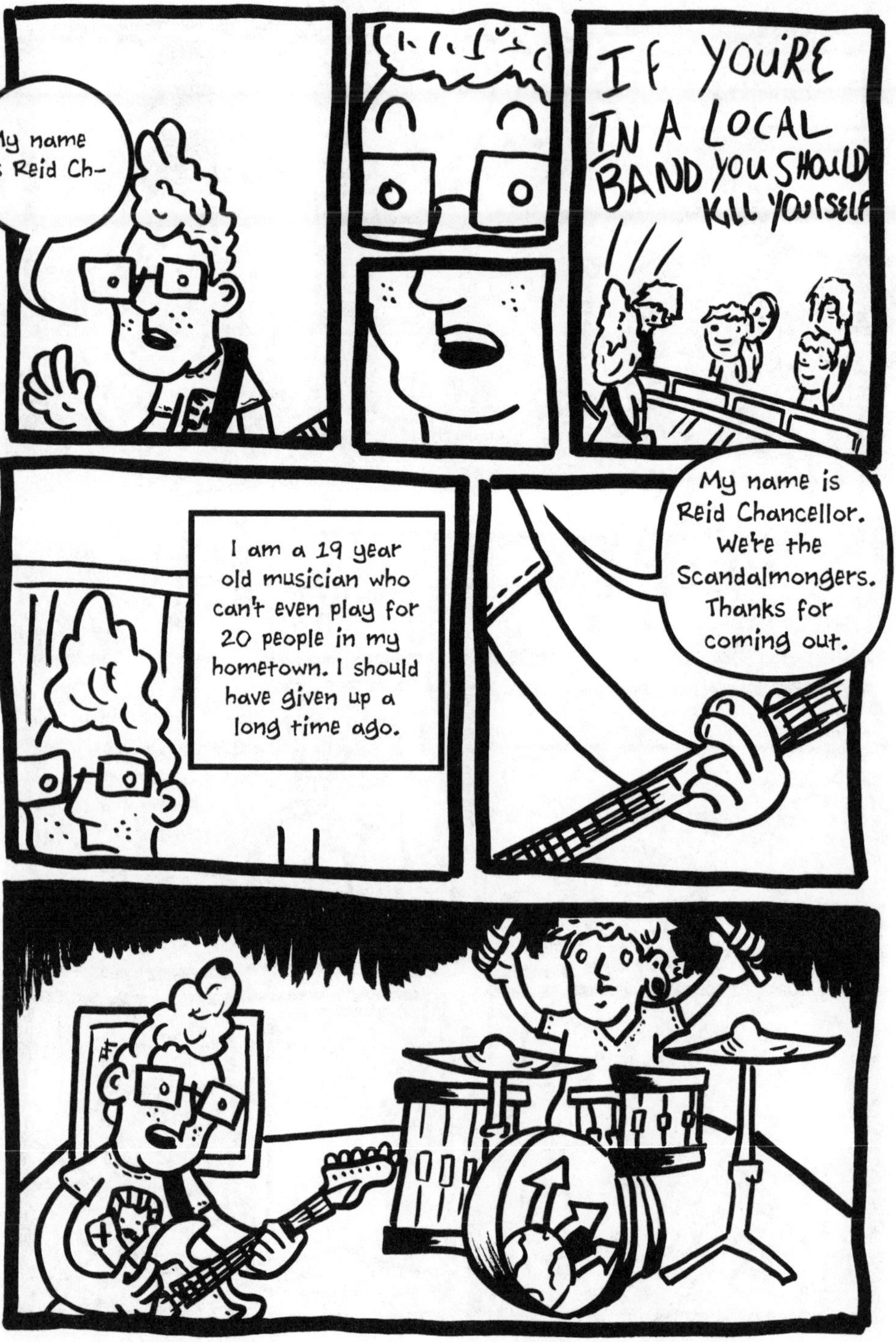
My name is Reid Ch-
IF YOU'RE IN A LOCAL BAND YOU SHOULD KILL YOURSELF
I am a 19 year old musician who can't even play for 20 people in my hometown. I should have given up a long time ago.
My name is Reid Chancellor. We're the Scandalmongers. Thanks for coming out.

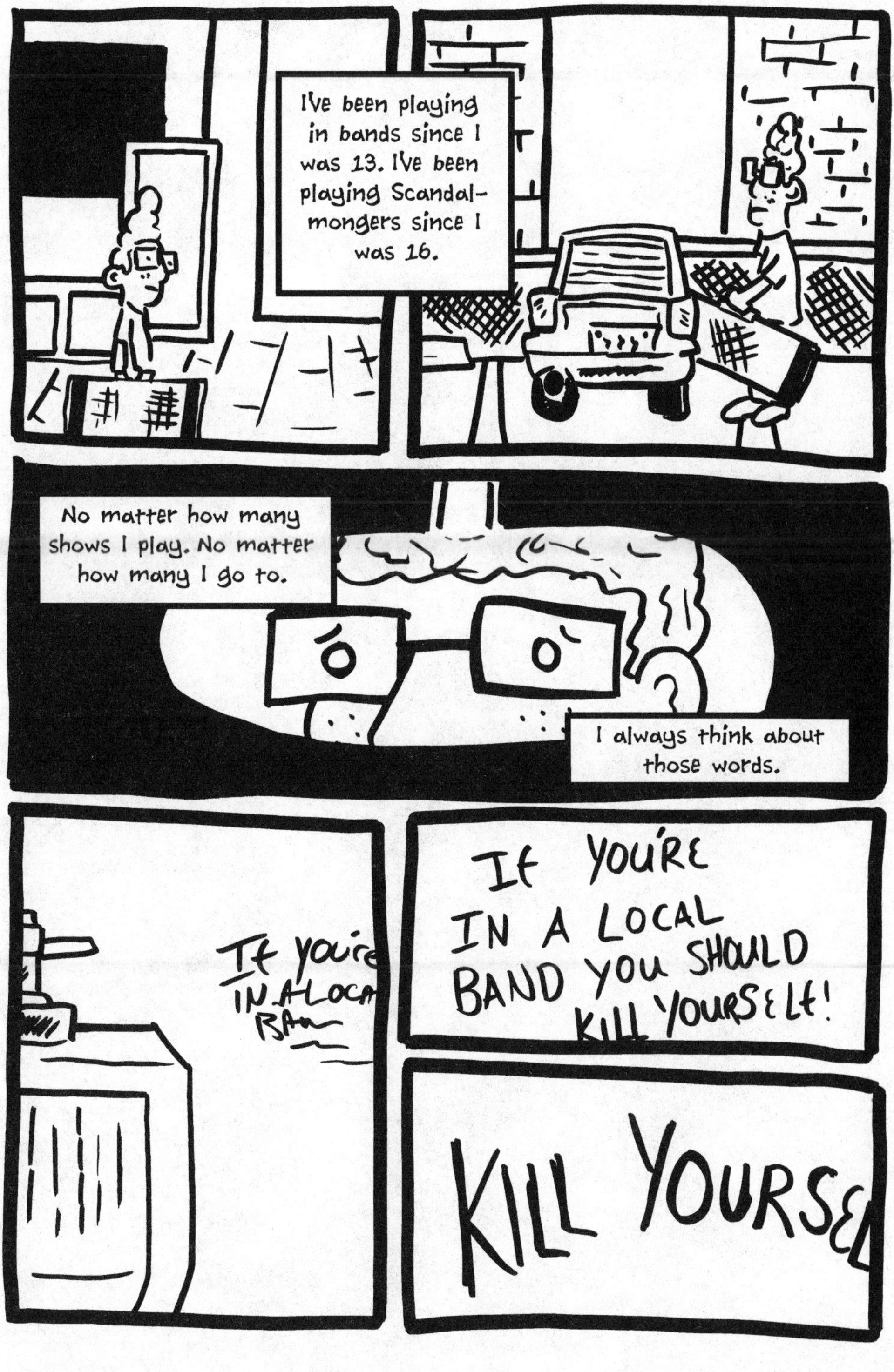
I've been playing in bands since I was 13. I've been playing Scandal-mongers since I was 16.
No matter how many shows I play. No matter how many I go to.
I always think about those words.
If you're IN A LOCA BA
IF YOU'RE IN A LOCAL BAND YOU SHOULD KILL YOURSELF!
KILL YOURSE

Part 1

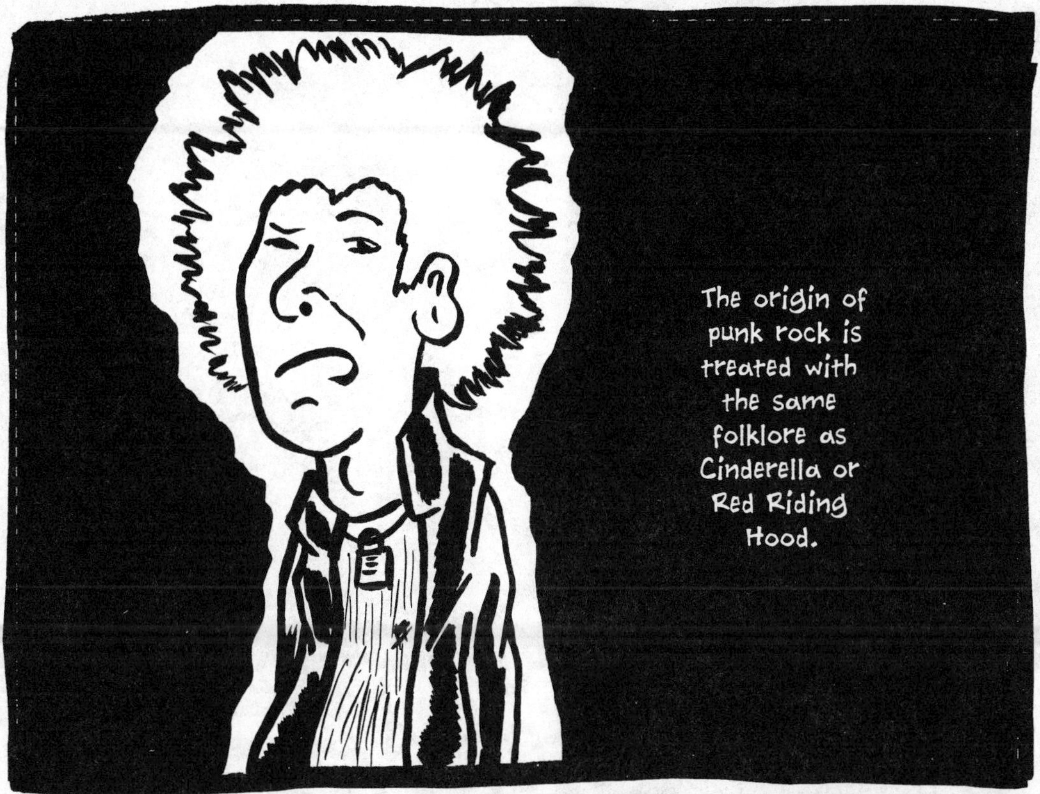
The origin of punk rock is treated with the same folklore as Cinderella or Red Riding Hood.

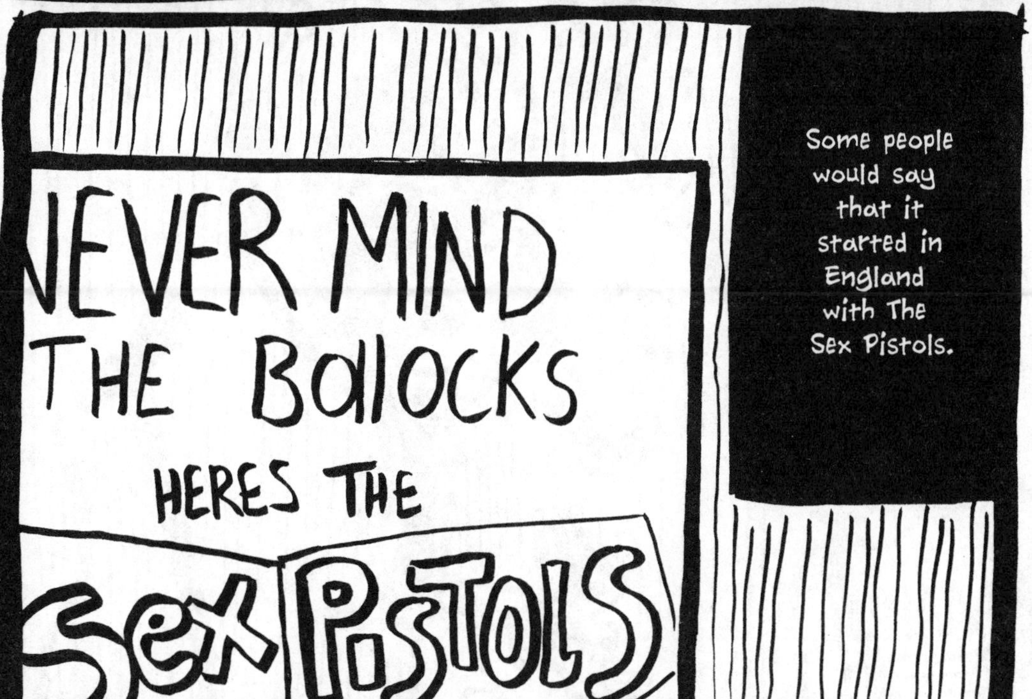
NEVER MIND
THE Bollocks
HERES THE
Sex Pistols
Some people would say that it started in England with The Sex Pistols.

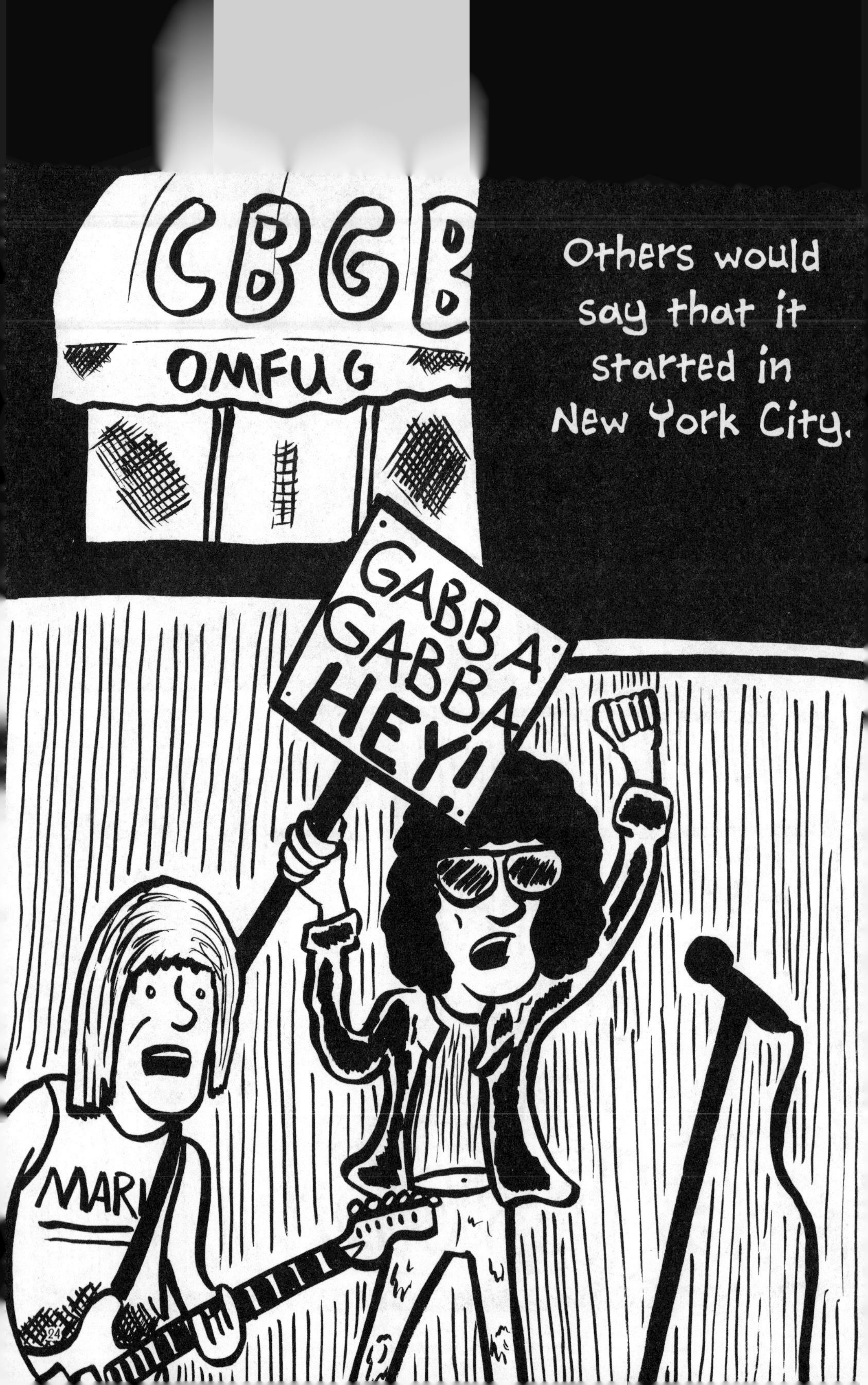
CBGB
OMFUG
Others would say that it started in New York City.
GABBA GABBA HEY!

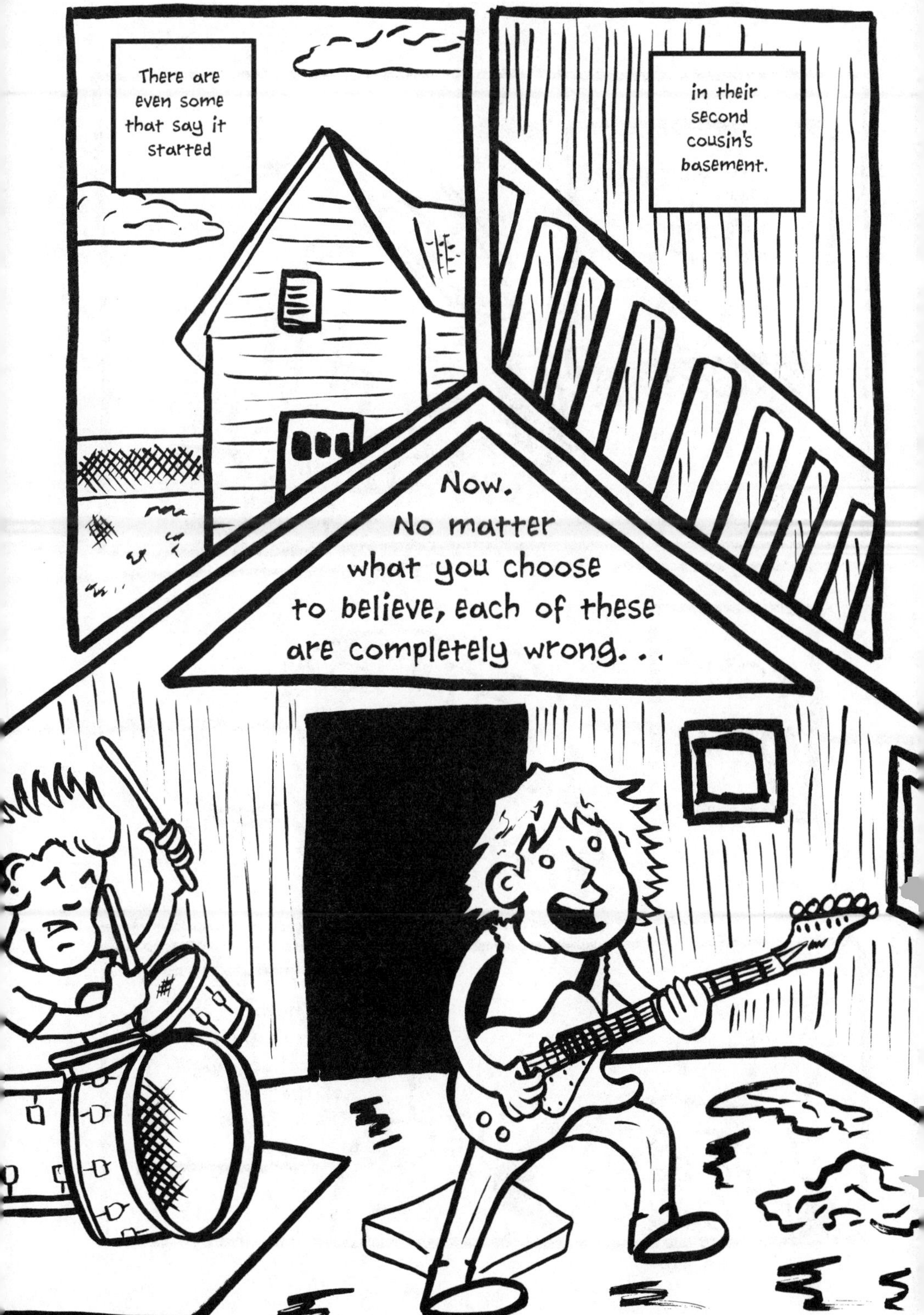
There are even some that say it started
in their second cousin's basement.
Now. No matter what you choose to believe, each of these are completely wrong...

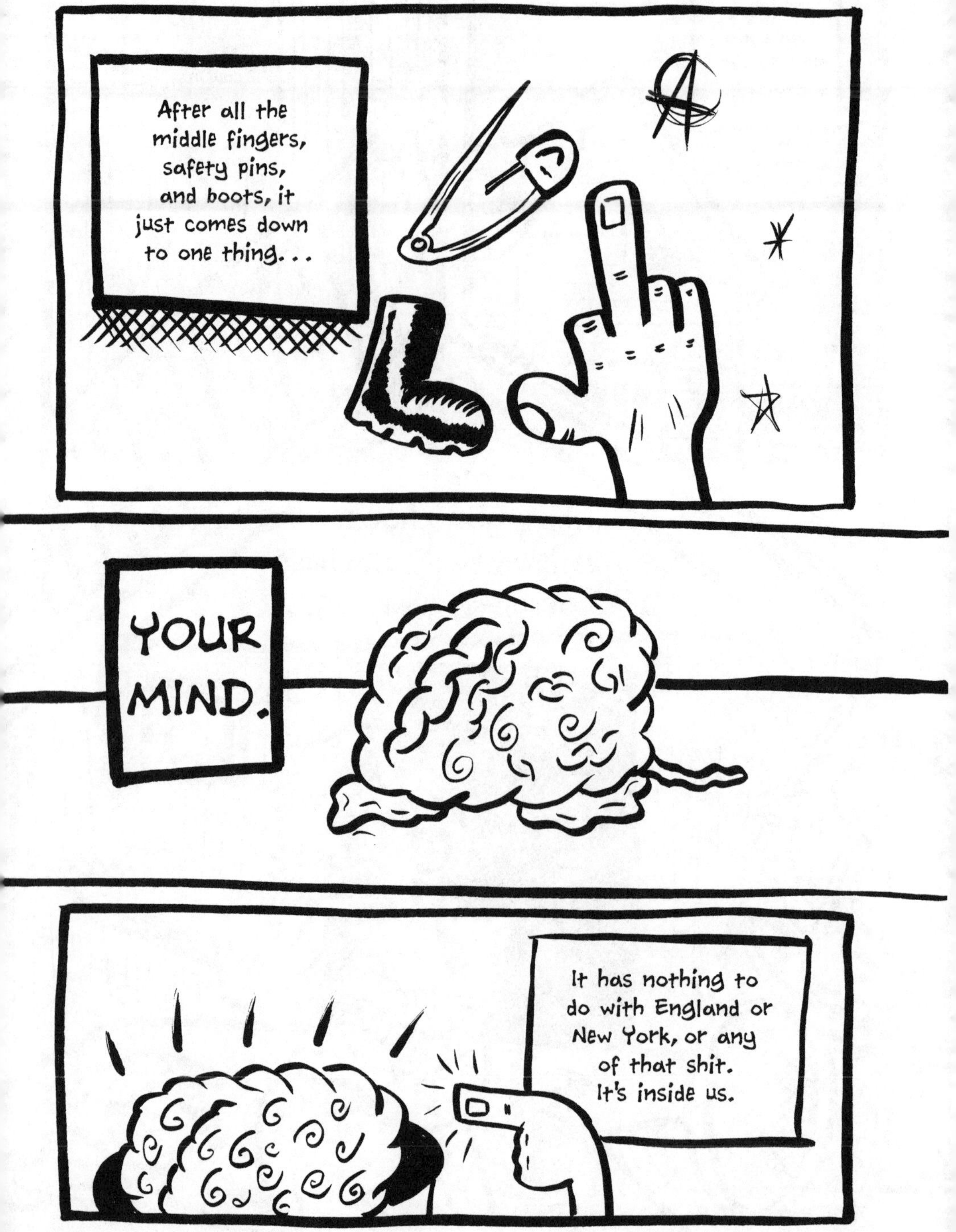
After all the middle fingers, safety pins, and boots, it just comes down to one thing...
YOUR MIND.
It has nothing to do with England or New York, or any of that shit. It's inside us.

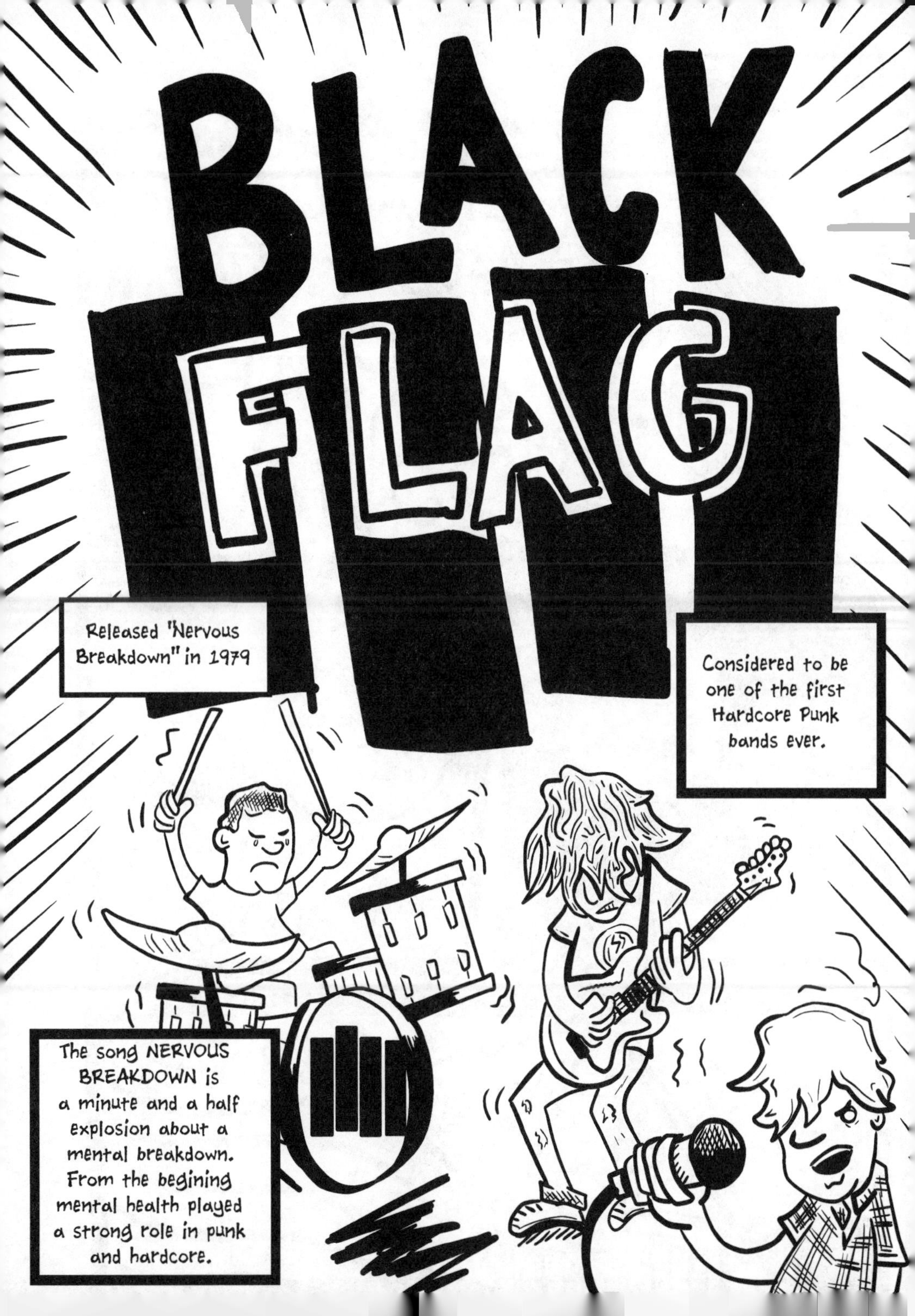
BLACK FLAG
Released "Nervous Breakdown" in 1979
Considered to be one of the first Hardcore Punk bands ever.
The song NERVOUS BREAKDOWN is a minute and a half explosion about a mental breakdown. From the begining mental health played a strong role in punk and hardcore.

Black Flag worked hard from the start. Keith Morris was the first singer on songs like "Nervous Breakdown"

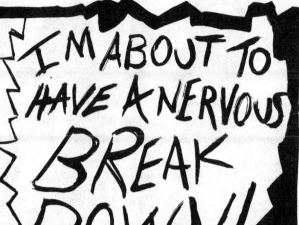

I'M ABOUT TO HAVE A NERVOUS BREAK DOWN!

Alright Keith, let's practice the songs again.

Greg Ginn

Chill Greg. I'm gonna have another beer and then we can start.

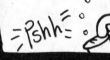

=Pshh=

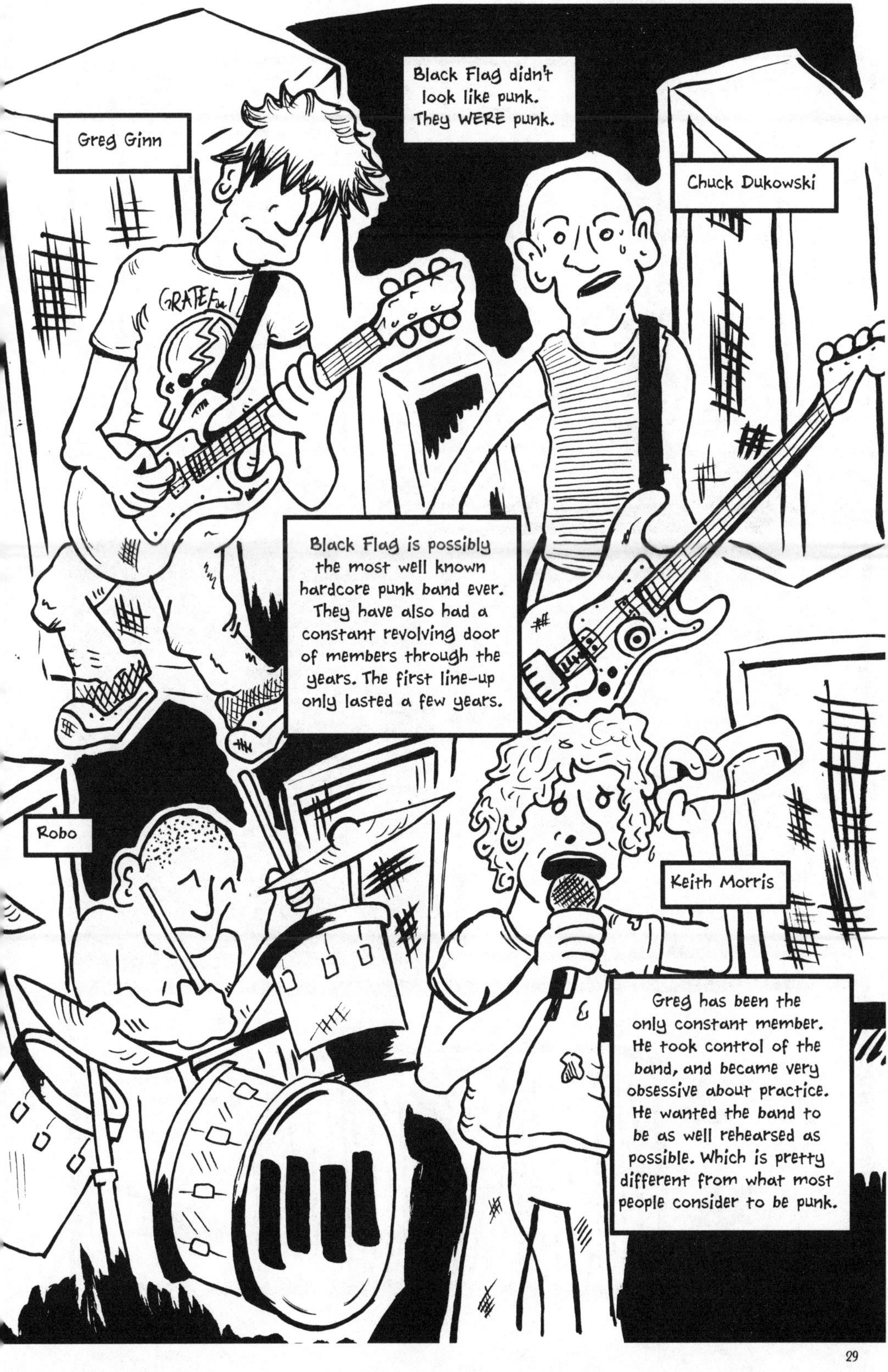

Black Flag didn't look like punk. They WERE punk.
Greg Ginn
Chuck Dukowski
Black Flag is possibly the most well known hardcore punk band ever. They have also had a constant revolving door of members through the years. The first line-up only lasted a few years.
Robo
Keith Morris
Greg has been the only constant member. He took control of the band, and became very obsessive about practice. He wanted the band to be as well rehearsed as possible. Which is pretty different from what most people consider to be punk.

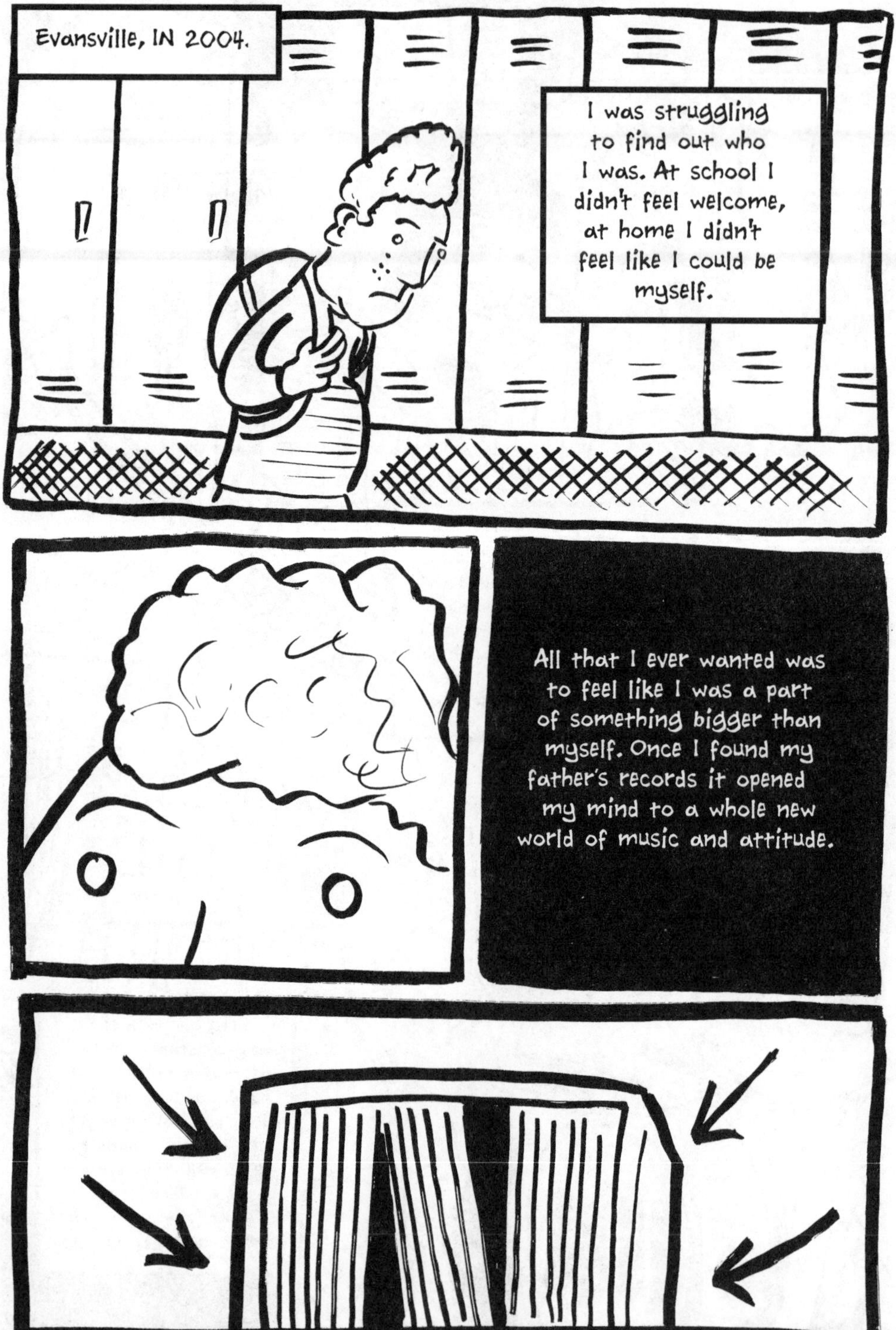
Evansville, IN 2004.
I was struggling to find out who I was. At school I didn't feel welcome, at home I didn't feel like I could be myself.
All that I ever wanted was to feel like I was a part of something bigger than myself. Once I found my father's records it opened my mind to a whole new world of music and attitude.

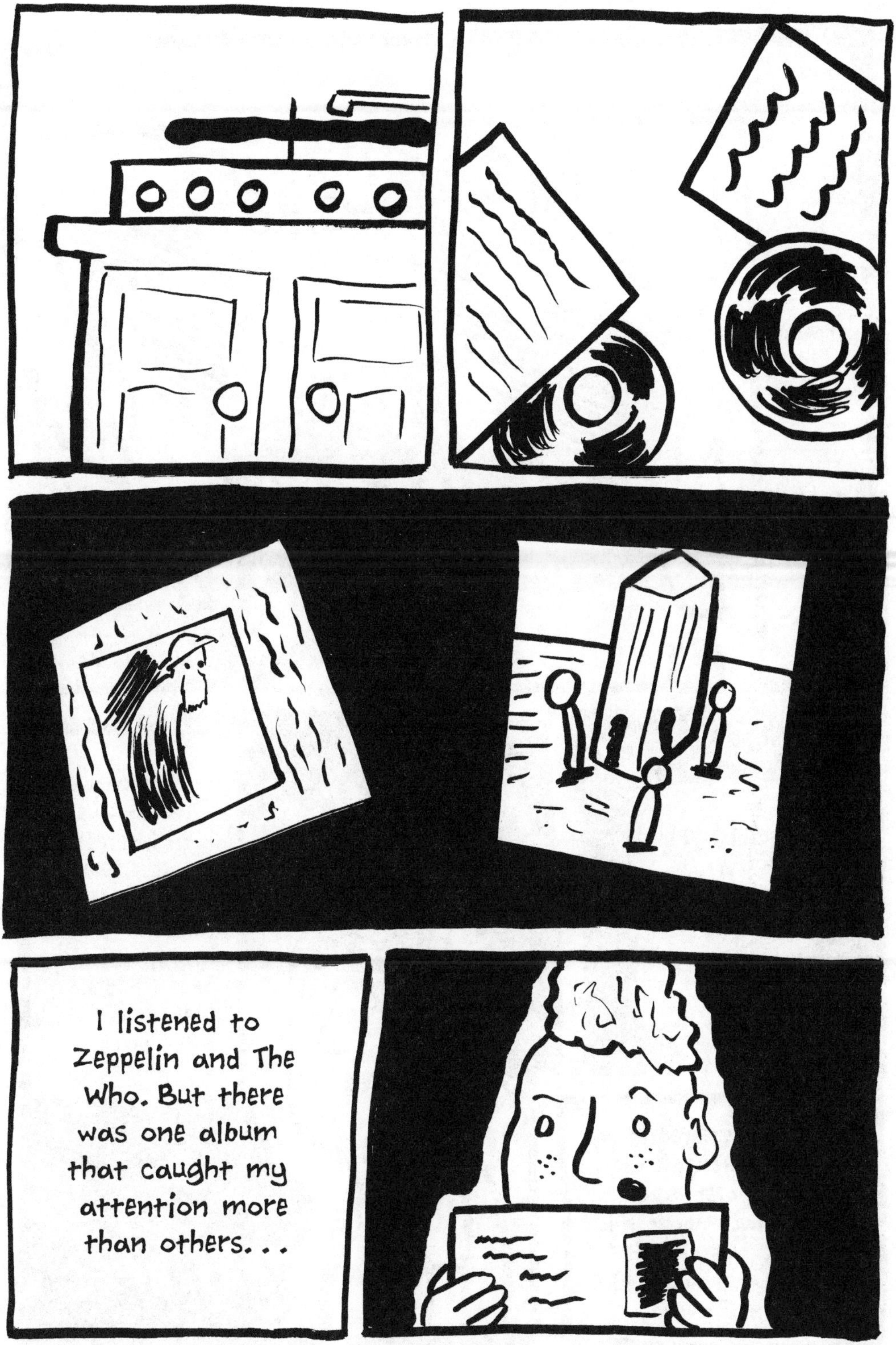
I listened to Zeppelin and The Who. But there was one album that caught my attention more than others. . .

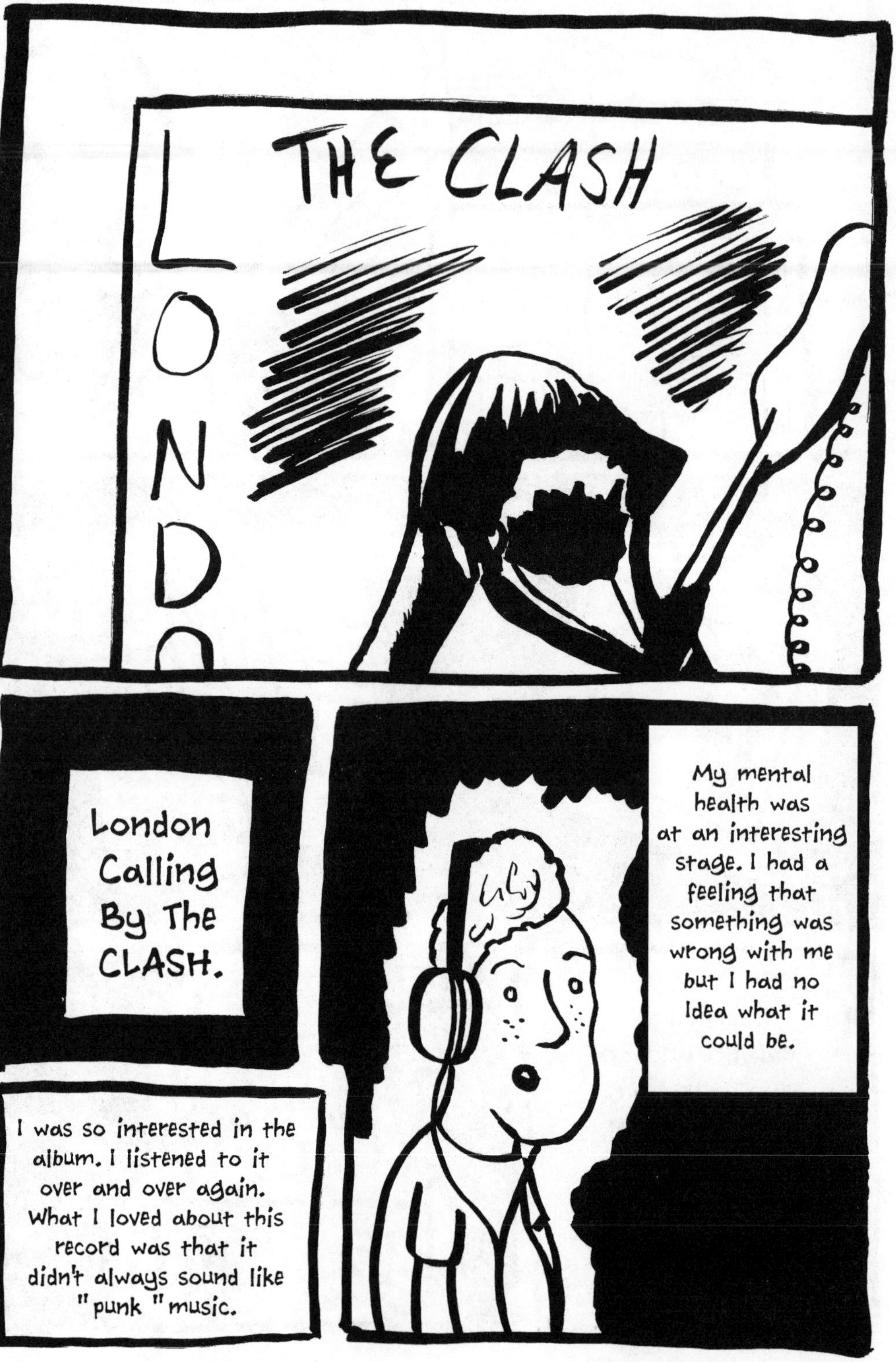
THE CLASH
LOND
London Calling By The CLASH.
I was so interested in the album. I listened to it over and over again. What I loved about this record was that it didn't always sound like "punk" music.
My mental health was at an interesting stage. I had a feeling that something was wrong with me but I had no Idea what it could be.

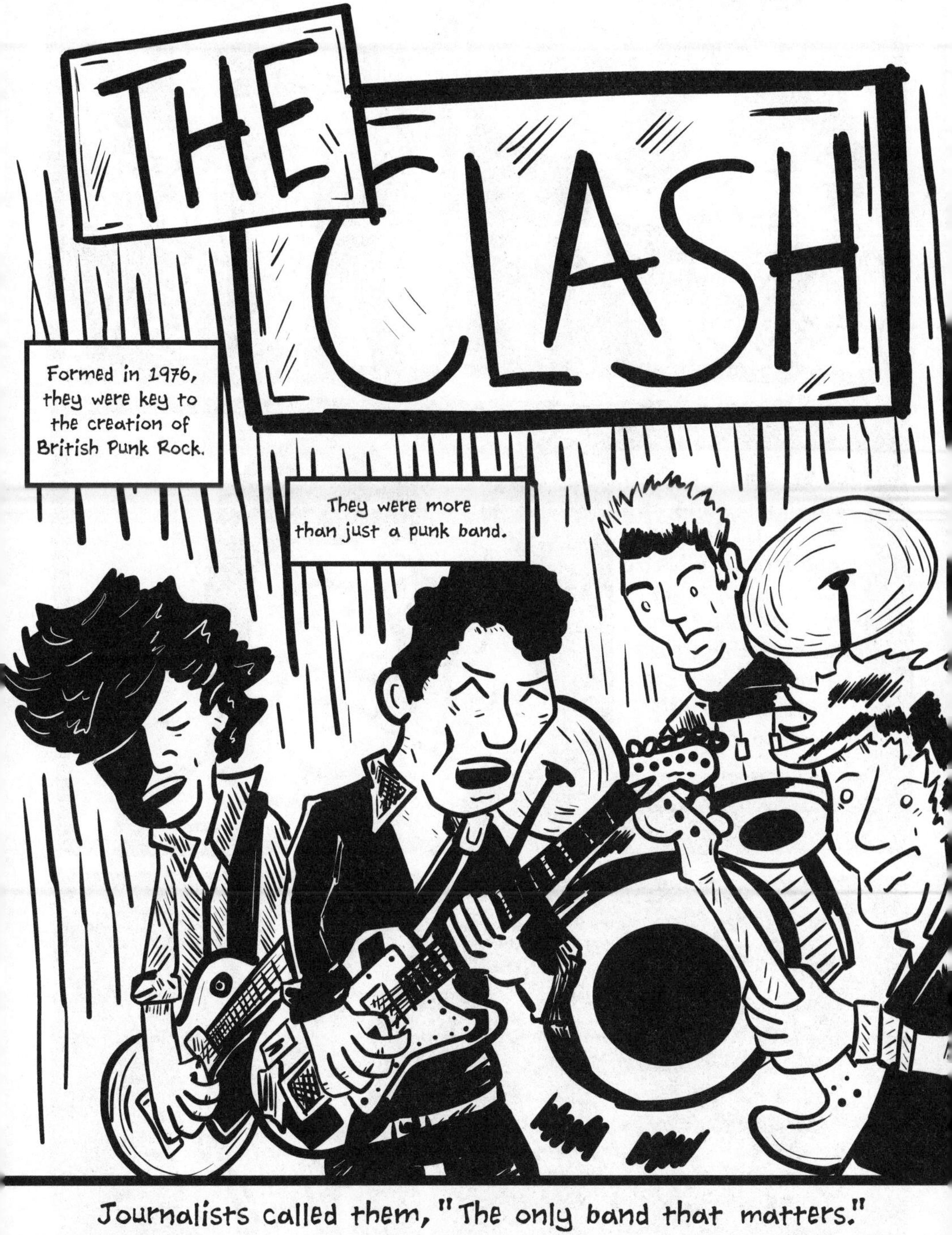
THE CLASH
Formed in 1976, they were key to the creation of British Punk Rock.
They were more than just a punk band.
Journalists called them, "The only band that matters."

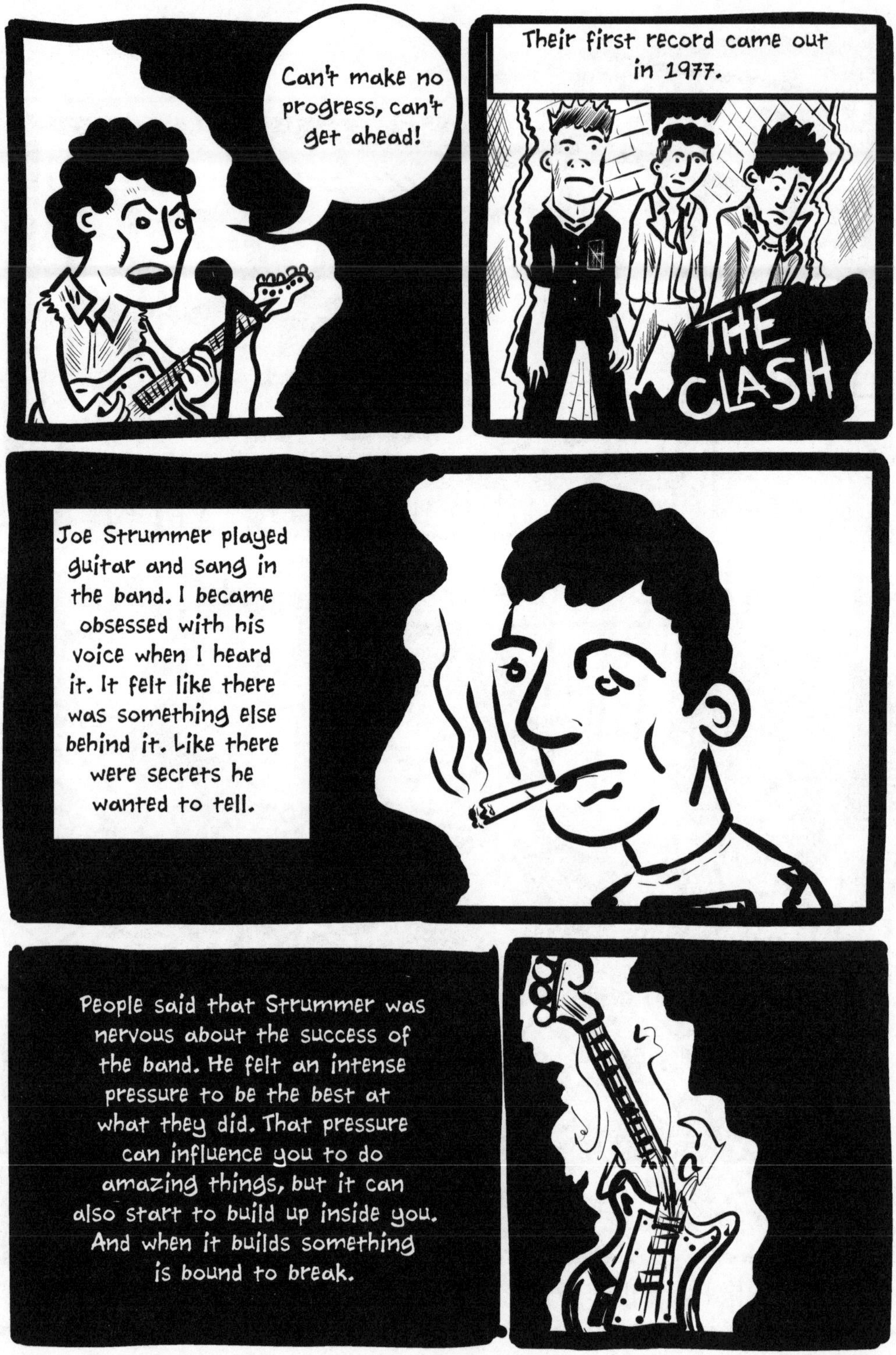

Can't make no progress, can't get ahead!
Their first record came out in 1977.
THE CLASH
Joe Strummer played guitar and sang in the band. I became obsessed with his voice when I heard it. It felt like there was something else behind it. Like there were secrets he wanted to tell.
People said that Strummer was nervous about the success of the band. He felt an intense pressure to be the best at what they did. That pressure can influence you to do amazing things, but it can also start to build up inside you. And when it builds something is bound to break.

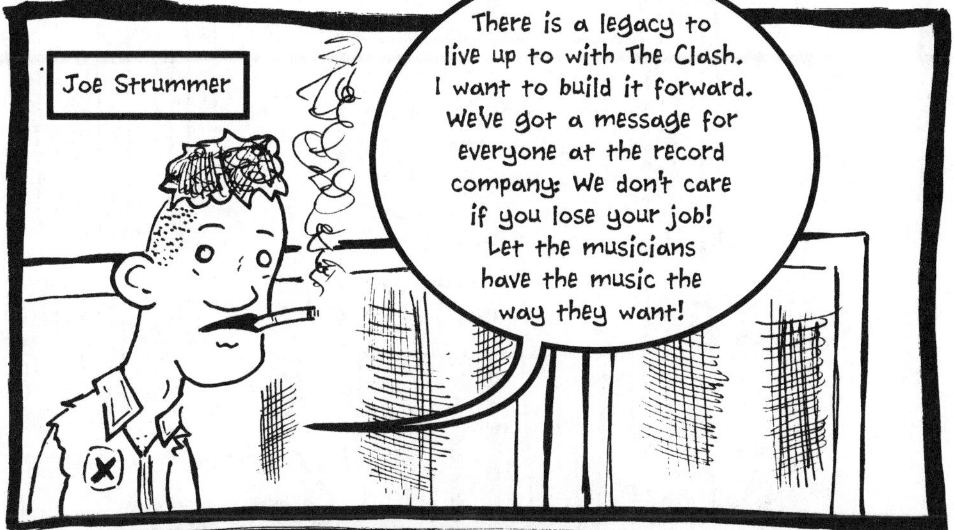
Joe Strummer
There is a legacy to live up to with The Clash. I want to build it forward. We've got a message for everyone at the record company: We don't care if you lose your job! Let the musicians have the music the way they want!

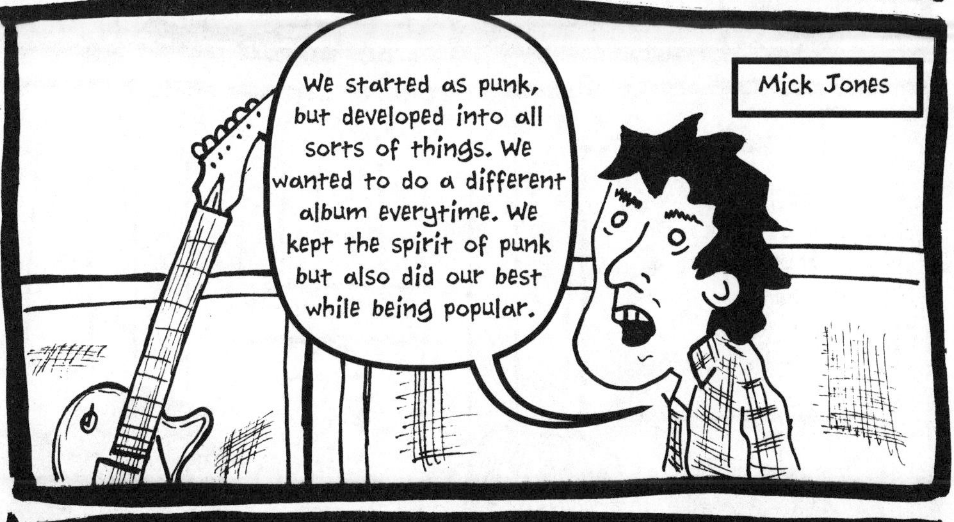
Mick Jones
We started as punk, but developed into all sorts of things. We wanted to do a different album everytime. We kept the spirit of punk but also did our best while being popular.

The Clash are a gateway drug to punk music. The attitudes and the sheer motivation to make something that no body had ever heard before. When I found The Clash I felt like I had finally found something REAL. The Clash's mental health was fairly focused, which is odd for a punk band. But I find it incredibly important to include them because of the impact they had on punk rock culture and mental health. They showed us that there is always something to sing about. I can always look at The Clash and think "Man, there is a band the fucking did it." Joe Strummer once said about why he wrote songs, "a song is something you write because you can't sleep unless you write it."

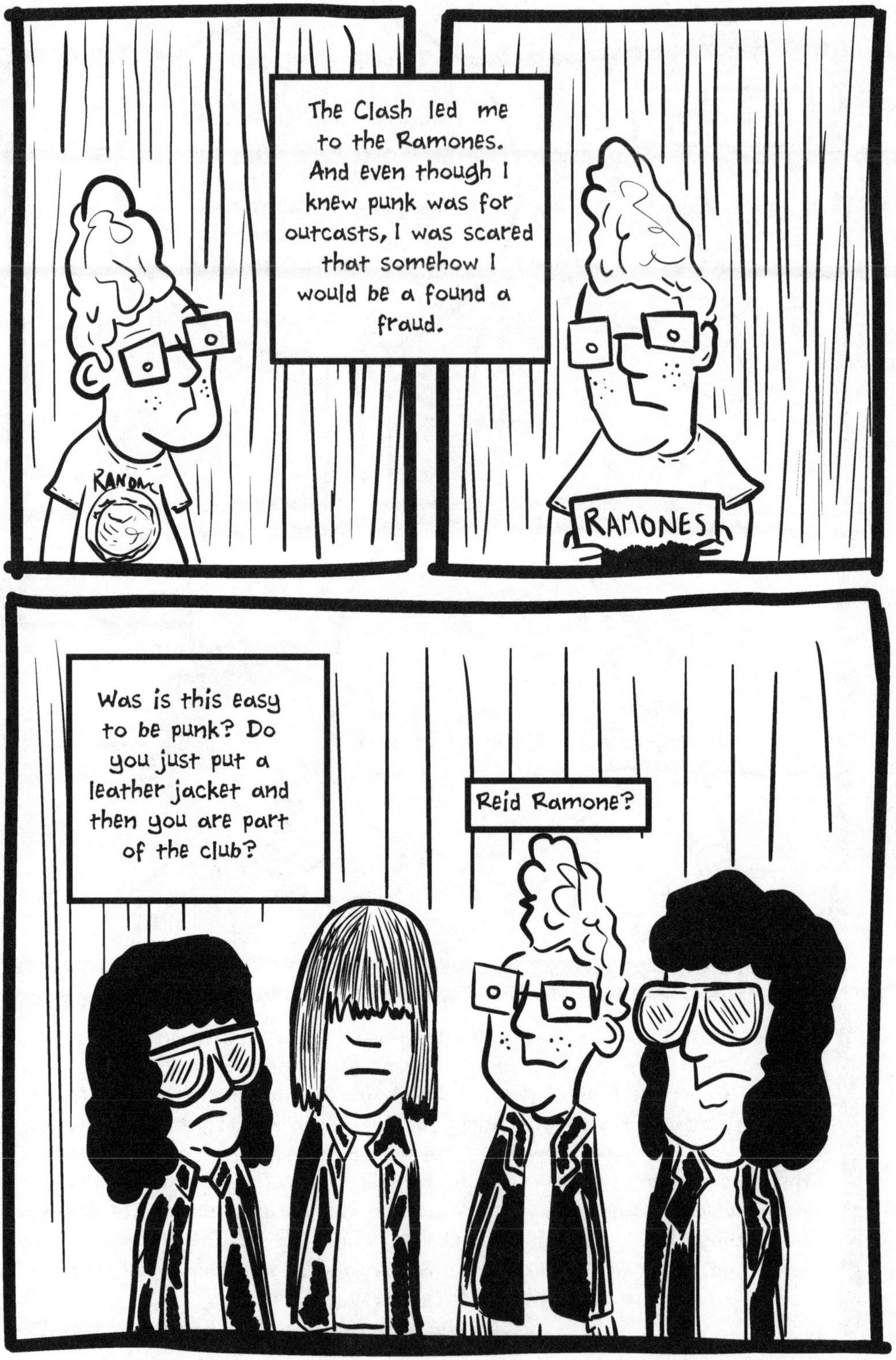
The Clash led me to the Ramones. And even though I knew punk was for outcasts, I was scared that somehow I would be a found a fraud.
RAMONES
Was is this easy to be punk? Do you just put a leather jacket and then you are part of the club?
Reid Ramone?

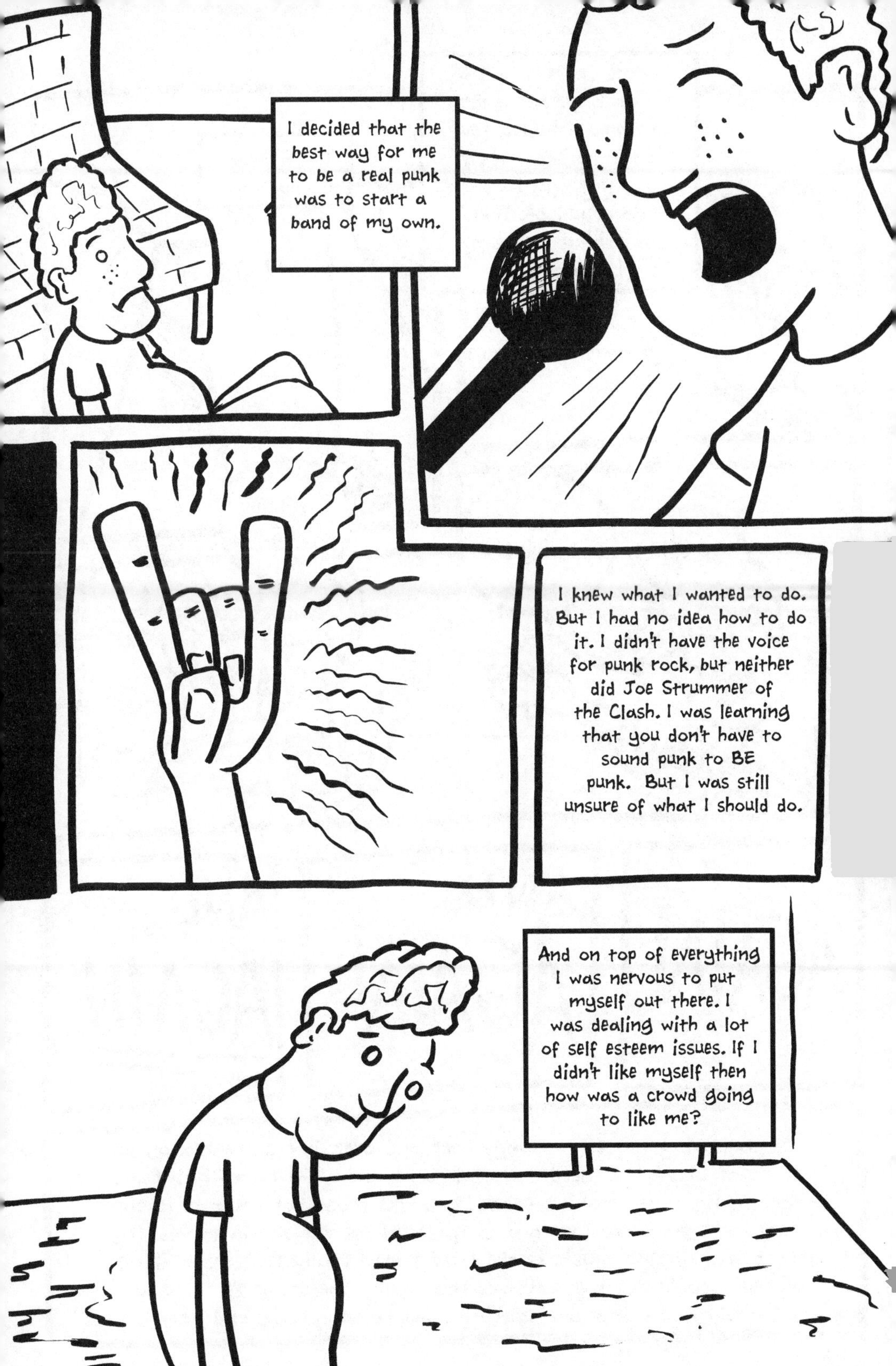
I decided that the best way for me to be a real punk was to start a band of my own.
I knew what I wanted to do. But I had no idea how to do it. I didn't have the voice for punk rock, but neither did Joe Strummer of the Clash. I was learning that you don't have to sound punk to BE punk. But I was still unsure of what I should do.
And on top of everything I was nervous to put myself out there. I was dealing with a lot of self esteem issues. If I didn't like myself then how was a crowd going to like me?

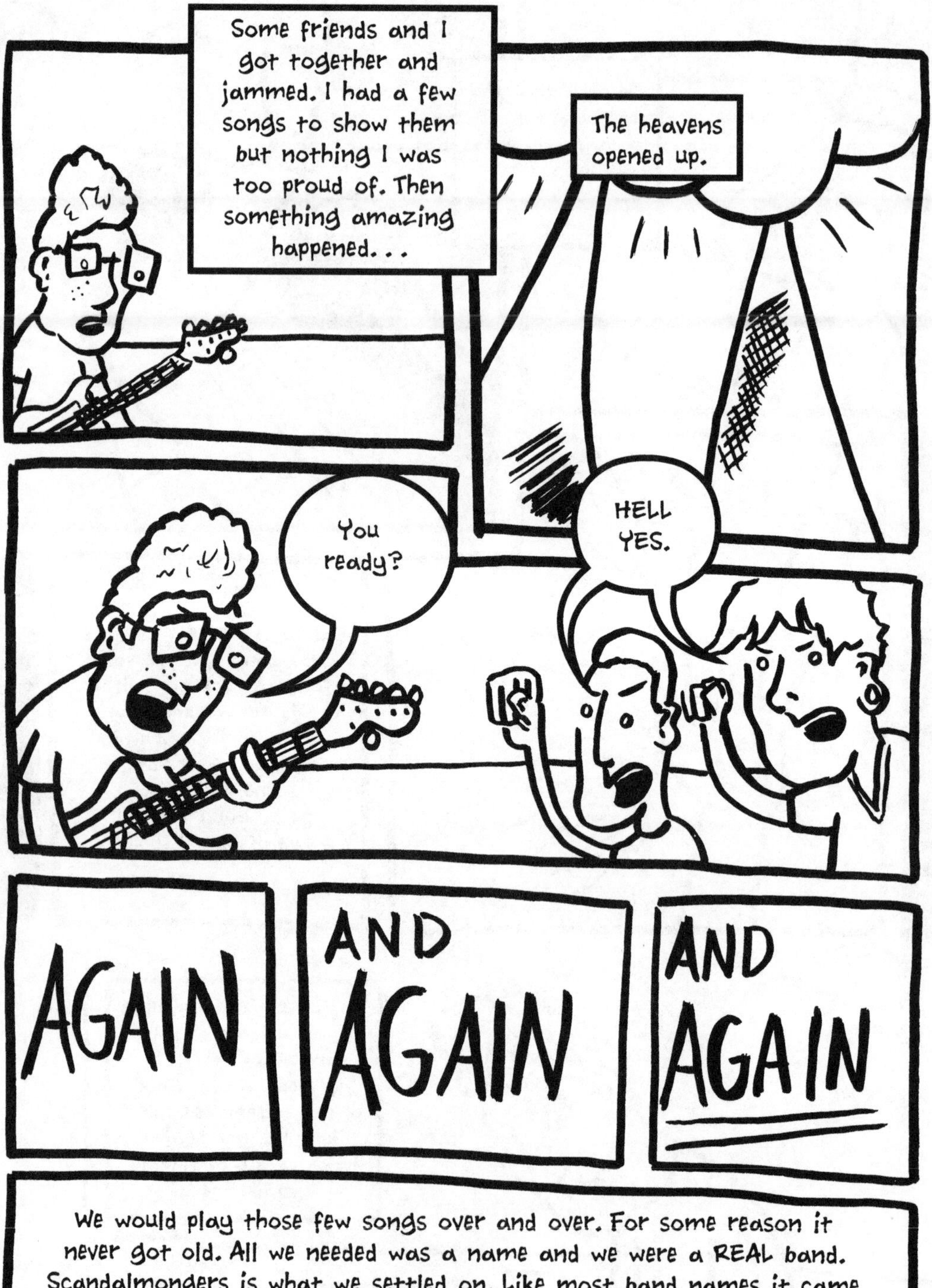
Some friends and I got together and jammed. I had a few songs to show them but nothing I was too proud of. Then something amazing happened. . .
The heavens opened up.
You ready?
HELL YES.
AGAIN
AND AGAIN
AND AGAIN

We would play those few songs over and over. For some reason it never got old. All we needed was a name and we were a REAL band. Scandalmongers is what we settled on. Like most band names it came from some place random and silly. (Our bass player Matt's history text book.) Playing music is the first time I really remember liking myself. I could become someone else easily. The stage felt like an entirely new world, one where I could be cool, sexy, and happy.

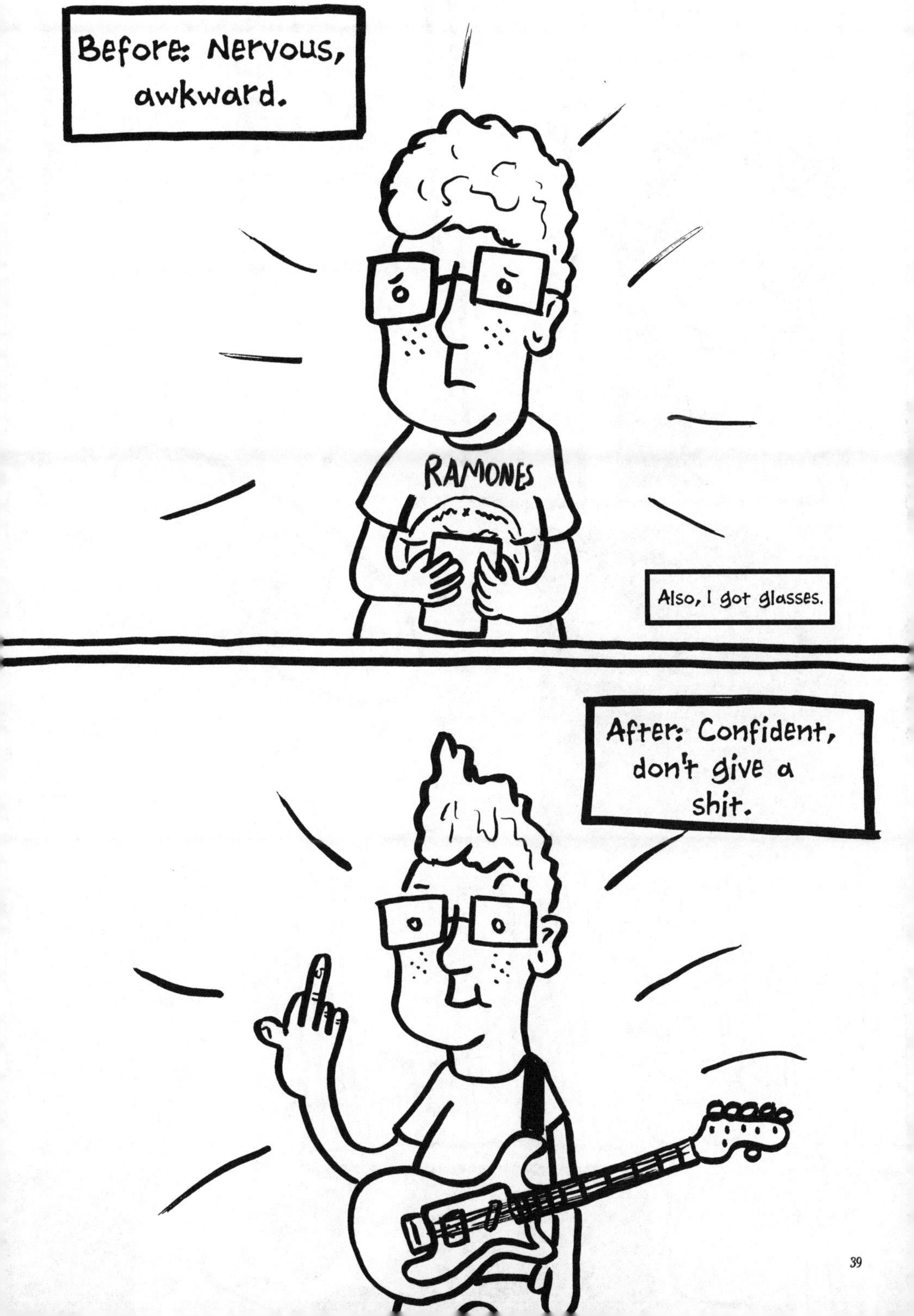
Before: Nervous, awkward.
RAMONES
Also, I got glasses.
After: Confident, don't give a shit.

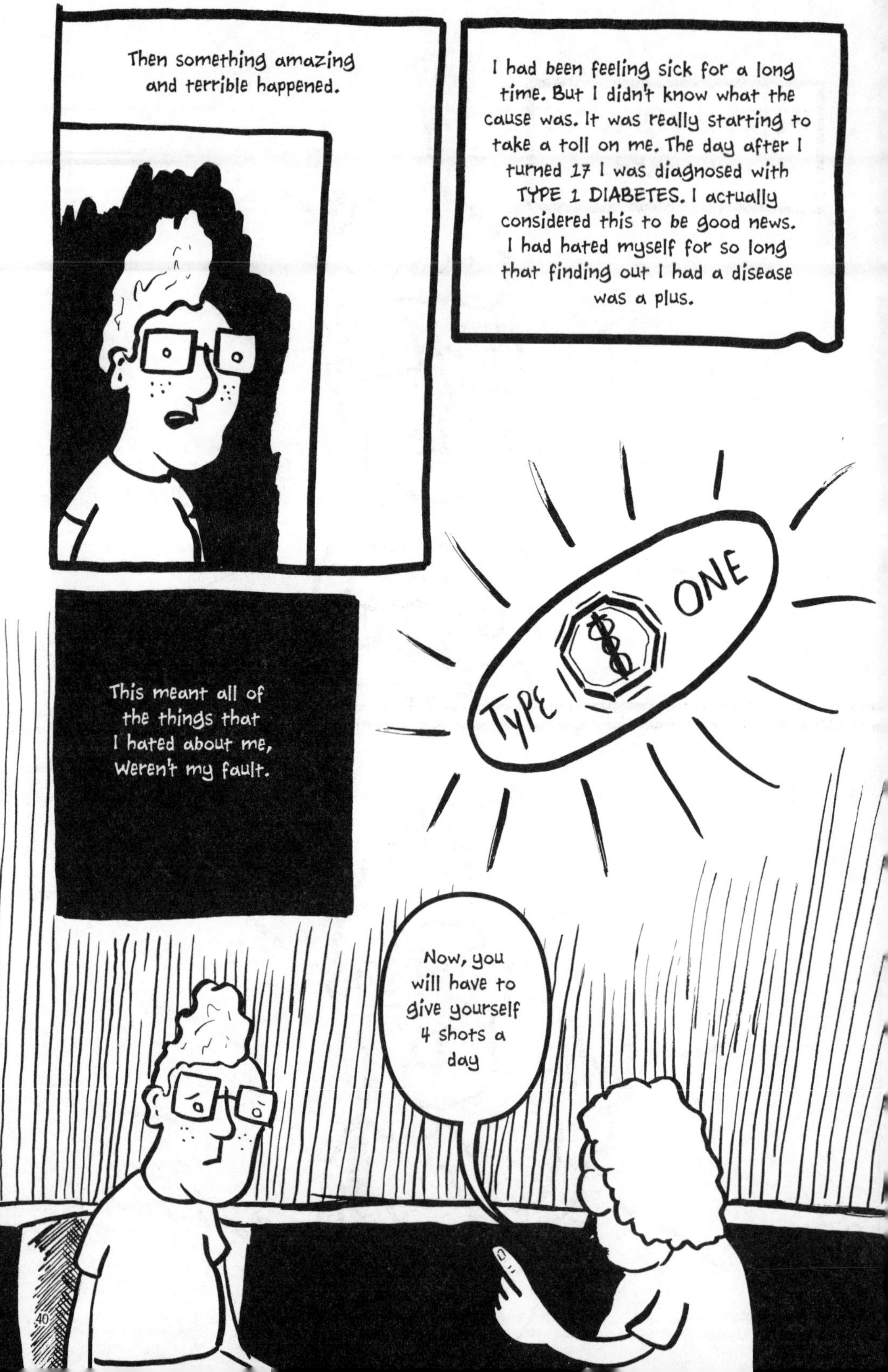
Then something amazing and terrible happened.
I had been feeling sick for a long time. But I didn't know what the cause was. It was really starting to take a toll on me. The day after I turned 17 I was diagnosed with TYPE 1 DIABETES. I actually considered this to be good news. I had hated myself for so long that finding out I had a disease was a plus.
This meant all of the things that I hated about me, Weren't my fault.
TYPE ONE
Now, you will have to give yourself 4 shots a day

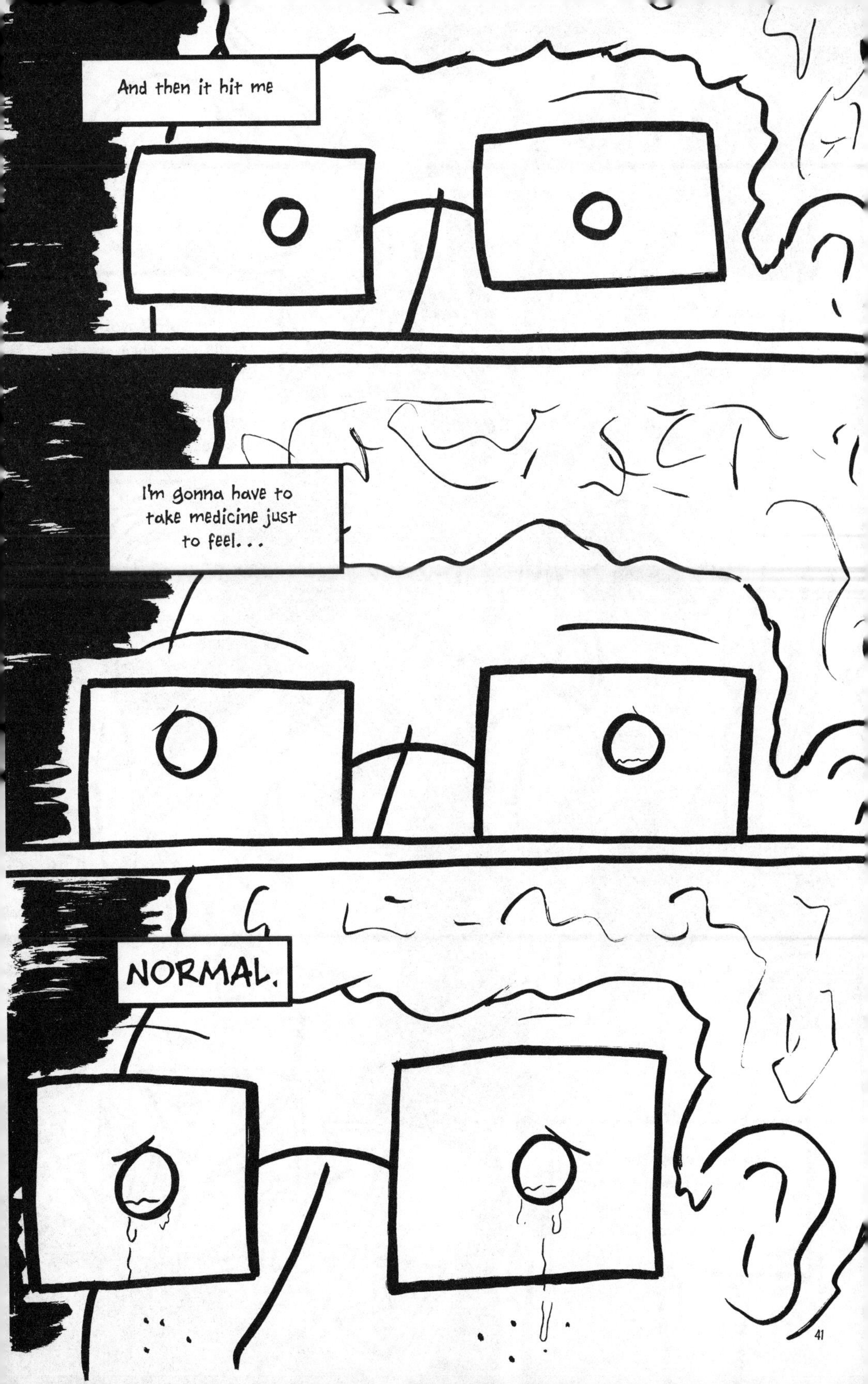
And then it hit me
I'm gonna have to take medicine just to feel...
NORMAL.

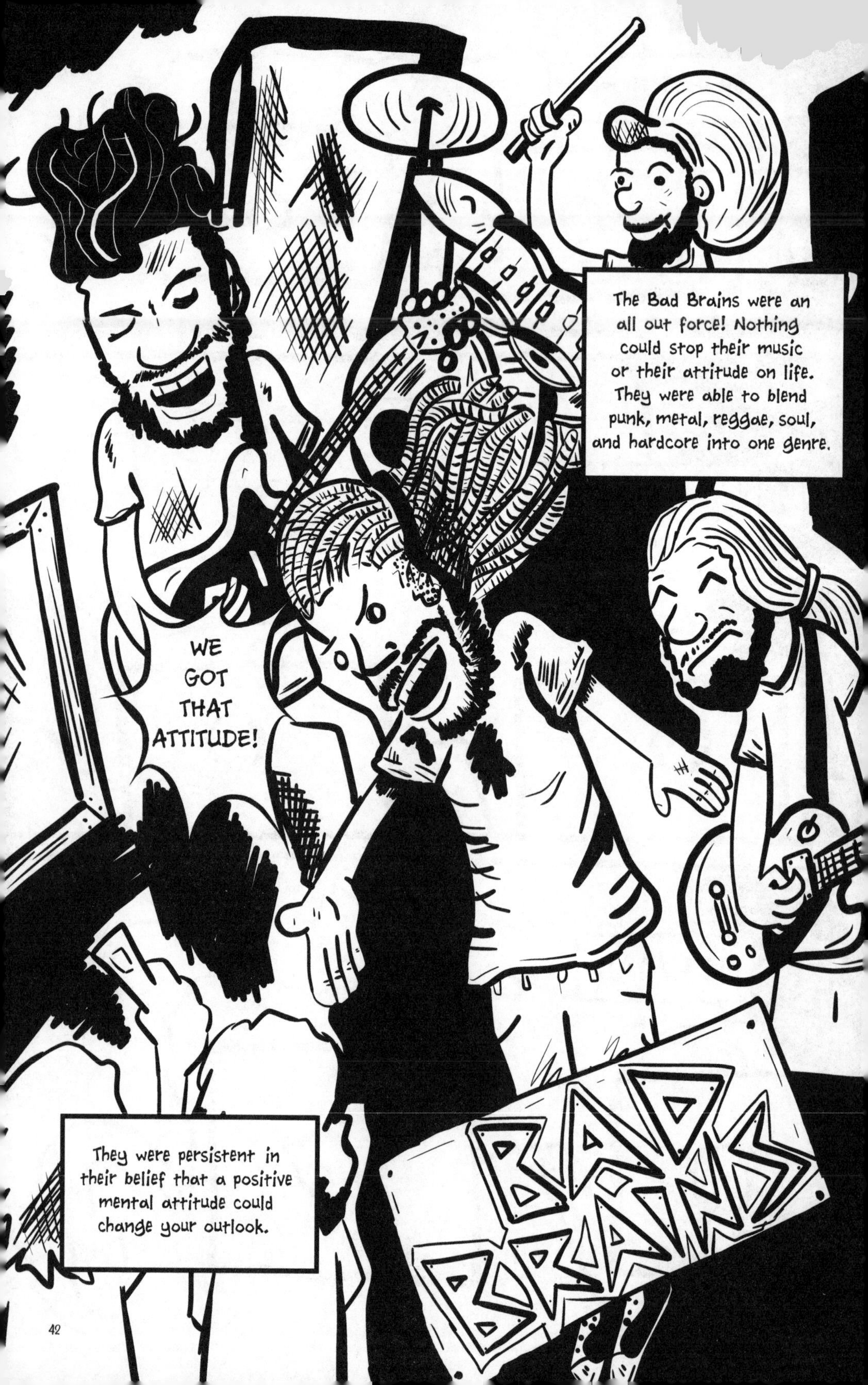
The Bad Brains were an all out force! Nothing could stop their music or their attitude on life. They were able to blend punk, metal, reggae, soul, and hardcore into one genre.
WE GOT THAT ATTITUDE!
They were persistent in their belief that a positive mental attitude could change your outlook.
BAD BRAINS

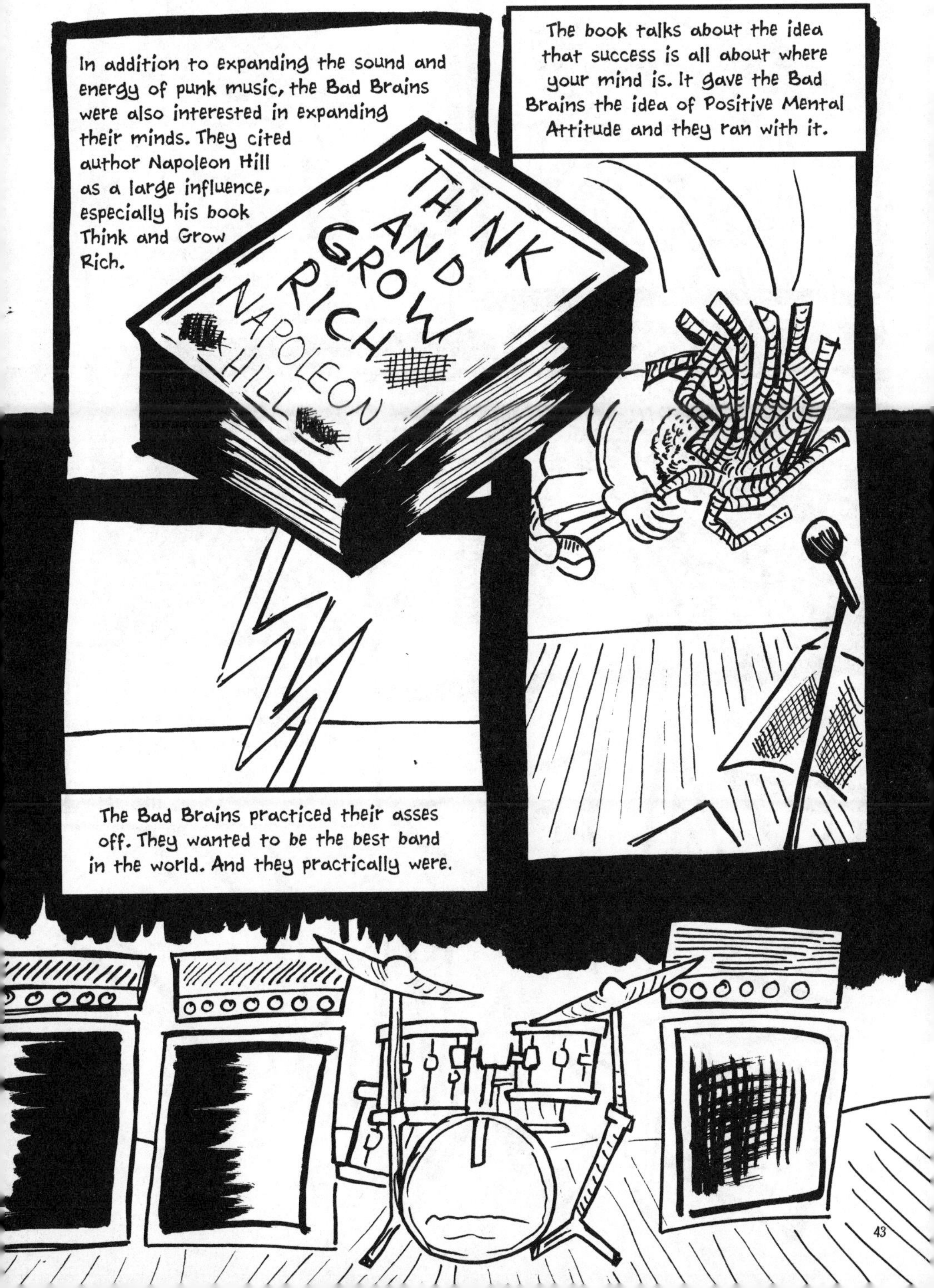

In addition to expanding the sound and energy of punk music, the Bad Brains were also interested in expanding their minds. They cited author Napoleon Hill as a large influence, especially his book Think and Grow Rich.
THINK AND GROW RICH
NAPOLEON HILL
The book talks about the idea that success is all about where your mind is. It gave the Bad Brains the idea of Positive Mental Attitude and they ran with it.
The Bad Brains practiced their asses off. They wanted to be the best band in the world. And they practically were.

HR, the lead singer of the Bad Brains, had his share of troubles. He suffers from schizophrenia and SUNCT syndrome.

SUNCT is a rare disorder that causes extreme headaches out of nowhere.

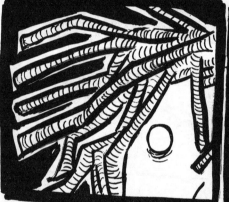

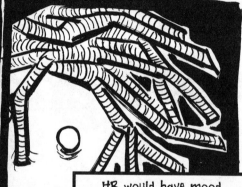

HR would have mood swings and caused some of his bandmates stress. But when HR took the stage. . . There was nothing like it!

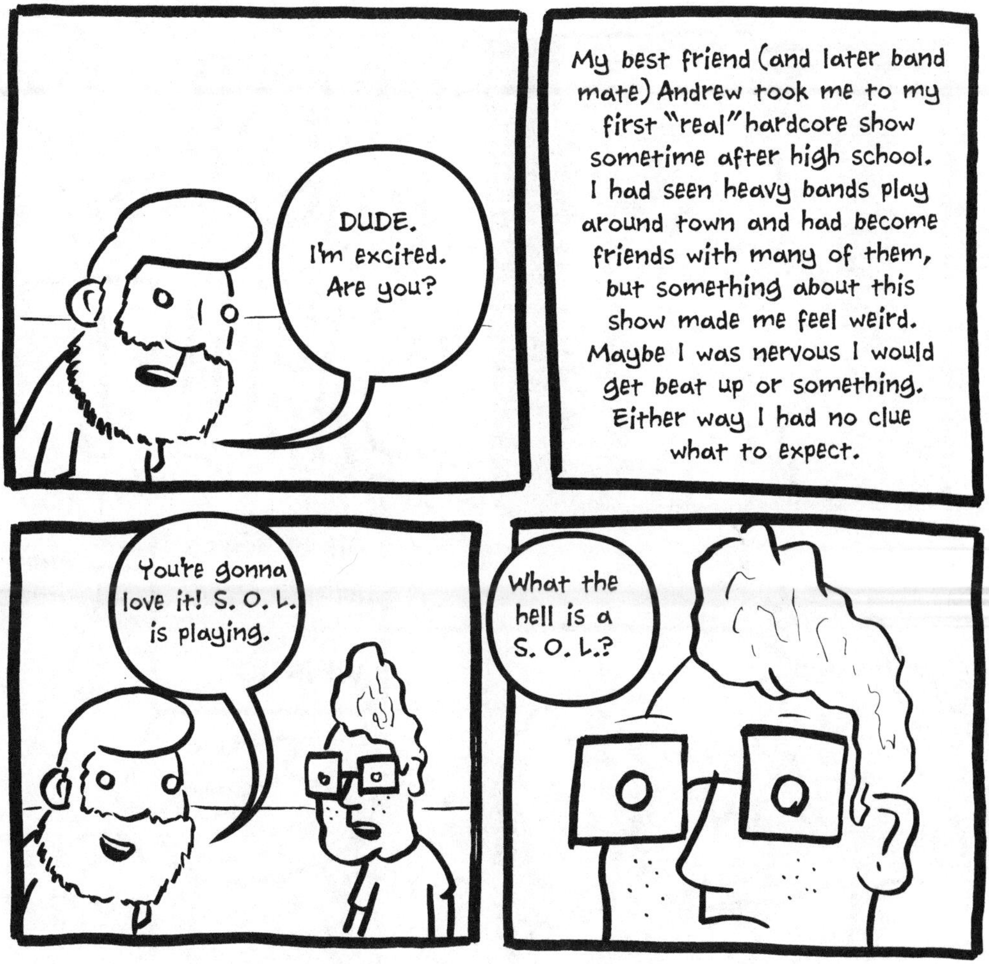
DUDE. I'm excited. Are you?
My best friend (and later band mate) Andrew took me to my first "real" hardcore show sometime after high school. I had seen heavy bands play around town and had become friends with many of them, but something about this show made me feel weird. Maybe I was nervous I would get beat up or something. Either way I had no clue what to expect.
You're gonna love it! S. O. L. is playing.
What the hell is a S. O. L.?

For some reason or another I had built up anxiety about the entire show. Maybe it stems from my fear of being found out as an imposter in the punk world. I wanted to be a part of the secret club that all the punk and hardcore kids were. But what if they didn't accept me? However when Andrew opened the door to that venue it looked. . .

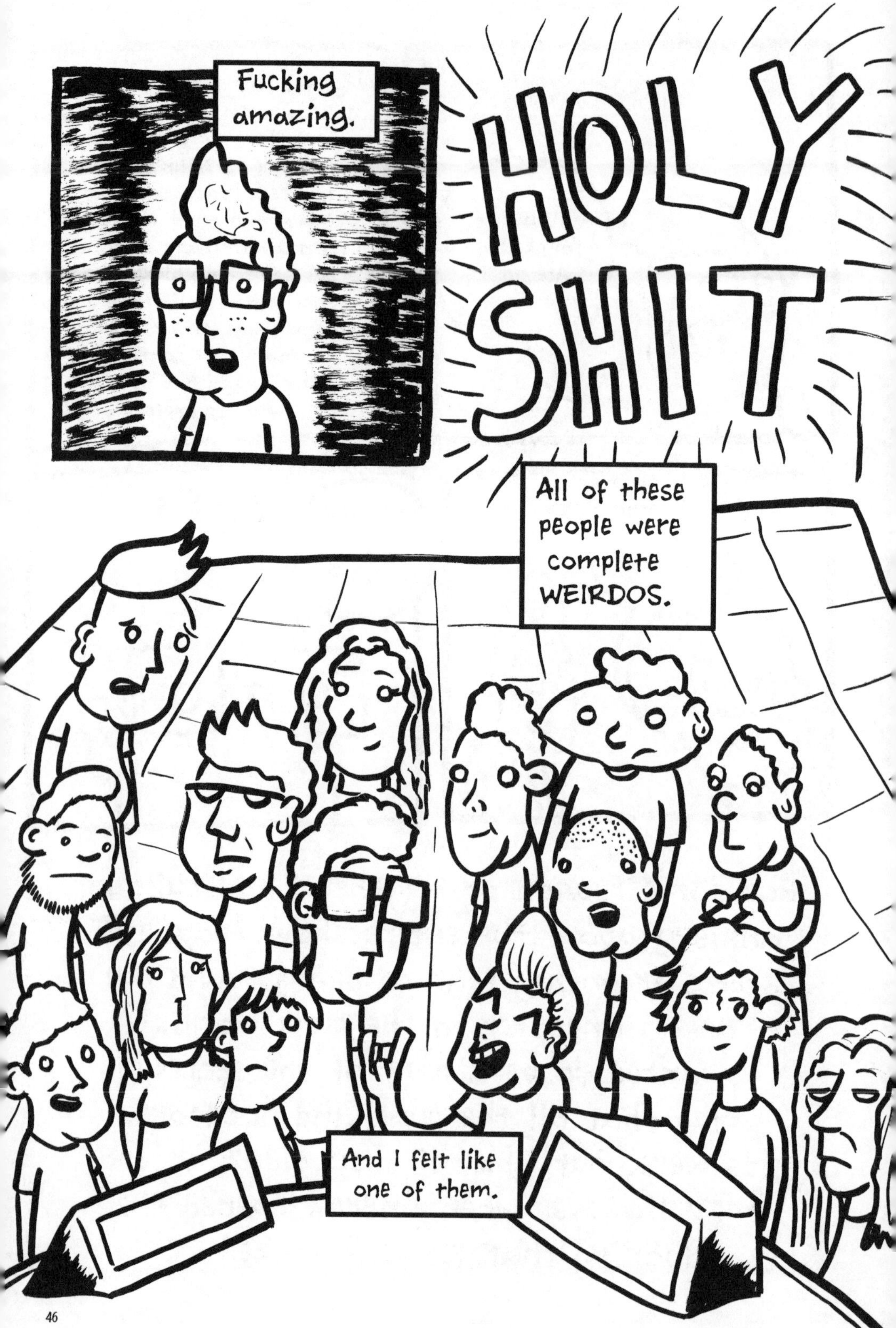

Fucking amazing.
HOLY SHIT
All of these people were complete WEIRDOS.
And I felt like one of them.

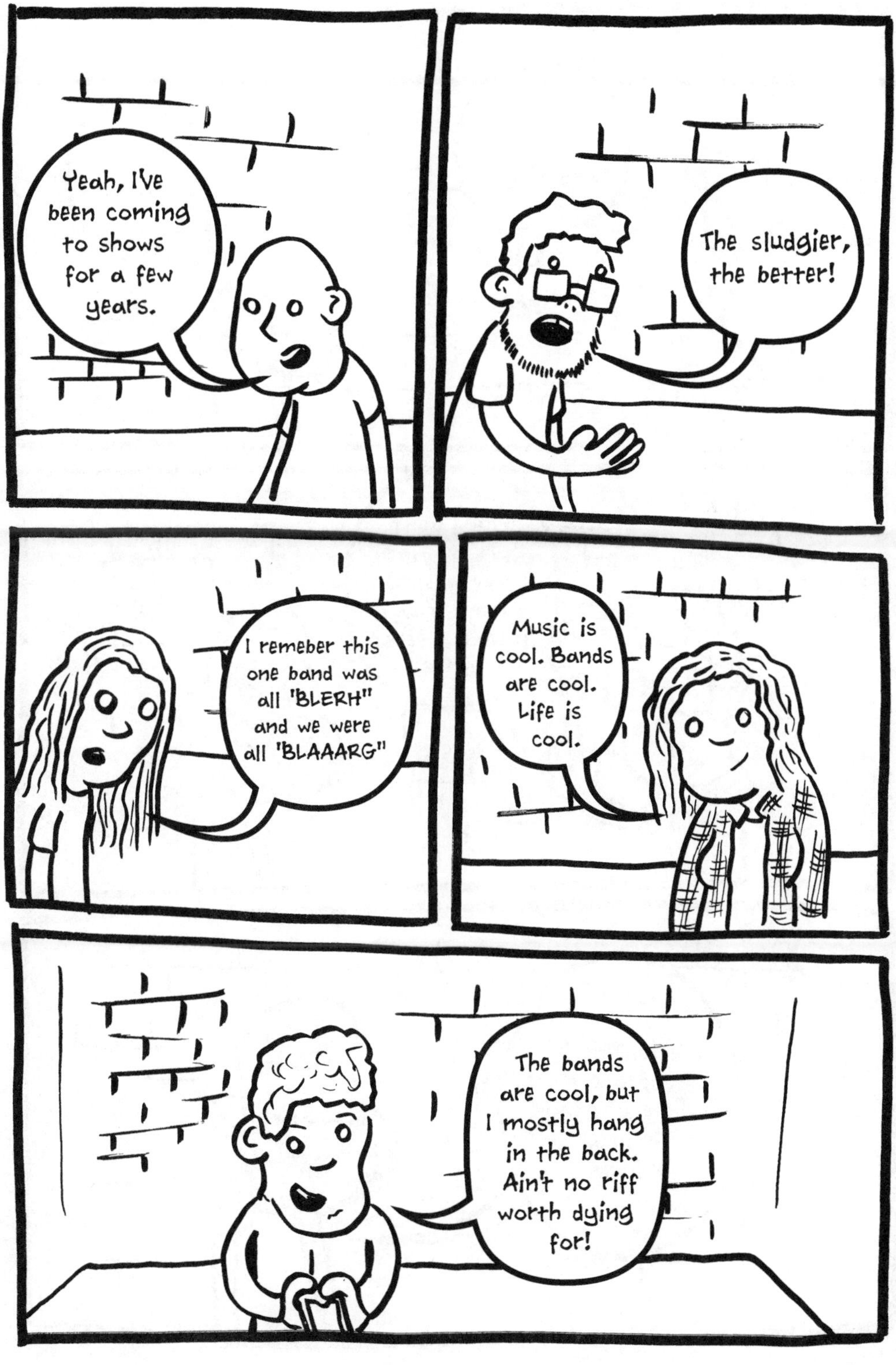
Yeah, I've been coming to shows for a few years.
The sludgier, the better!
I remeber this one band was all "BLERH" and we were all "BLAAARG"
Music is cool. Bands are cool. Life is cool.
The bands are cool, but I mostly hang in the back. Ain't no riff worth dying for!

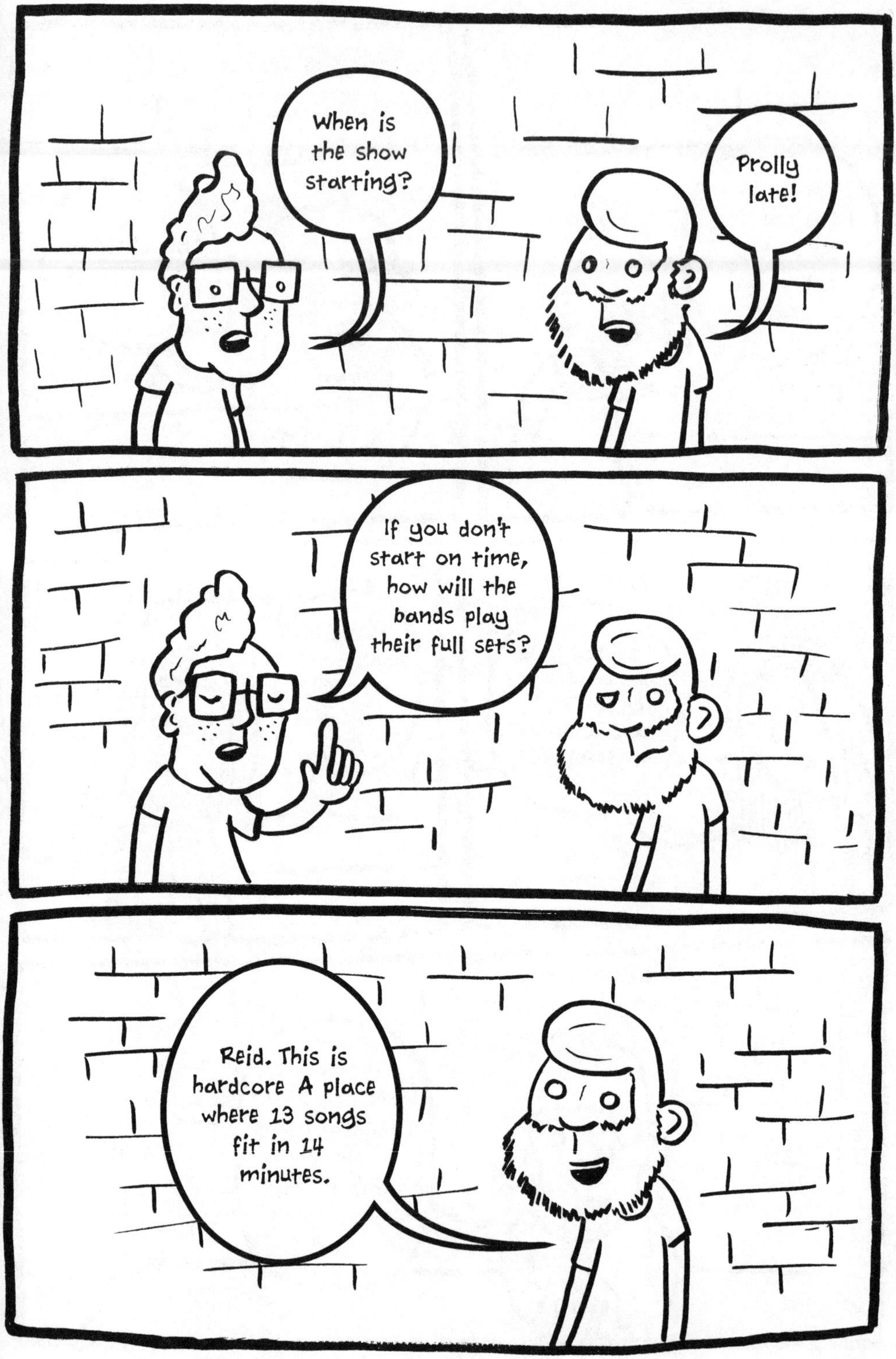
When is the show starting?
Prolly late!
If you don't start on time, how will the bands play their full sets?
Reid. This is hardcore A place where 13 songs fit in 14 minutes.

The style was different. It was unlike anything I had ever seen. Both awesome and terrifying.
The longer I watched the more welcome I felt. I was starting to understand.
MOSH
MOSH

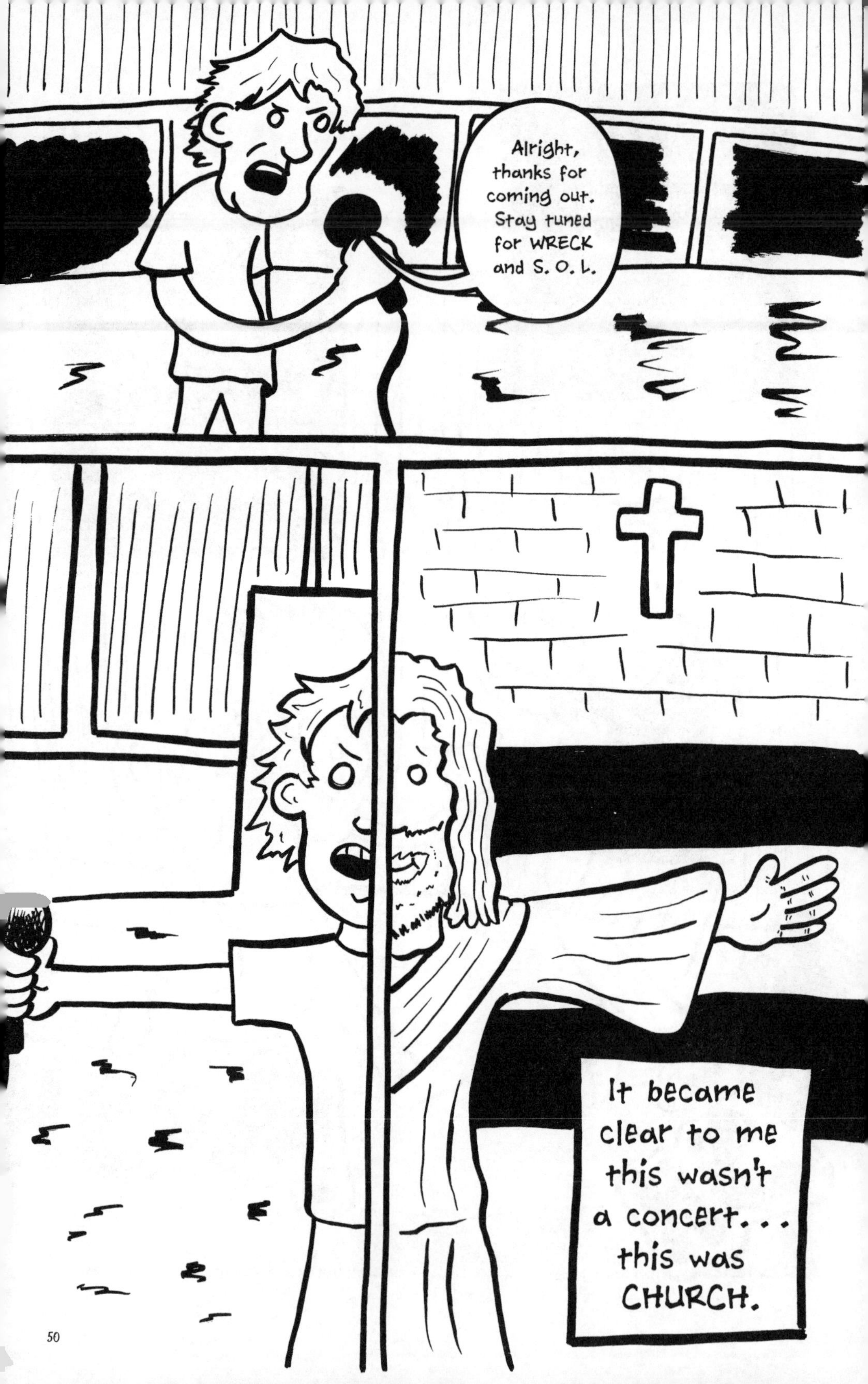
Alright, thanks for coming out. Stay tuned for WRECK and S. O. L.
It became clear to me this wasn't a concert... this was CHURCH.

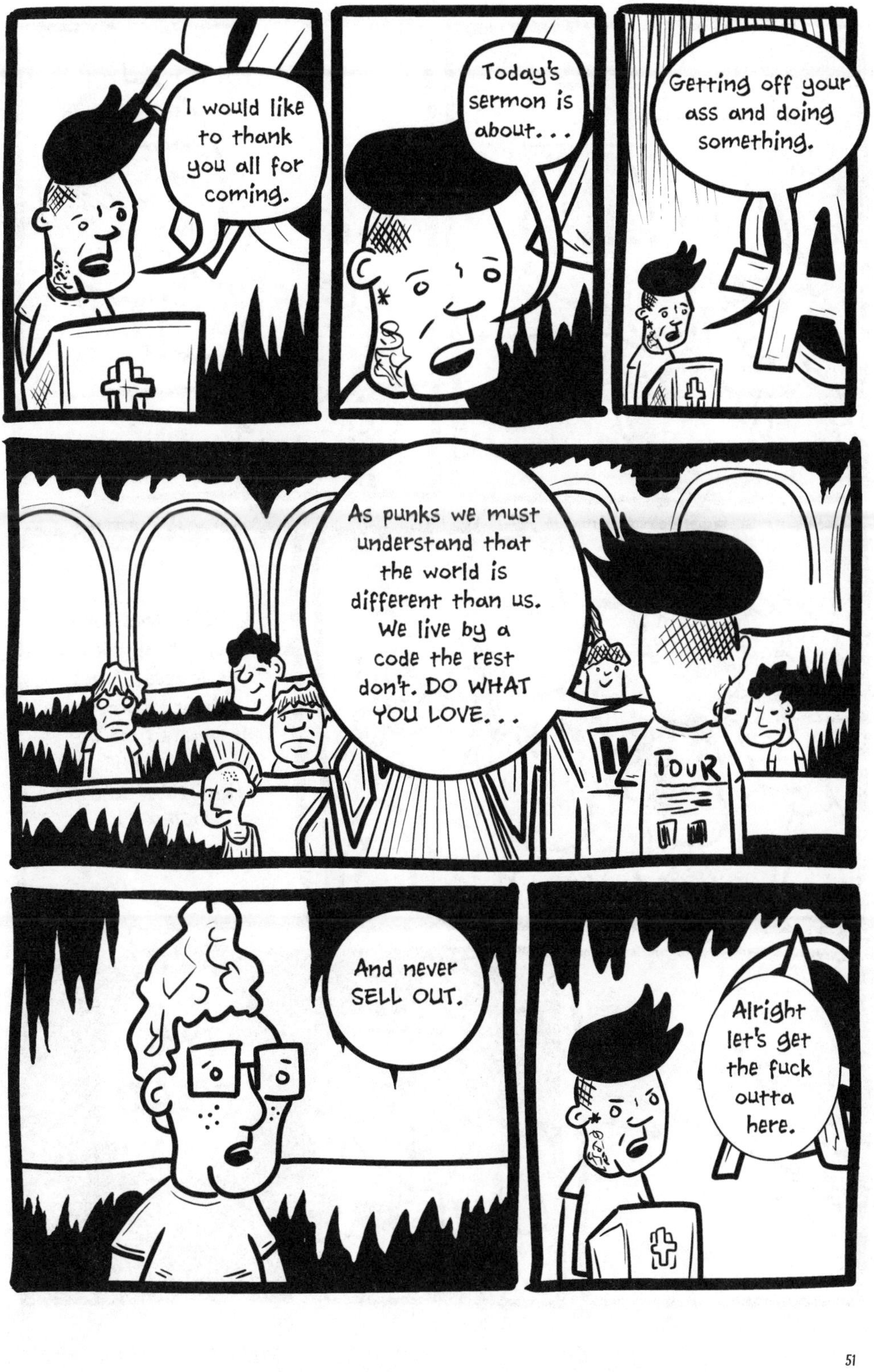
I would like to thank you all for coming.
Today's sermon is about...
Getting off your ass and doing something.
As punks we must understand that the world is different than us. We live by a code the rest don't. DO WHAT YOU LOVE...
TOUR
And never SELL OUT.
Alright let's get the fuck outta here.

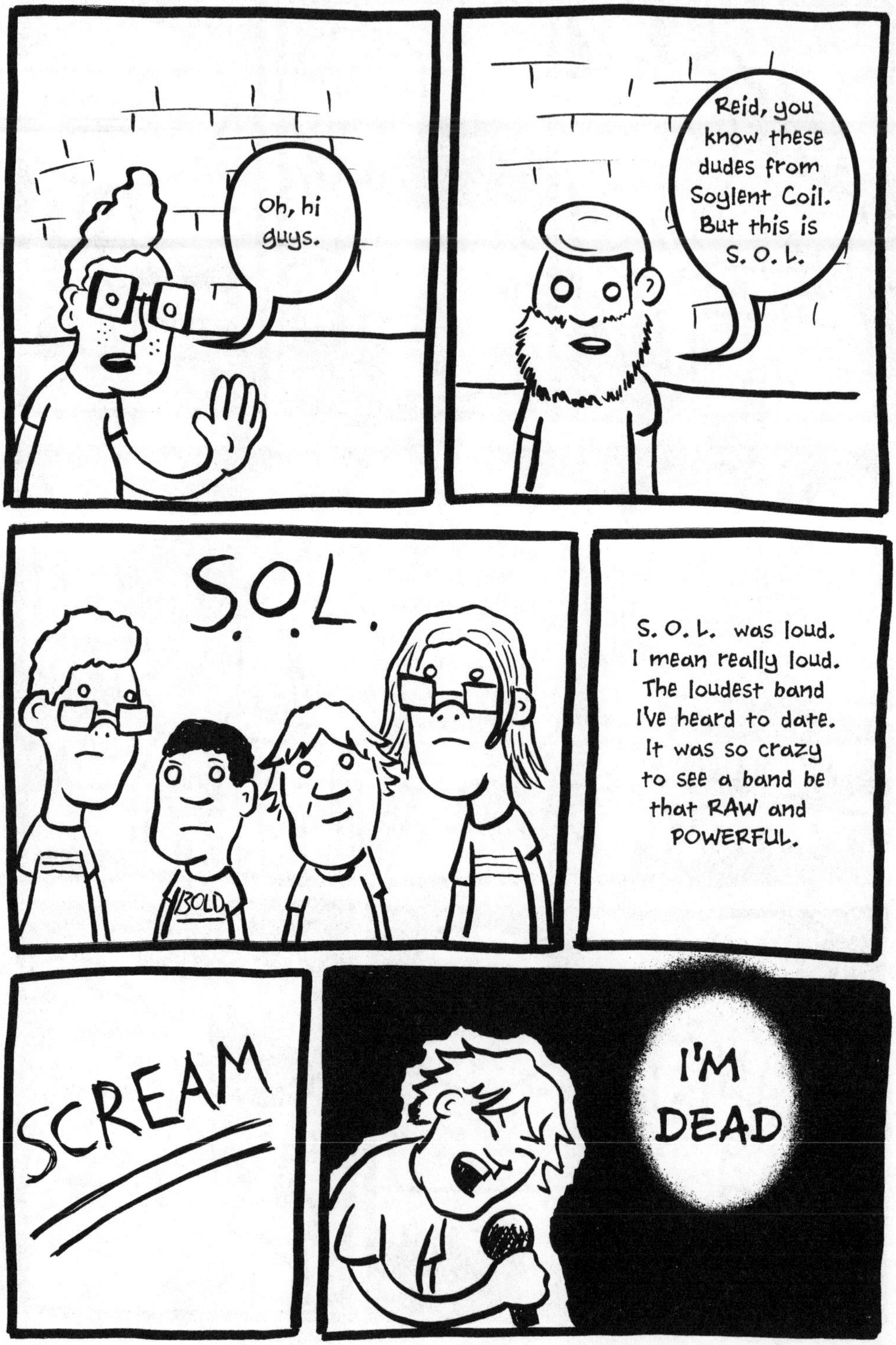
Oh, hi guys.
Reid, you know these dudes from Soylent Coil. But this is S.O.L.
S.O.L.
BOLD
S.O.L. was loud. I mean really loud. The loudest band I've heard to date. It was so crazy to see a band be that RAW and POWERFUL.
SCREAM
I'M DEAD

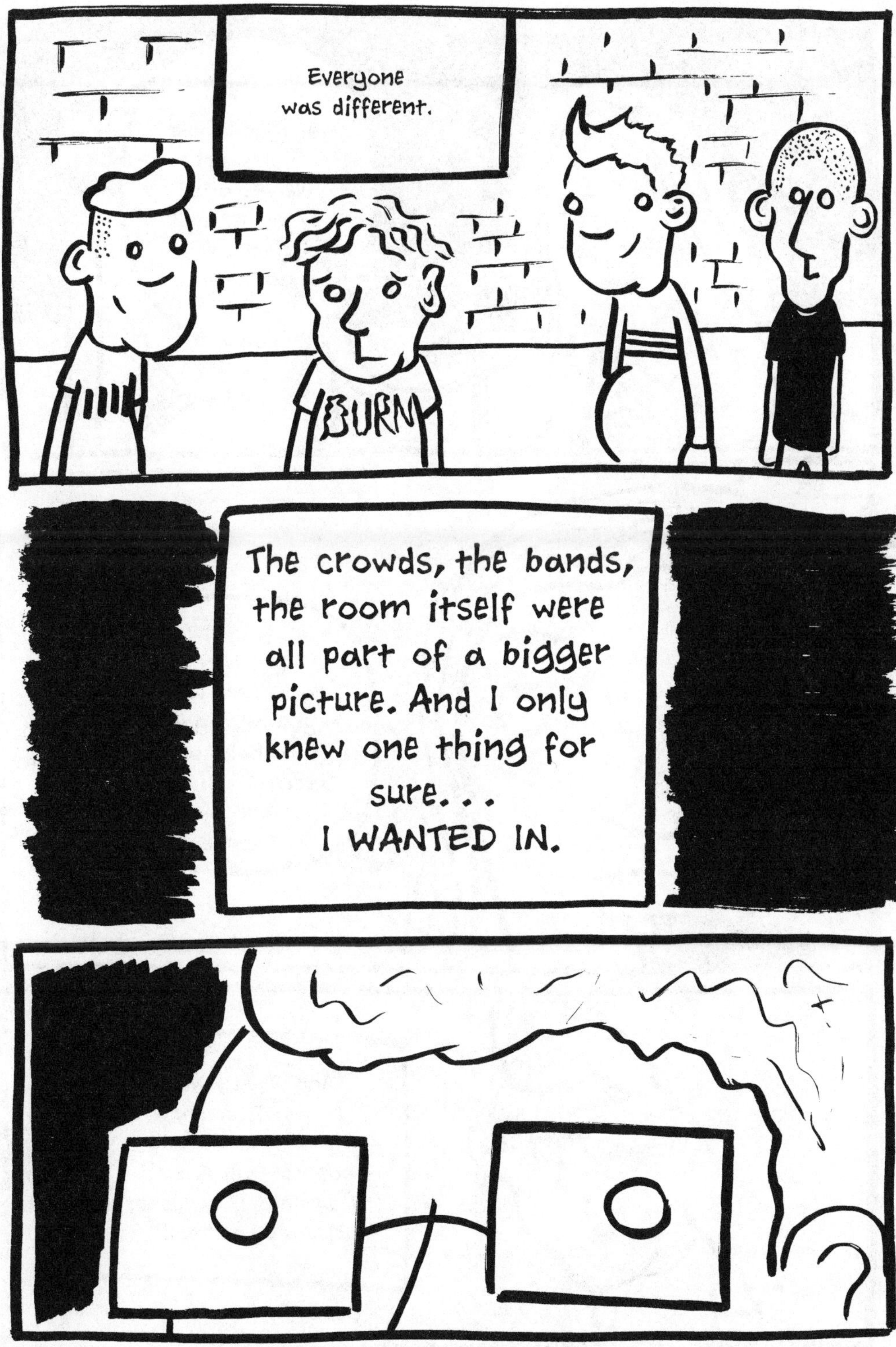
Everyone was different.
BURN
The crowds, the bands, the room itself were all part of a bigger picture. And I only knew one thing for sure...
I WANTED IN.

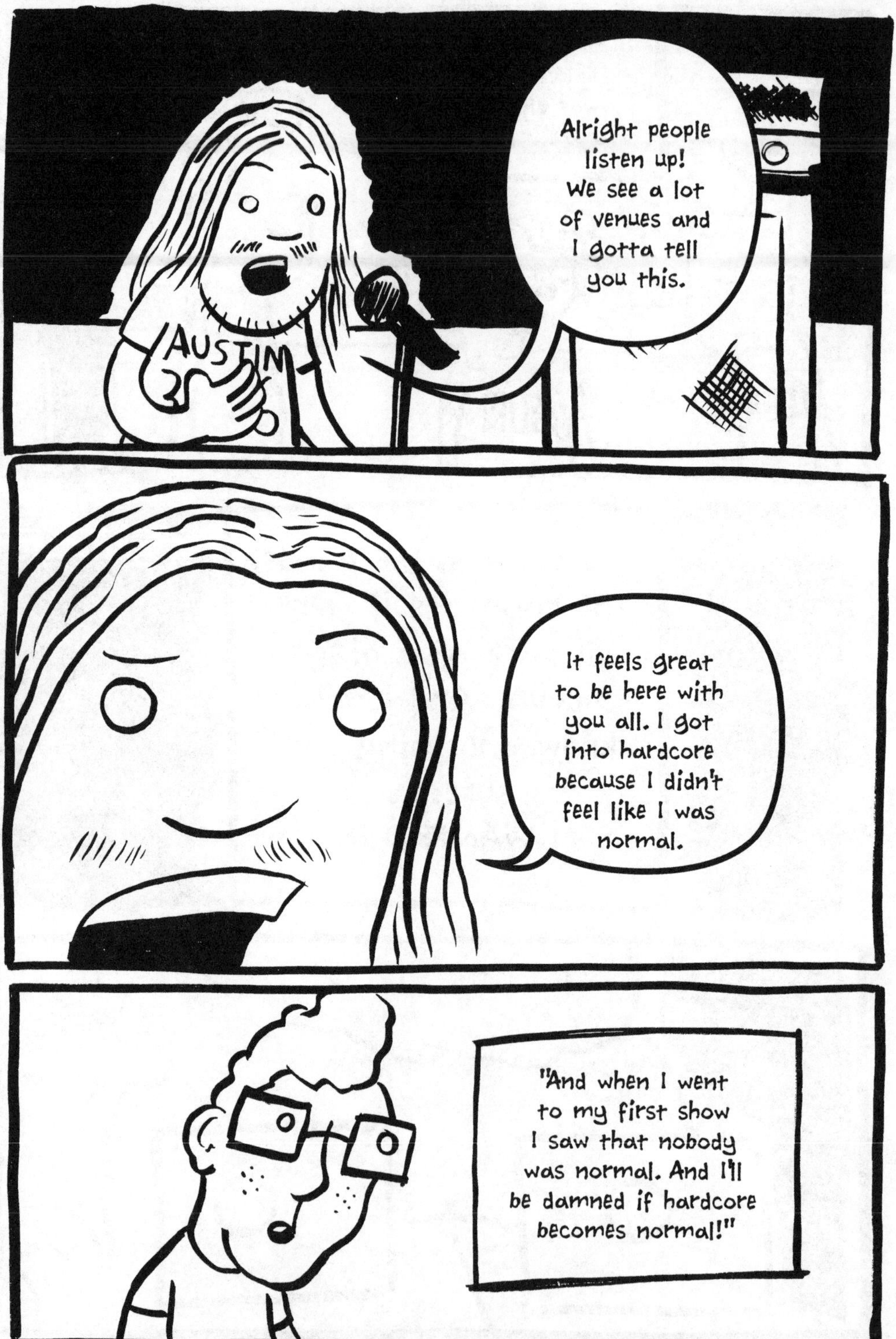

Alright people listen up! We see a lot of venues and I gotta tell you this.
AUSTIN
It feels great to be here with you all. I got into hardcore because I didn't feel like I was normal.
"And when I went to my first show I saw that nobody was normal. And I'll be damned if hardcore becomes normal!"

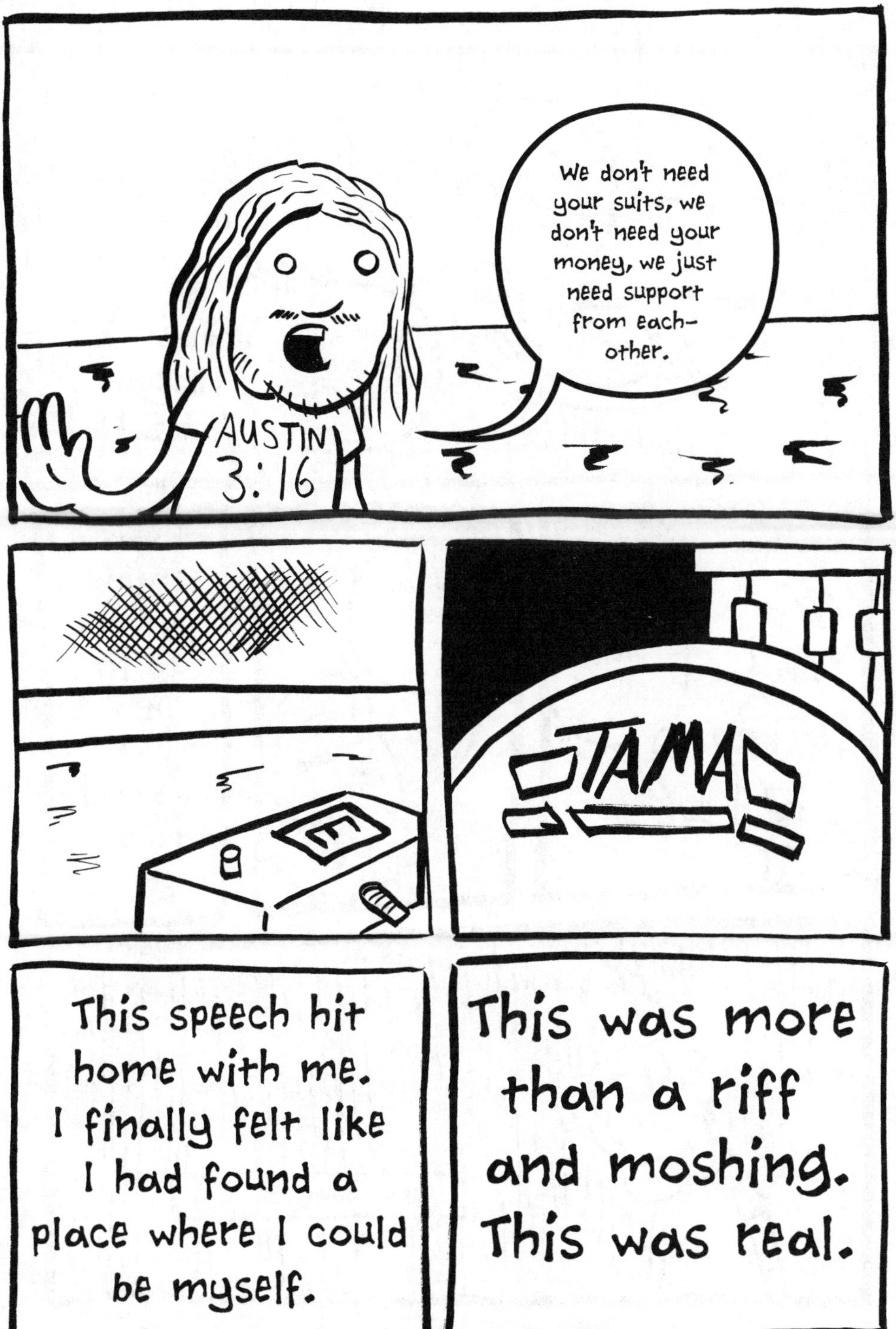
We don't need your suits, we don't need your money, we just need support from each-other.
AUSTIN 3:16
TAMA
This speech hit home with me. I finally felt like I had found a place where I could be myself.
This was more than a riff and moshing. This was real.

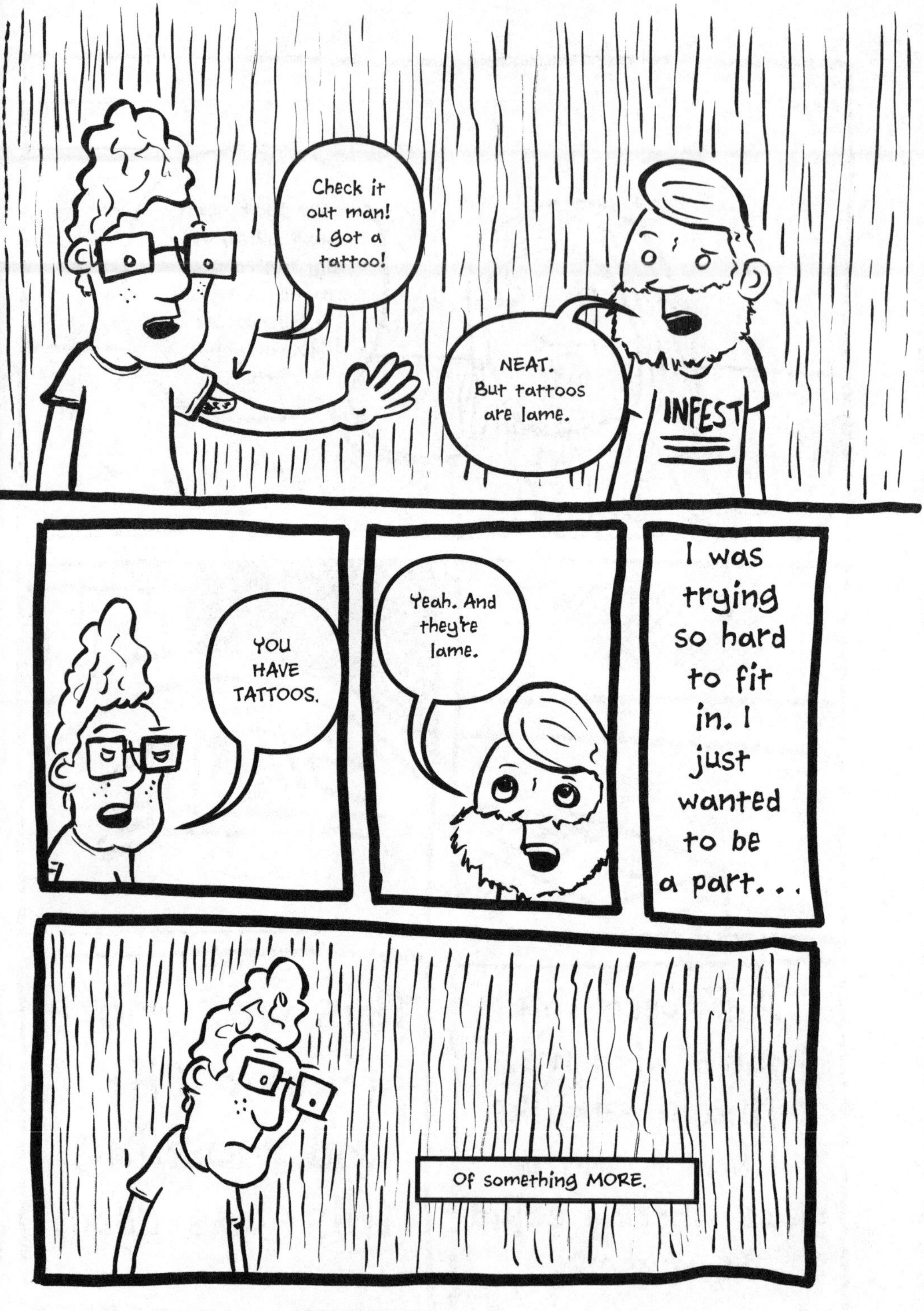
Check it out man! I got a tattoo!
NEAT. But tattoos are lame.
INFEST
YOU HAVE TATTOOS.
Yeah. And they're lame.
I was trying so hard to fit in. I just wanted to be a part...
Of something MORE.

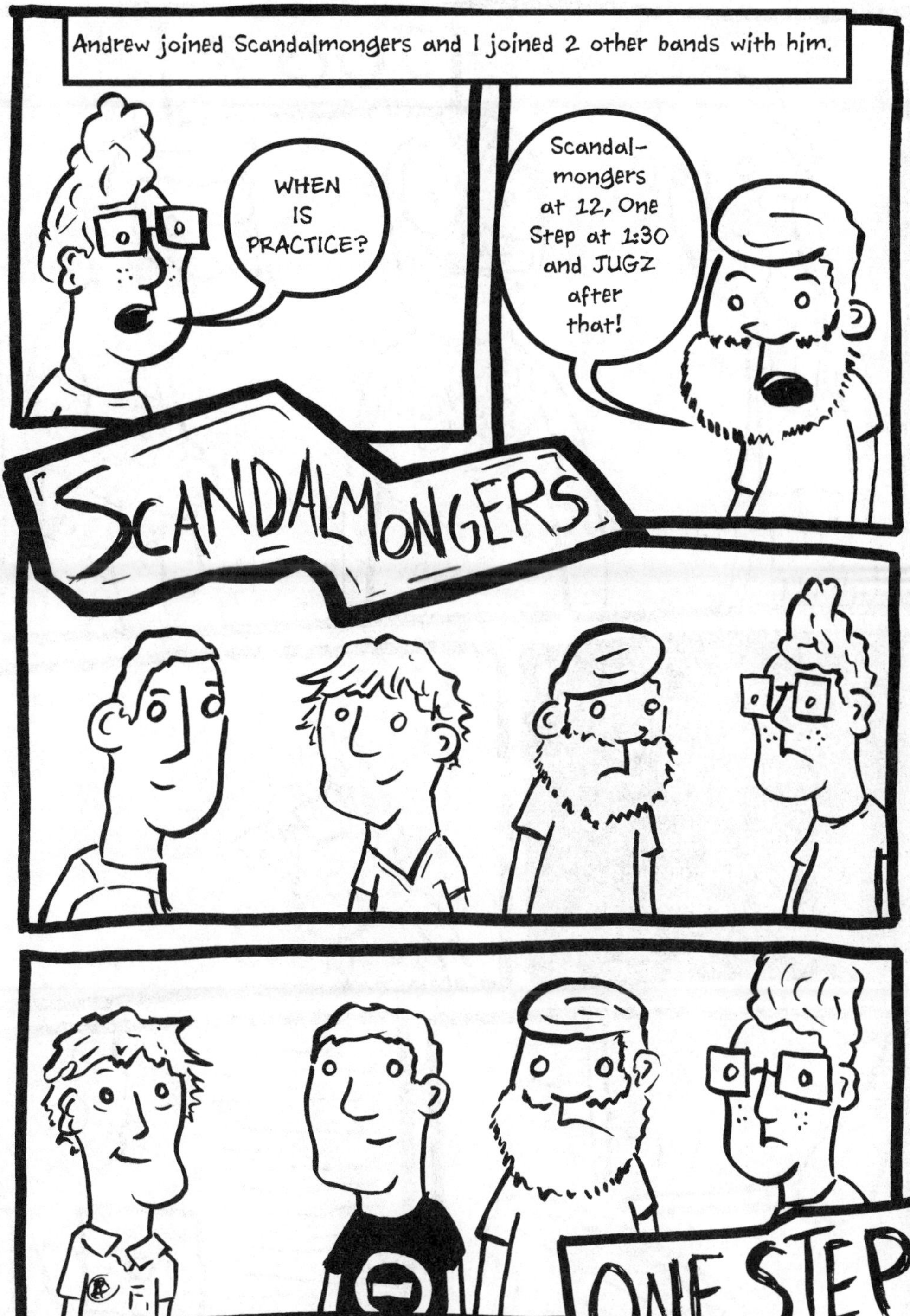
Andrew joined Scandalmongers and I joined 2 other bands with him.
WHEN IS PRACTICE?
Scandal-mongers at 12, One Step at 1:30 and JUGZ after that!
SCANDALMONGERS
ONE STEP

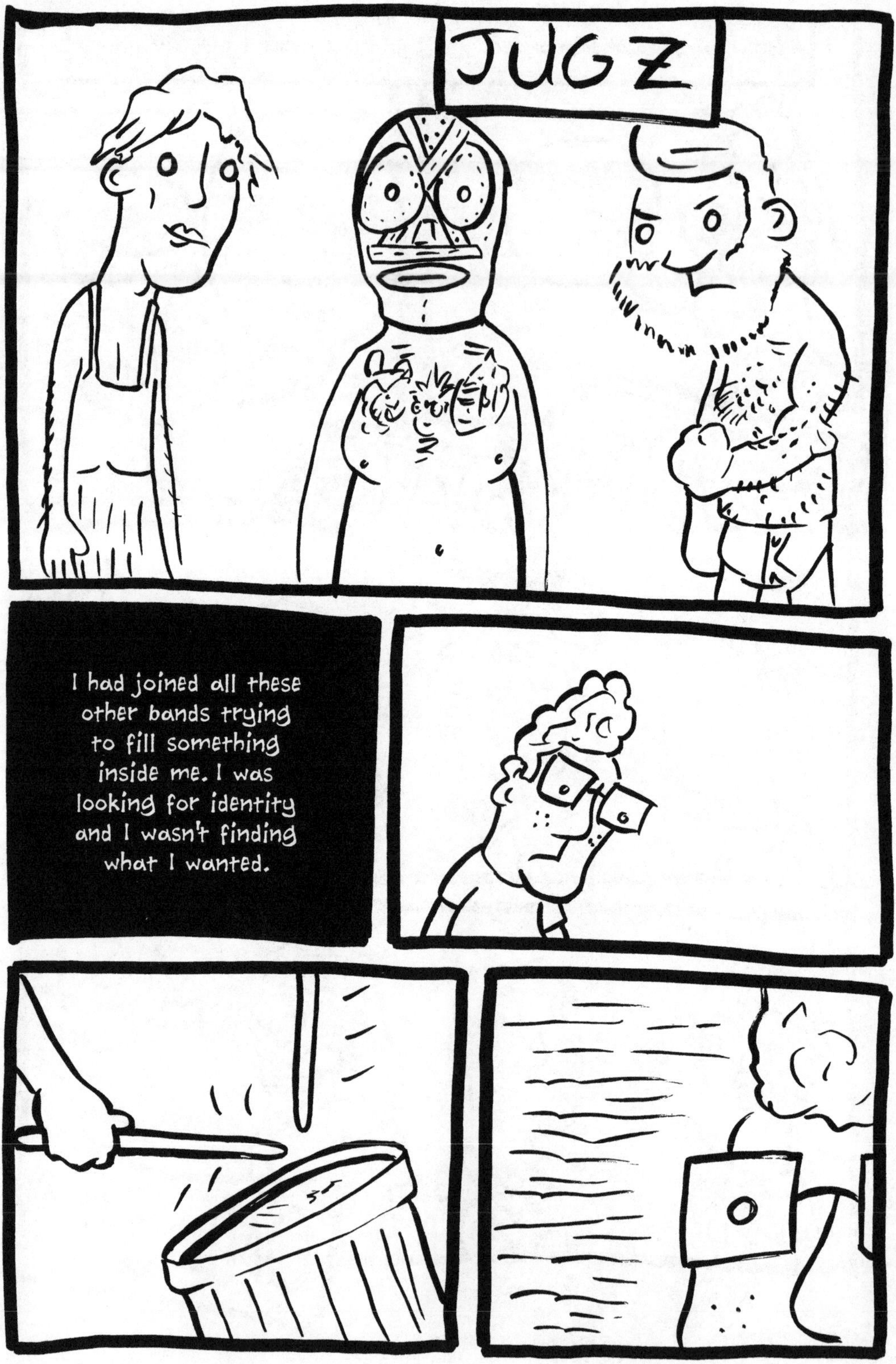
JUGZ
I had joined all these other bands trying to fill something inside me. I was looking for identity and I wasn't finding what I wanted.

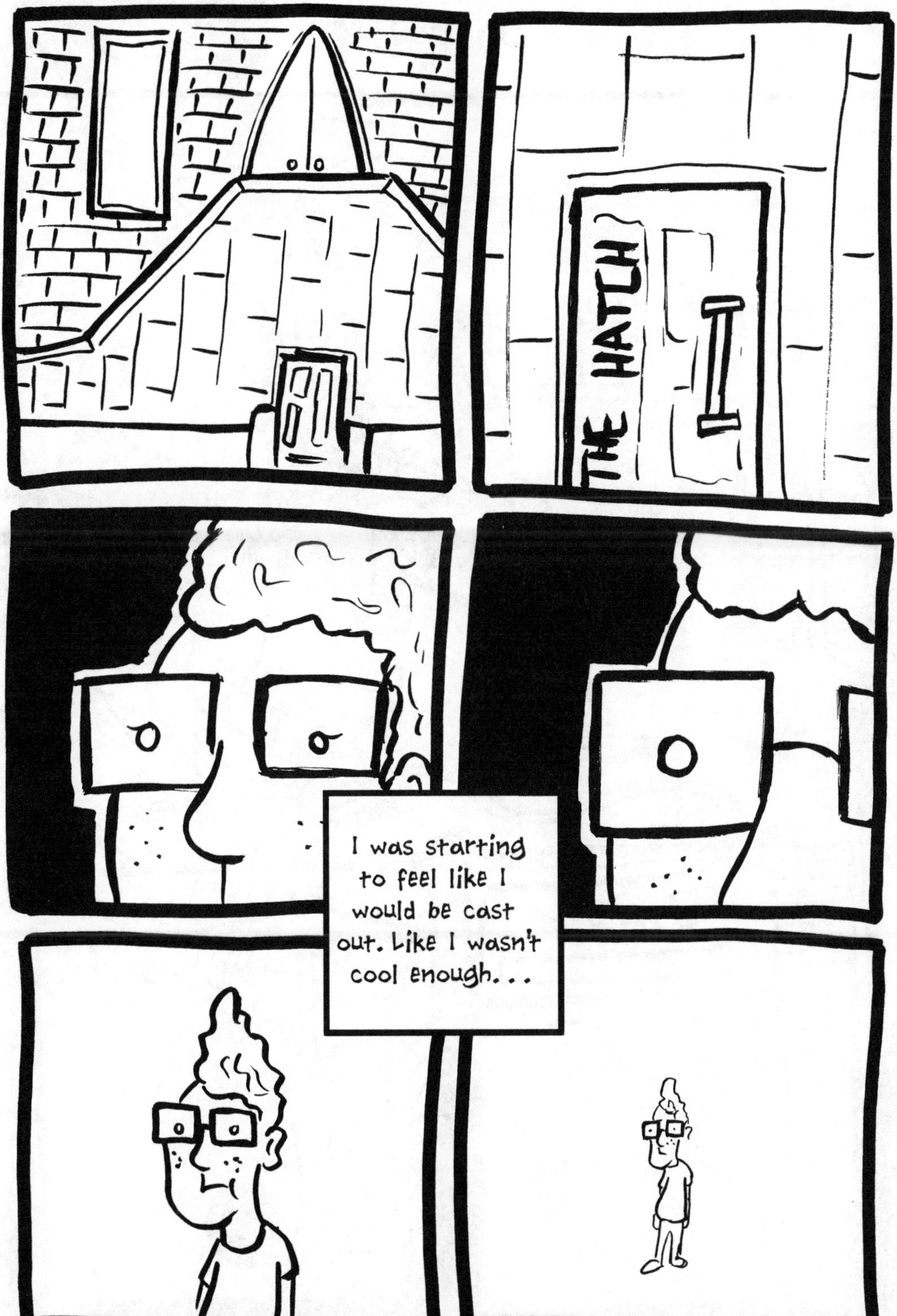
THE HATCH
I was starting to feel like I would be cast out. Like I wasn't cool enough...

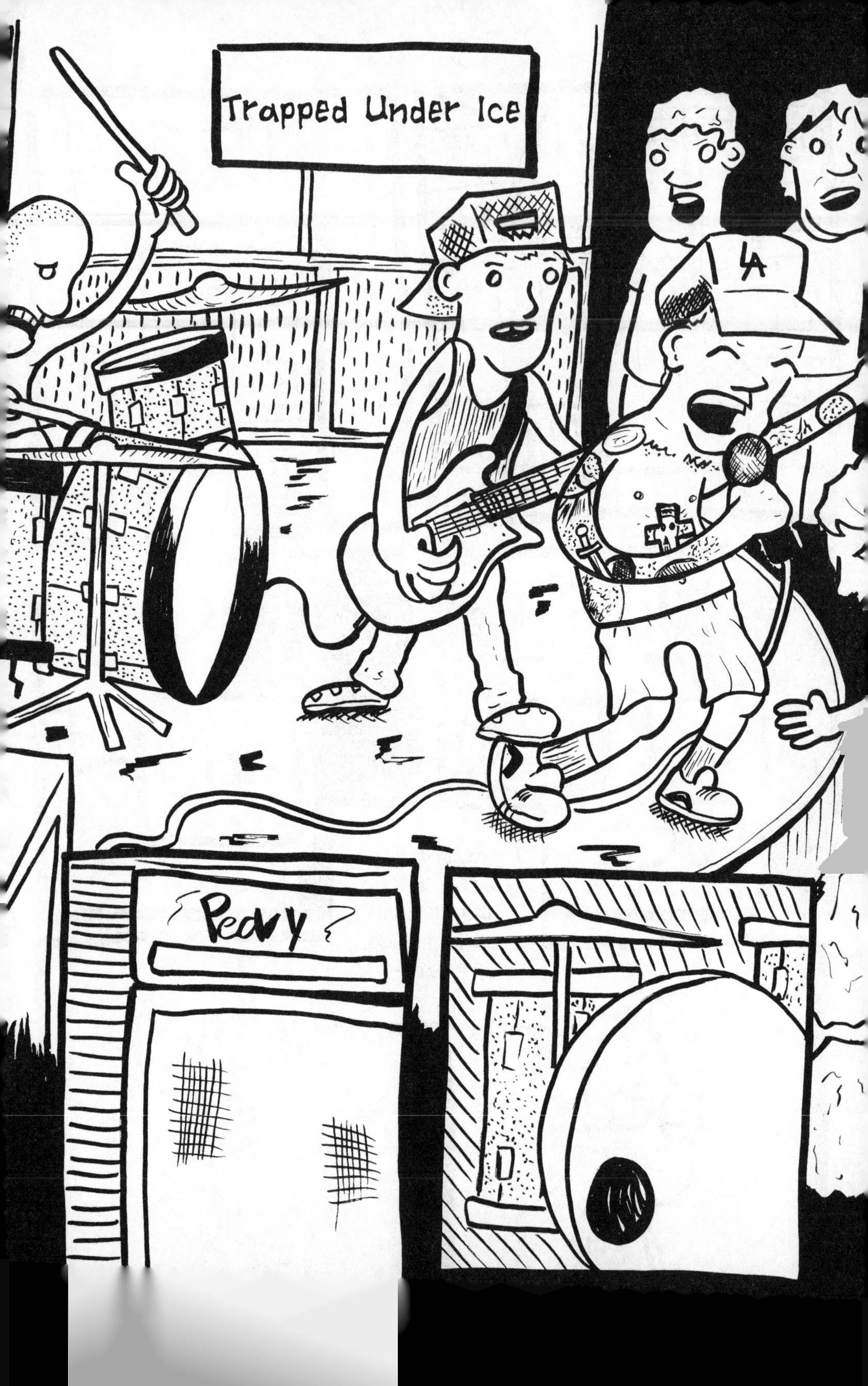
Trapped Under Ice
LA
Peavy

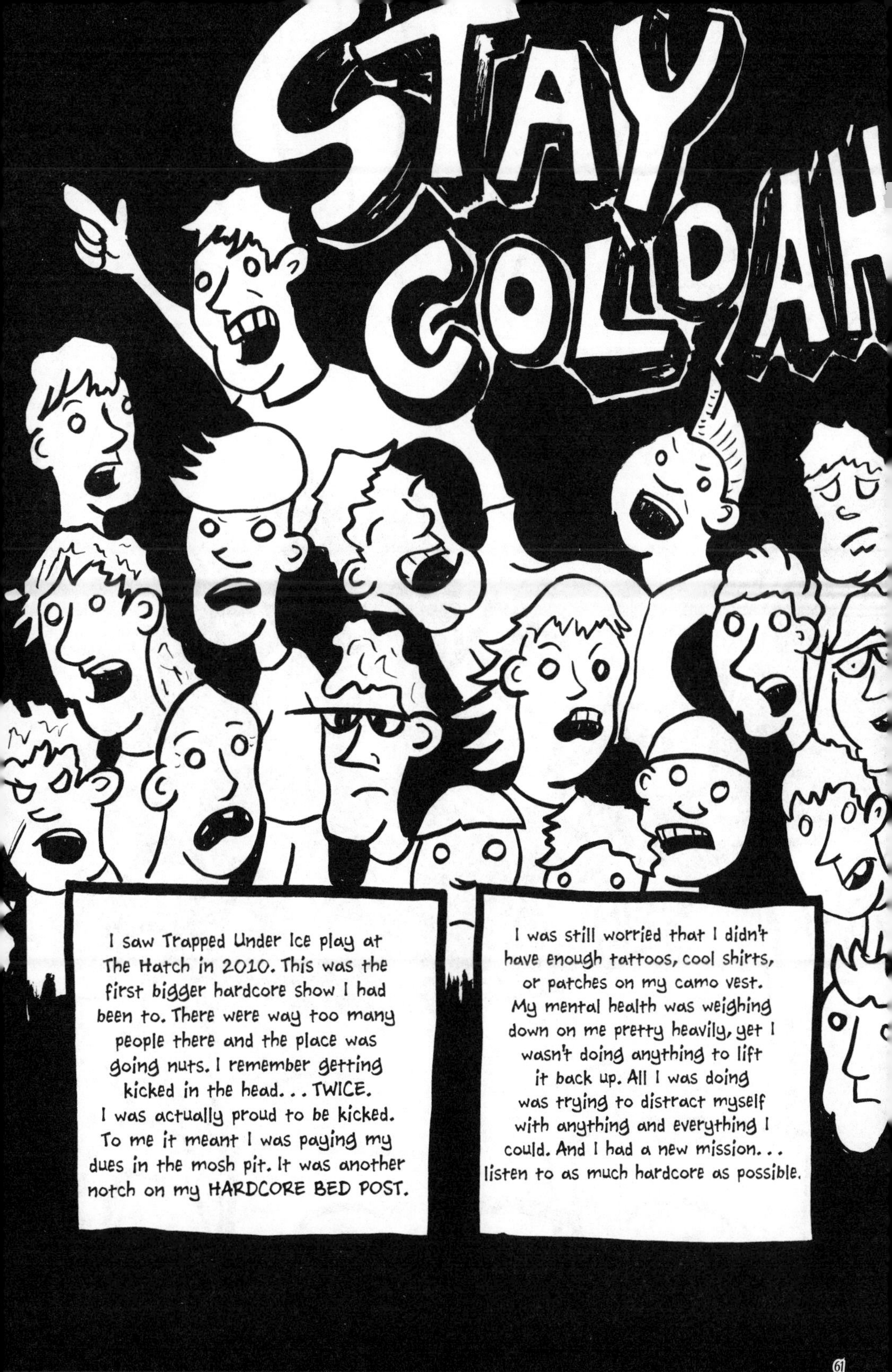
STAY COLLDAH
I saw Trapped Under Ice play at The Hatch in 2010. This was the first bigger hardcore show I had been to. There were way too many people there and the place was going nuts. I remember getting kicked in the head. . . TWICE. I was actually proud to be kicked. To me it meant I was paying my dues in the mosh pit. It was another notch on my HARDCORE BED POST.
I was still worried that I didn't have enough tattoos, cool shirts, or patches on my camo vest. My mental health was weighing down on me pretty heavily, yet I wasn't doing anything to lift it back up. All I was doing was trying to distract myself with anything and everything I could. And I had a new mission. . . listen to as much hardcore as possible.

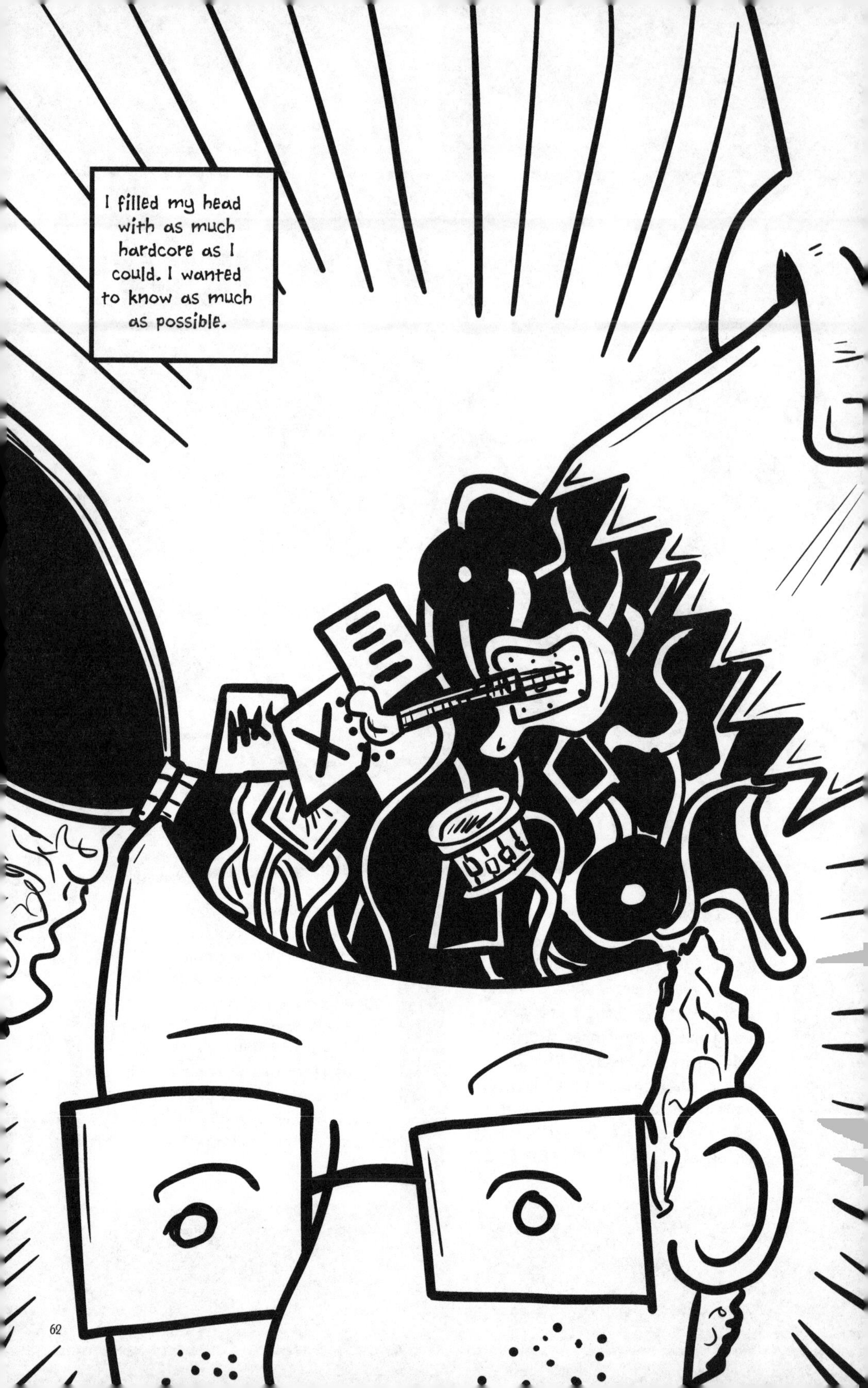
I filled my head with as much hardcore as I could. I wanted to know as much as possible.

Part 2

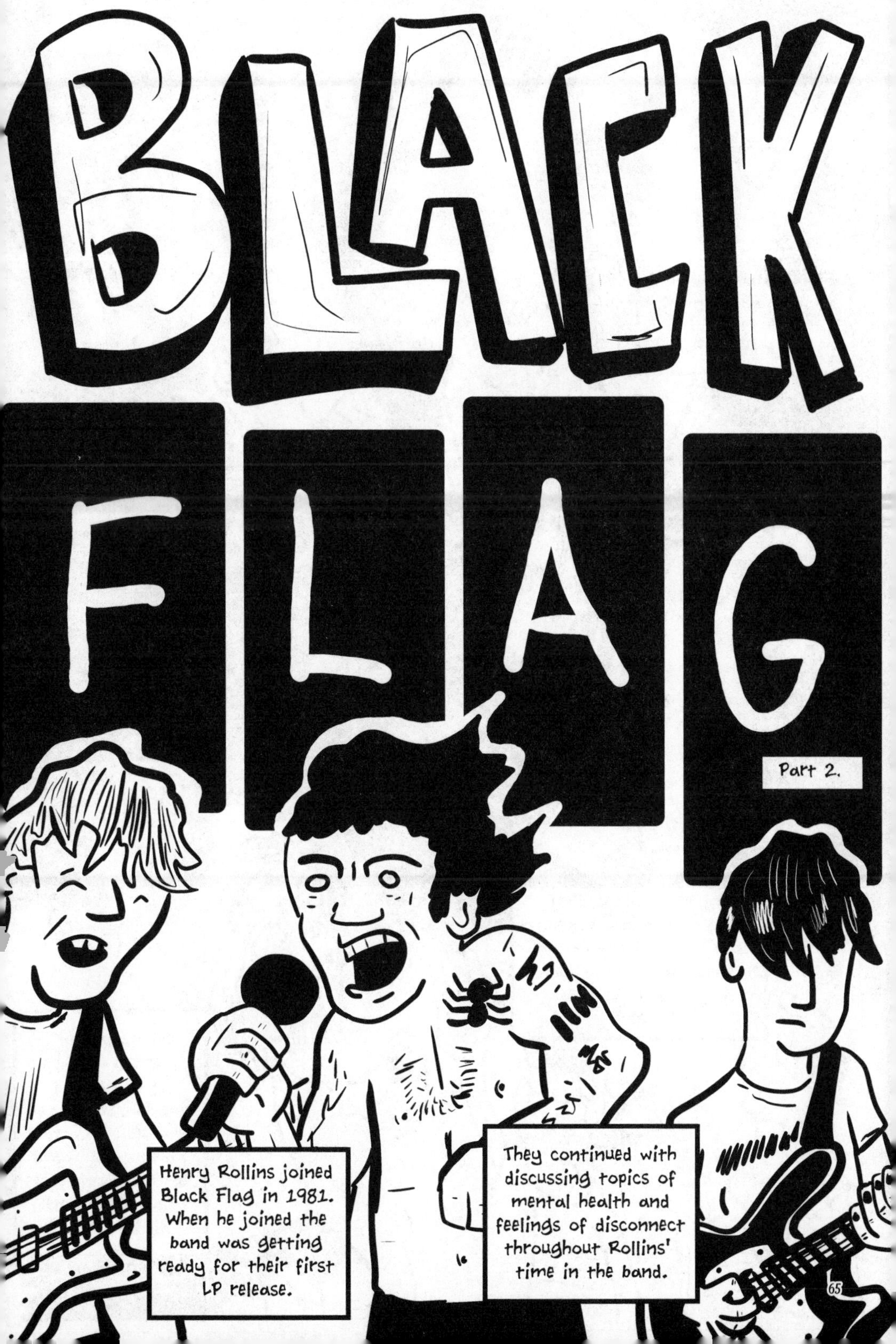

BLACK
FLAG
Part 2.
Henry Rollins joined Black Flag in 1981. When he joined the band was getting ready for their first LP release.
They continued with discussing topics of mental health and feelings of disconnect throughout Rollins' time in the band.

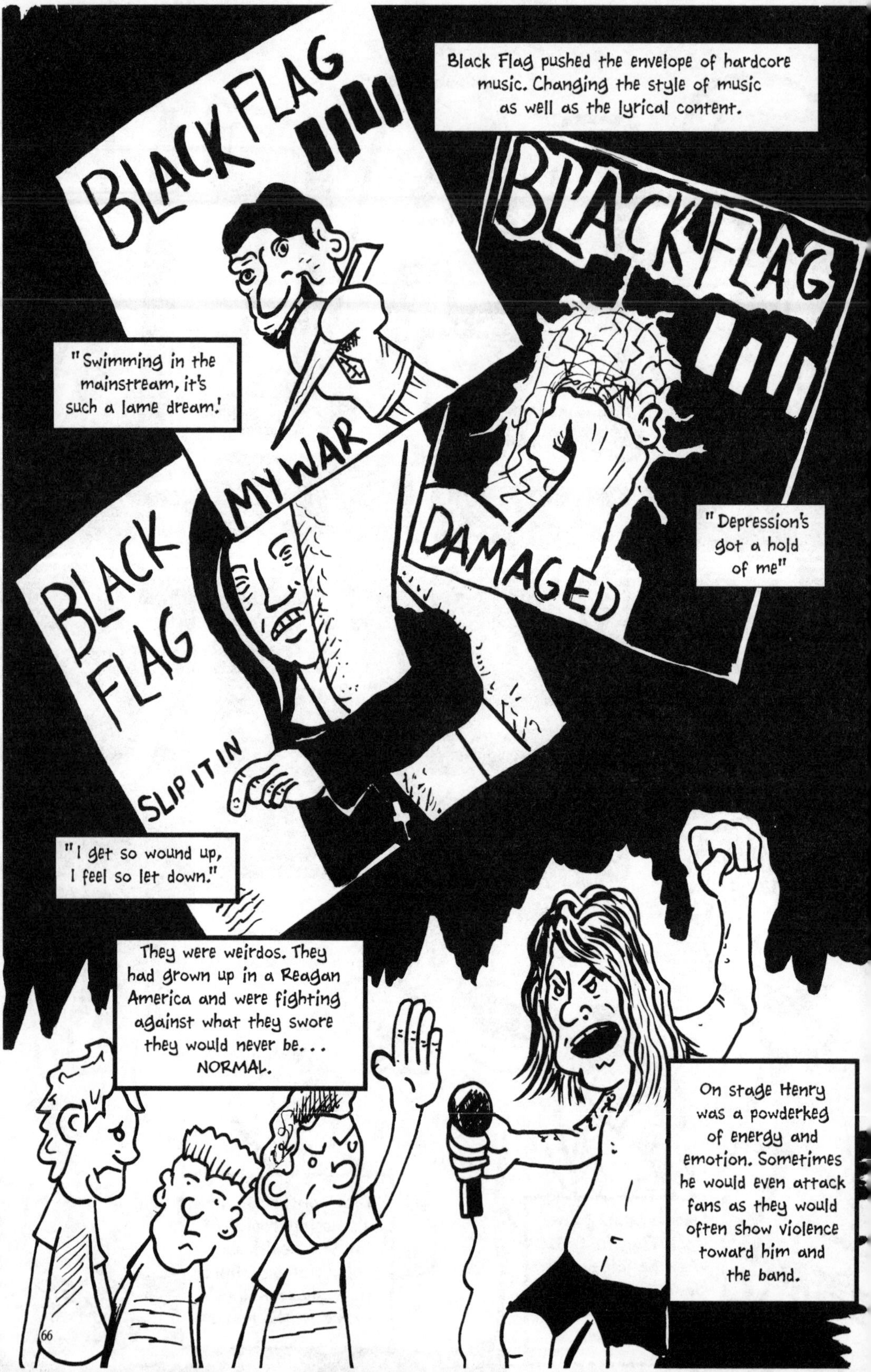
BLACK FLAG
MY WAR
Black Flag pushed the envelope of hardcore music. Changing the style of music as well as the lyrical content.
BLACK FLAG
DAMAGED
"Swimming in the mainstream, it's such a lame dream!
BLACK FLAG
SLIP IT IN
"Depression's got a hold of me"
"I get so wound up, I feel so let down."
They were weirdos. They had grown up in a Reagan America and were fighting against what they swore they would never be... NORMAL.
On stage Henry was a powderkeg of energy and emotion. Sometimes he would even attack fans as they would often show violence toward him and the band.

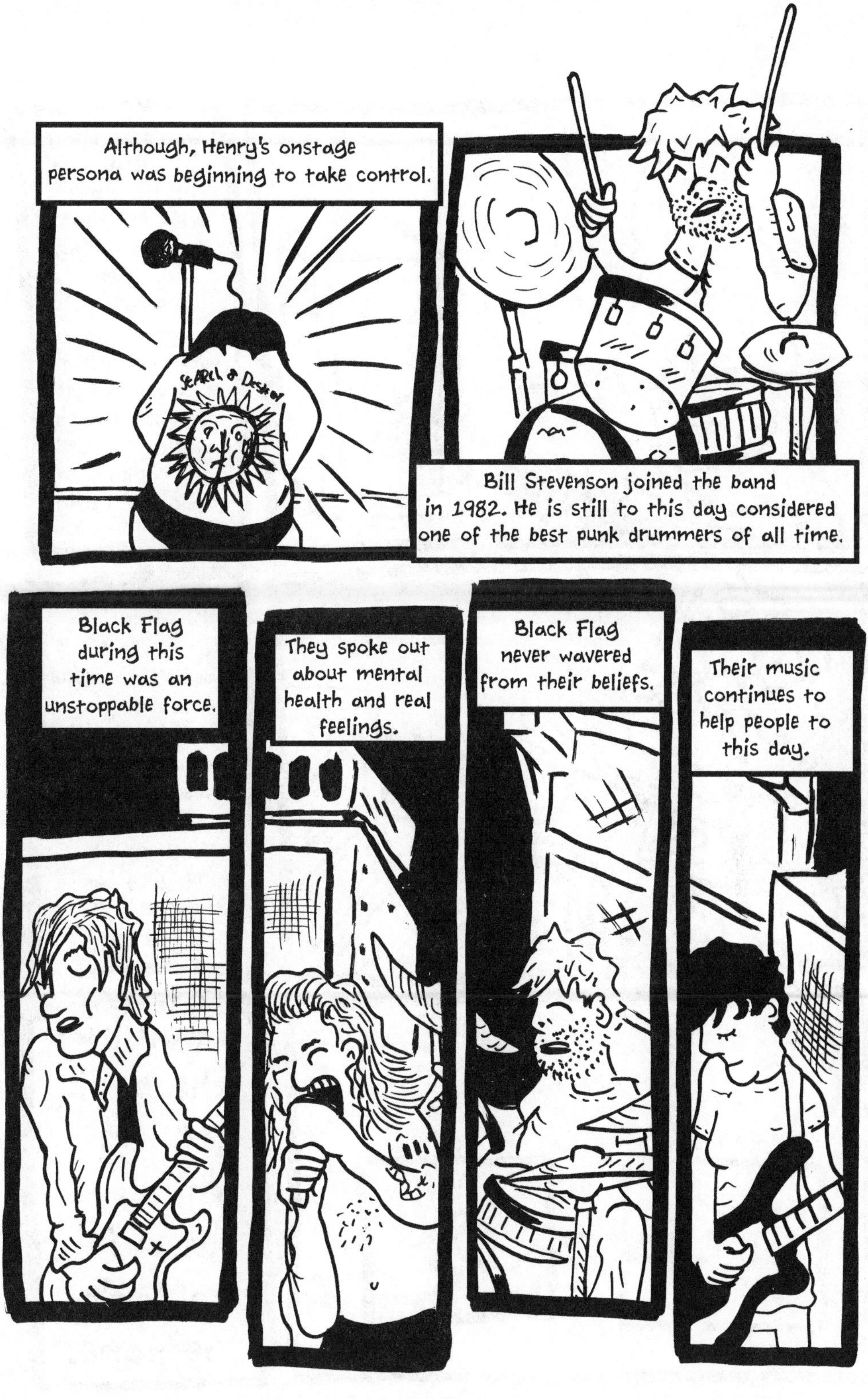
Although, Henry's onstage persona was beginning to take control.
SEARCH & Destroy
Bill Stevenson joined the band in 1982. He is still to this day considered one of the best punk drummers of all time.
Black Flag during this time was an unstoppable force.
They spoke out about mental health and real feelings.
Black Flag never wavered from their beliefs.
Their music continues to help people to this day.

I was practicing with every band all the time. I figured that if I was feeling busy, then I was feeling something. I was desperate to create something amazing for the world. I wanted my shot to do music for a living.

I had no idea if it was even possible to make this dream a reality. But I always had one rule. . . Practice and perform like you are playing for thousands every single time.

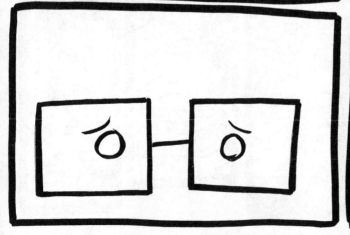

But in the back of my mind, I knew it couldn't be done.

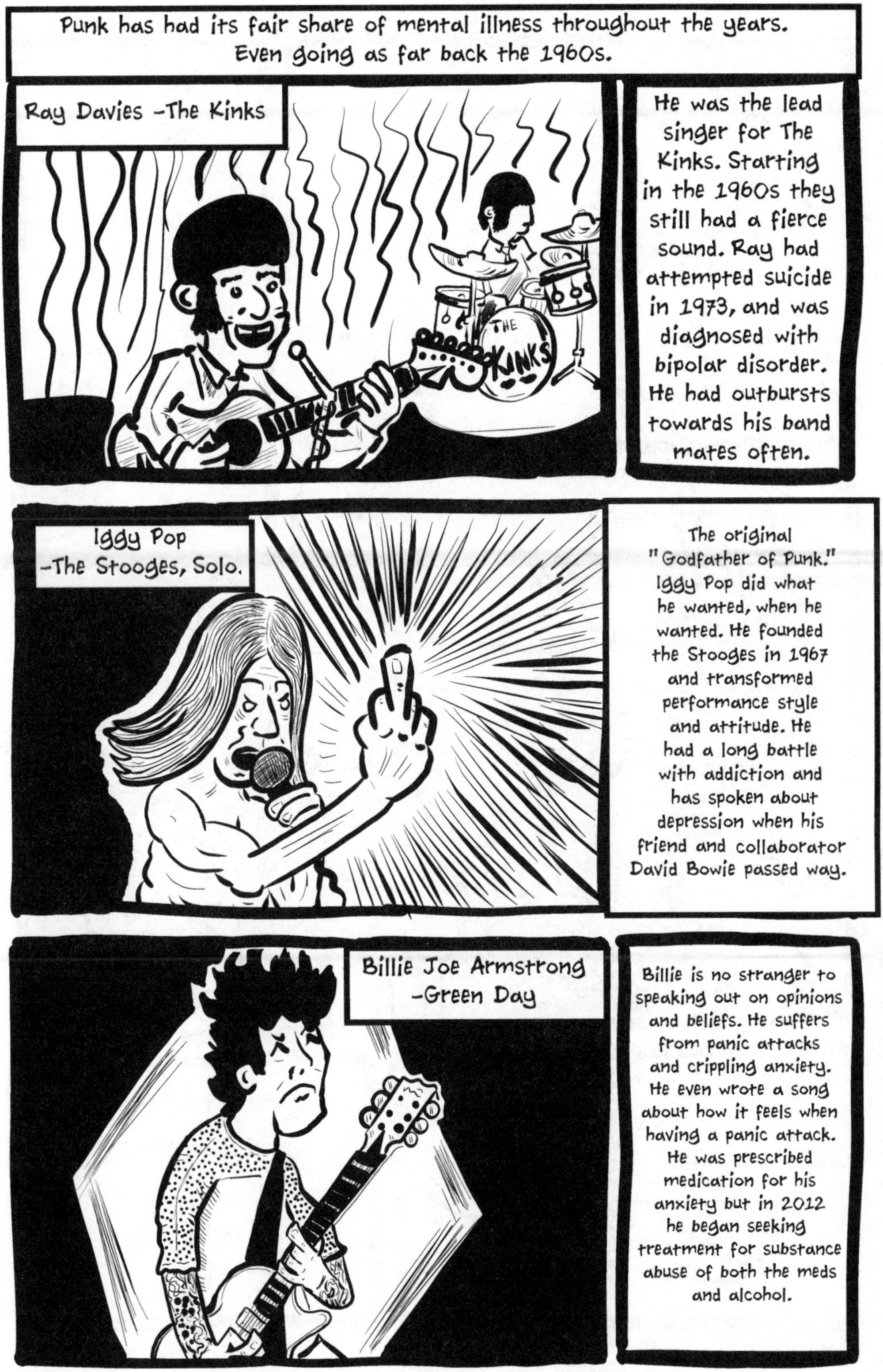
Punk has had its fair share of mental illness throughout the years. Even going as far back the 1960s.
Ray Davies -The Kinks
THE KINKS
He was the lead singer for The Kinks. Starting in the 1960s they still had a fierce sound. Ray had attempted suicide in 1973, and was diagnosed with bipolar disorder. He had outbursts towards his band mates often.
Iggy Pop -The Stooges, Solo.
The original "Godfather of Punk." Iggy Pop did what he wanted, when he wanted. He founded the Stooges in 1967 and transformed performance style and attitude. He had a long battle with addiction and has spoken about depression when his friend and collaborator David Bowie passed way.
Billie Joe Armstrong -Green Day
Billie is no stranger to speaking out on opinions and beliefs. He suffers from panic attacks and crippling anxiety. He even wrote a song about how it feels when having a panic attack. He was prescribed medication for his anxiety but in 2012 he began seeking treatment for substance abuse of both the meds and alcohol.

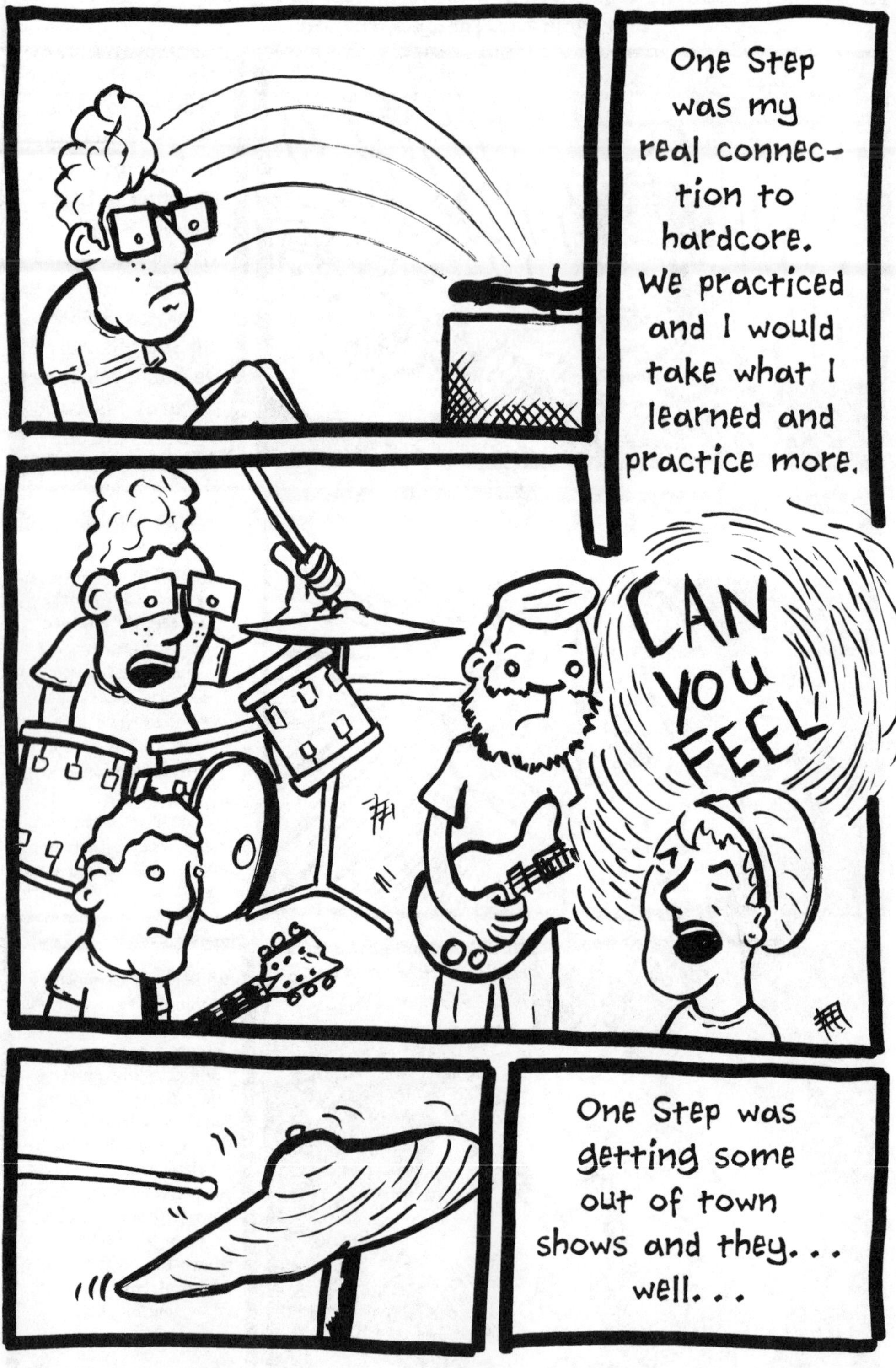
One Step was my real connection to hardcore. We practiced and I would take what I learned and practice more.
CAN YOU FEEL
One Step was getting some out of town shows and they... well...

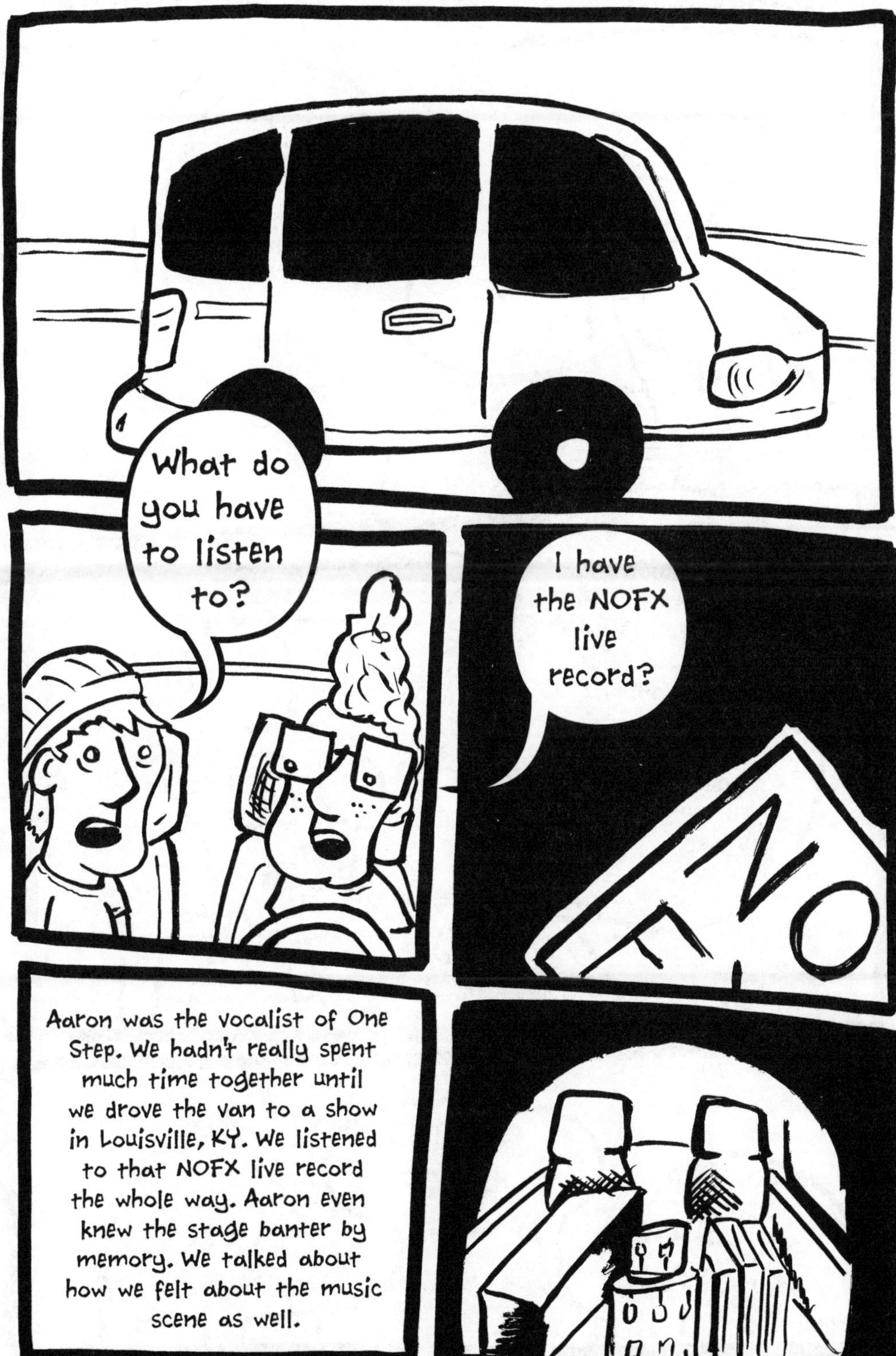
What do you have to listen to?
I have the NOFX live record?
NO F
Aaron was the vocalist of One Step. We hadn't really spent much time together until we drove the van to a show in Louisville, KY. We listened to that NOFX live record the whole way. Aaron even knew the stage banter by memory. We talked about how we felt about the music scene as well.

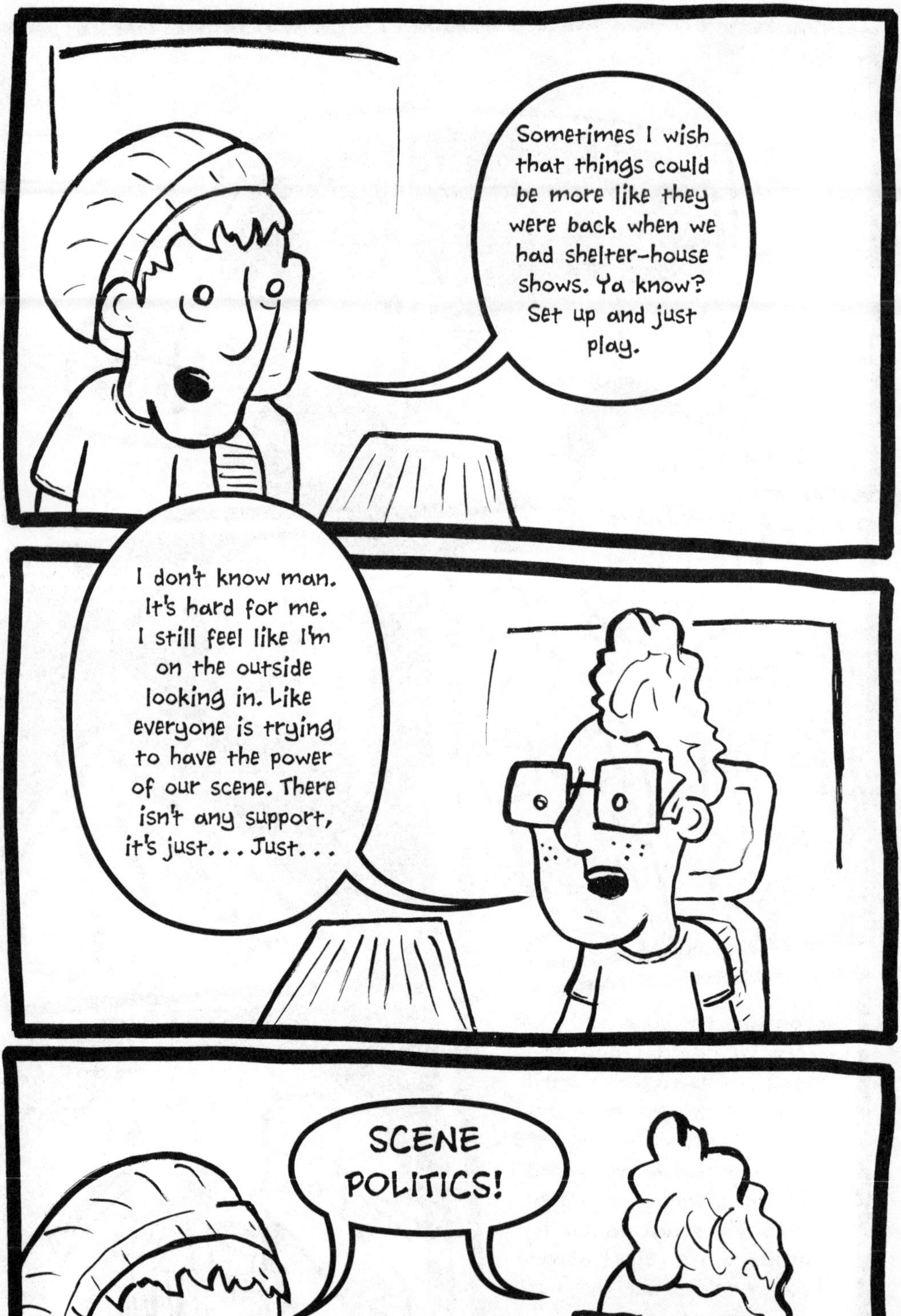
Sometimes I wish that things could be more like they were back when we had shelter-house shows. Ya know? Set up and just play.
I don't know man. It's hard for me. I still feel like I'm on the outside looking in. Like everyone is trying to have the power of our scene. There isn't any support, it's just... Just...
SCENE POLITICS!

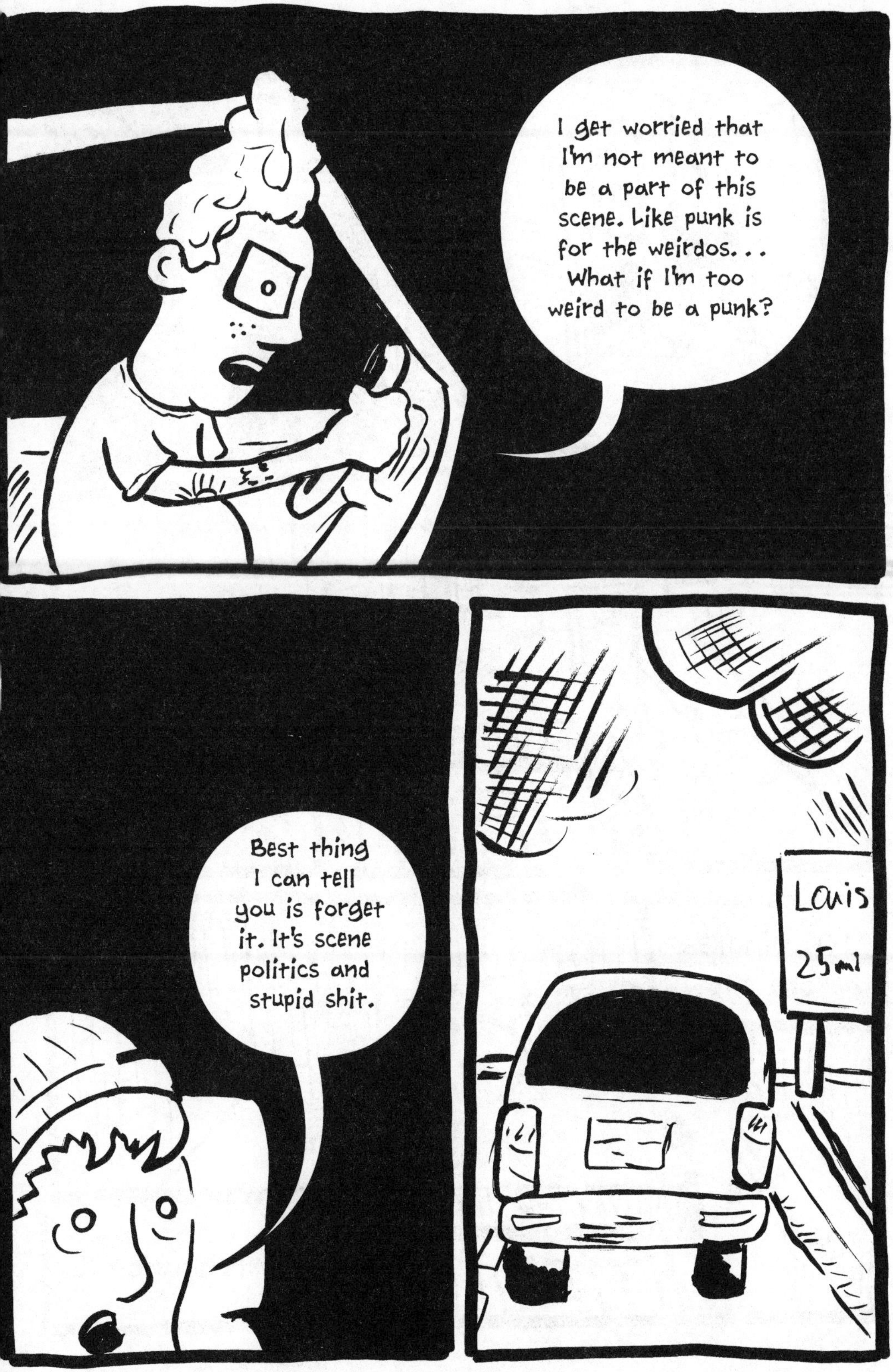
I get worried that I'm not meant to be a part of this scene. Like punk is for the weirdos... What if I'm too weird to be a punk?
Best thing I can tell you is forget it. It's scene politics and stupid shit.
Louis
25 mi

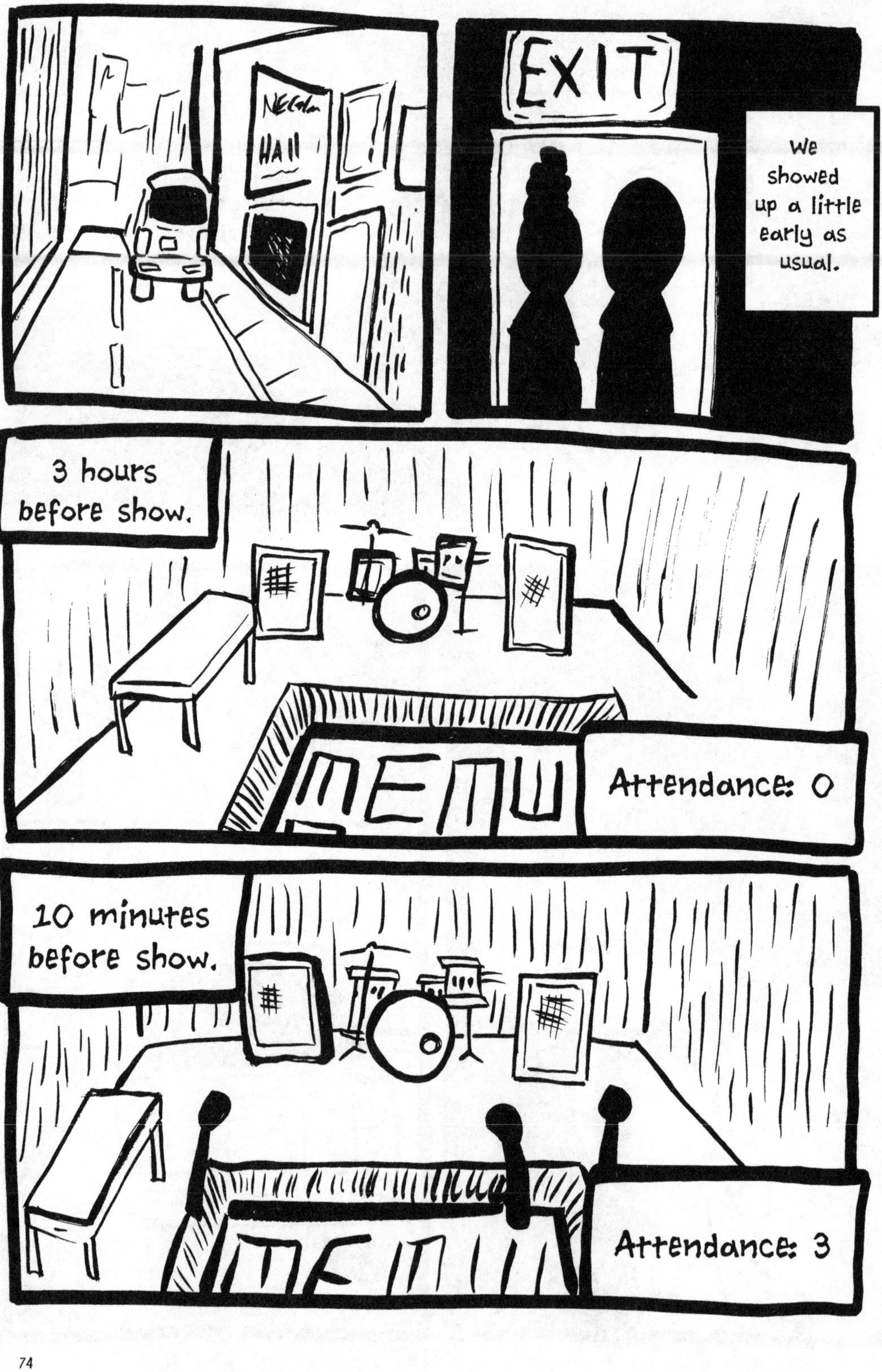
EXIT
We showed up a little early as usual.
3 hours before show.
MENU
Attendance: 0
10 minutes before show.
Attendance: 3

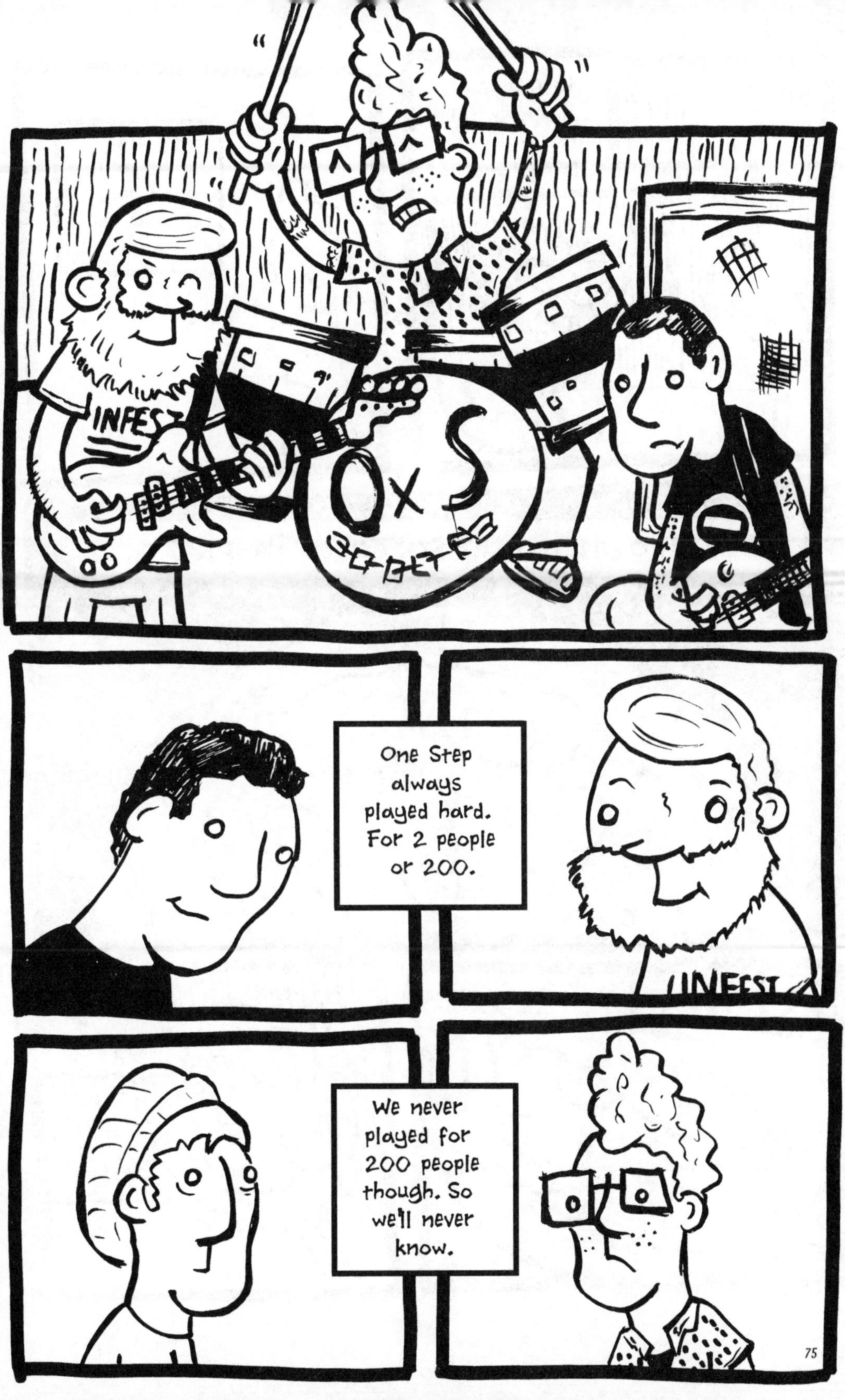
INFEST
OxS
One Step always played hard. For 2 people or 200.
INFEST
We never played for 200 people though. So we'll never know.

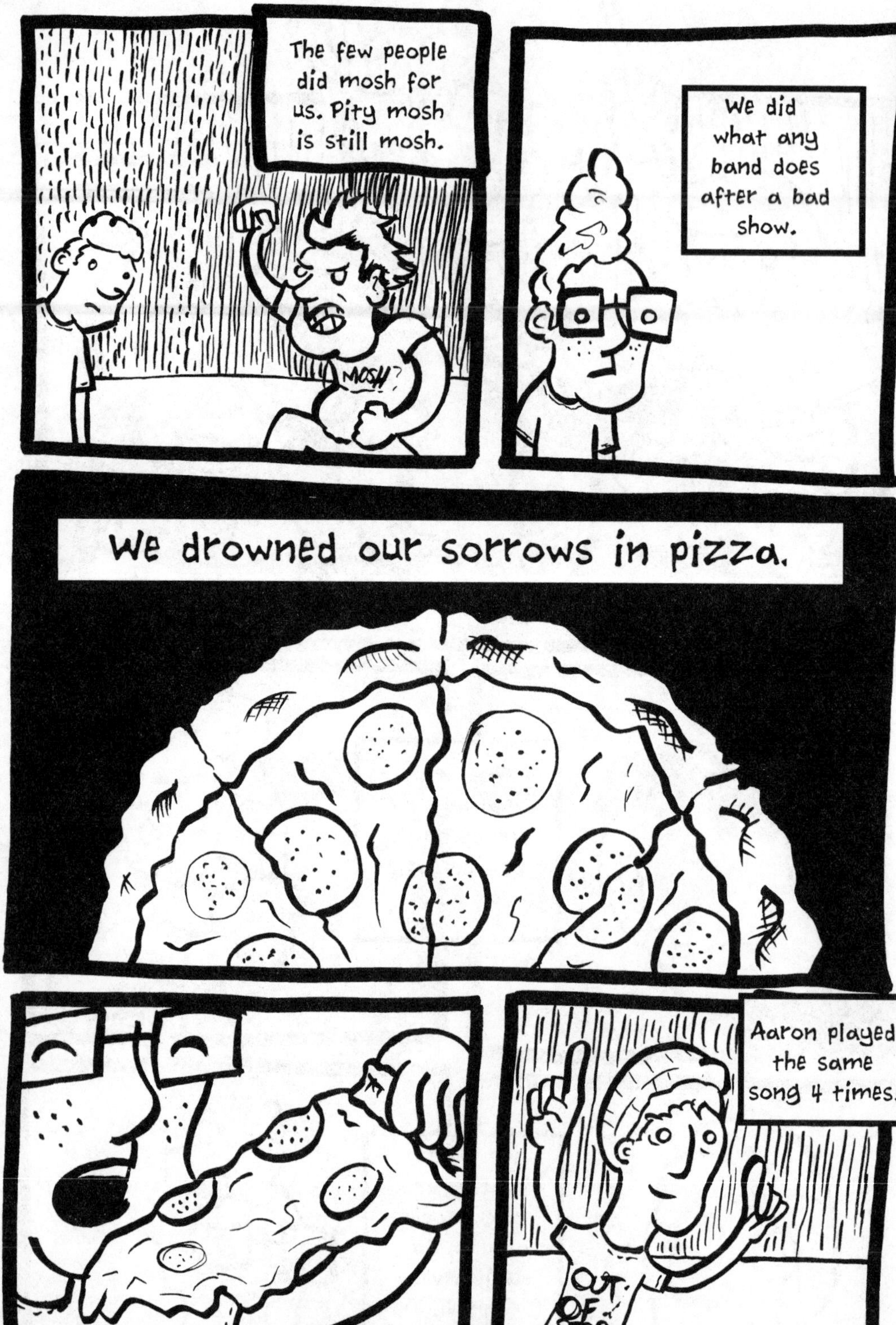
The few people did mosh for us. Pity mosh is still mosh.
MOSH?
We did what any band does after a bad show.
We drowned our sorrows in pizza.
Aaron played the same song 4 times.
OUT OF STEP

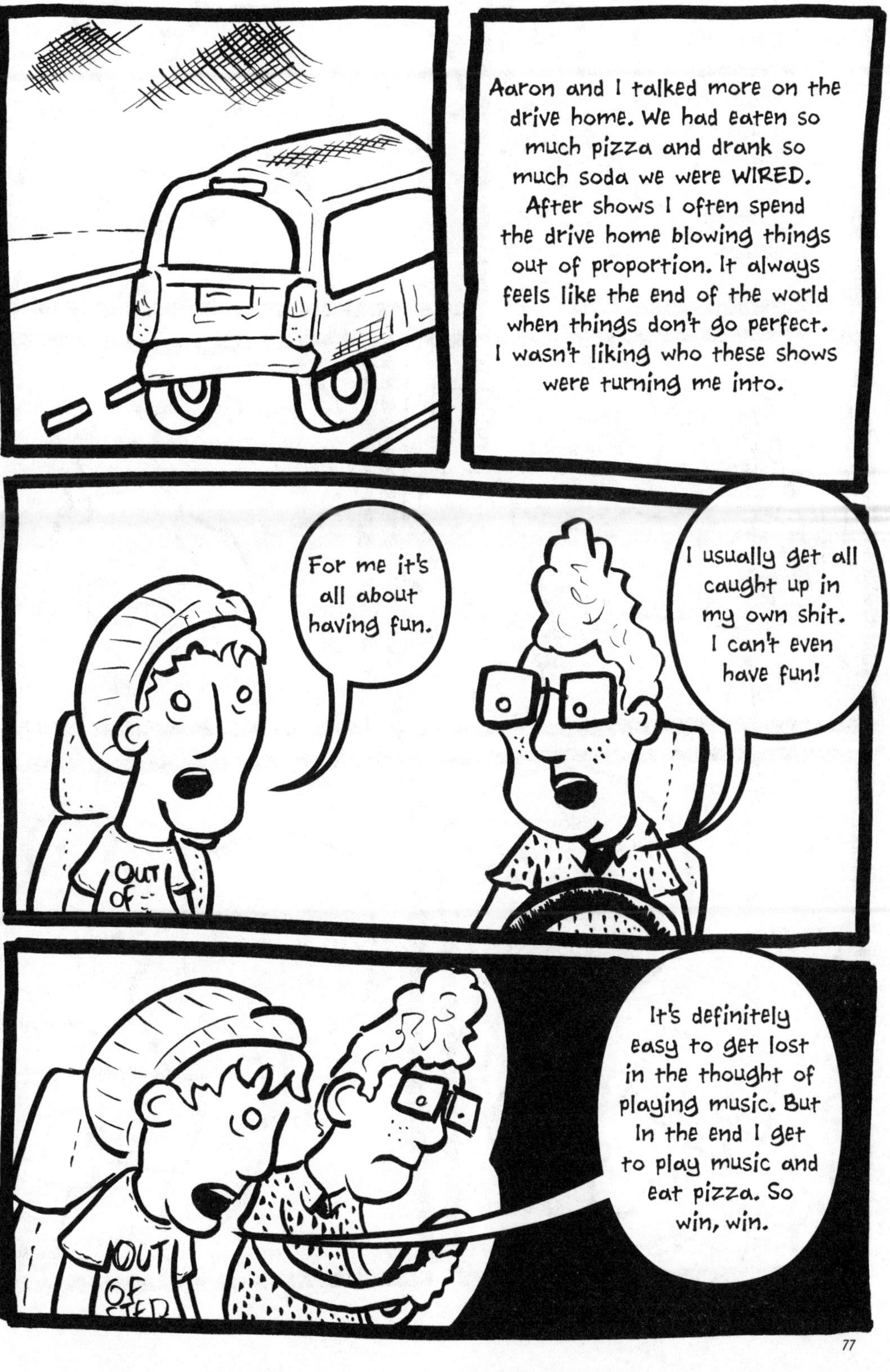
Aaron and I talked more on the drive home. We had eaten so much pizza and drank so much soda we were WIRED. After shows I often spend the drive home blowing things out of proportion. It always feels like the end of the world when things don't go perfect. I wasn't liking who these shows were turning me into.
For me it's all about having fun.
I usually get all caught up in my own shit. I can't even have fun!
It's definitely easy to get lost in the thought of playing music. But In the end I get to play music and eat pizza. So win, win.

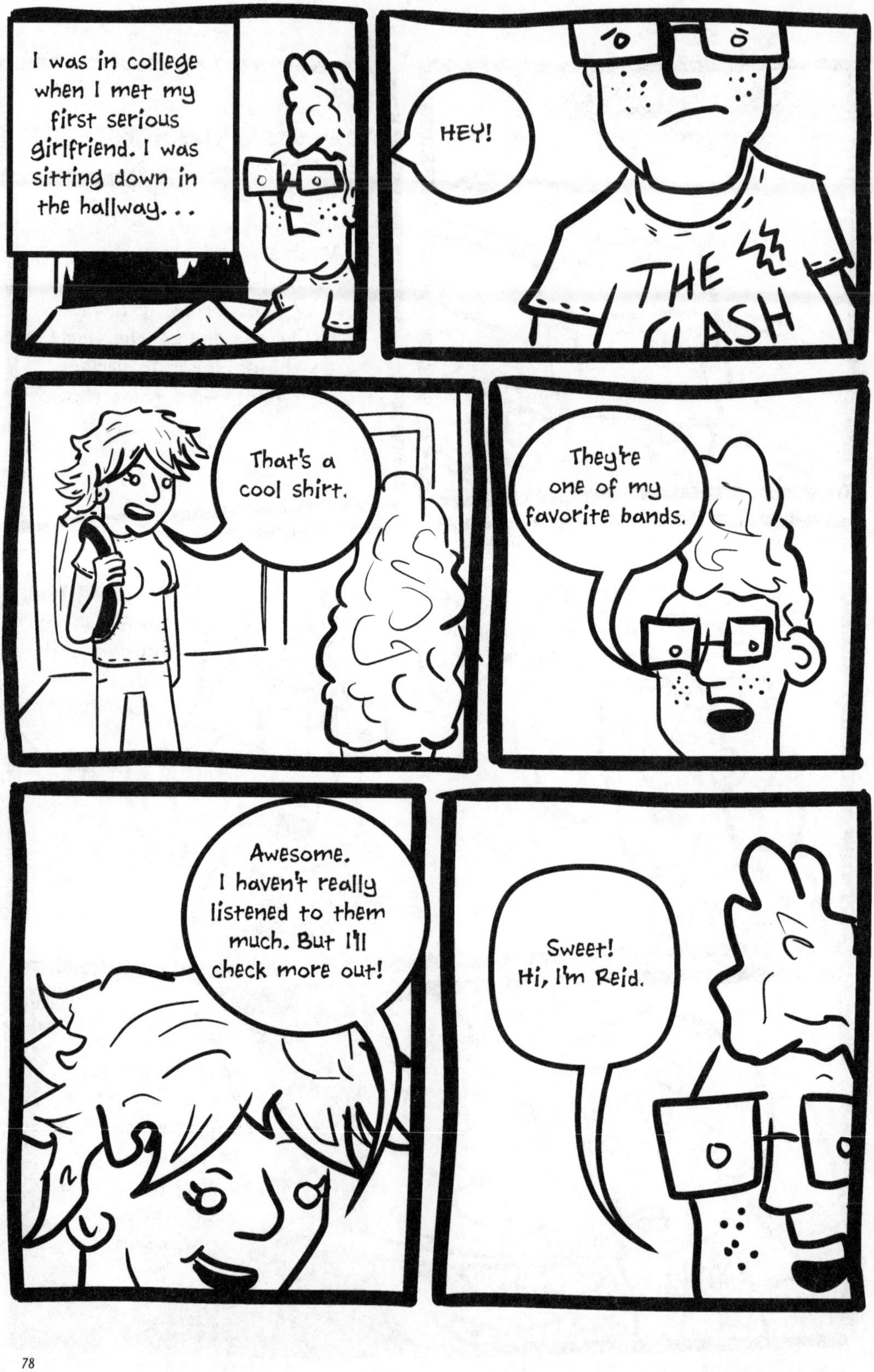
I was in college when I met my first serious girlfriend. I was sitting down in the hallway. . .
HEY!
THE CLASH
That's a cool shirt.
They're one of my favorite bands.
Awesome. I haven't really listened to them much. But I'll check more out!
Sweet! Hi, I'm Reid.

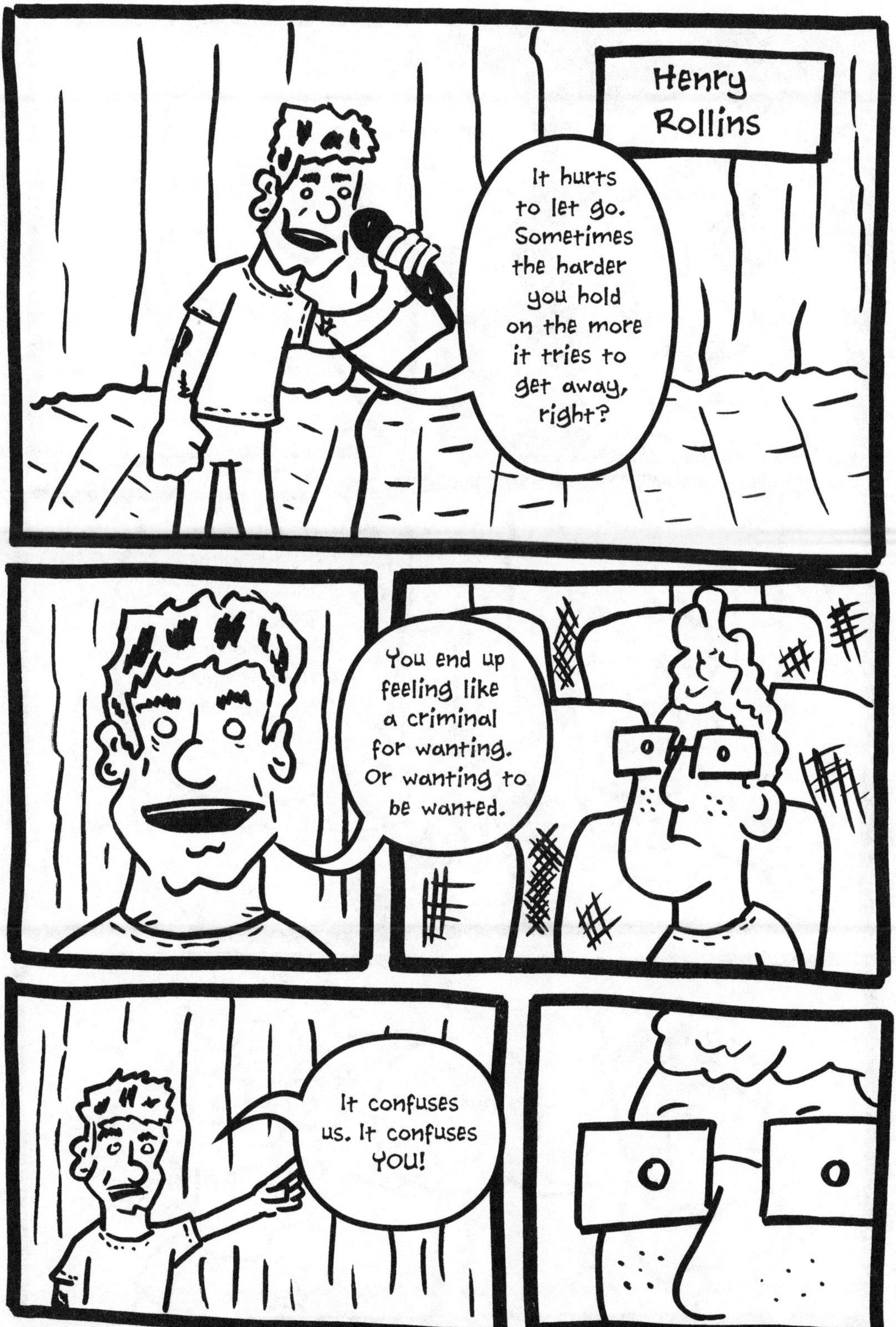
Henry Rollins
It hurts to let go. Sometimes the harder you hold on the more it tries to get away, right?
You end up feeling like a criminal for wanting. Or wanting to be wanted.
It confuses us. It confuses YOU!

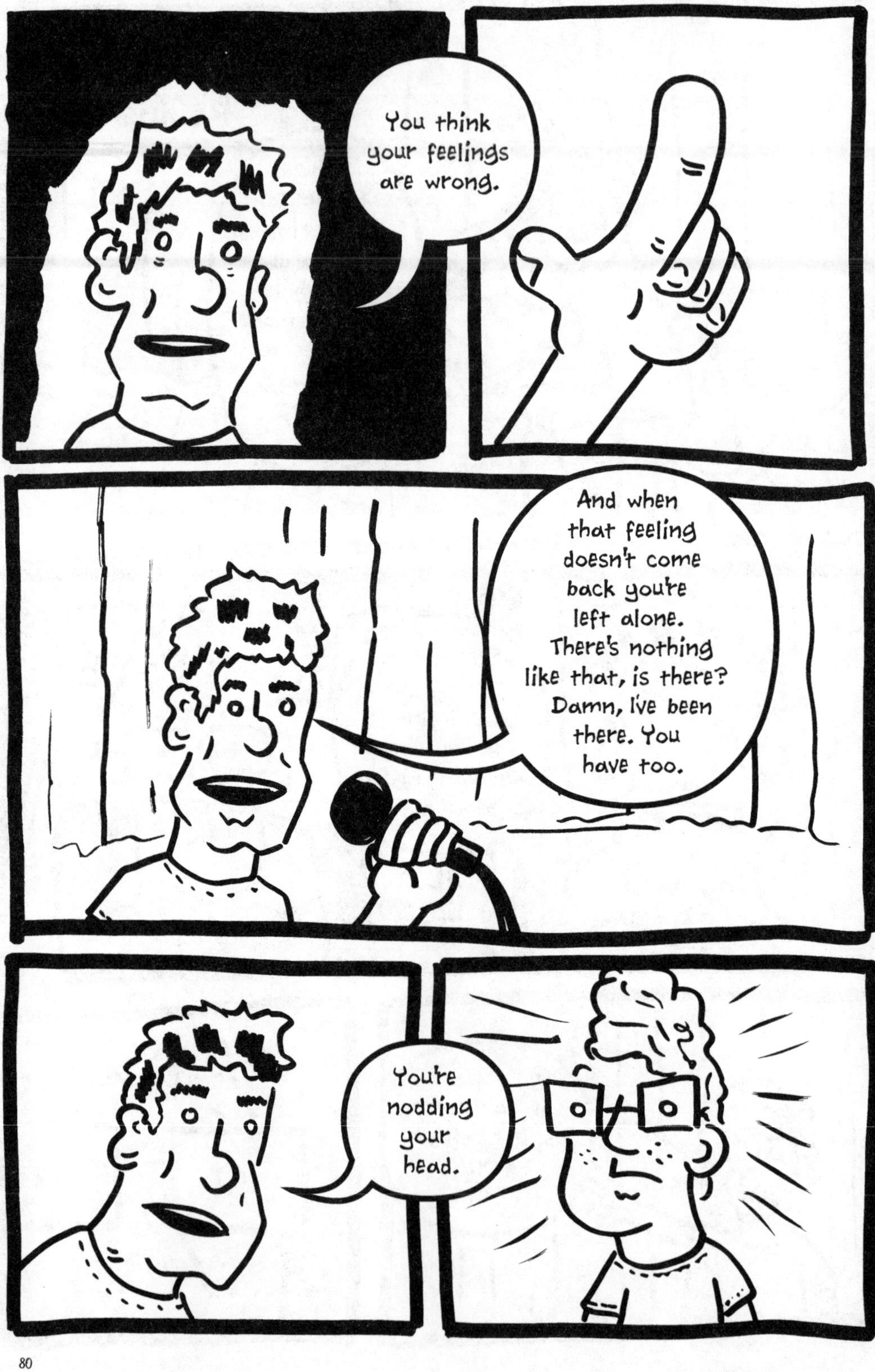
You think your feelings are wrong.
And when that feeling doesn't come back you're left alone. There's nothing like that, is there? Damn, I've been there. You have too.
You're nodding your head.

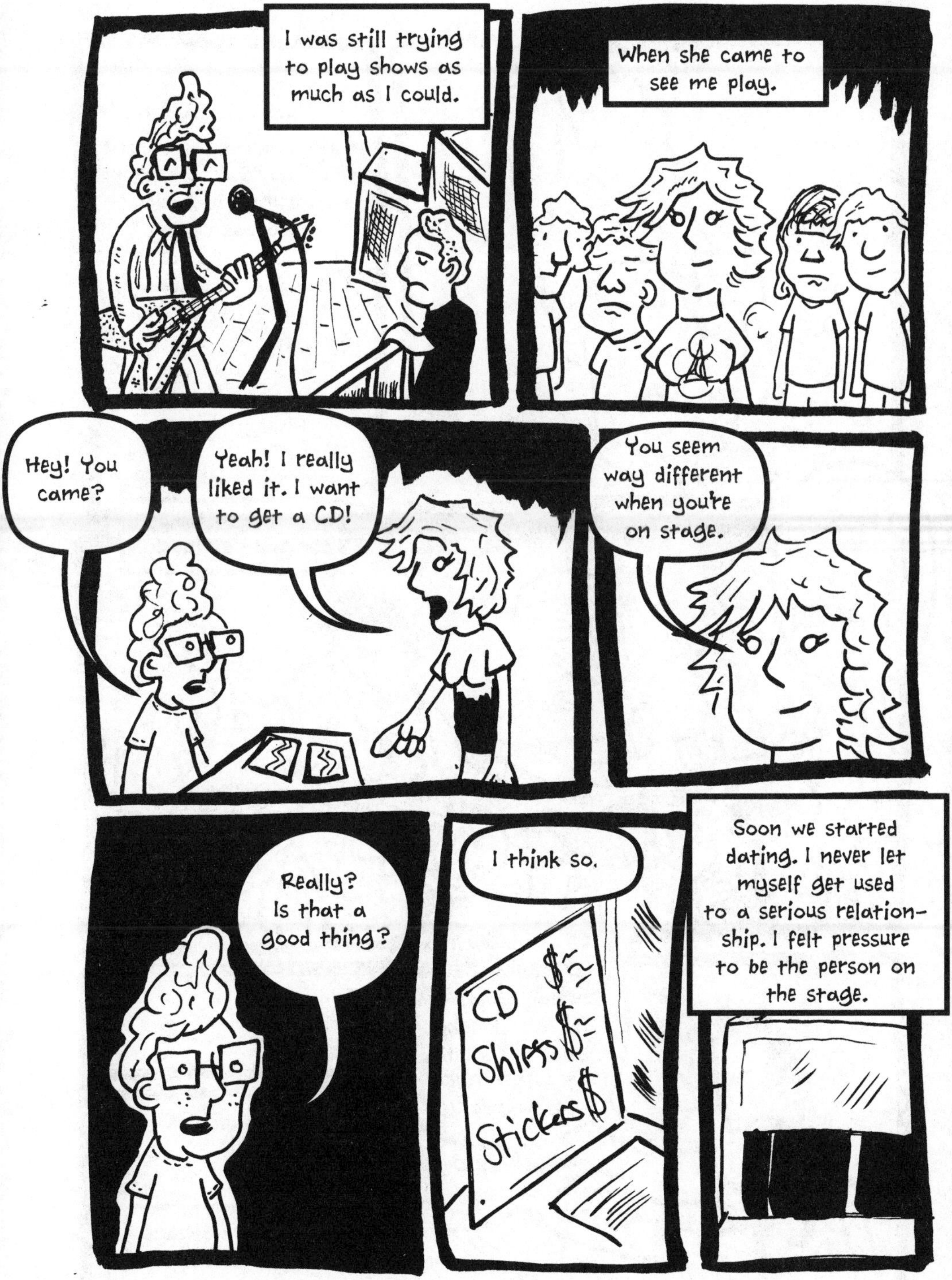
I was still trying to play shows as much as I could.
When she came to see me play.
Hey! You came?
Yeah! I really liked it. I want to get a CD!
You seem way different when you're on stage.
Really? Is that a good thing?
I think so.
CD $
Shirts $
Stickers $
Soon we started dating. I never let myself get used to a serious relationship. I felt pressure to be the person on the stage.

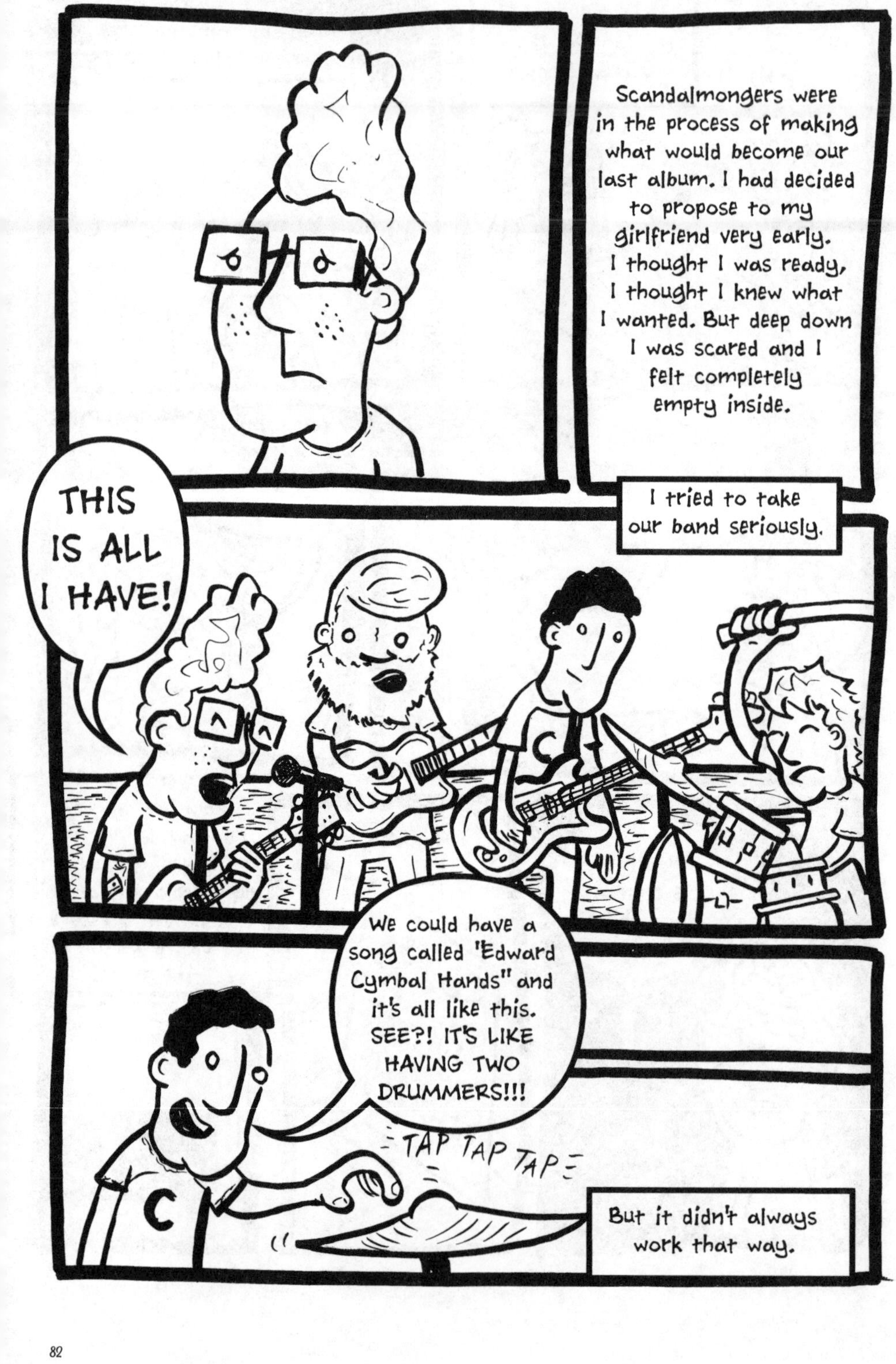
Scandalmongers were in the process of making what would become our last album. I had decided to propose to my girlfriend very early. I thought I was ready, I thought I knew what I wanted. But deep down I was scared and I felt completely empty inside.
THIS IS ALL I HAVE!
I tried to take our band seriously.
We could have a song called "Edward Cymbal Hands" and it's all like this. SEE?! IT'S LIKE HAVING TWO DRUMMERS!!!
TAP TAP TAP
But it didn't always work that way.

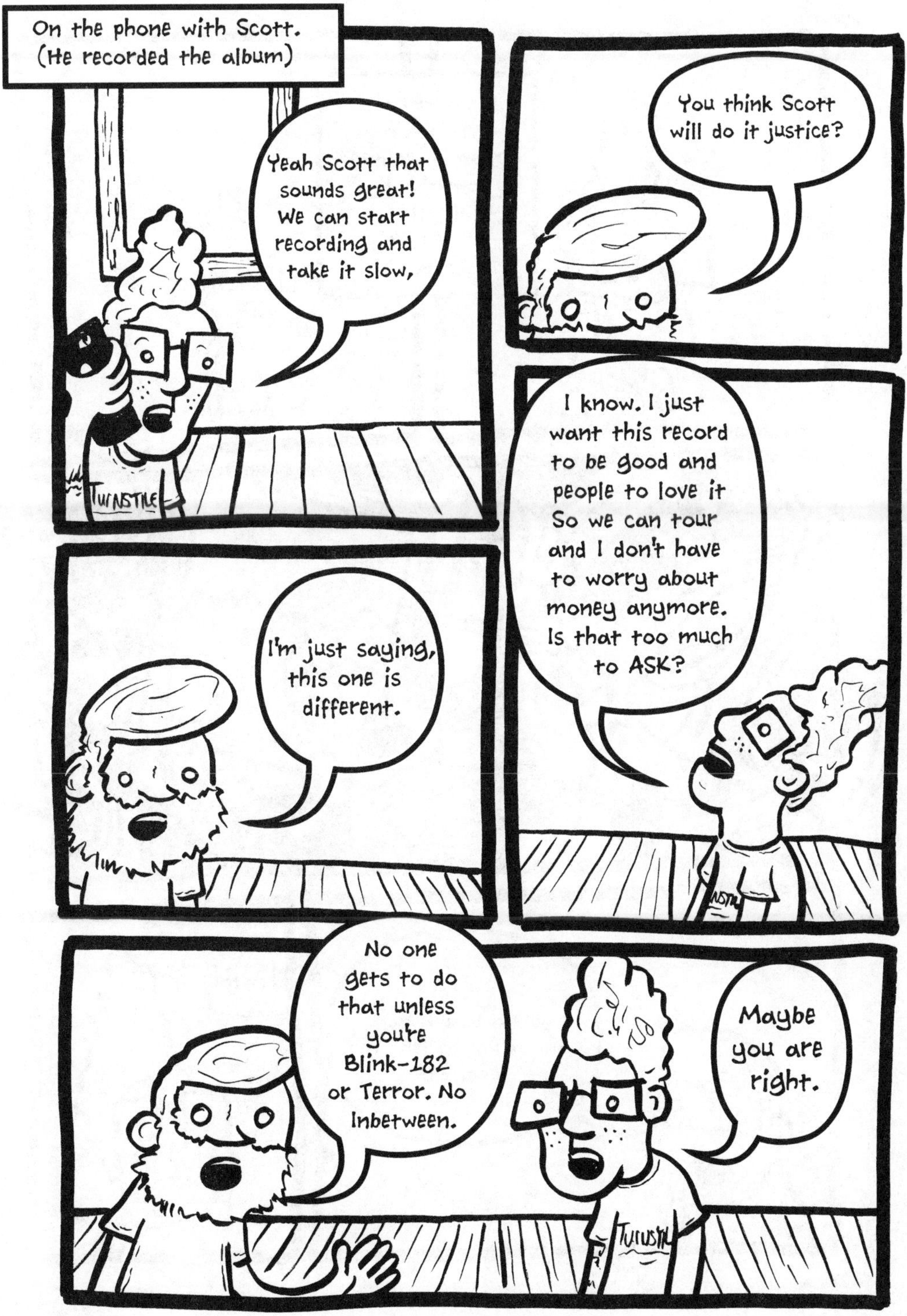
On the phone with Scott. (He recorded the album)
Yeah Scott that sounds great! We can start recording and take it slow,
TURNSTILE
You think Scott will do it justice?
I know. I just want this record to be good and people to love it So we can tour and I don't have to worry about money anymore. Is that too much to ASK?
I'm just saying, this one is different.
No one gets to do that unless you're Blink-182 or Terror. No Inbetween.
Maybe you are right.

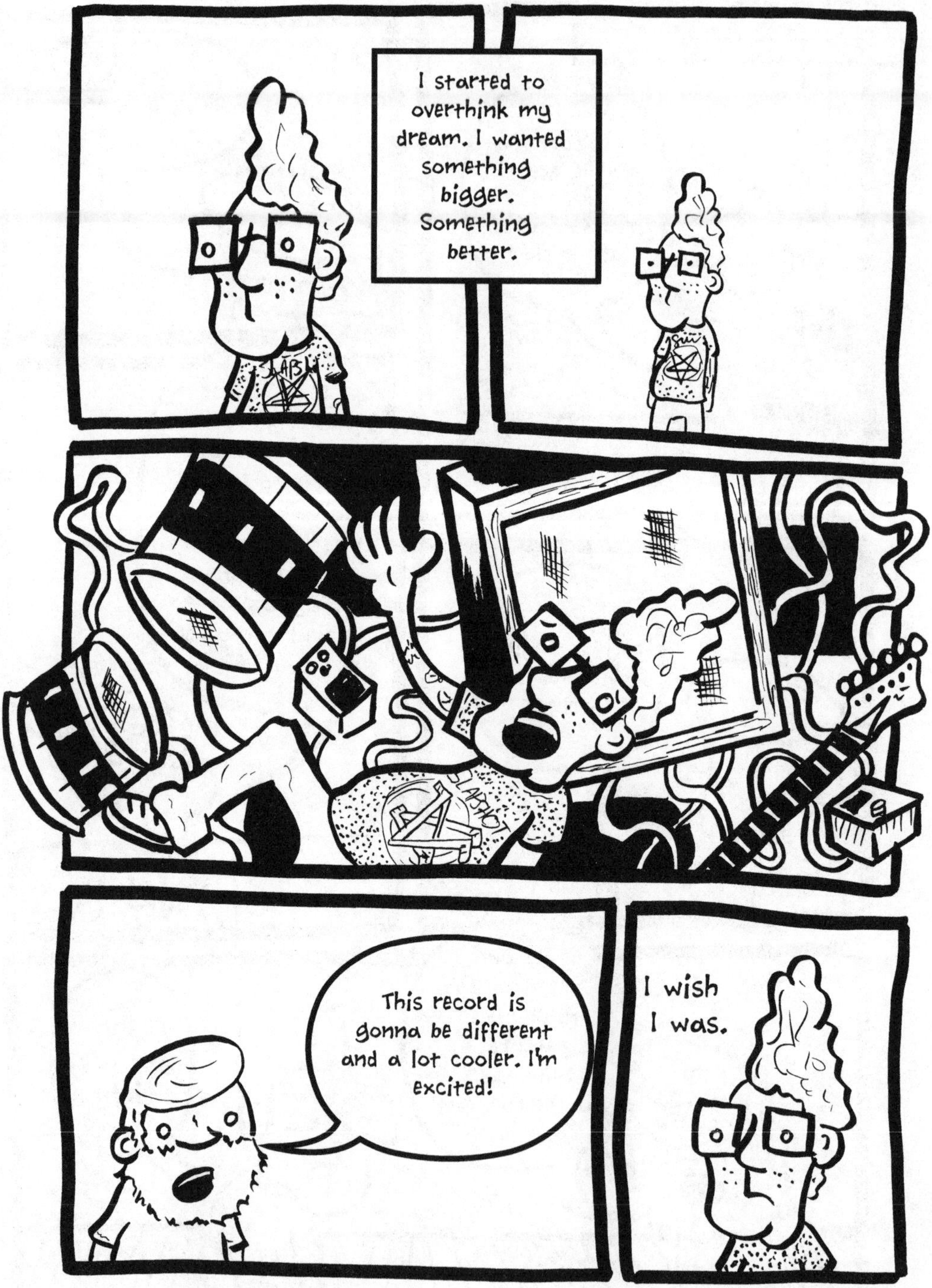
I started to overthink my dream. I wanted something bigger. Something better.
SLAPSHOT
This record is gonna be different and a lot cooler. I'm excited!
I wish I was.

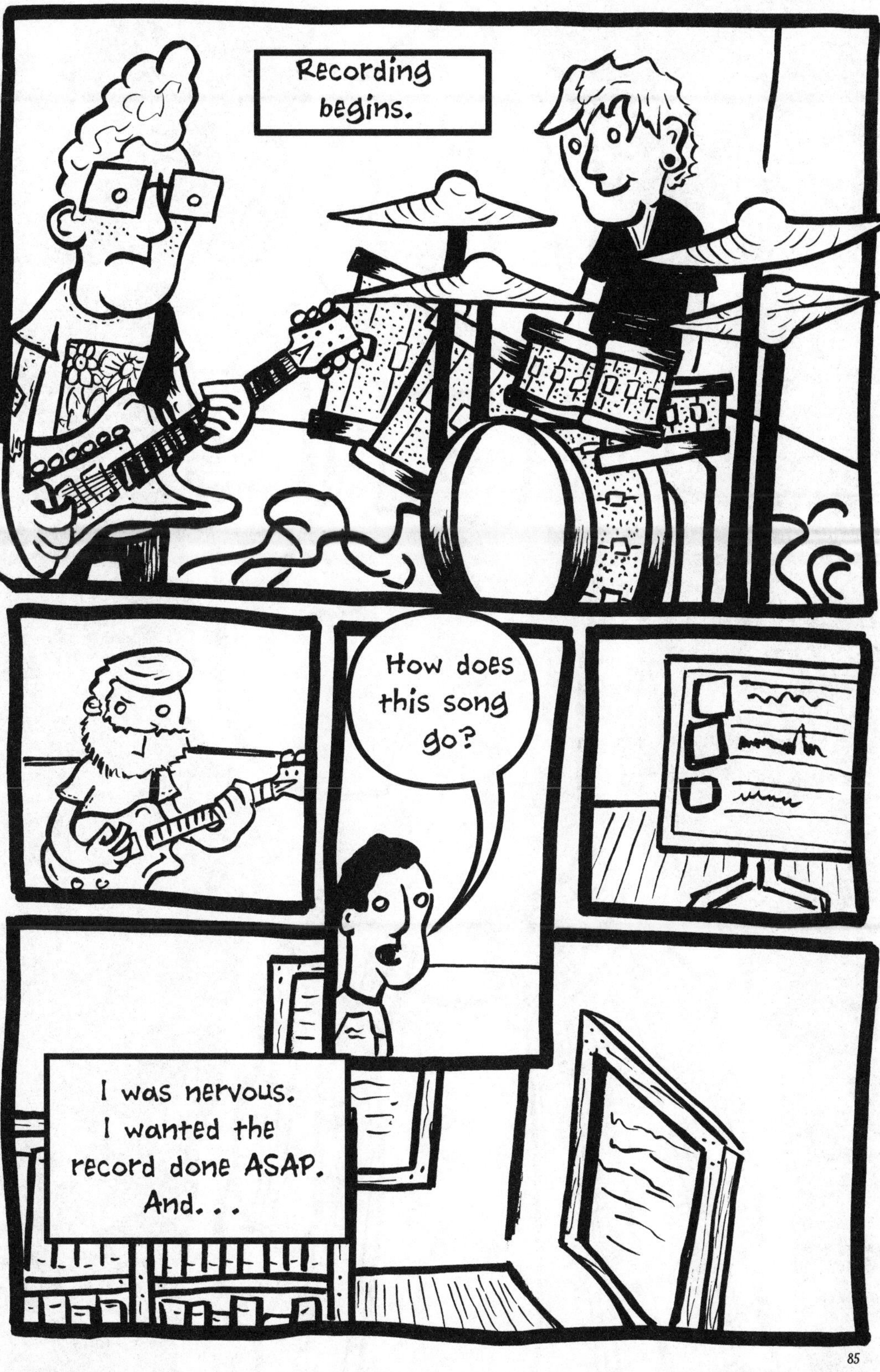
Recording begins.
How does this song go?
I was nervous. I wanted the record done ASAP. And...

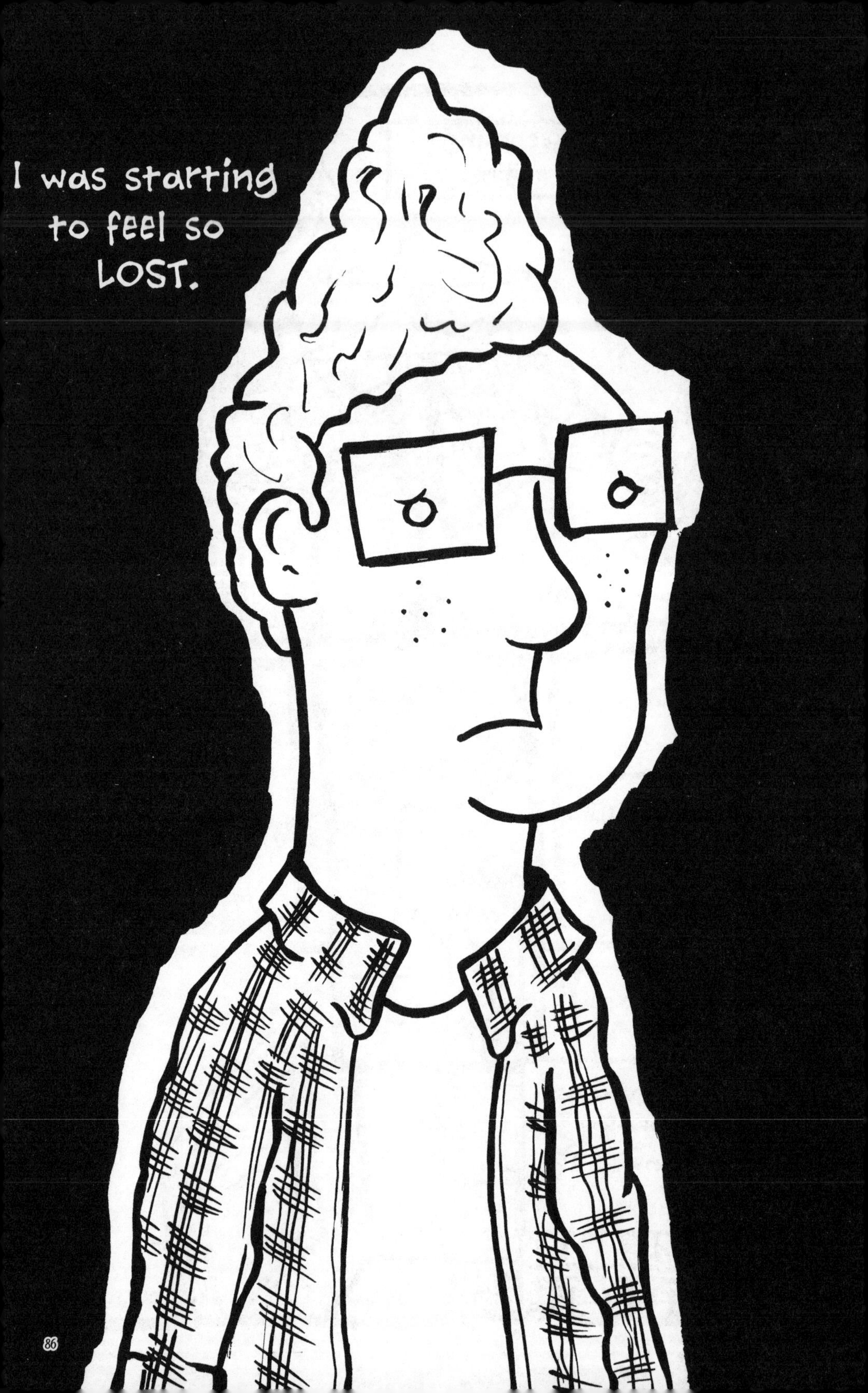
I was starting to feel so LOST.

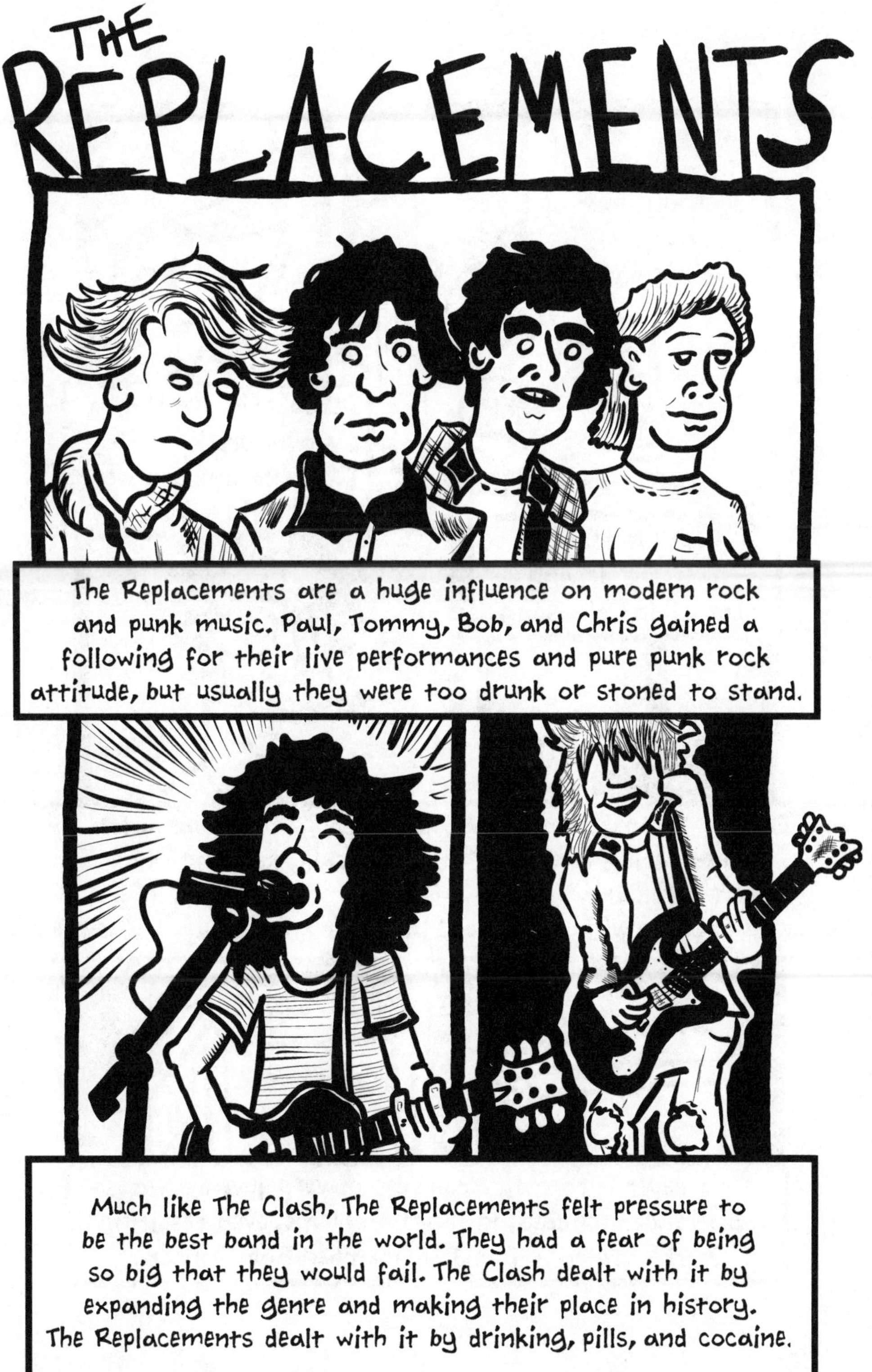
THE REPLACEMENTS
The Replacements are a huge influence on modern rock and punk music. Paul, Tommy, Bob, and Chris gained a following for their live performances and pure punk rock attitude, but usually they were too drunk or stoned to stand.
Much like The Clash, The Replacements felt pressure to be the best band in the world. They had a fear of being so big that they would fail. The Clash dealt with it by expanding the genre and making their place in history. The Replacements dealt with it by drinking, pills, and cocaine.

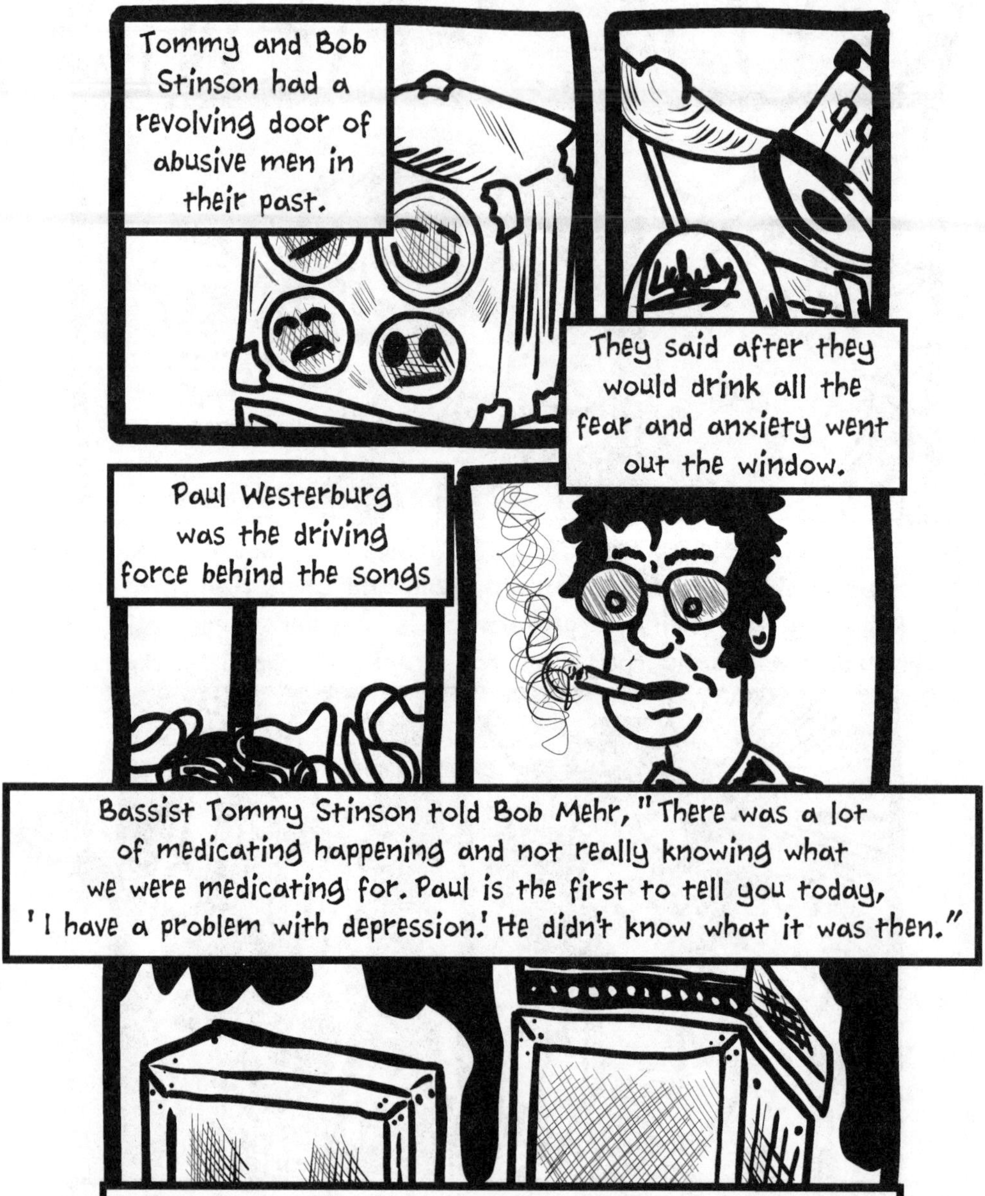
Tommy and Bob Stinson had a revolving door of abusive men in their past.
They said after they would drink all the fear and anxiety went out the window.
Paul Westerburg was the driving force behind the songs
Bassist Tommy Stinson told Bob Mehr, "There was a lot of medicating happening and not really knowing what we were medicating for. Paul is the first to tell you today, 'I have a problem with depression.' He didn't know what it was then."
They dealt with their problems in very juvenile ways and it ended up causing more problems, even resulting in the death of founding member Bob Stinson.

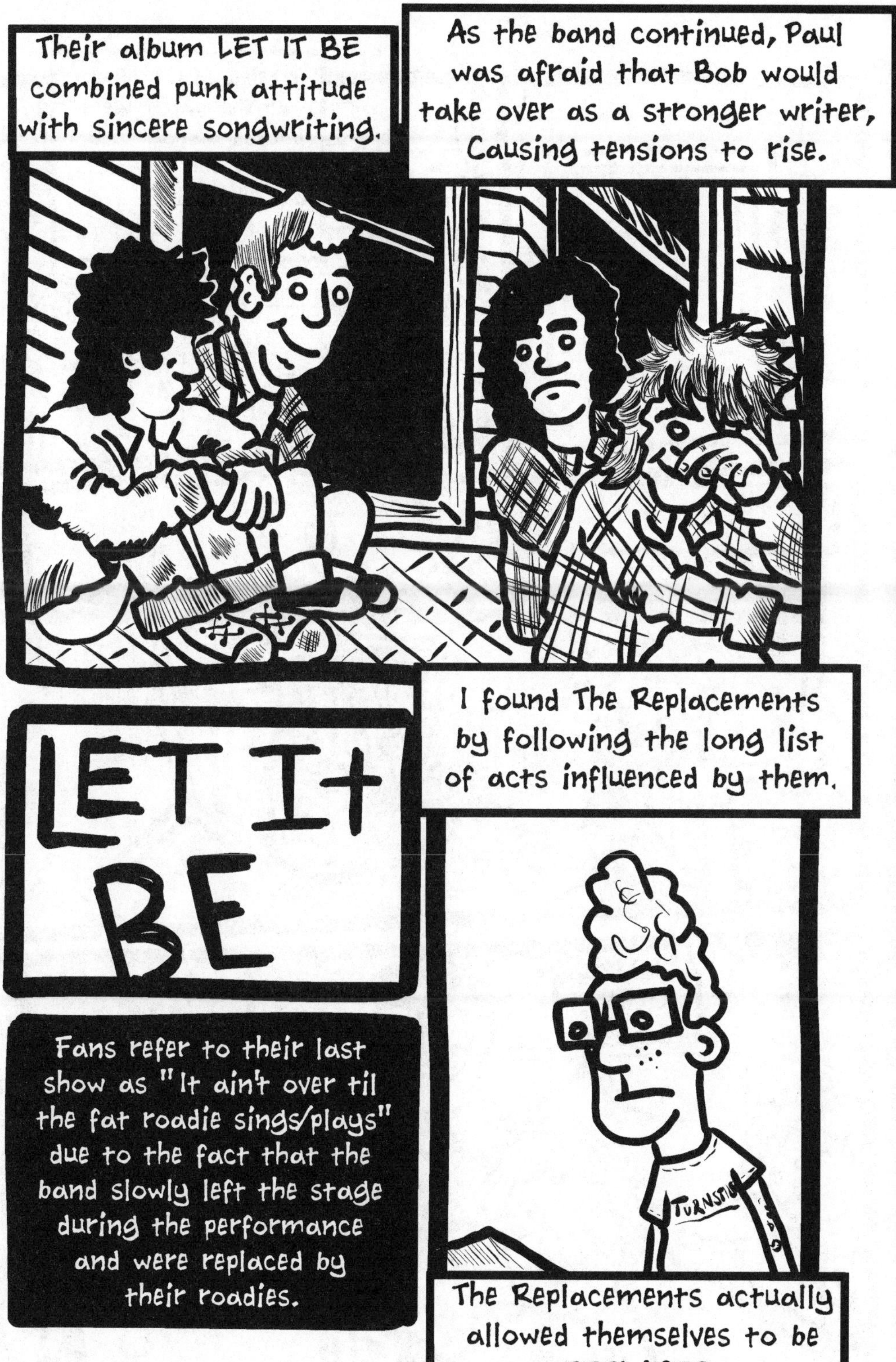
Their album LET IT BE combined punk attitude with sincere songwriting.
As the band continued, Paul was afraid that Bob would take over as a stronger writer, Causing tensions to rise.
LET It BE
I found The Replacements by following the long list of acts influenced by them.
Fans refer to their last show as "It ain't over til the fat roadie sings/plays" due to the fact that the band slowly left the stage during the performance and were replaced by their roadies.
The Replacements actually allowed themselves to be REPLACED.

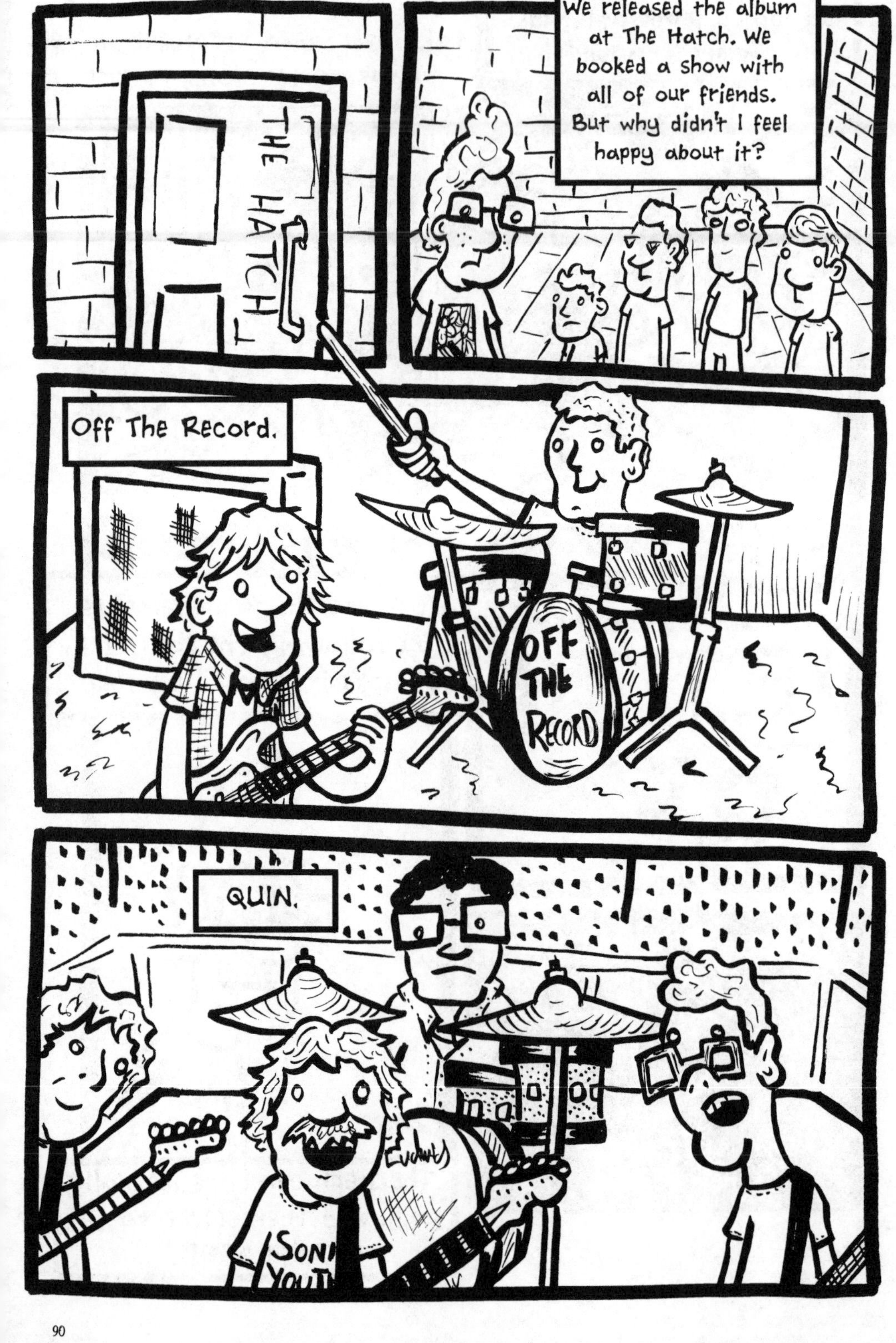
THE HATCH
We released the album at The Hatch. We booked a show with all of our friends. But why didn't I feel happy about it?
Off The Record.
OFF THE RECORD
QUIN.
SONI
YOUT

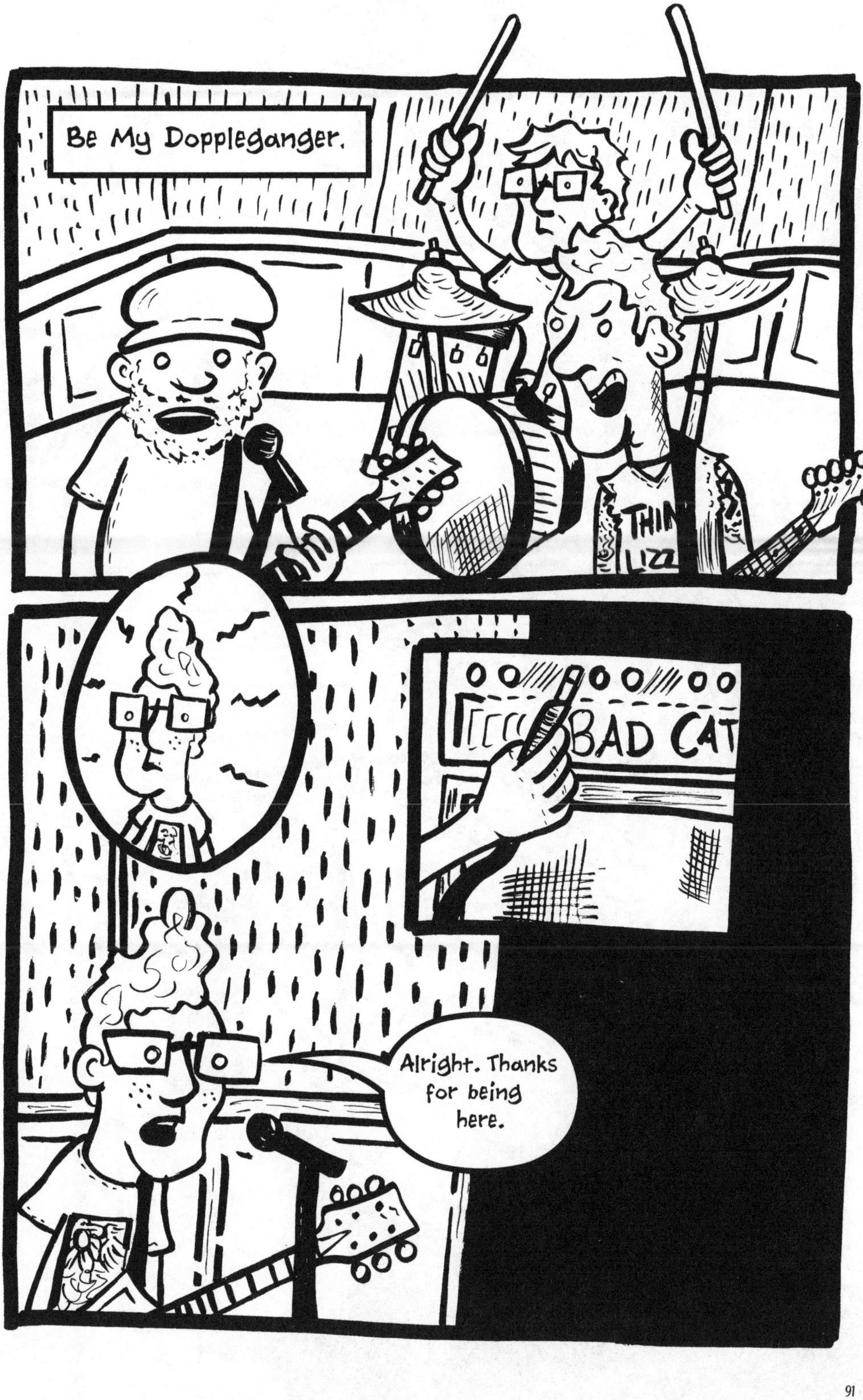
Be My Doppleganger.
THIN LIZZ
BAD CAT
Alright. Thanks for being here.

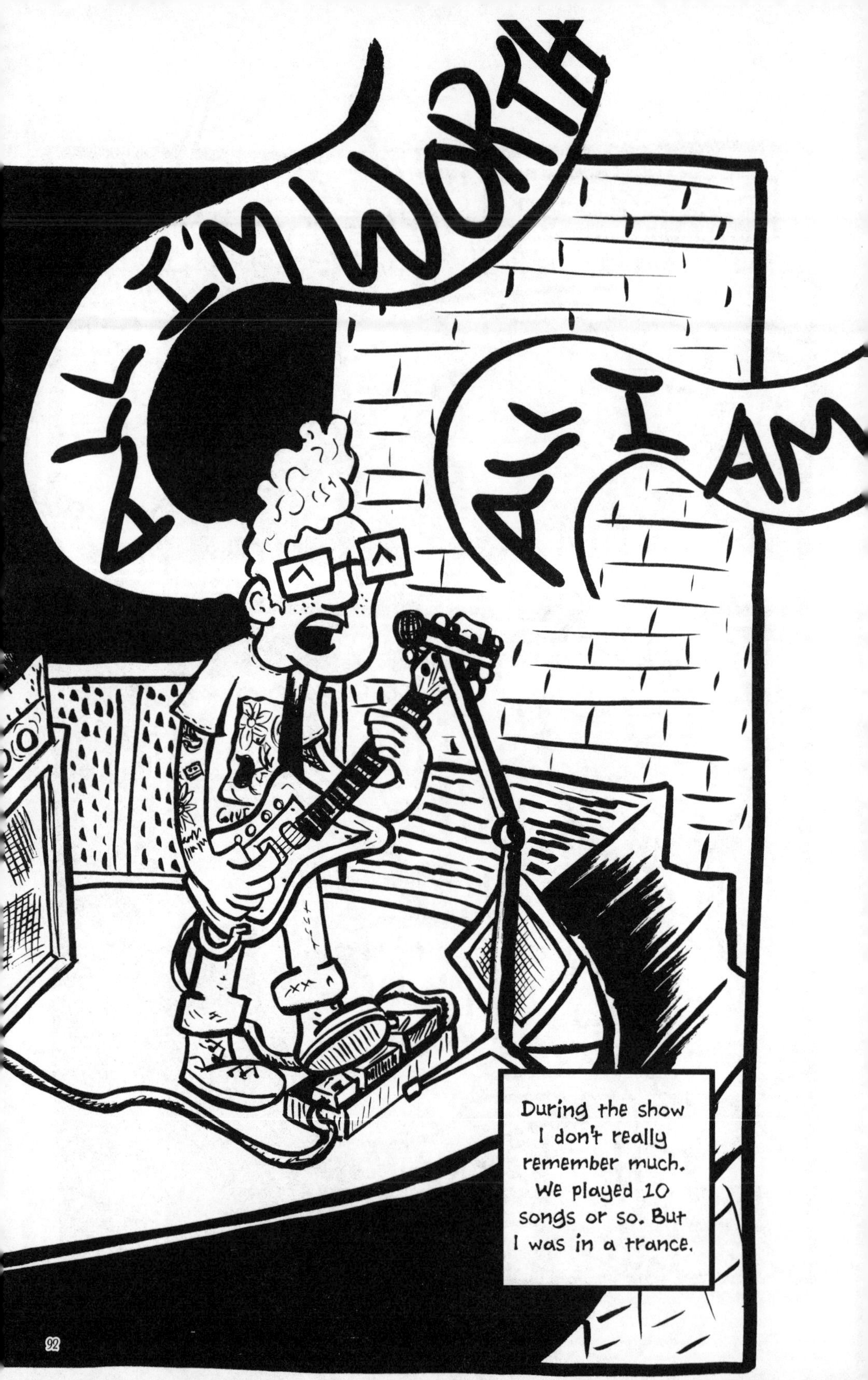
ALL I'M WORTH
ALL I AM
During the show I don't really remember much. We played 10 songs or so. But I was in a trance.

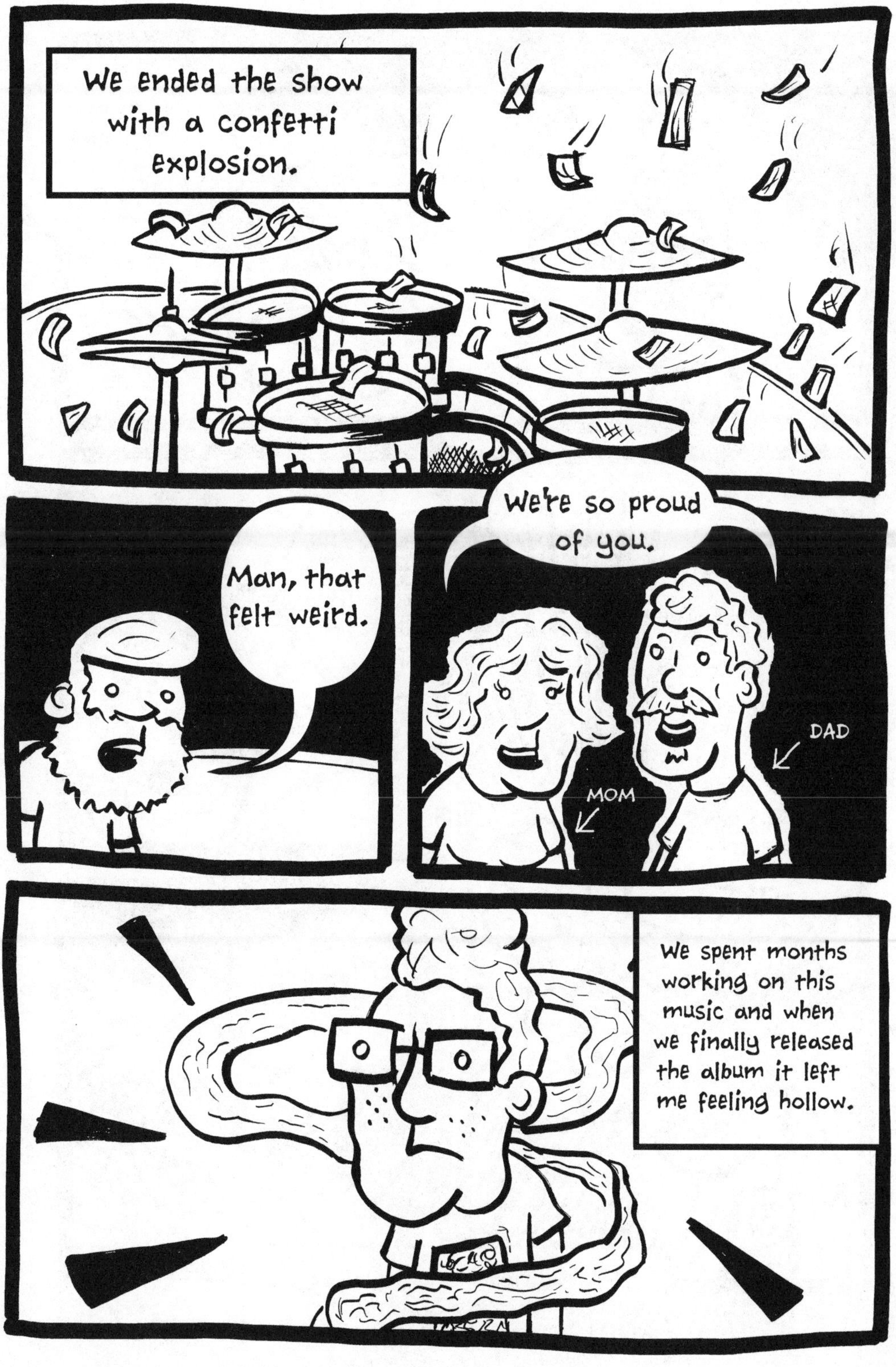
We ended the show with a confetti explosion.
Man, that felt weird.
We're so proud of you.
DAD
MOM
We spent months working on this music and when we finally released the album it left me feeling hollow.

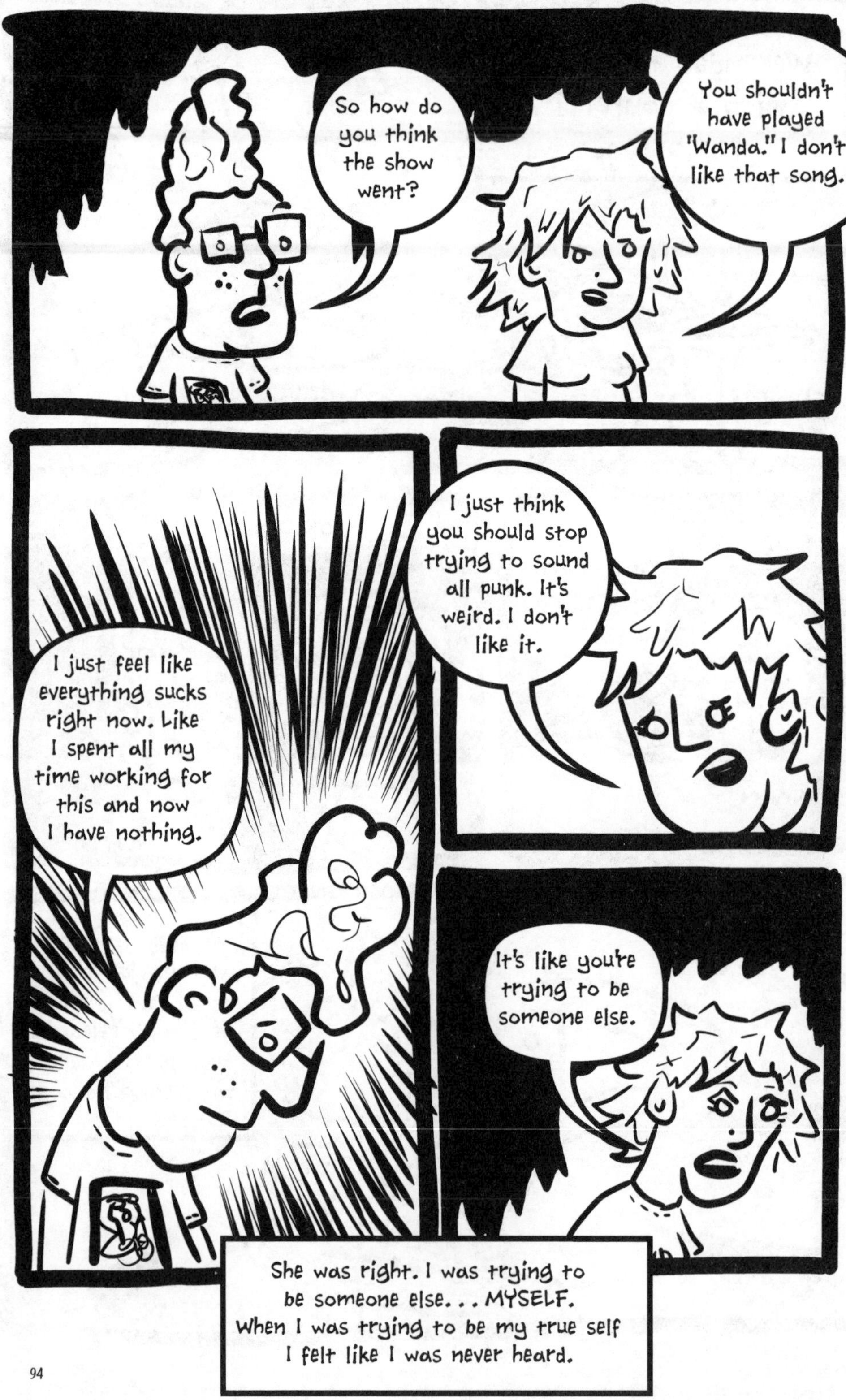
So how do you think the show went?
You shouldn't have played "Wanda." I don't like that song.
I just feel like everything sucks right now. Like I spent all my time working for this and now I have nothing.
I just think you should stop trying to sound all punk. It's weird. I don't like it.
It's like you're trying to be someone else.
She was right. I was trying to be someone else. . . MYSELF. When I was trying to be my true self I felt like I was never heard.

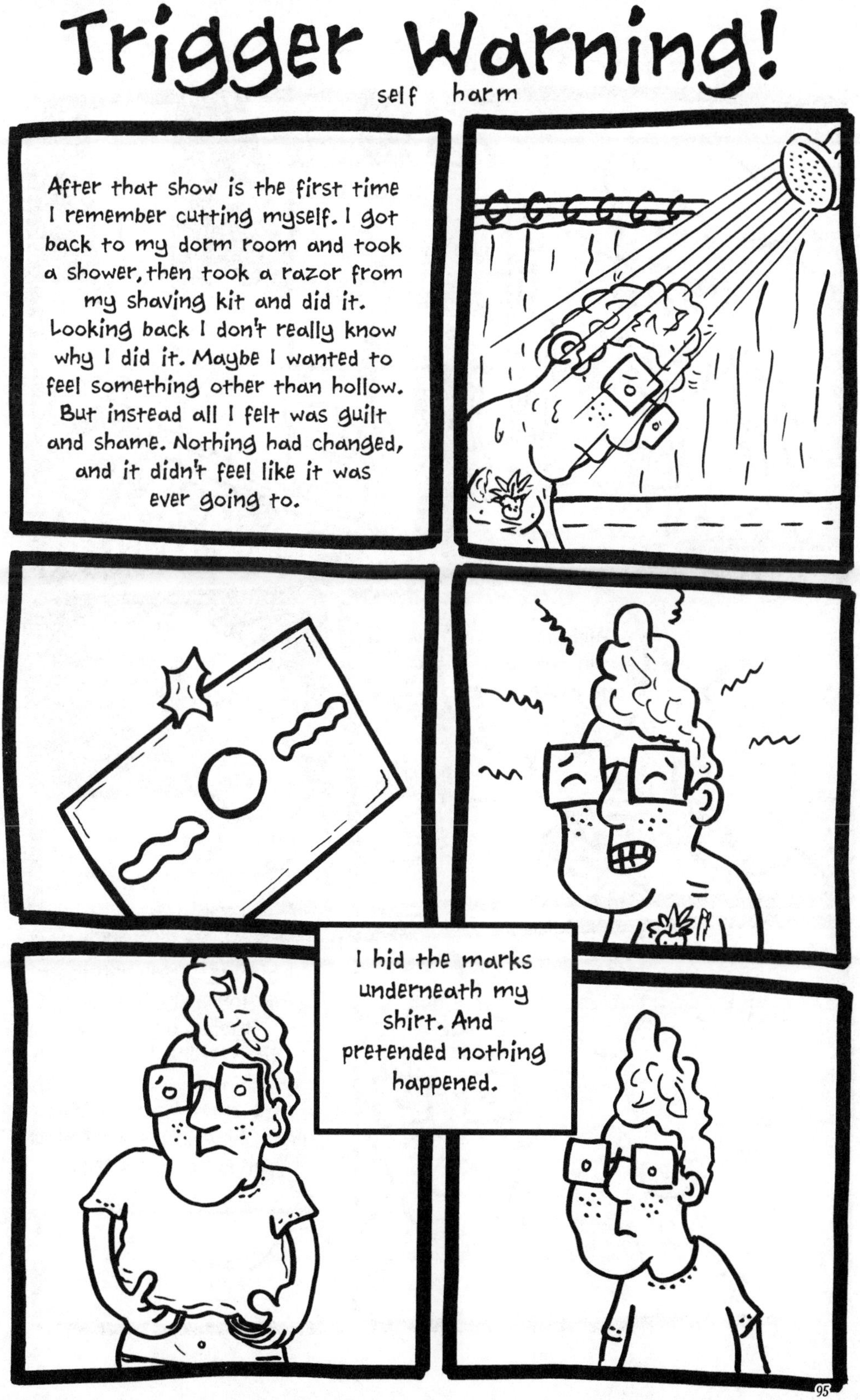
Trigger Warning!
self harm
After that show is the first time I remember cutting myself. I got back to my dorm room and took a shower, then took a razor from my shaving kit and did it. Looking back I don't really know why I did it. Maybe I wanted to feel something other than hollow. But instead all I felt was guilt and shame. Nothing had changed, and it didn't feel like it was ever going to.
I hid the marks underneath my shirt. And pretended nothing happened.

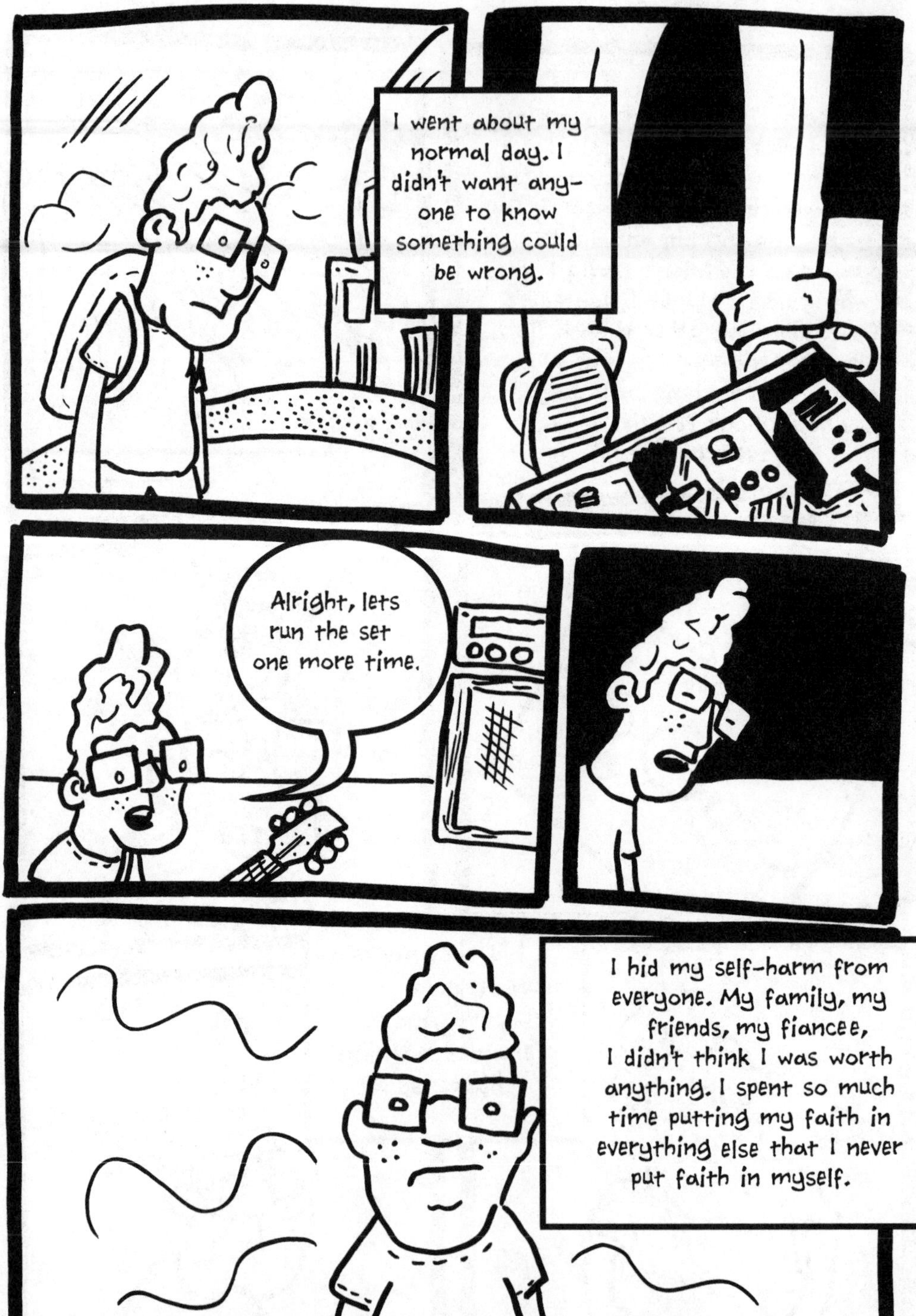
I went about my normal day. I didn't want any-one to know something could be wrong.
Alright, lets run the set one more time.
I hid my self-harm from everyone. My family, my friends, my fiancee, I didn't think I was worth anything. I spent so much time putting my faith in everything else that I never put faith in myself.

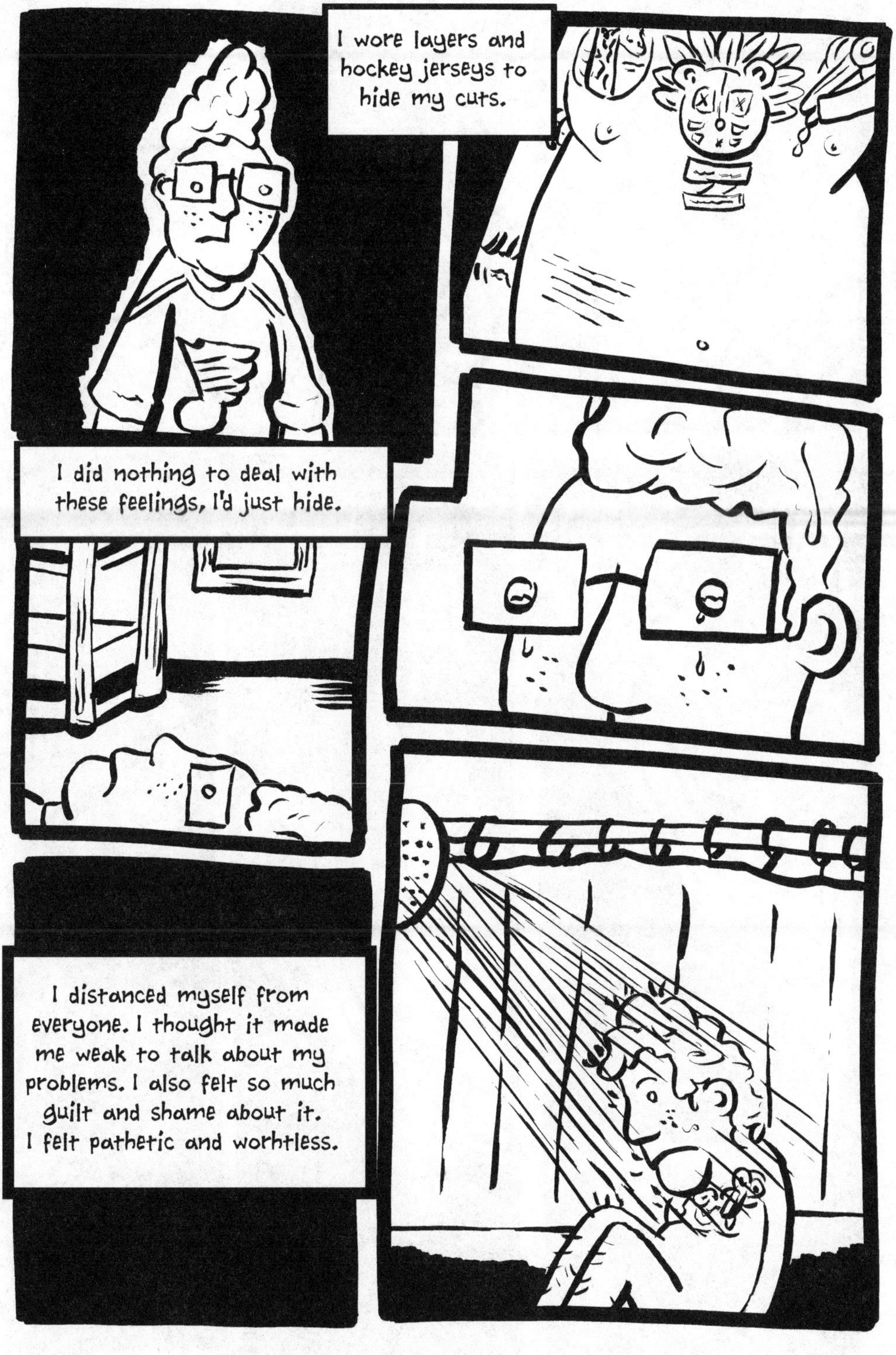
I wore layers and hockey jerseys to hide my cuts.
I did nothing to deal with these feelings, I'd just hide.
I distanced myself from everyone. I thought it made me weak to talk about my problems. I also felt so much guilt and shame about it. I felt pathetic and worhtless.

Everything was crumbling underneath me.

I was falling.

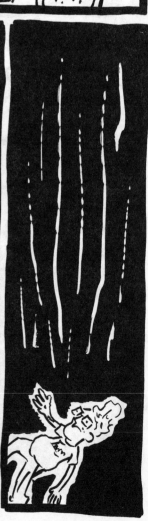

Part 3

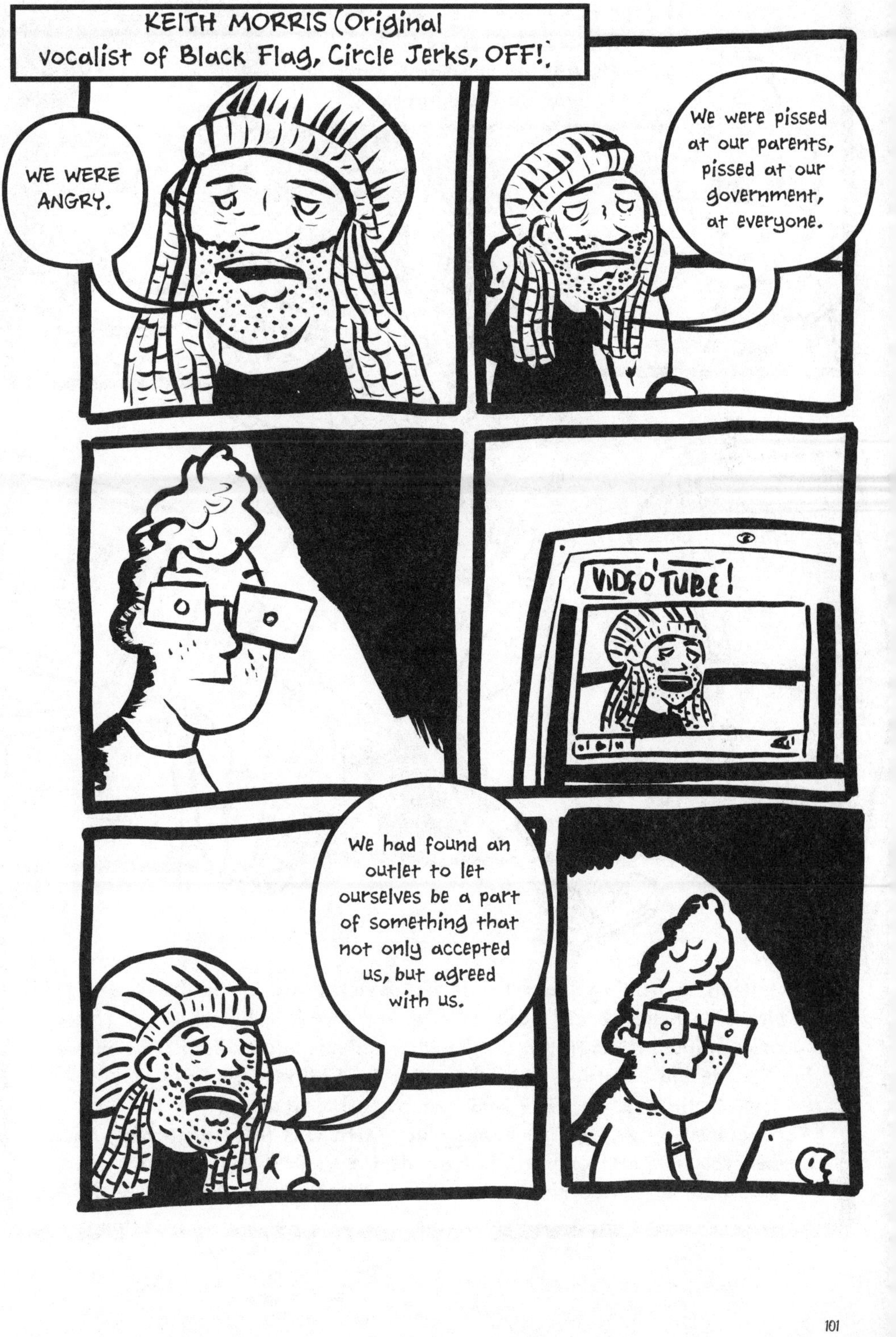
KEITH MORRIS (Original vocalist of Black Flag, Circle Jerks, OFF!)
WE WERE ANGRY.
We were pissed at our parents, pissed at our government, at everyone.
VIDEO TUBE!
We had found an outlet to let ourselves be a part of something that not only accepted us, but agreed with us.

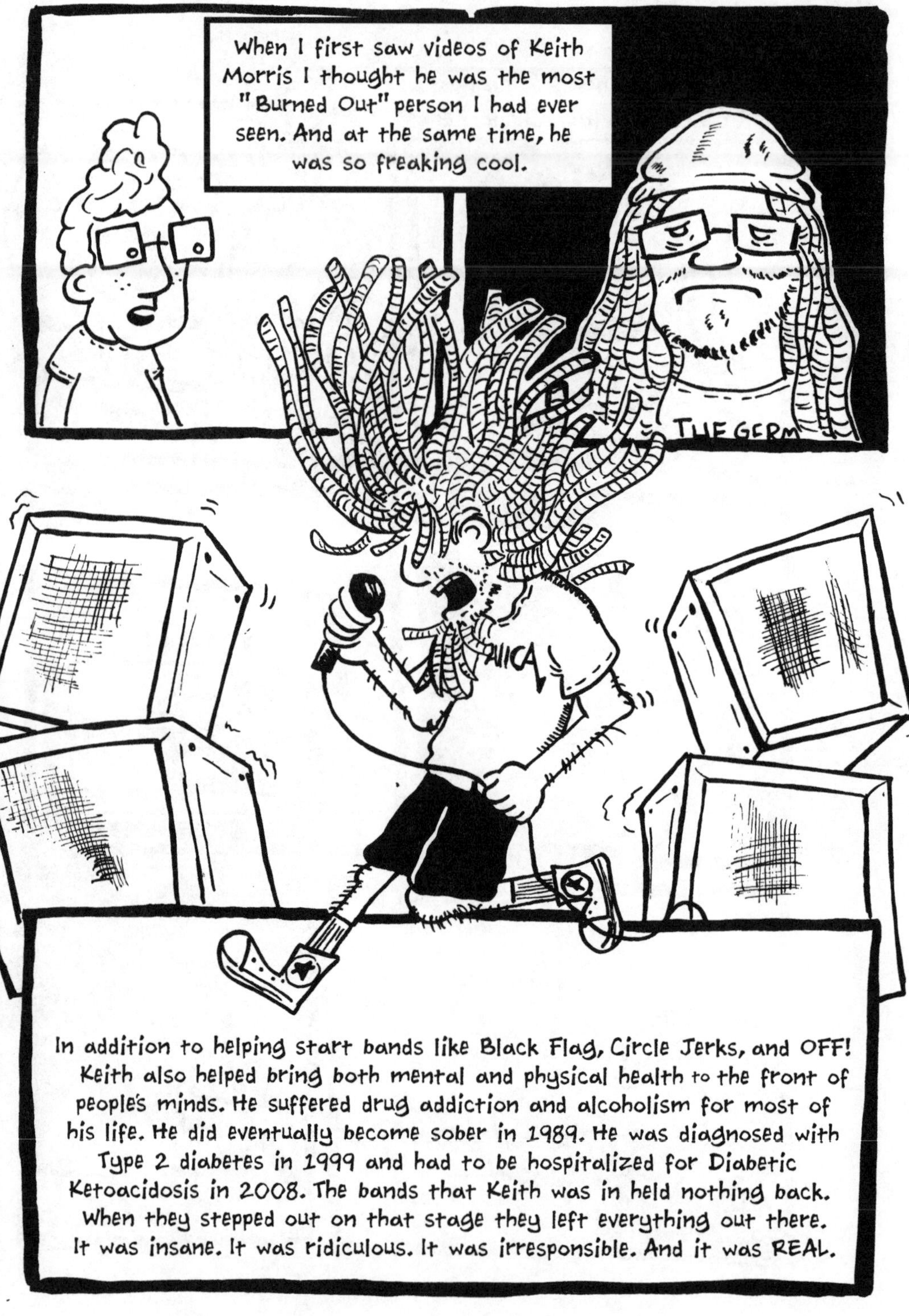
When I first saw videos of Keith Morris I thought he was the most "Burned Out" person I had ever seen. And at the same time, he was so freaking cool.
THE GERM
In addition to helping start bands like Black Flag, Circle Jerks, and OFF! Keith also helped bring both mental and physical health to the front of people's minds. He suffered drug addiction and alcoholism for most of his life. He did eventually become sober in 1989. He was diagnosed with Type 2 diabetes in 1999 and had to be hospitalized for Diabetic Ketoacidosis in 2008. The bands that Keith was in held nothing back. When they stepped out on that stage they left everything out there. It was insane. It was ridiculous. It was irresponsible. And it was REAL.

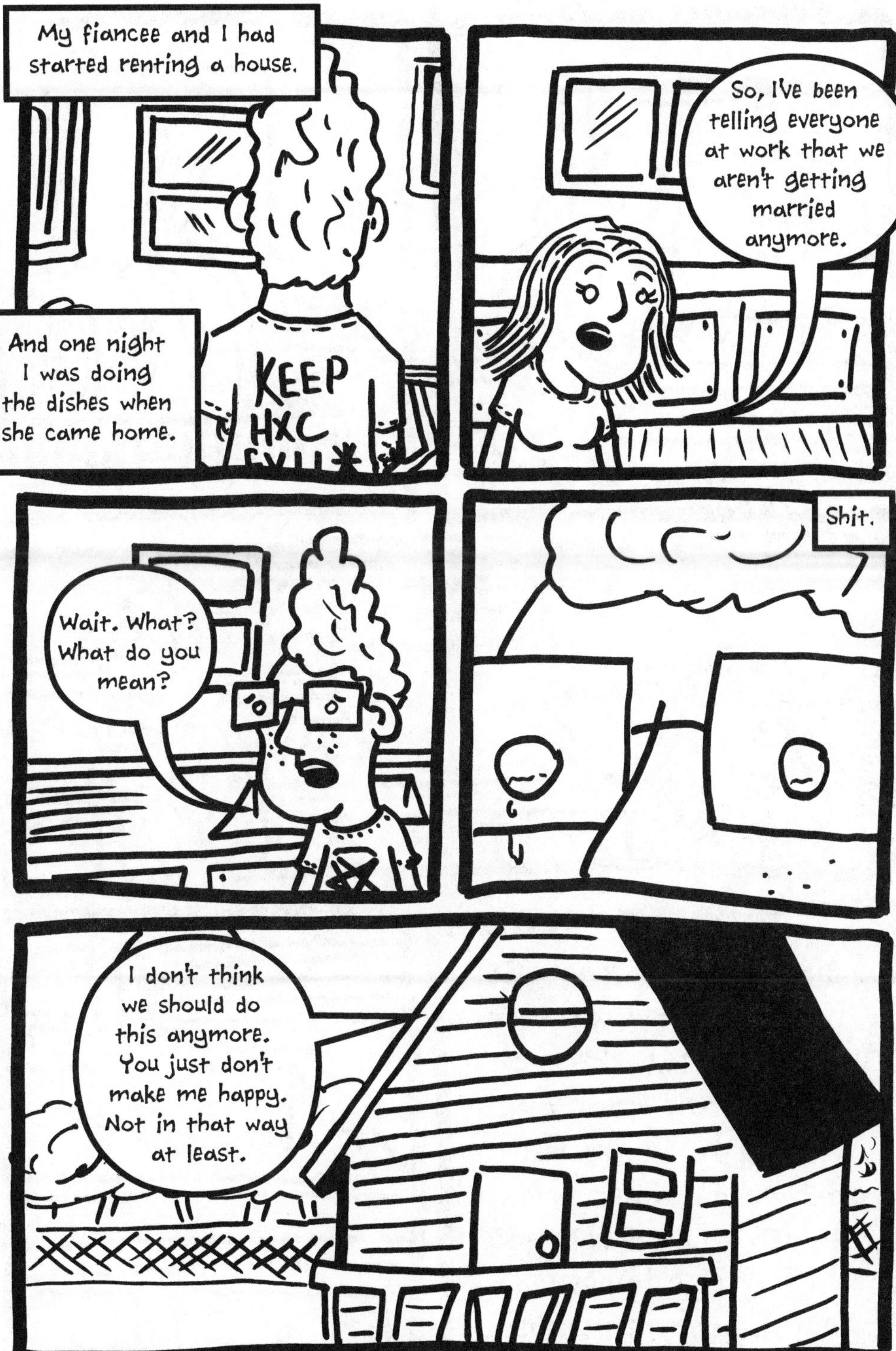

My fiancee and I had started renting a house.
And one night I was doing the dishes when she came home.
KEEP HXC
So, I've been telling everyone at work that we aren't getting married anymore.
Wait. What? What do you mean?
Shit.
I don't think we should do this anymore. You just don't make me happy. Not in that way at least.

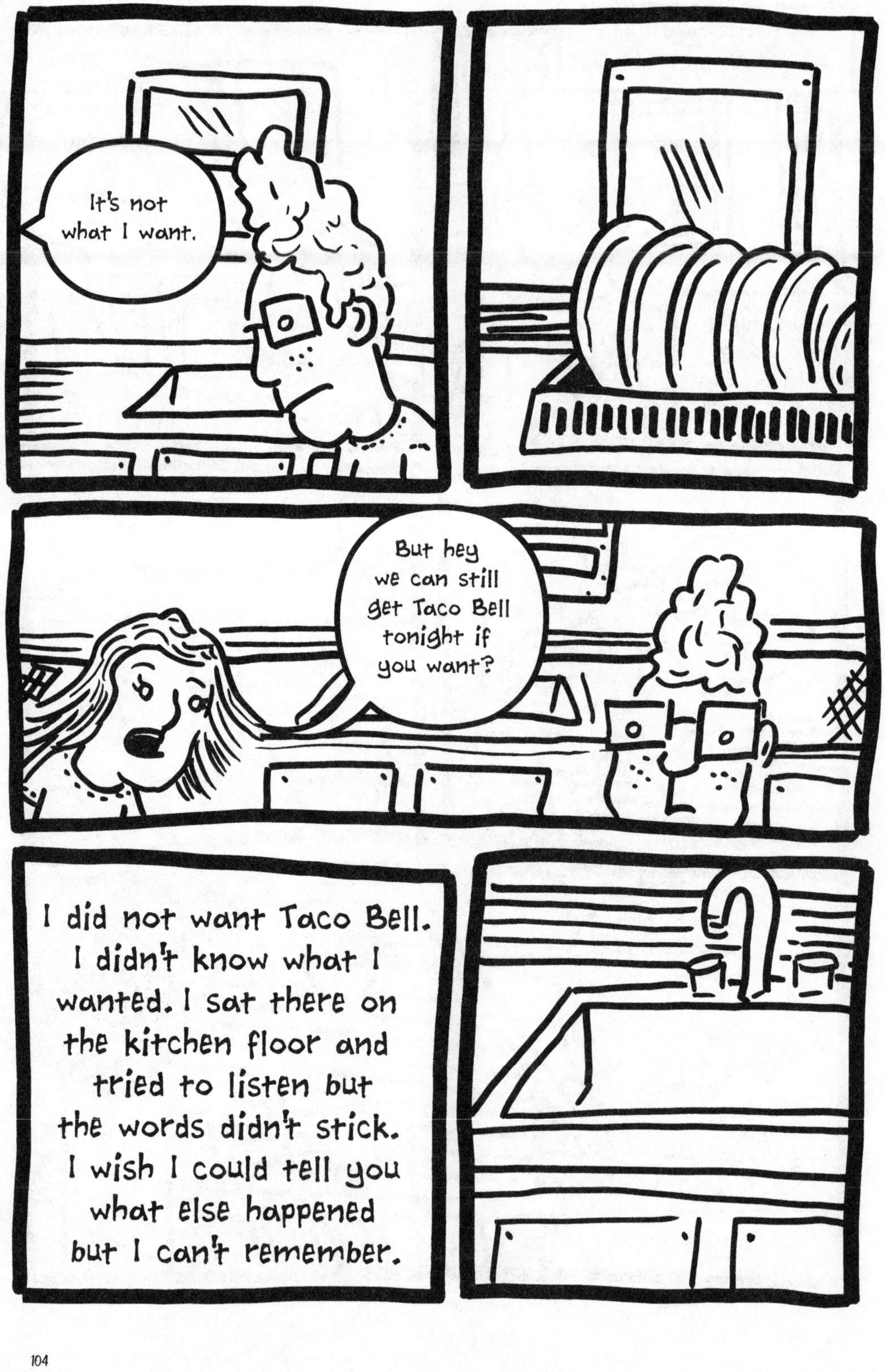
It's not what I want.
But hey we can still get Taco Bell tonight if you want?
I did not want Taco Bell. I didn't know what I wanted. I sat there on the kitchen floor and tried to listen but the words didn't stick. I wish I could tell you what else happened but I can't remember.

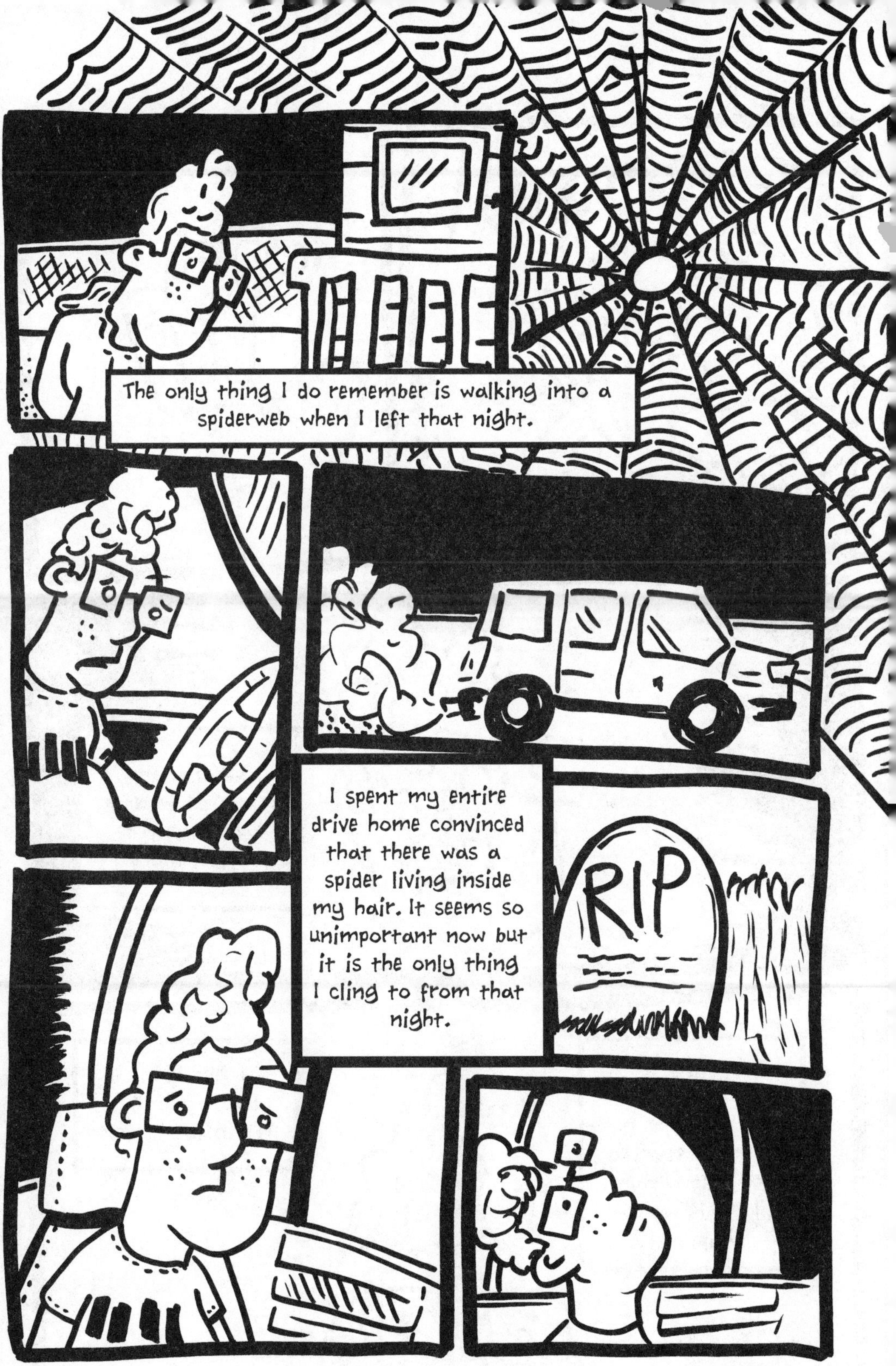
The only thing I do remember is walking into a spiderweb when I left that night.
I spent my entire drive home convinced that there was a spider living inside my hair. It seems so unimportant now but it is the only thing I cling to from that night.
RIP

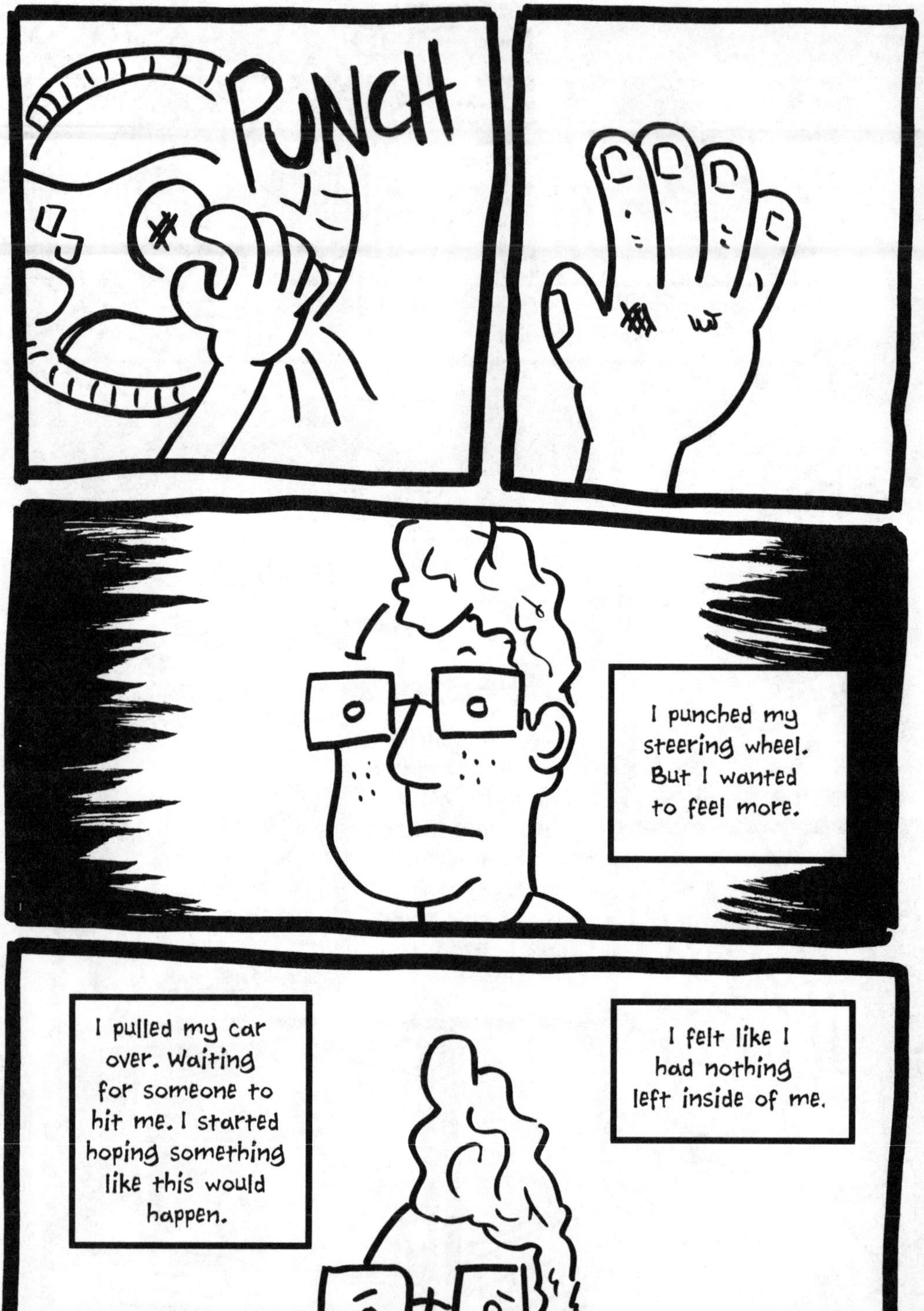
PUNCH
I punched my steering wheel. But I wanted to feel more.
I pulled my car over. Waiting for someone to hit me. I started hoping something like this would happen.
I felt like I had nothing left inside of me.

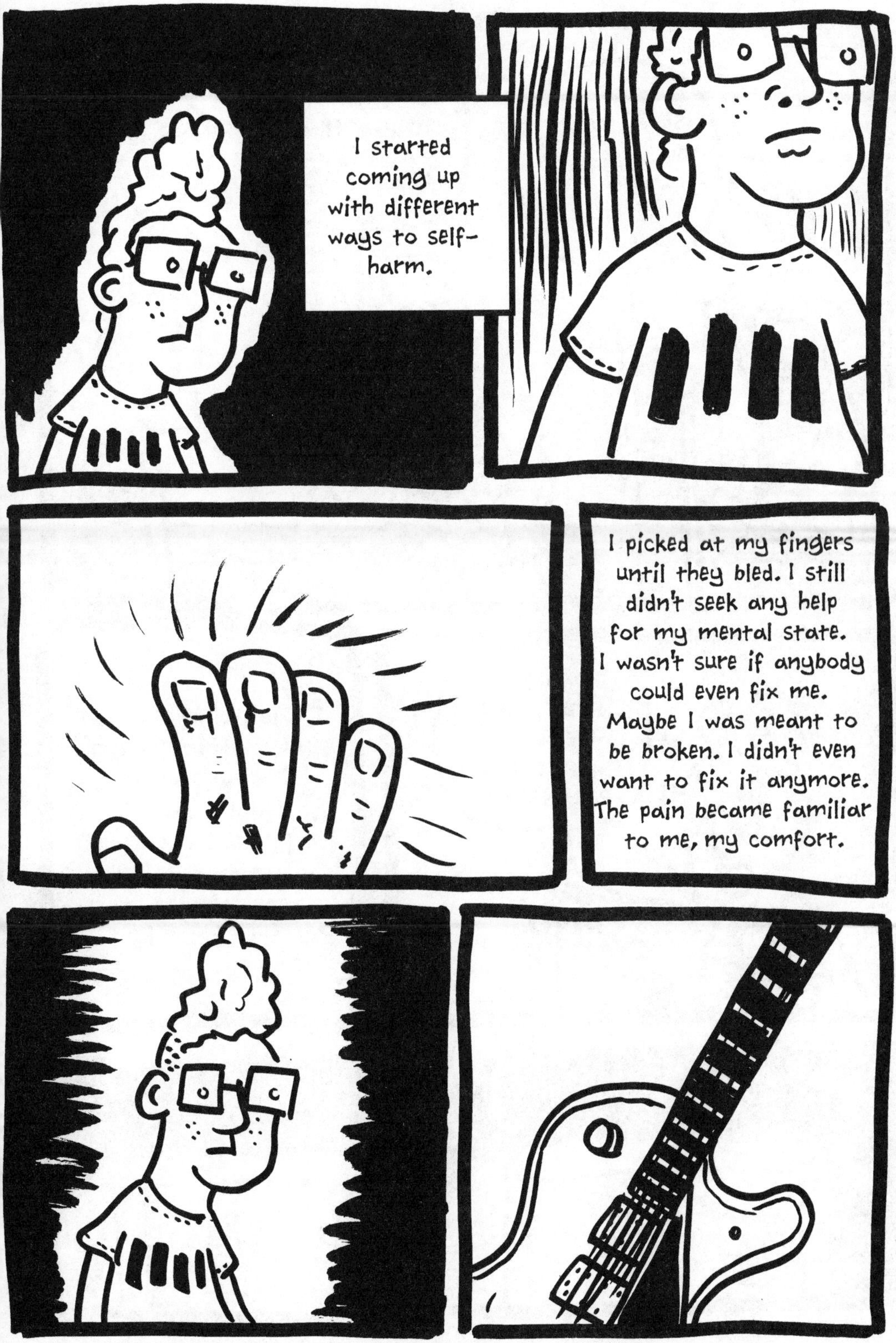
I started coming up with different ways to self-harm.
I picked at my fingers until they bled. I still didn't seek any help for my mental state. I wasn't sure if anybody could even fix me. Maybe I was meant to be broken. I didn't even want to fix it anymore. The pain became familiar to me, my comfort.

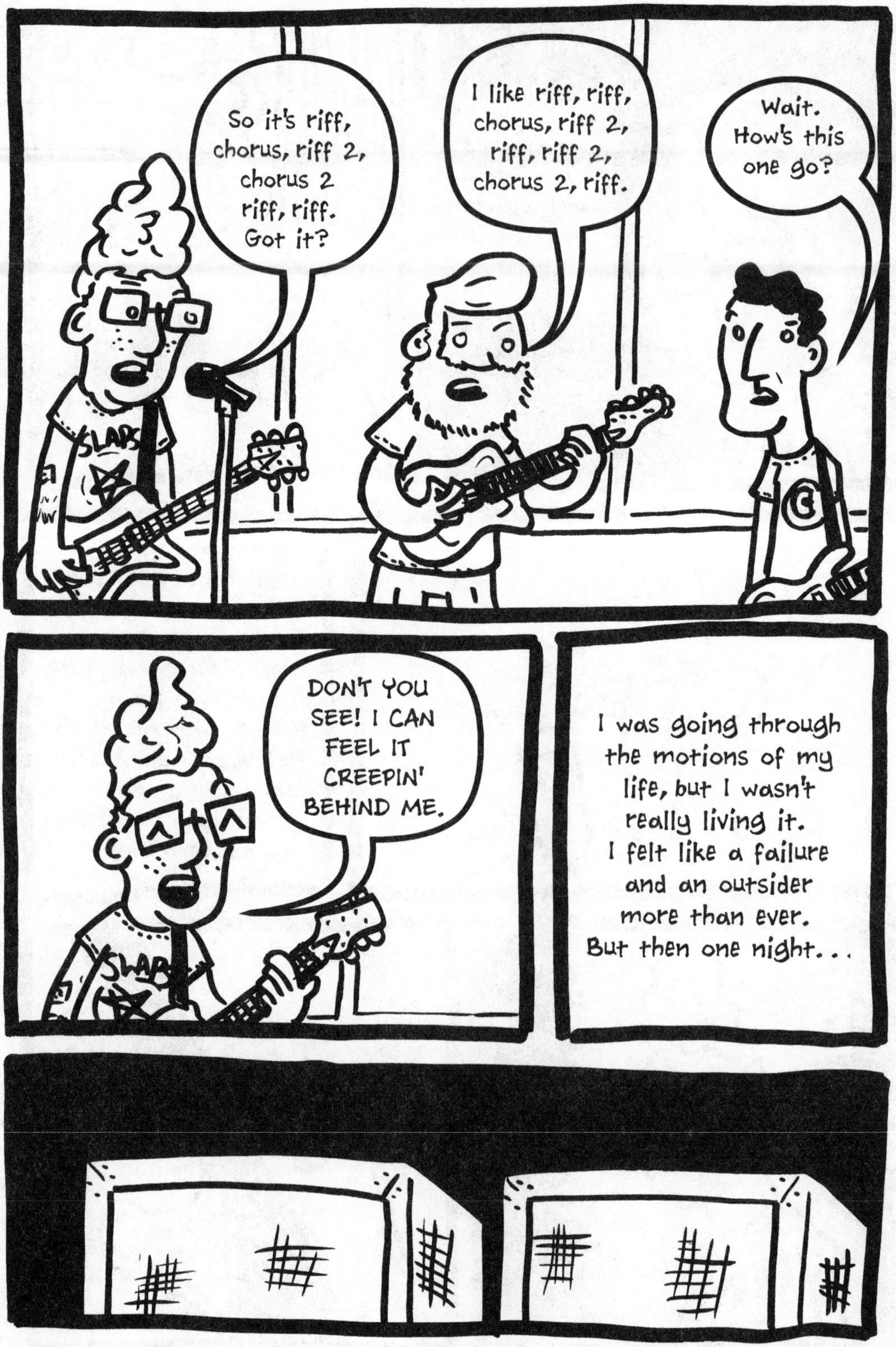
So it's riff, chorus, riff 2, chorus 2 riff, riff. Got it?
I like riff, riff, chorus, riff 2, riff, riff 2, chorus 2, riff.
Wait. How's this one go?
SLAPS
DON'T YOU SEE! I CAN FEEL IT CREEPIN' BEHIND ME.
SLAPS
I was going through the motions of my life, but I wasn't really living it. I felt like a failure and an outsider more than ever. But then one night. . .

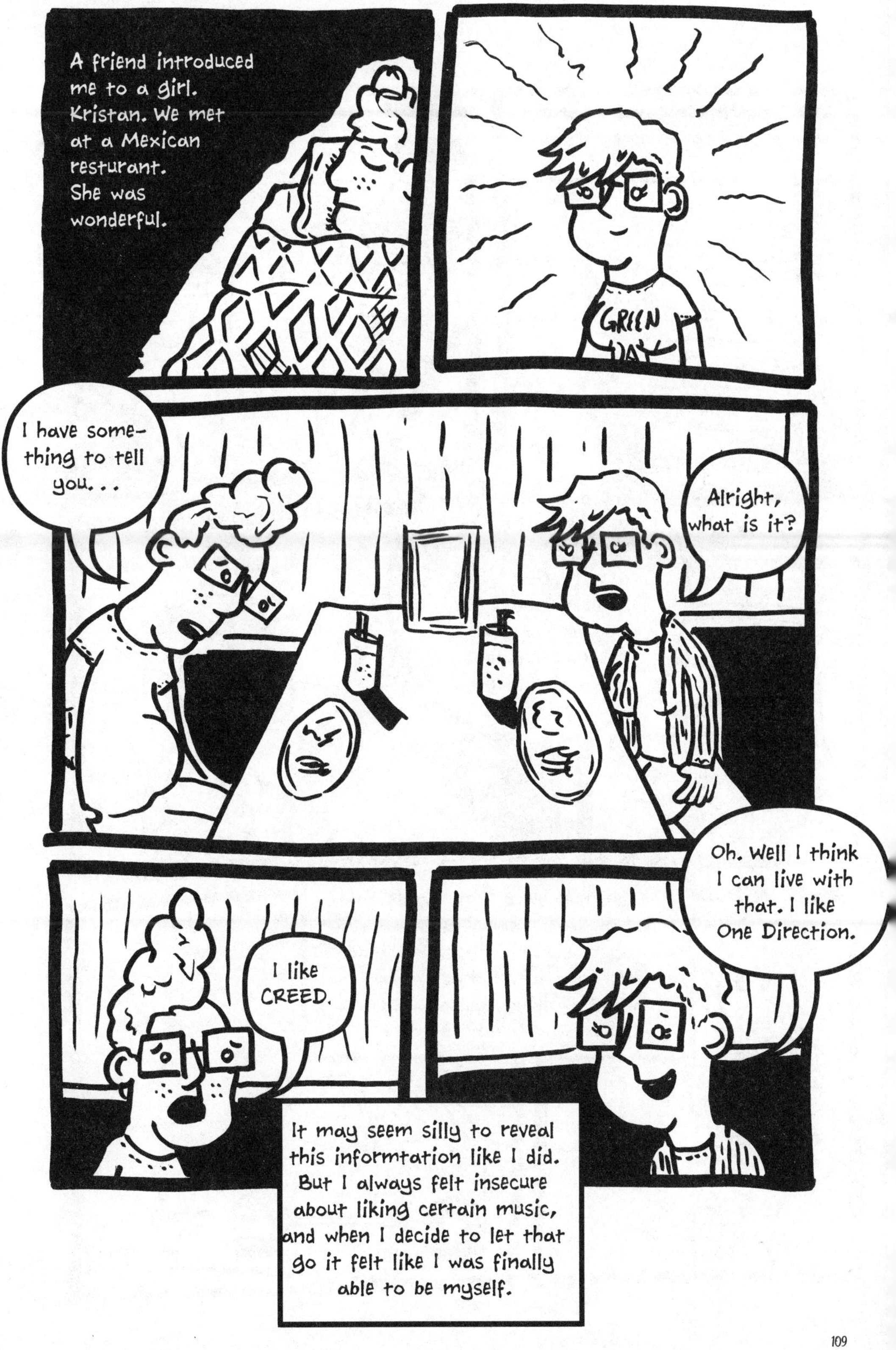
A friend introduced me to a girl. Kristan. We met at a Mexican resturant. She was wonderful.
GREEN DAY
I have something to tell you. . .
Alright, what is it?
I like CREED.
Oh. Well I think I can live with that. I like One Direction.
It may seem silly to reveal this informtation like I did. But I always felt insecure about liking certain music, and when I decide to let that go it felt like I was finally able to be myself.

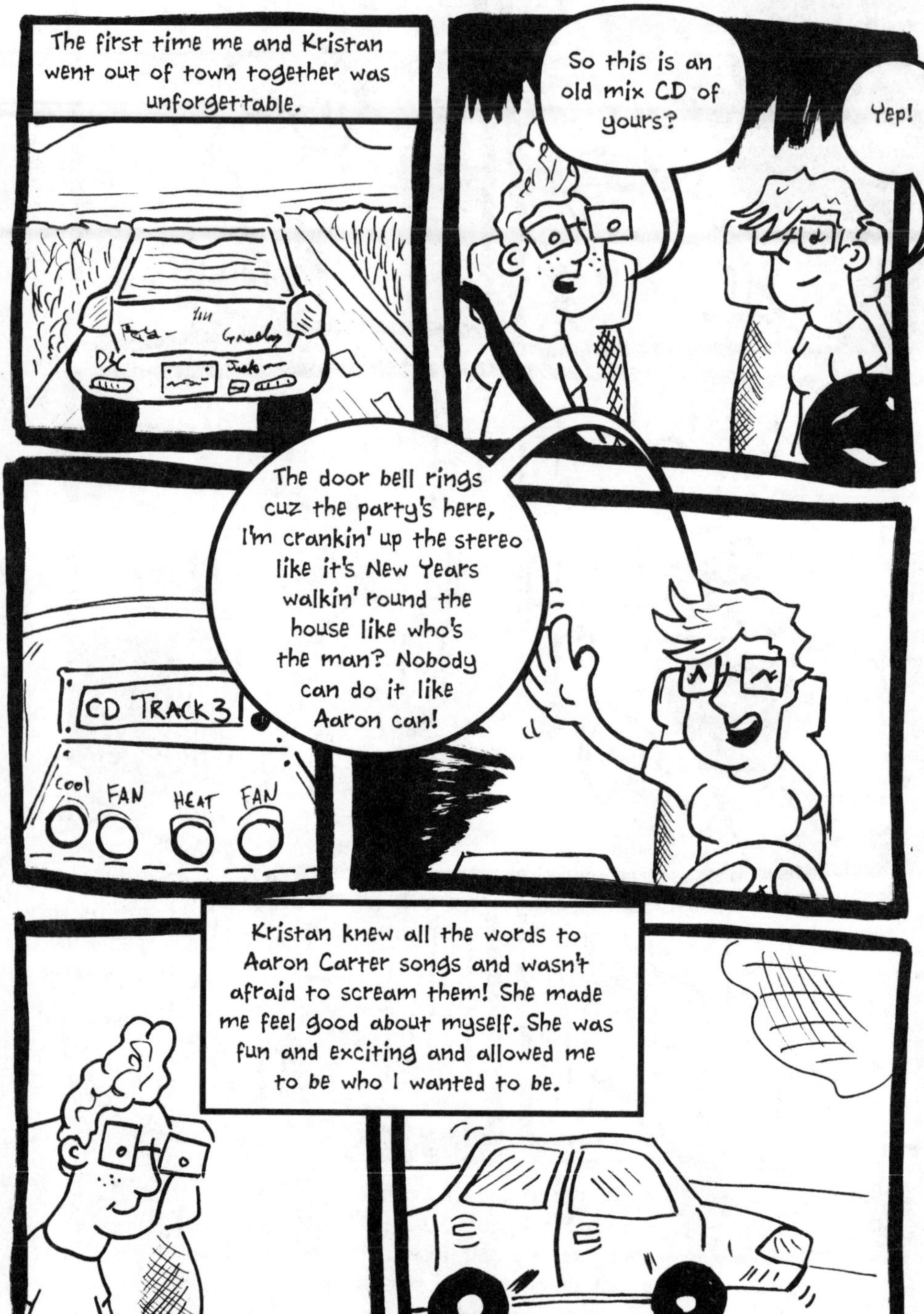

The first time me and Kristan went out of town together was unforgettable.
So this is an old mix CD of yours?
Yep!
The door bell rings cuz the party's here, I'm crankin' up the stereo like it's New Years walkin' round the house like who's the man? Nobody can do it like Aaron can!
CD TRACK 3
COOL
FAN
HEAT
FAN
Kristan knew all the words to Aaron Carter songs and wasn't afraid to scream them! She made me feel good about myself. She was fun and exciting and allowed me to be who I wanted to be.

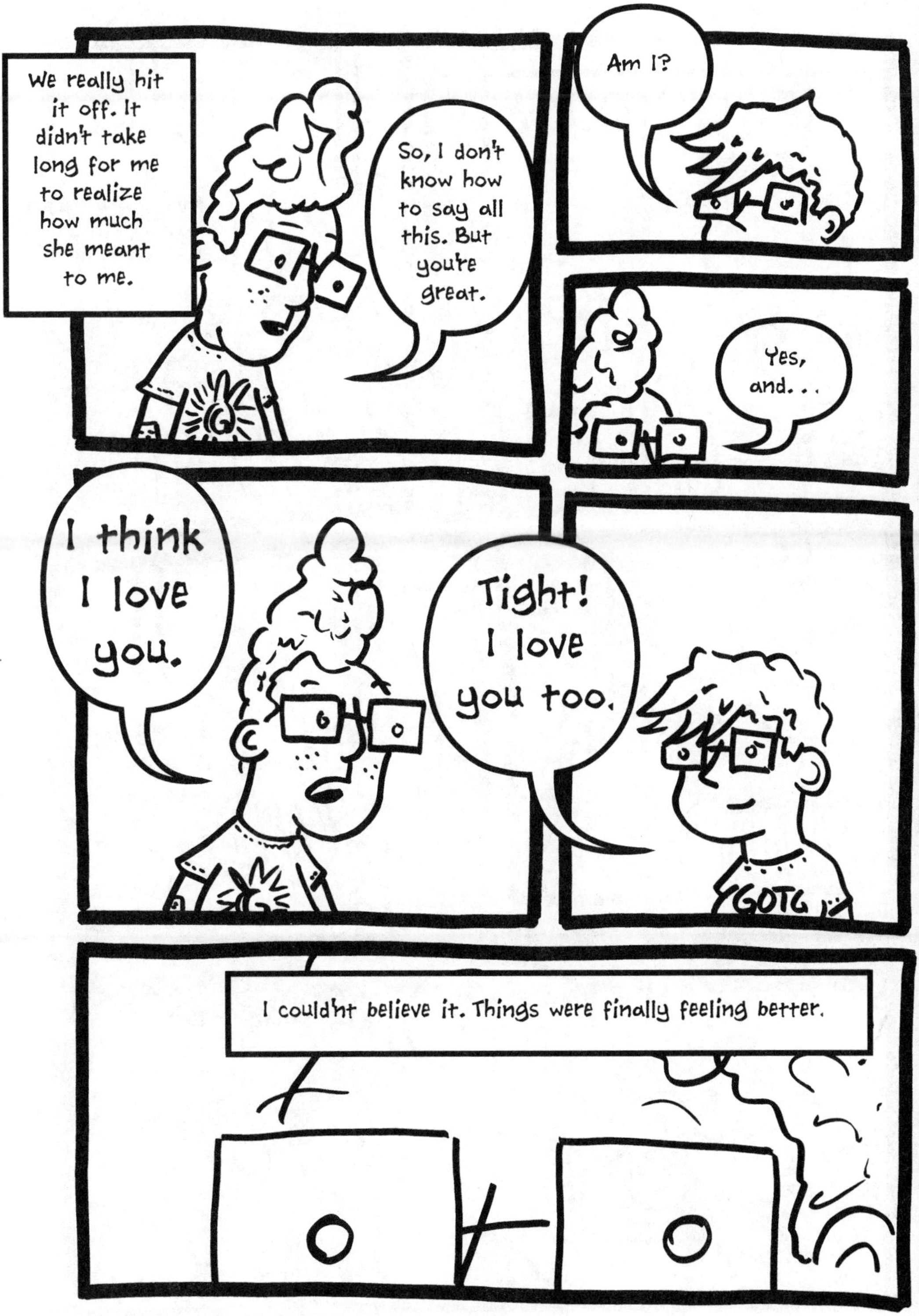
We really hit it off. It didn't take long for me to realize how much she meant to me.
So, I don't know how to say all this. But you're great.
Am I?
Yes, and...
I think I love you.
Tight! I love you too.
GOTG
I couldn't believe it. Things were finally feeling better.

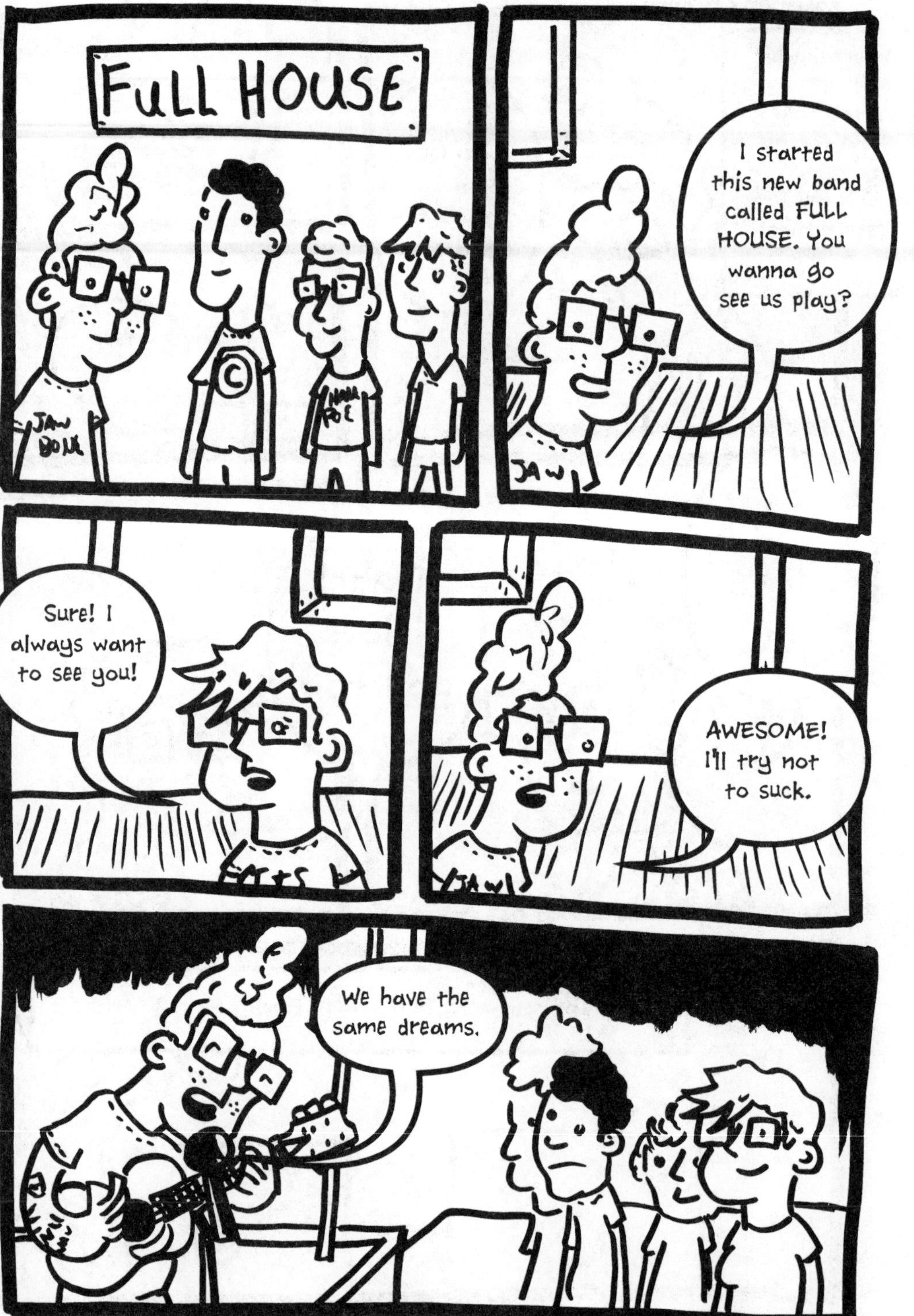
FULL HOUSE
I started this new band called FULL HOUSE. You wanna go see us play?
Sure! I always want to see you!
AWESOME! I'll try not to suck.
We have the same dreams.

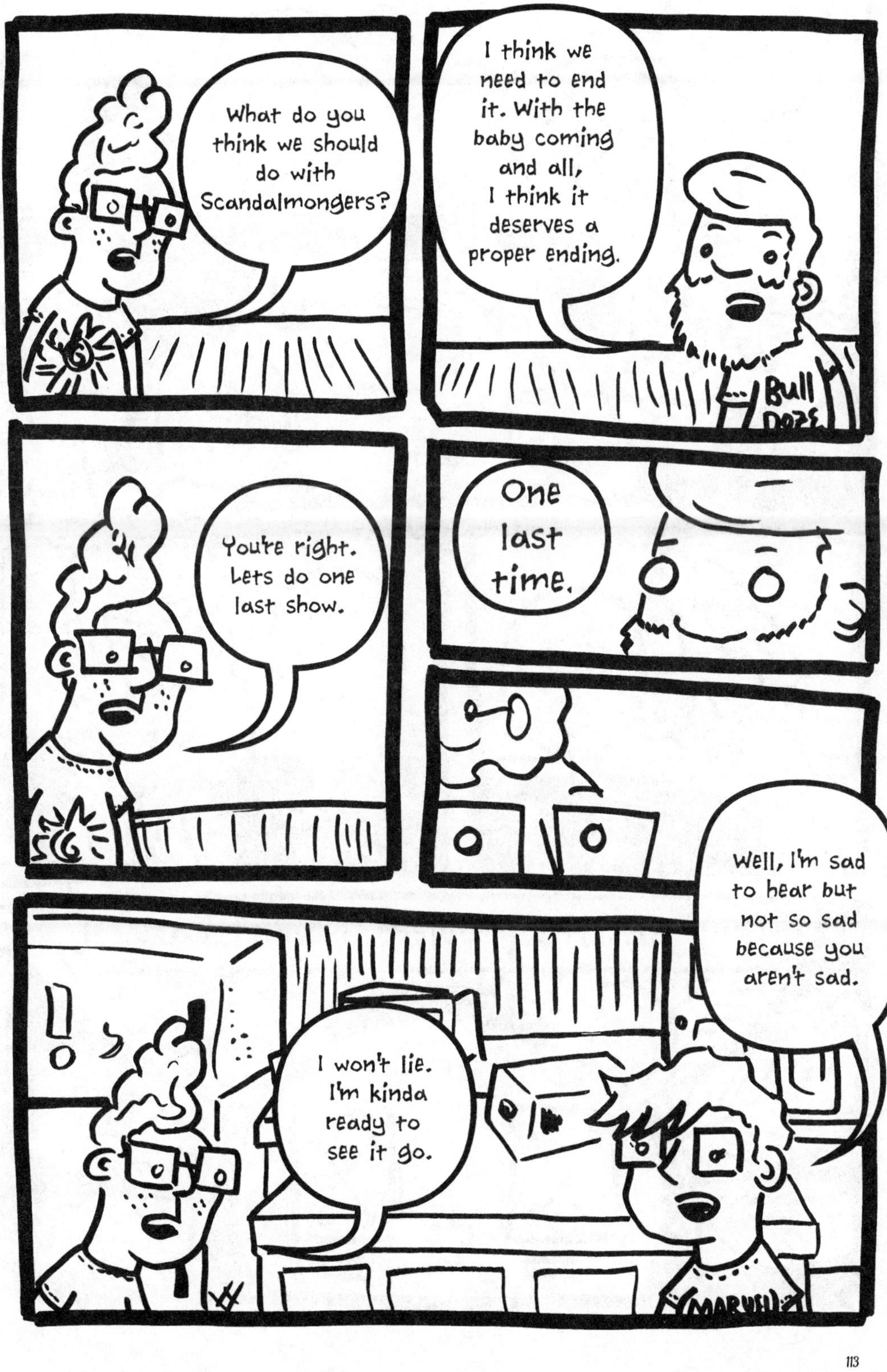
What do you think we should do with Scandalmongers?
I think we need to end it. With the baby coming and all, I think it deserves a proper ending.
BULL DOZE
You're right. Lets do one last show.
One last time.
!
Well, I'm sad to hear but not so sad because you aren't sad.
I won't lie. I'm kinda ready to see it go.
MARVEL

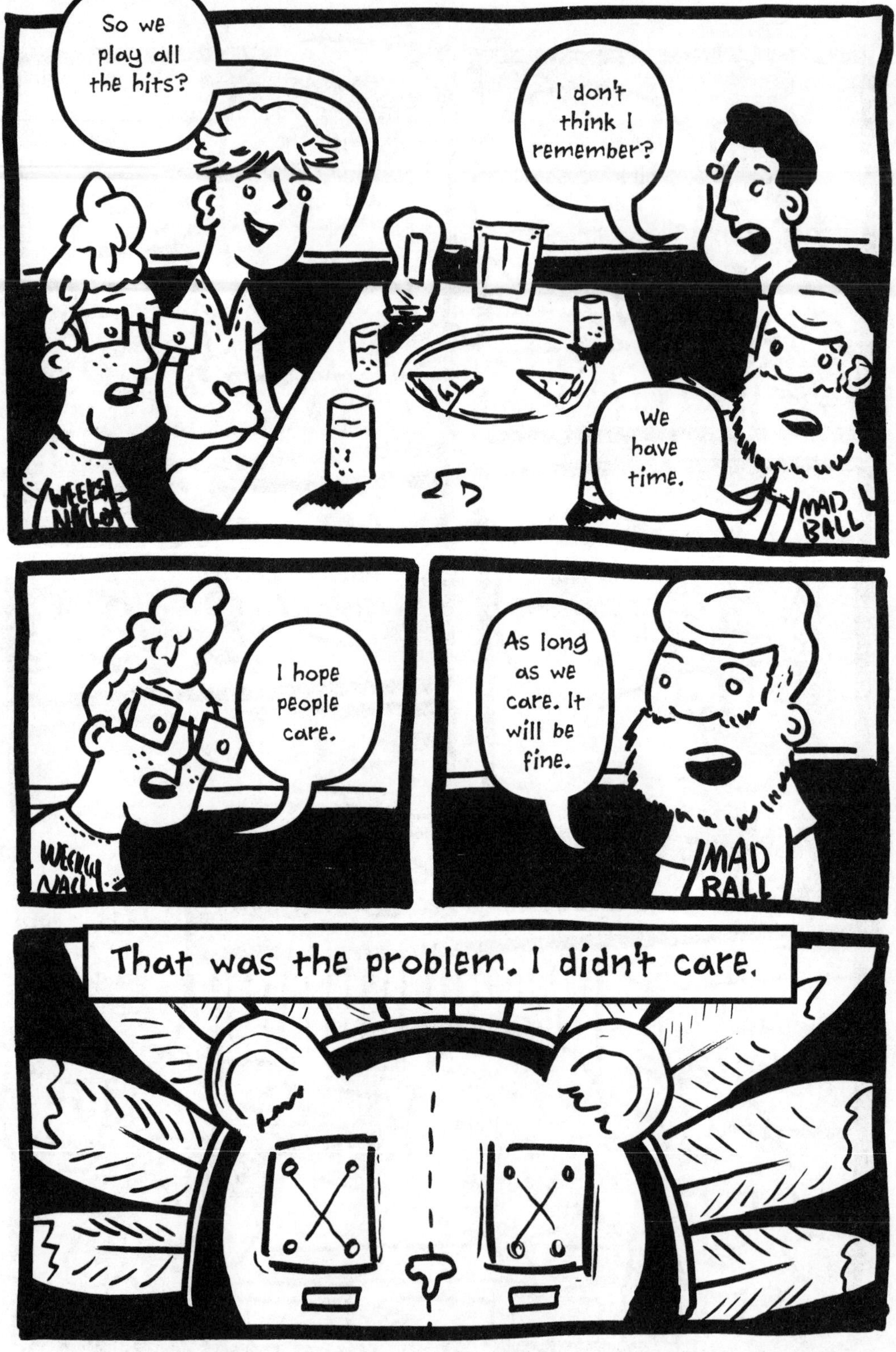
So we play all the hits?
I don't think I remember?
We have time.
WEEKLY NACHOS
MAD BALL
I hope people care.
WEEKLY NACH
As long as we care. It will be fine.
MAD BALL
That was the problem. I didn't care.

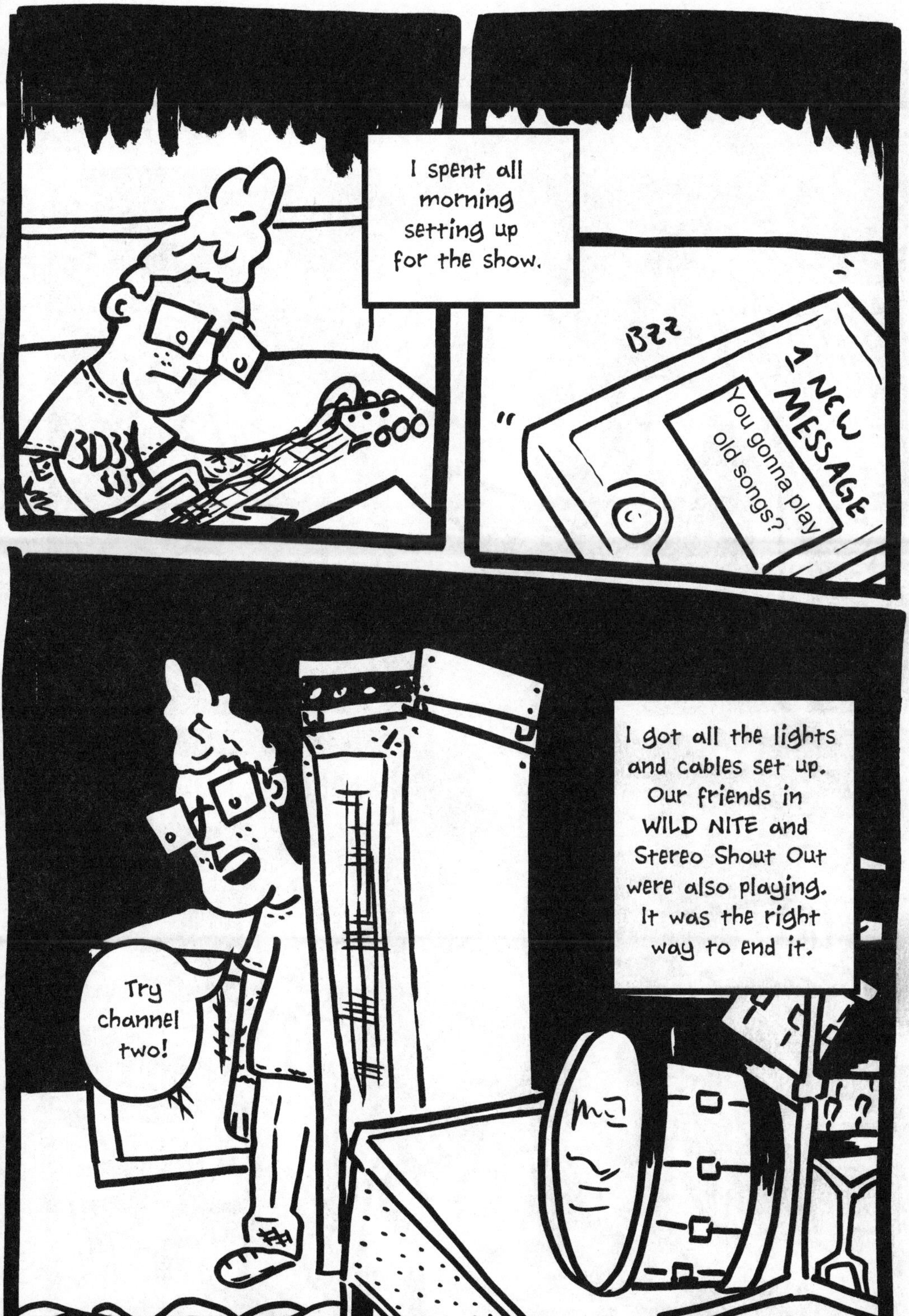
I spent all morning setting up for the show.
BZZ
1 NEW MESSAGE
You gonna play old songs?
I got all the lights and cables set up. Our friends in WILD NITE and Stereo Shout Out were also playing. It was the right way to end it.
Try channel two!

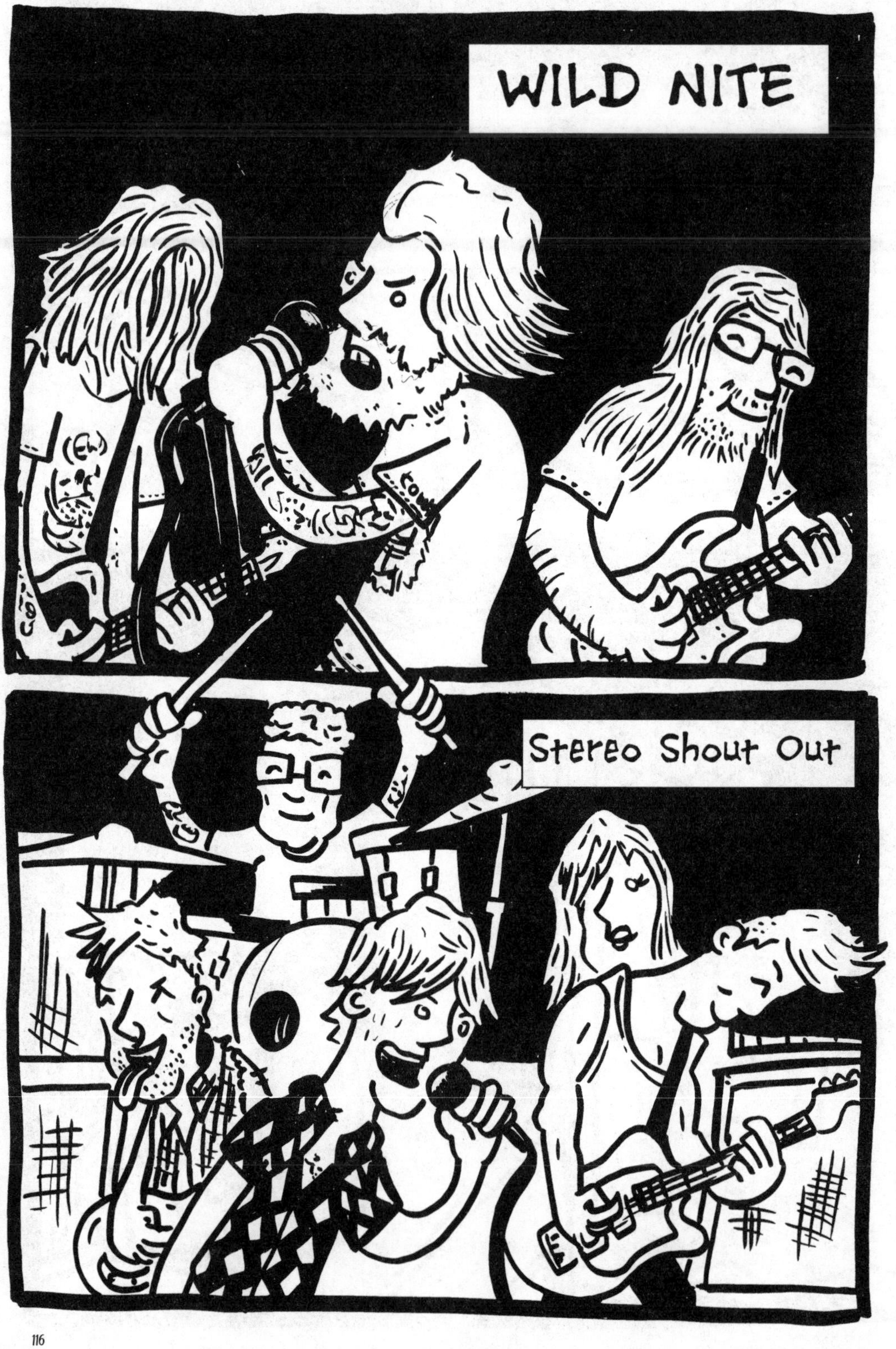
WILD NITE
Stereo Shout Out

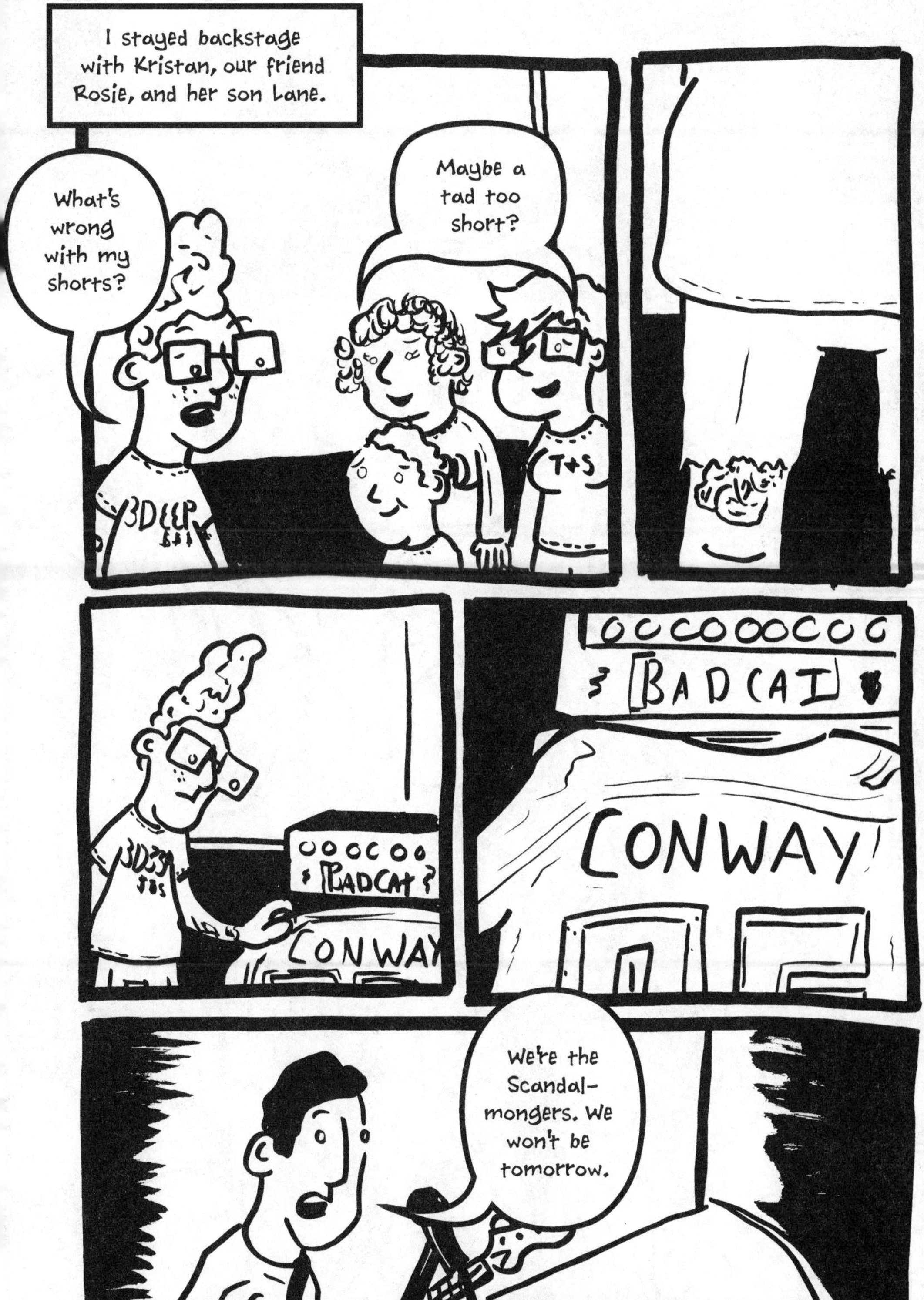
I stayed backstage with Kristan, our friend Rosie, and her son Lane.
What's wrong with my shorts?
Maybe a tad too short?
3DEEP
T+S
BADCAT
CONWAY
We're the Scandal-mongers. We won't be tomorrow.

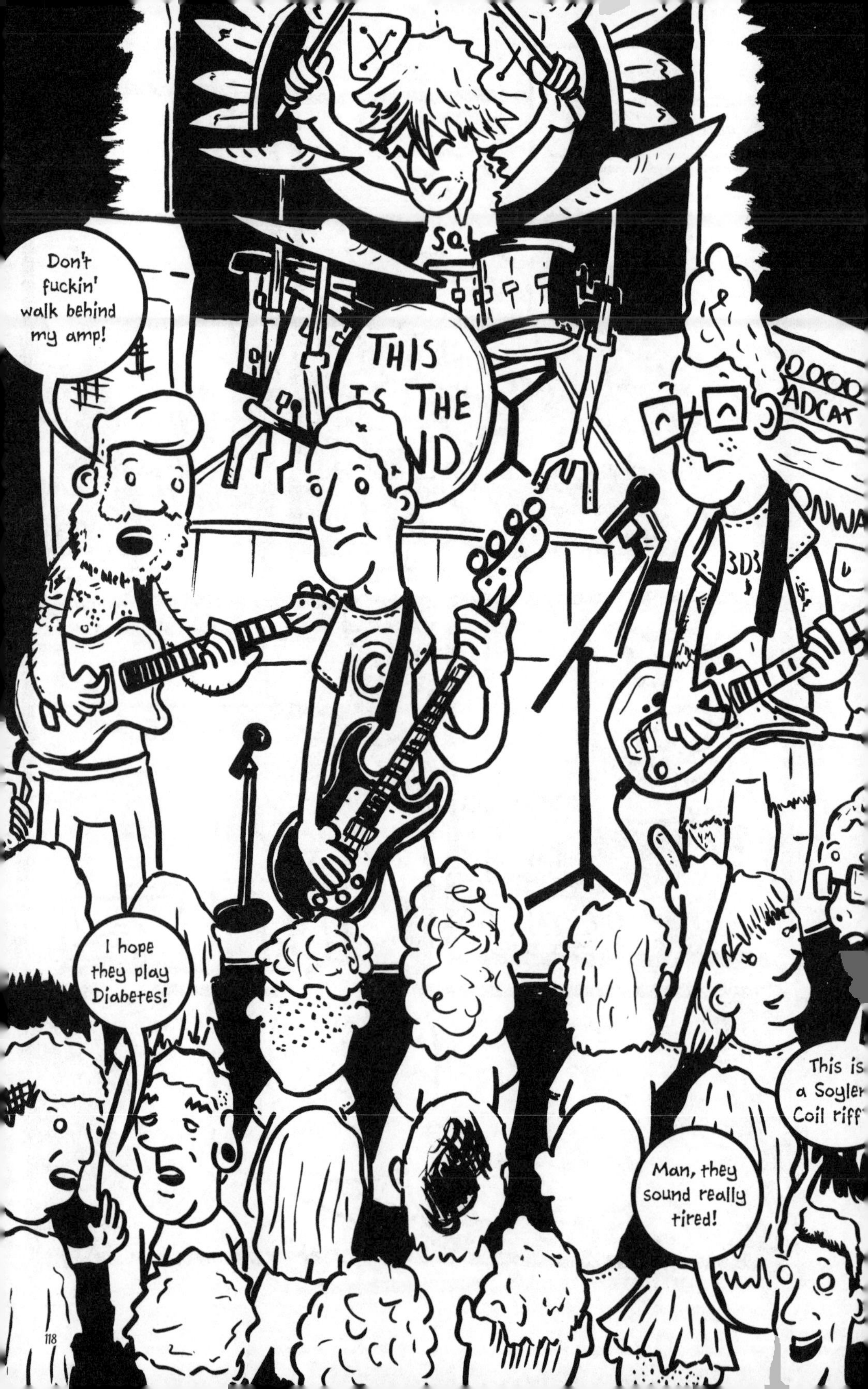
Don't fuckin' walk behind my amp!
I hope they play Diabetes!
This is a Soyler Coil riff
Man, they sound really tired!

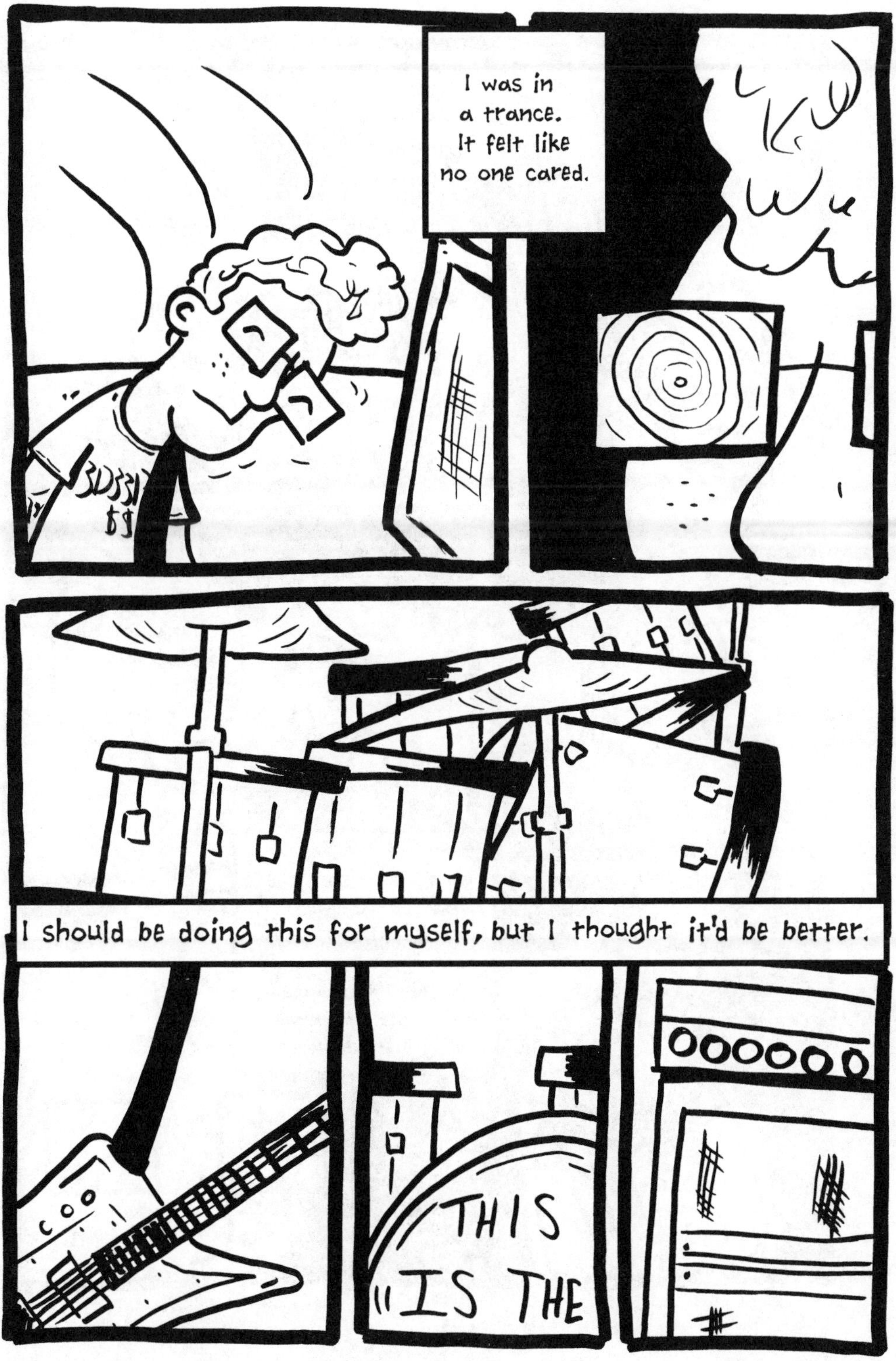
I was in a trance. It felt like no one cared.
I should be doing this for myself, but I thought it'd be better.
THIS IS THE

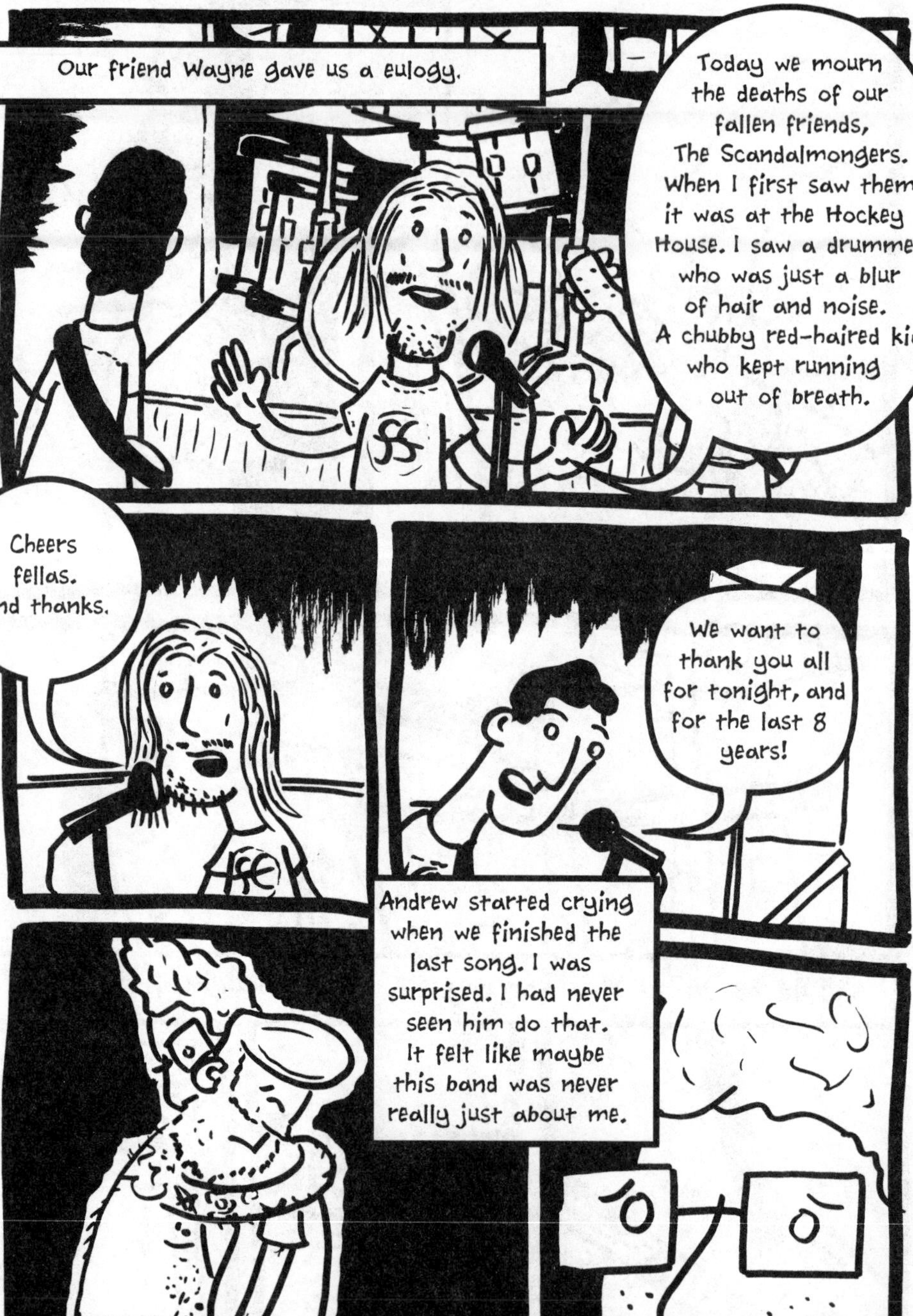
Our friend Wayne gave us a eulogy.
Today we mourn the deaths of our fallen friends, The Scandalmongers. When I first saw them it was at the Hockey House. I saw a drummer who was just a blur of hair and noise. A chubby red-haired kid who kept running out of breath.
Cheers fellas. And thanks.
We want to thank you all for tonight, and for the last 8 years!
Andrew started crying when we finished the last song. I was surprised. I had never seen him do that. It felt like maybe this band was never really just about me.

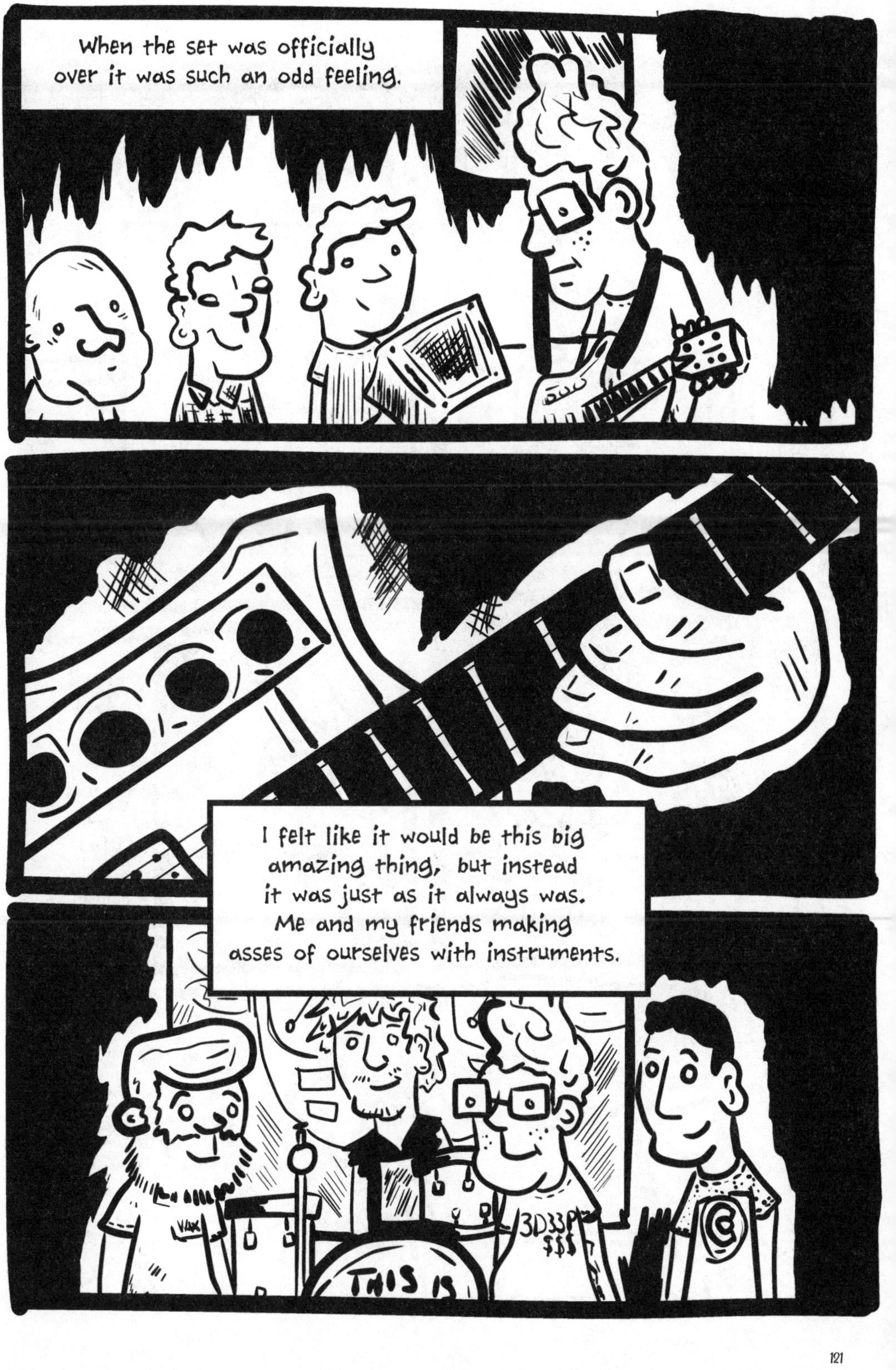
When the set was officially over it was such an odd feeling.
I felt like it would be this big amazing thing, but instead it was just as it always was. Me and my friends making asses of ourselves with instruments.
THIS IS

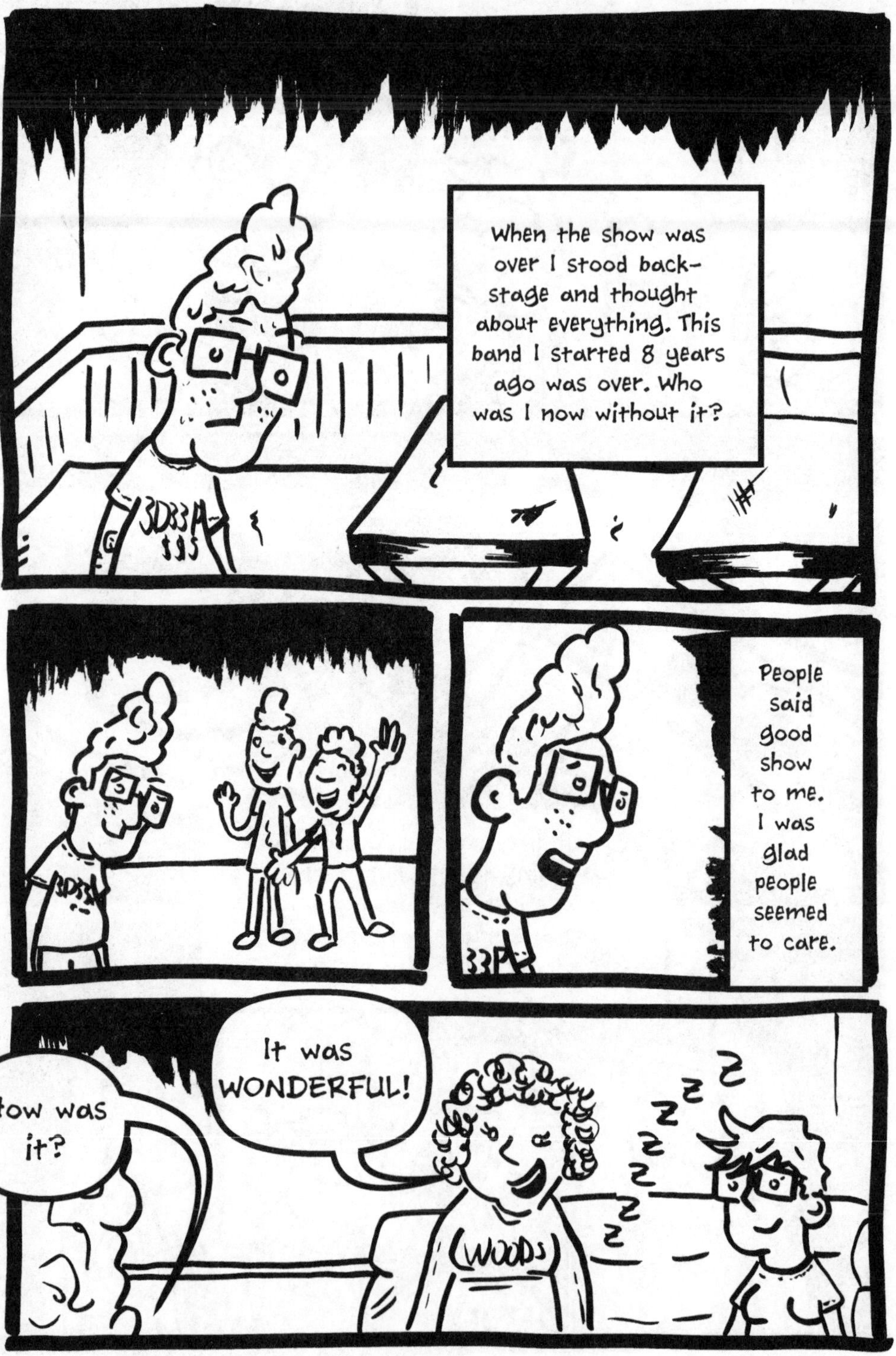

When the show was over I stood back-stage and thought about everything. This band I started 8 years ago was over. Who was I now without it?
People said good show to me. I was glad people seemed to care.
How was it?
It was WONDERFUL!
Z Z Z Z Z Z Z Z

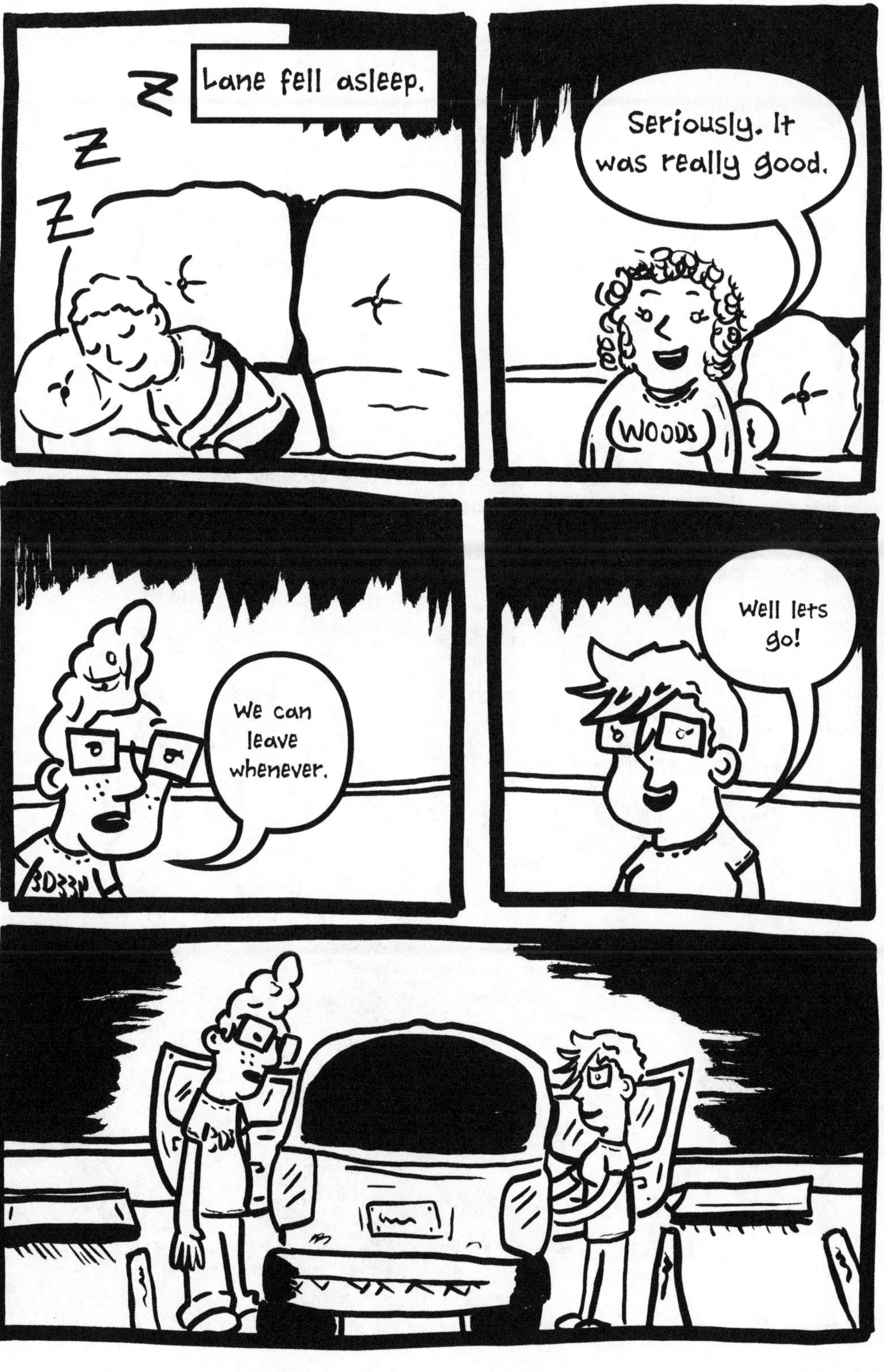
Lane fell asleep.
Z Z Z
Seriously. It was really good.
WOODS
We can leave whenever.
Well lets go!

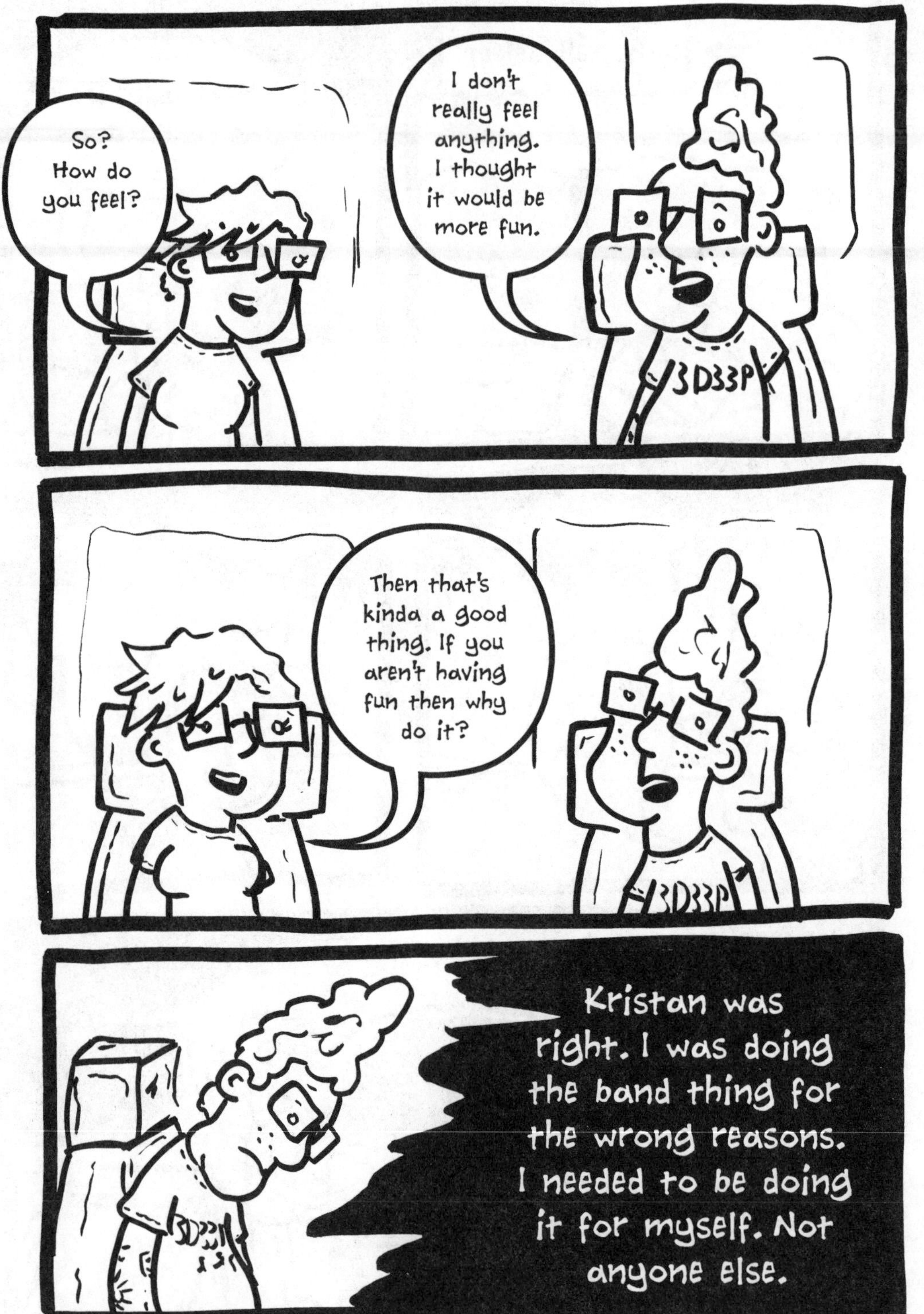
So? How do you feel?
I don't really feel anything. I thought it would be more fun.
3D33P
Then that's kinda a good thing. If you aren't having fun then why do it?
3D33P
Kristan was right. I was doing the band thing for the wrong reasons. I needed to be doing it for myself. Not anyone else.

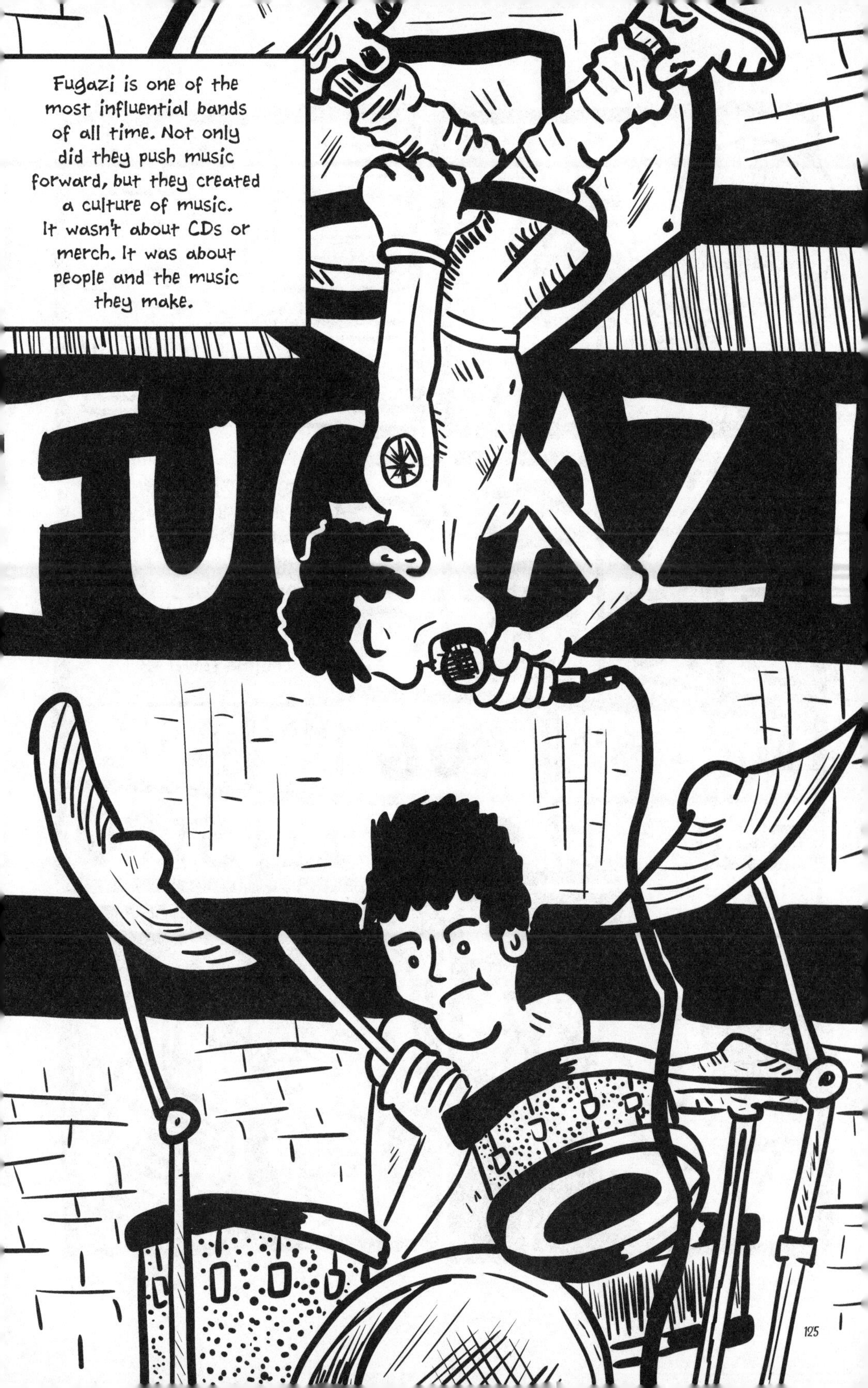
Fugazi is one of the most influential bands of all time. Not only did they push music forward, but they created a culture of music. It wasn't about CDs or merch. It was about people and the music they make.
FUGAZI

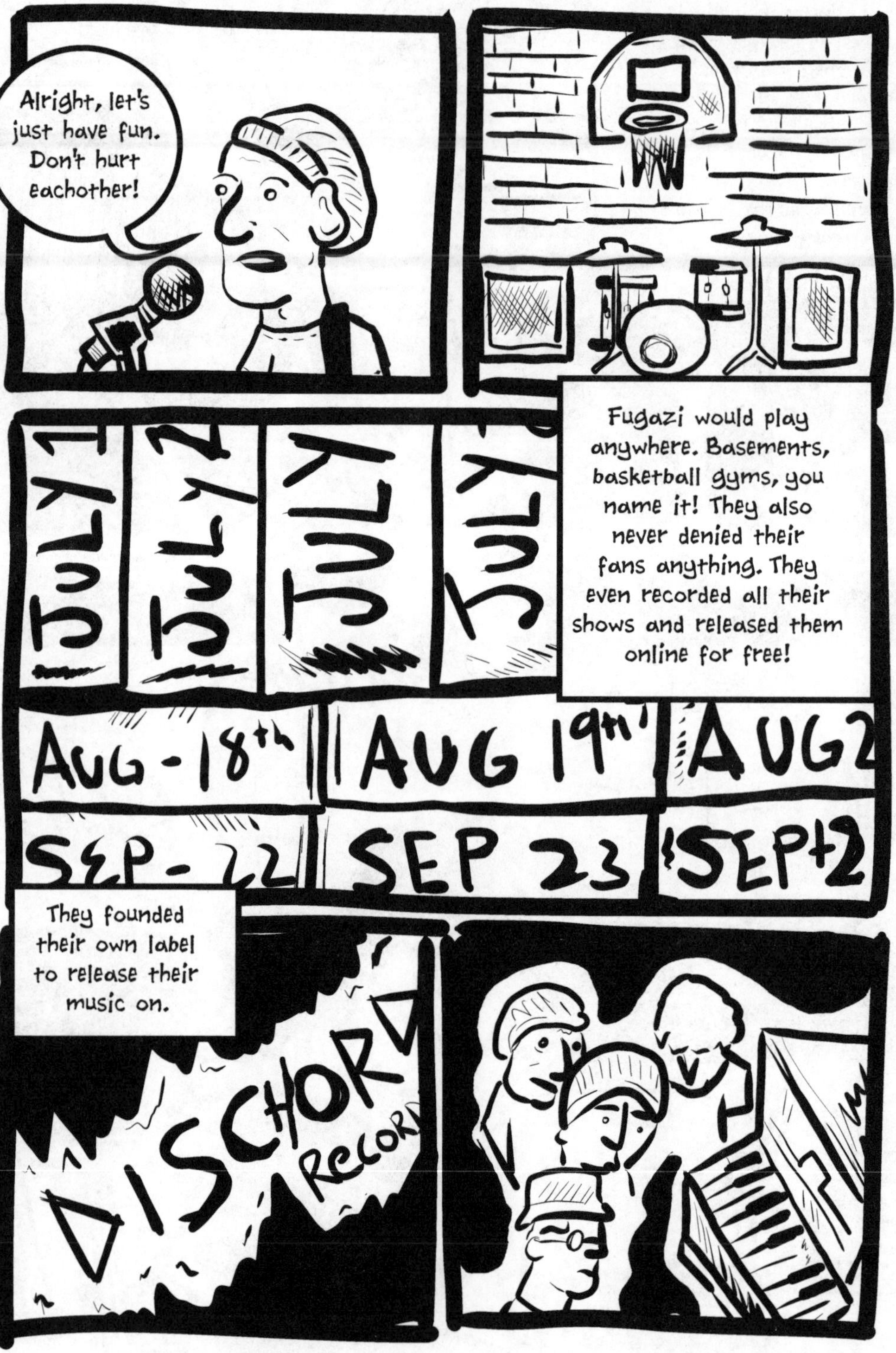

Alright, let's just have fun. Don't hurt eachother!
Fugazi would play anywhere. Basements, basketball gyms, you name it! They also never denied their fans anything. They even recorded all their shows and released them online for free!
JULY 1
JULY 2
JULY
JULY
AUG - 18th
AUG 19th
AUG 2
SEP - 22
SEP 23
SEP 2
They founded their own label to release their music on.
DISCHORD
RECORD

Fugazi believed in creating and nurturing a community of musicians and fans. After the end of groundbreaking punk band Minor Threat, Ian MacKaye felt like violence was taking over the punk world.

It wasn't until I read that Joe Strummer called Fugazi, "The only band that exemplified punk's spirit," that I really gave them a listen.

From the moment the record starts it builds something inside me.

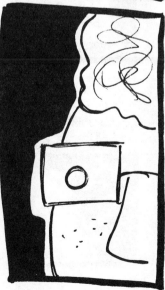

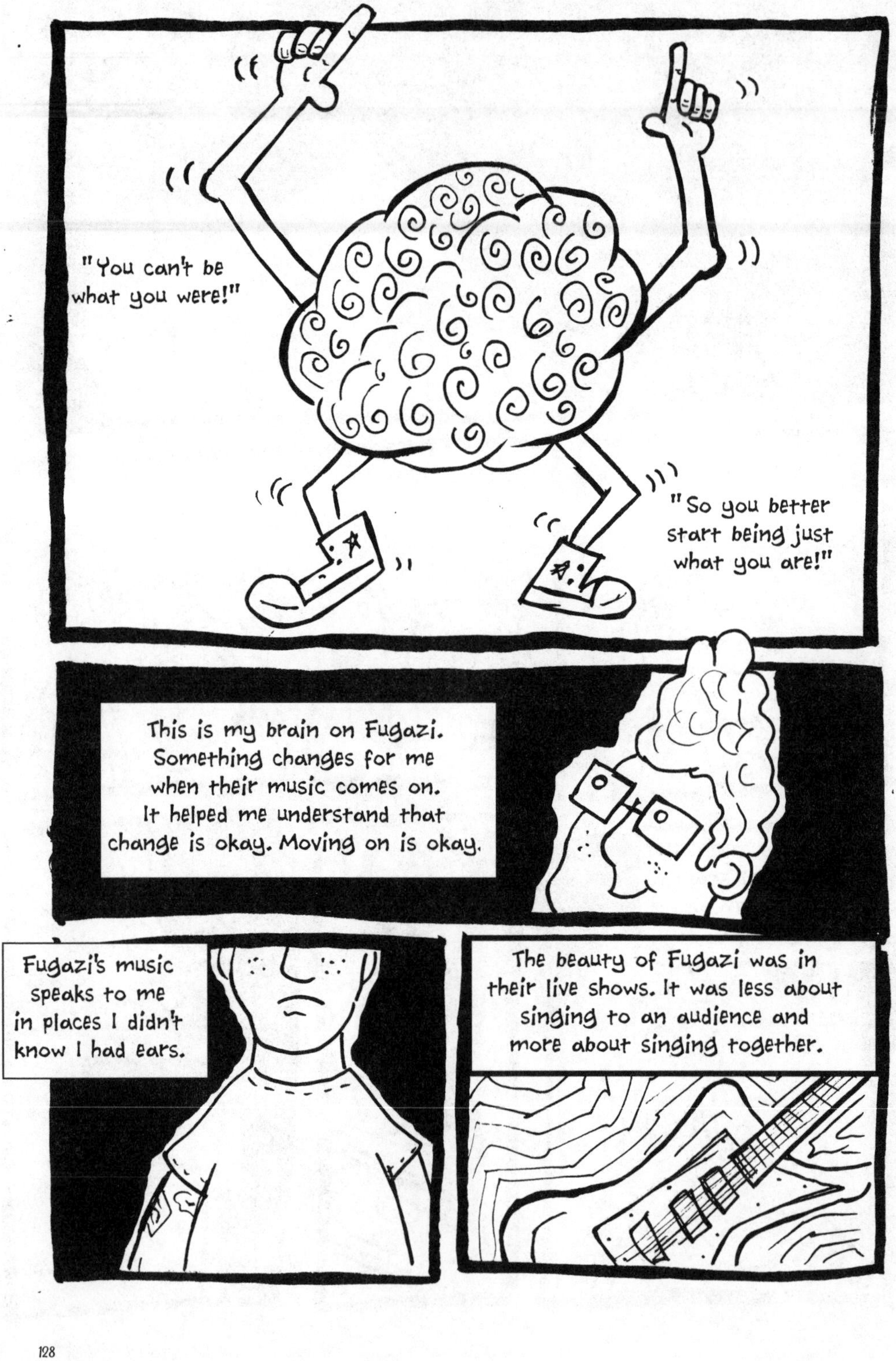
"You can't be what you were!"
"So you better start being just what you are!"
This is my brain on Fugazi. Something changes for me when their music comes on. It helped me understand that change is okay. Moving on is okay.
Fugazi's music speaks to me in places I didn't know I had ears.
The beauty of Fugazi was in their live shows. It was less about singing to an audience and more about singing together.

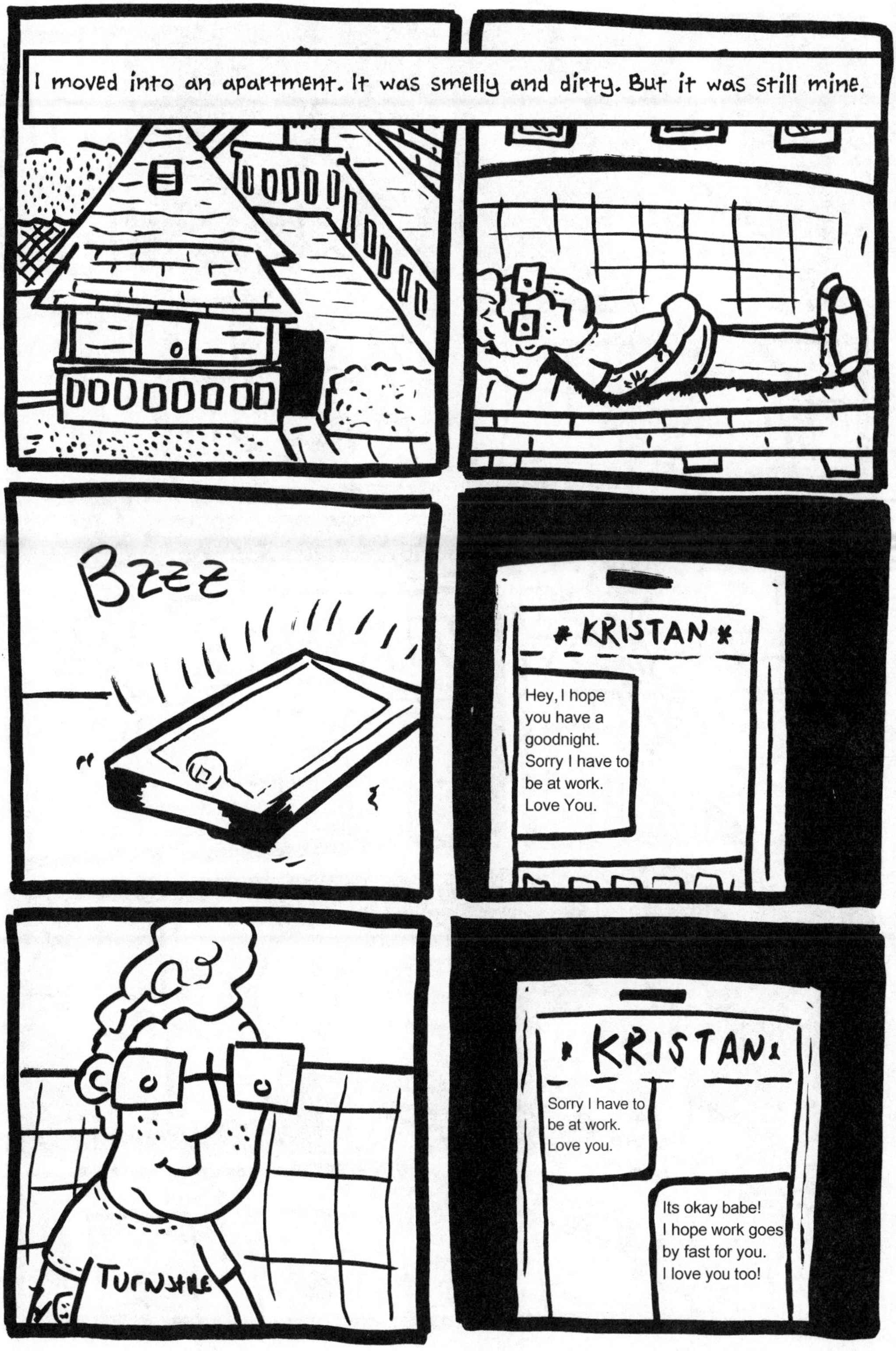
I moved into an apartment. It was smelly and dirty. But it was still mine.
BZZZ
KRISTAN
Hey, I hope you have a goodnight. Sorry I have to be at work. Love You.
TURNSTILE
KRISTAN
Sorry I have to be at work. Love you.
Its okay babe! I hope work goes by fast for you. I love you too!

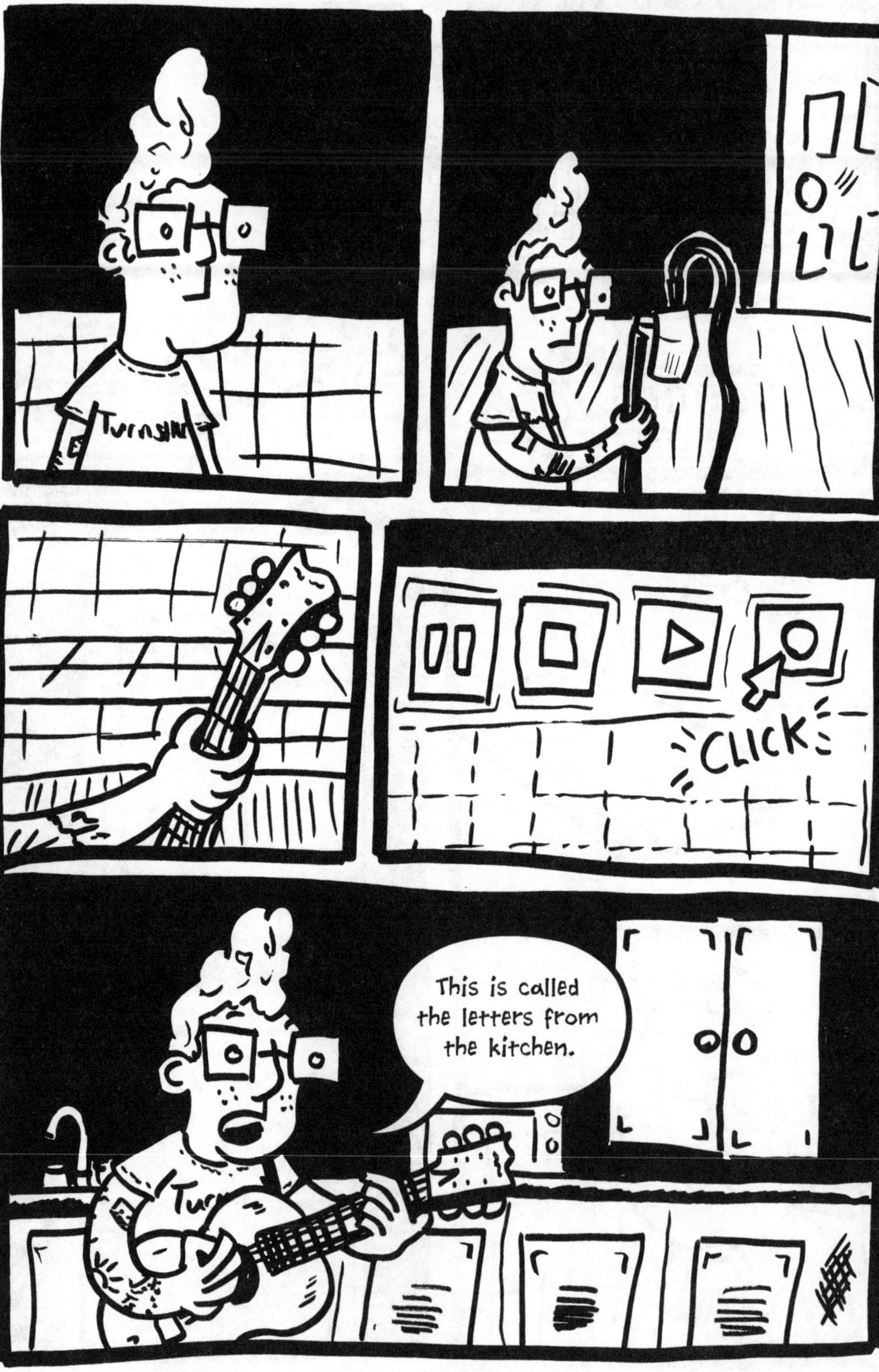
CLICK
This is called the letters from the kitchen.

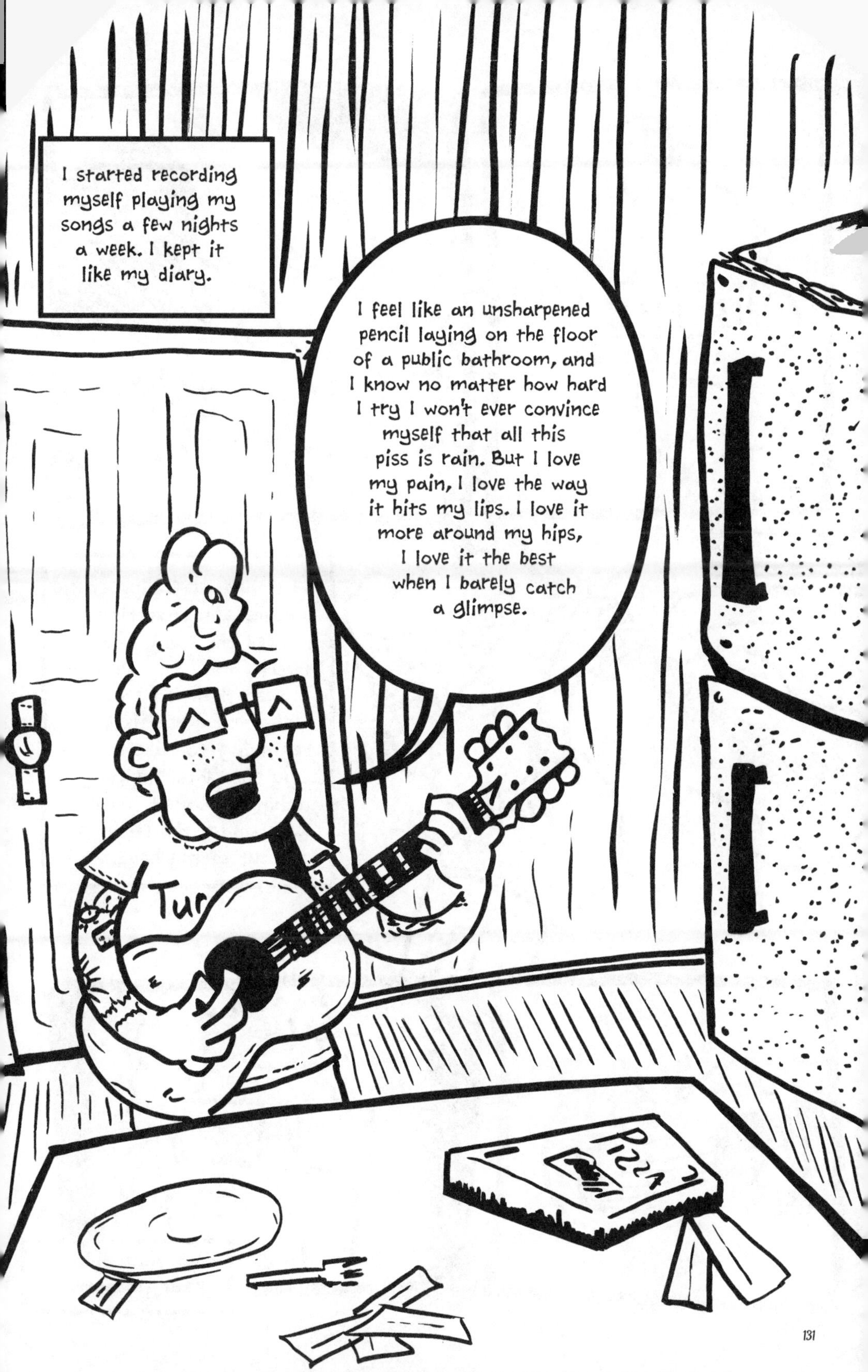
I started recording myself playing my songs a few nights a week. I kept it like my diary.
I feel like an unsharpened pencil laying on the floor of a public bathroom, and I know no matter how hard I try I won't ever convince myself that all this piss is rain. But I love my pain, I love the way it hits my lips. I love it more around my hips, I love it the best when I barely catch a glimpse.
Tur
Pizza

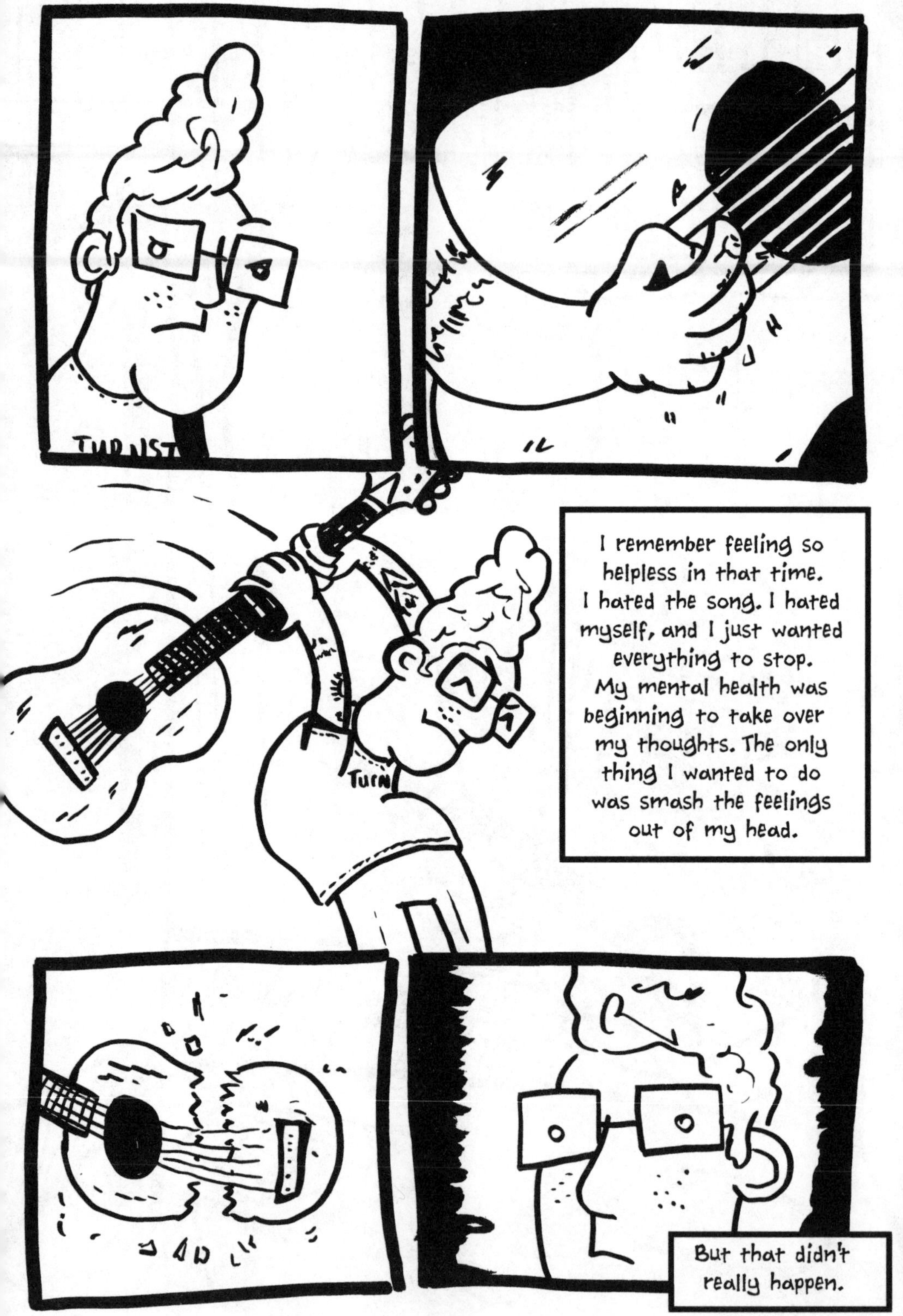
I remember feeling so helpless in that time. I hated the song. I hated myself, and I just wanted everything to stop. My mental health was beginning to take over my thoughts. The only thing I wanted to do was smash the feelings out of my head.
But that didn't really happen.

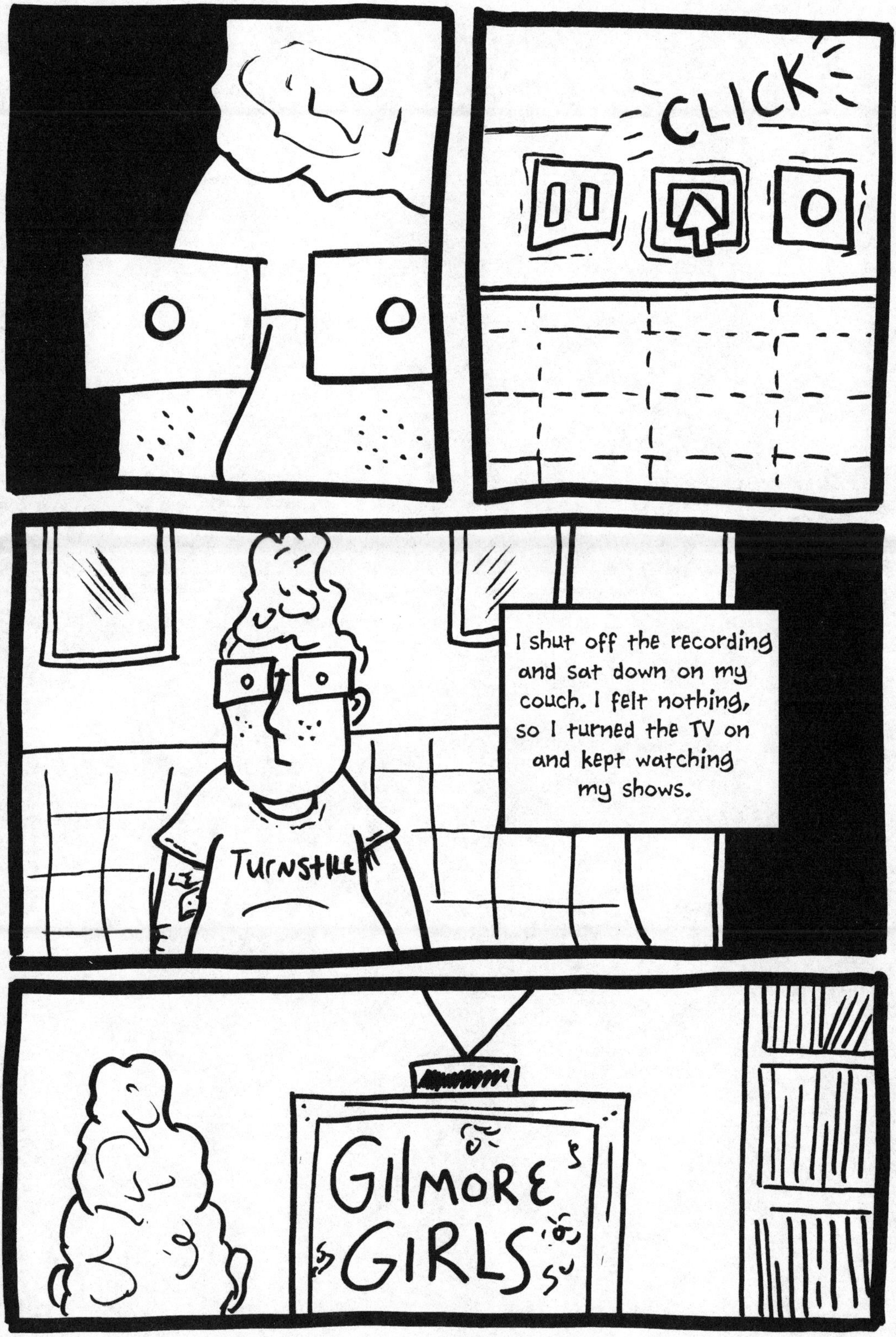
CLICK
I shut off the recording and sat down on my couch. I felt nothing, so I turned the TV on and kept watching my shows.
TURNSTILE
GILMORE GIRLS

Part 4

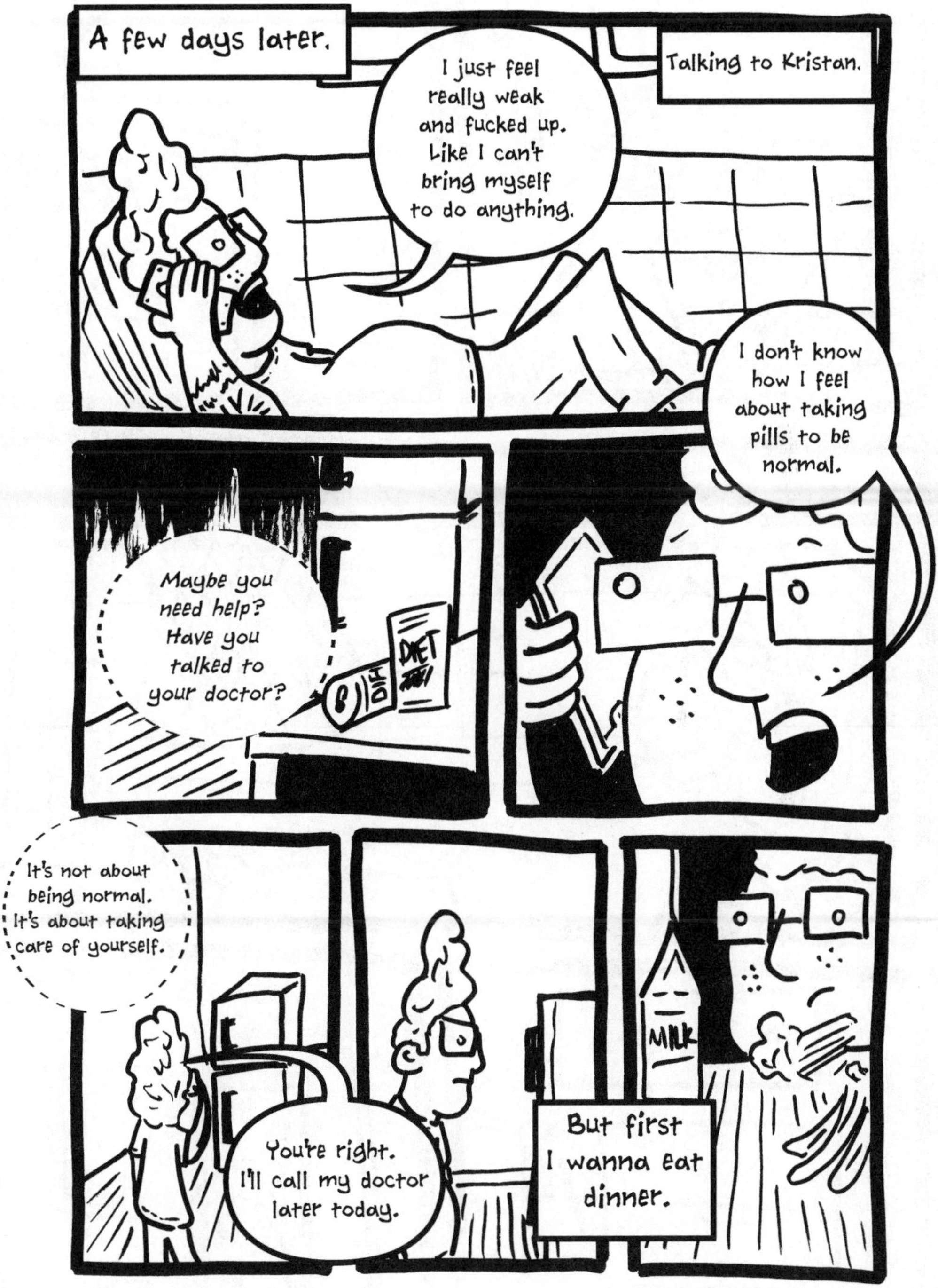
A few days later.
Talking to Kristan.
I just feel really weak and fucked up. Like I can't bring myself to do anything.
I don't know how I feel about taking pills to be normal.
Maybe you need help? Have you talked to your doctor?
DIET
It's not about being normal. It's about taking care of yourself.
You're right. I'll call my doctor later today.
But first I wanna eat dinner.
MILK

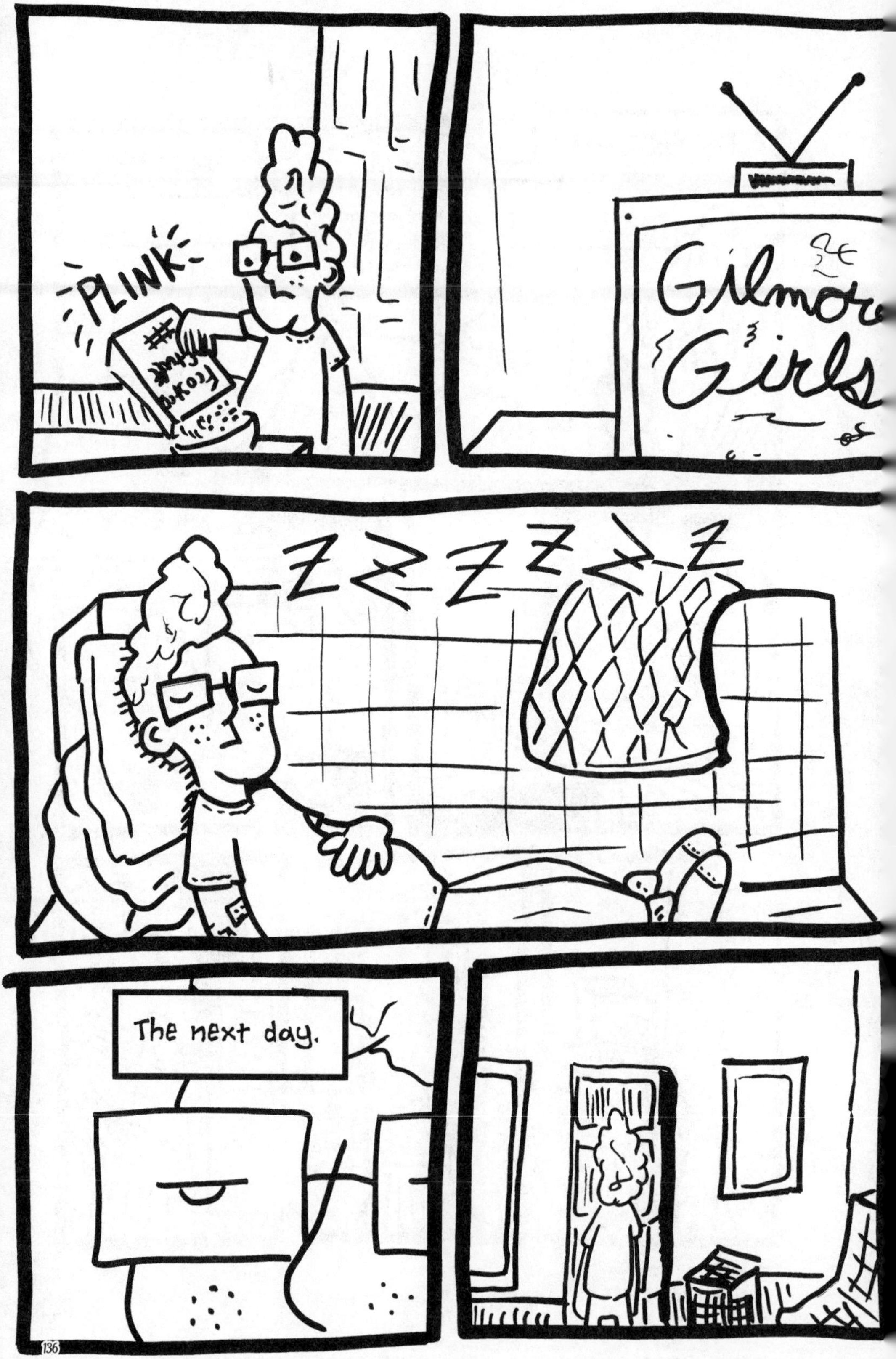
PLINK
Gilmore Girls
ZZZZZZ
The next day.

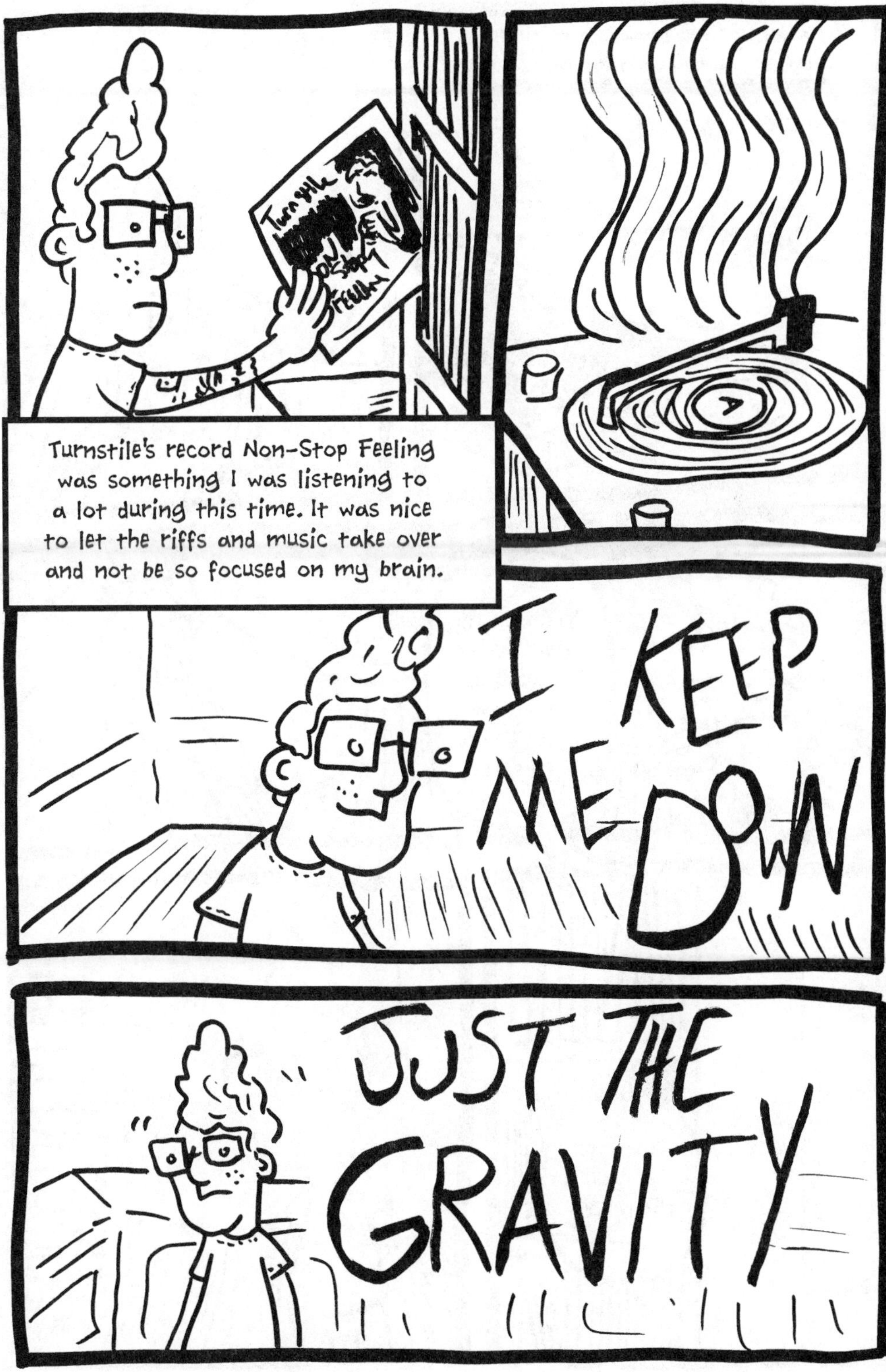
Turnstile
NON STOP FEELIN
Turnstile's record Non-Stop Feeling was something I was listening to a lot during this time. It was nice to let the riffs and music take over and not be so focused on my brain.
I KEEP ME DOWN
JUST THE GRAVITY

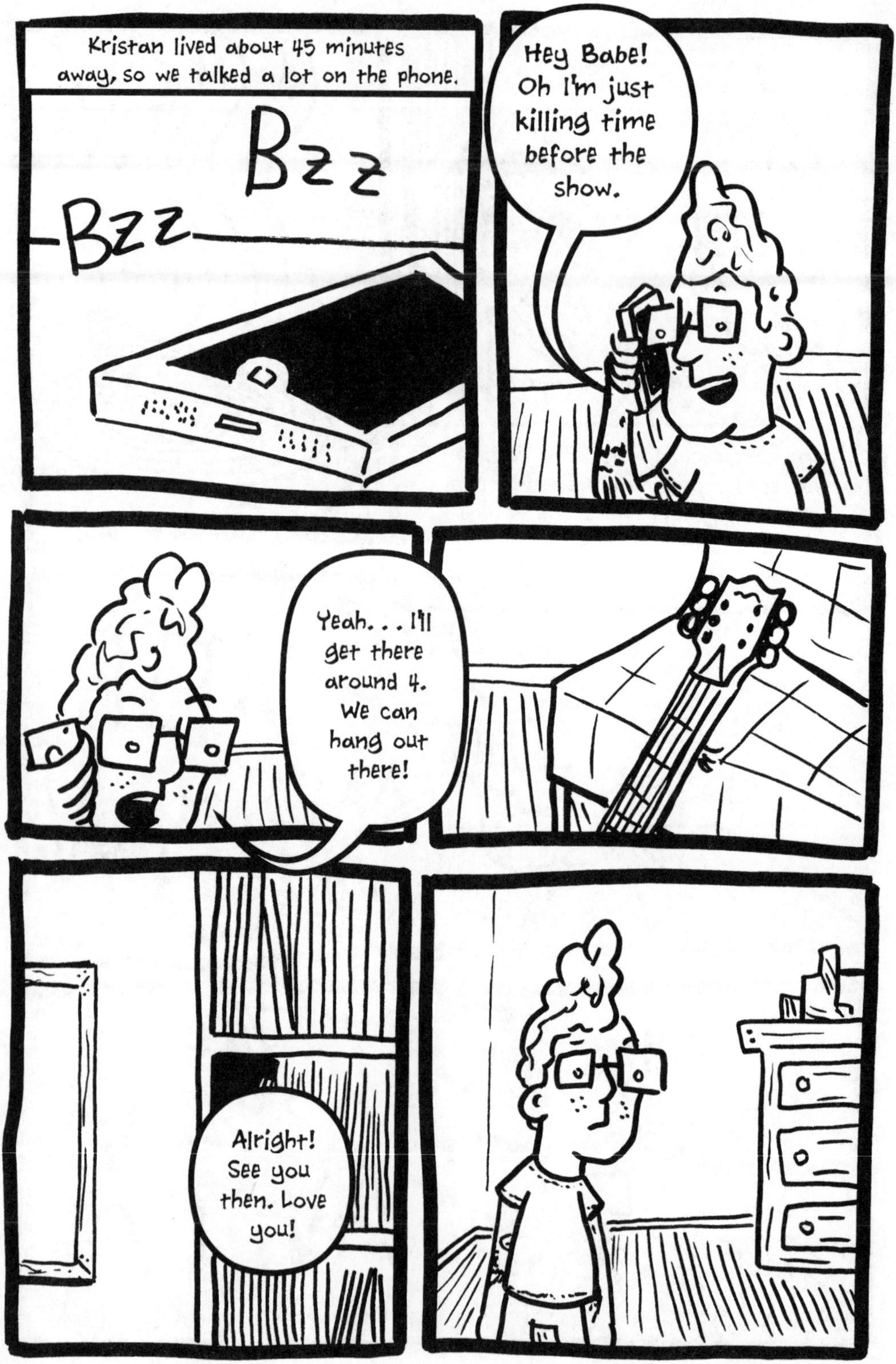
Kristan lived about 45 minutes away, so we talked a lot on the phone.
Bzz
Bzz
Hey Babe! Oh I'm just killing time before the show.
Yeah. . . I'll get there around 4. We can hang out there!
Alright! See you then. Love you!

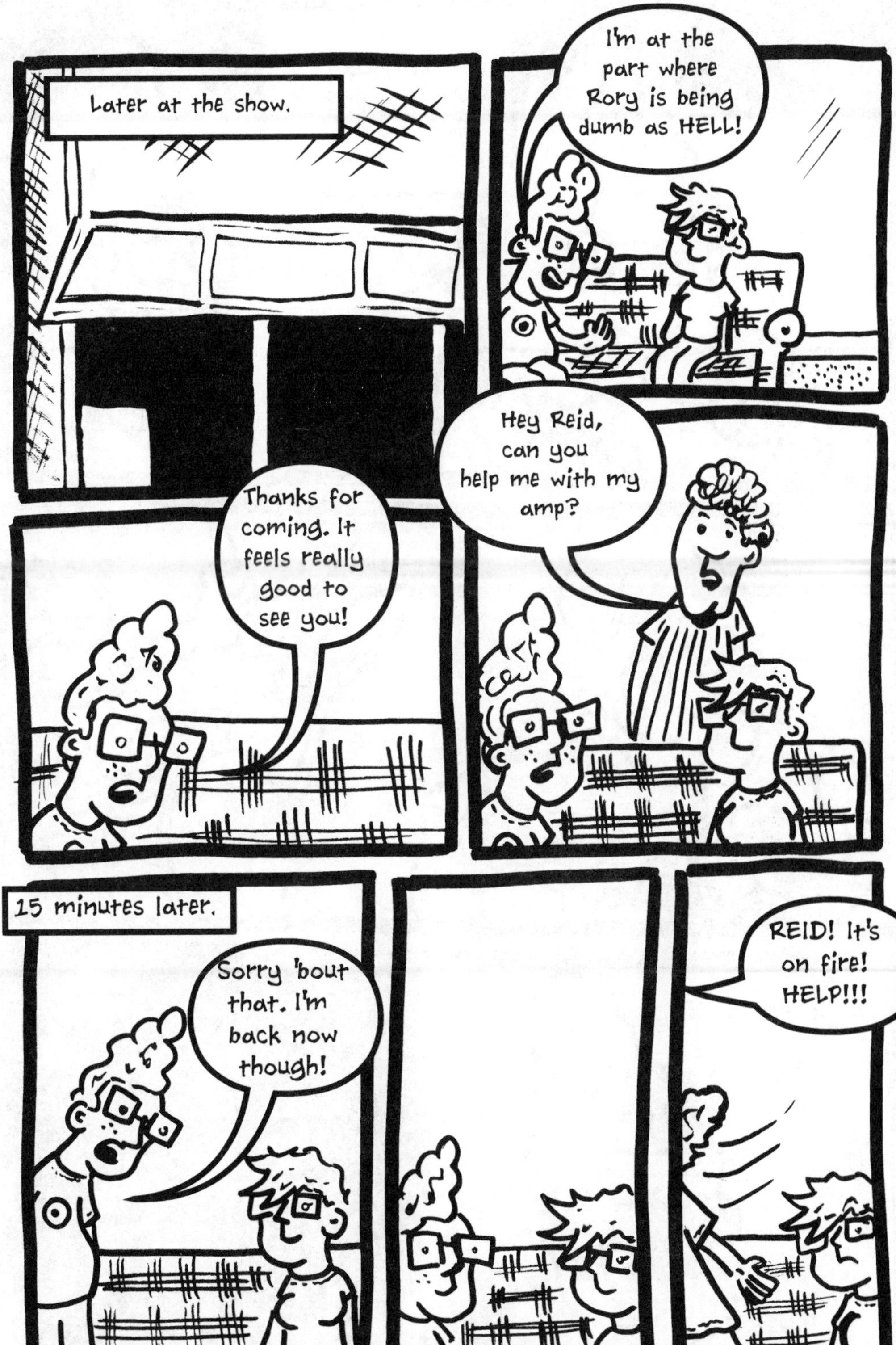
Later at the show.
I'm at the part where Rory is being dumb as HELL!
Thanks for coming. It feels really good to see you!
Hey Reid, can you help me with my amp?
15 minutes later.
Sorry 'bout that. I'm back now though!
REID! It's on fire! HELP!!!

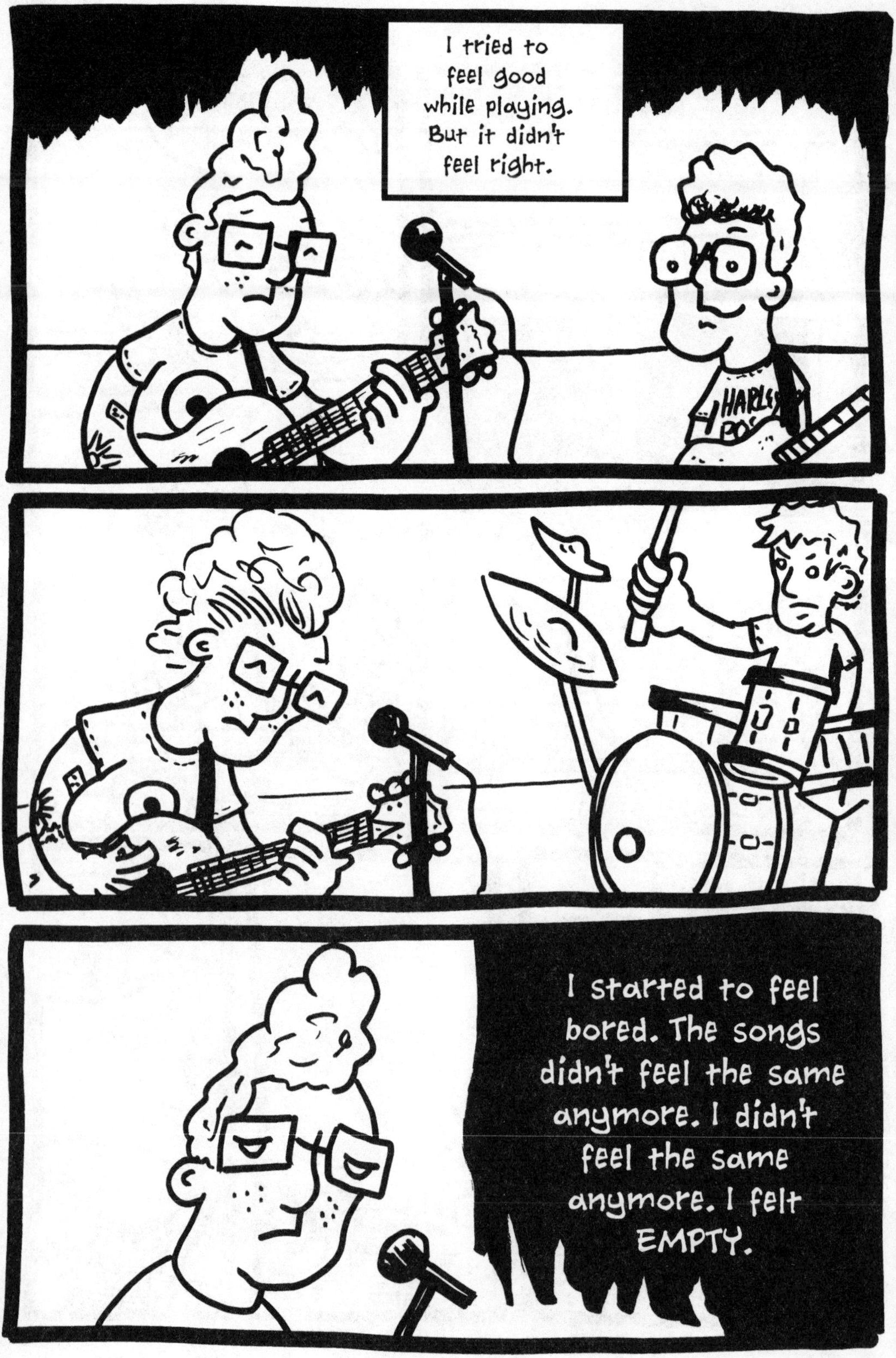
I tried to feel good while playing. But it didn't feel right.
HARLE
POS
I started to feel bored. The songs didn't feel the same anymore. I didn't feel the same anymore. I felt EMPTY.

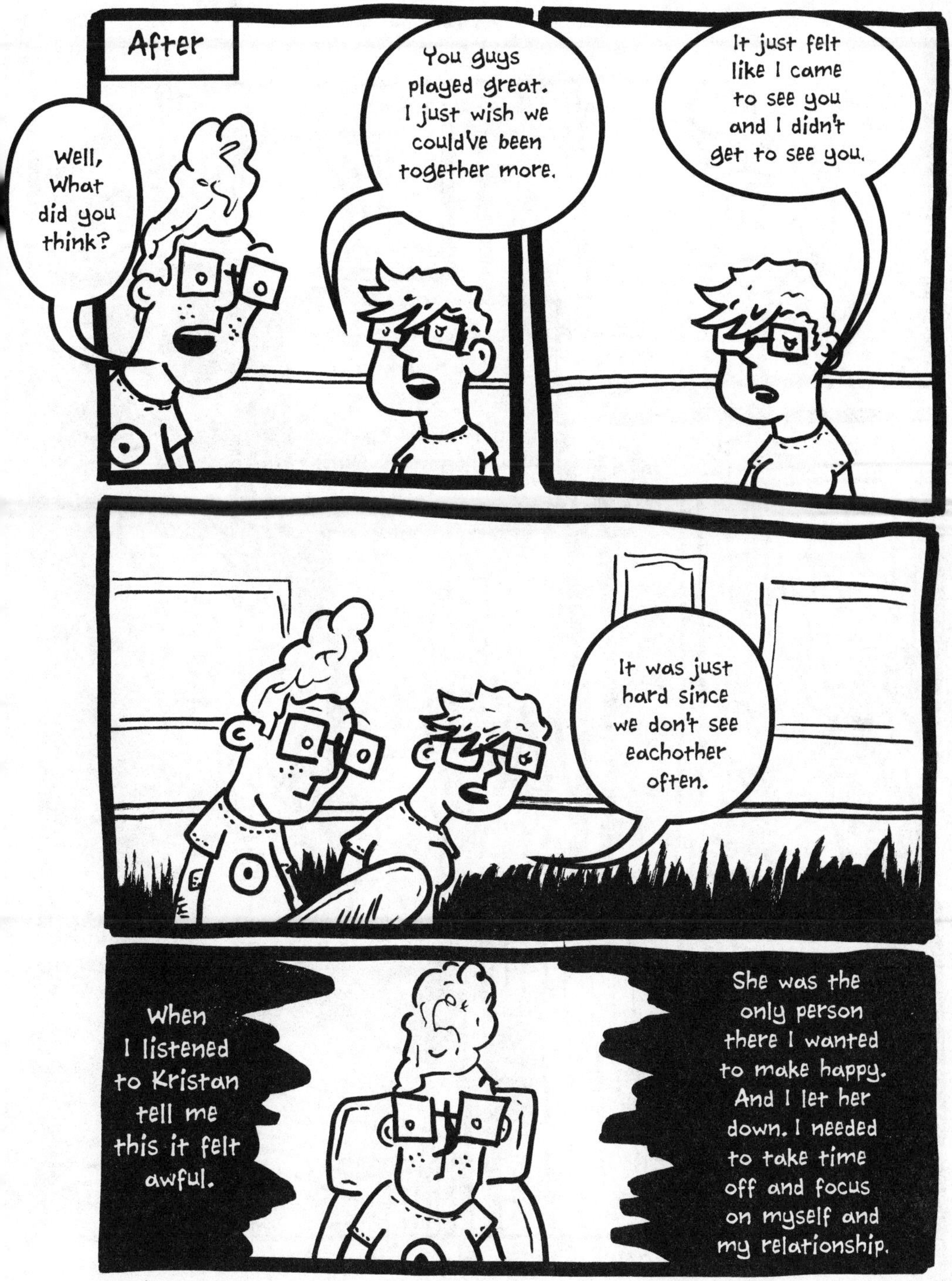
After
Well, What did you think?
You guys played great. I just wish we could've been together more.
It just felt like I came to see you and I didn't get to see you.
It was just hard since we don't see eachother often.
When I listened to Kristan tell me this it felt awful.
She was the only person there I wanted to make happy. And I let her down. I needed to take time off and focus on myself and my relationship.

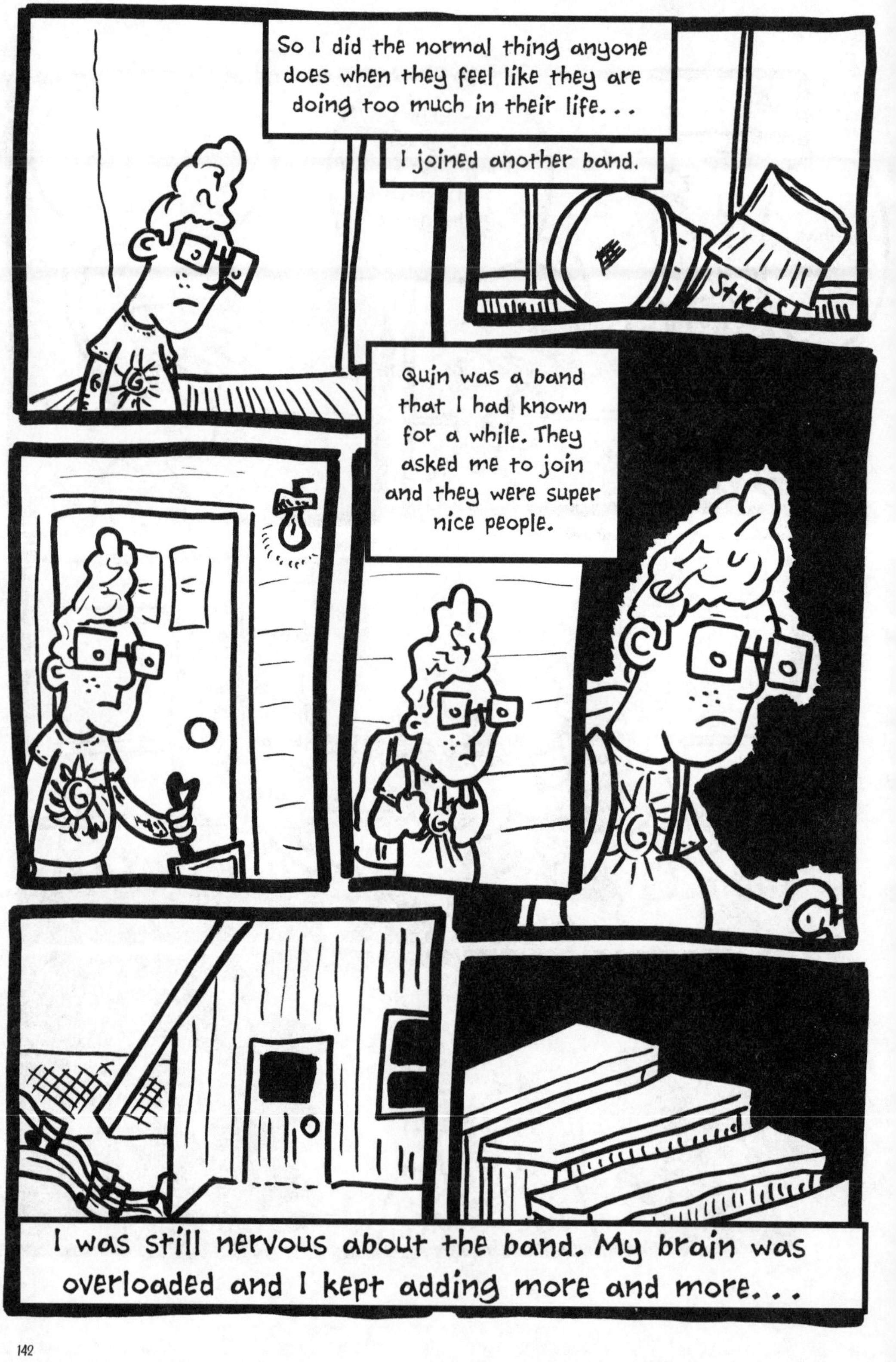
So I did the normal thing anyone does when they feel like they are doing too much in their life...
I joined another band.
STICKS!
Quin was a band that I had known for a while. They asked me to join and they were super nice people.
I was still nervous about the band. My brain was overloaded and I kept adding more and more...

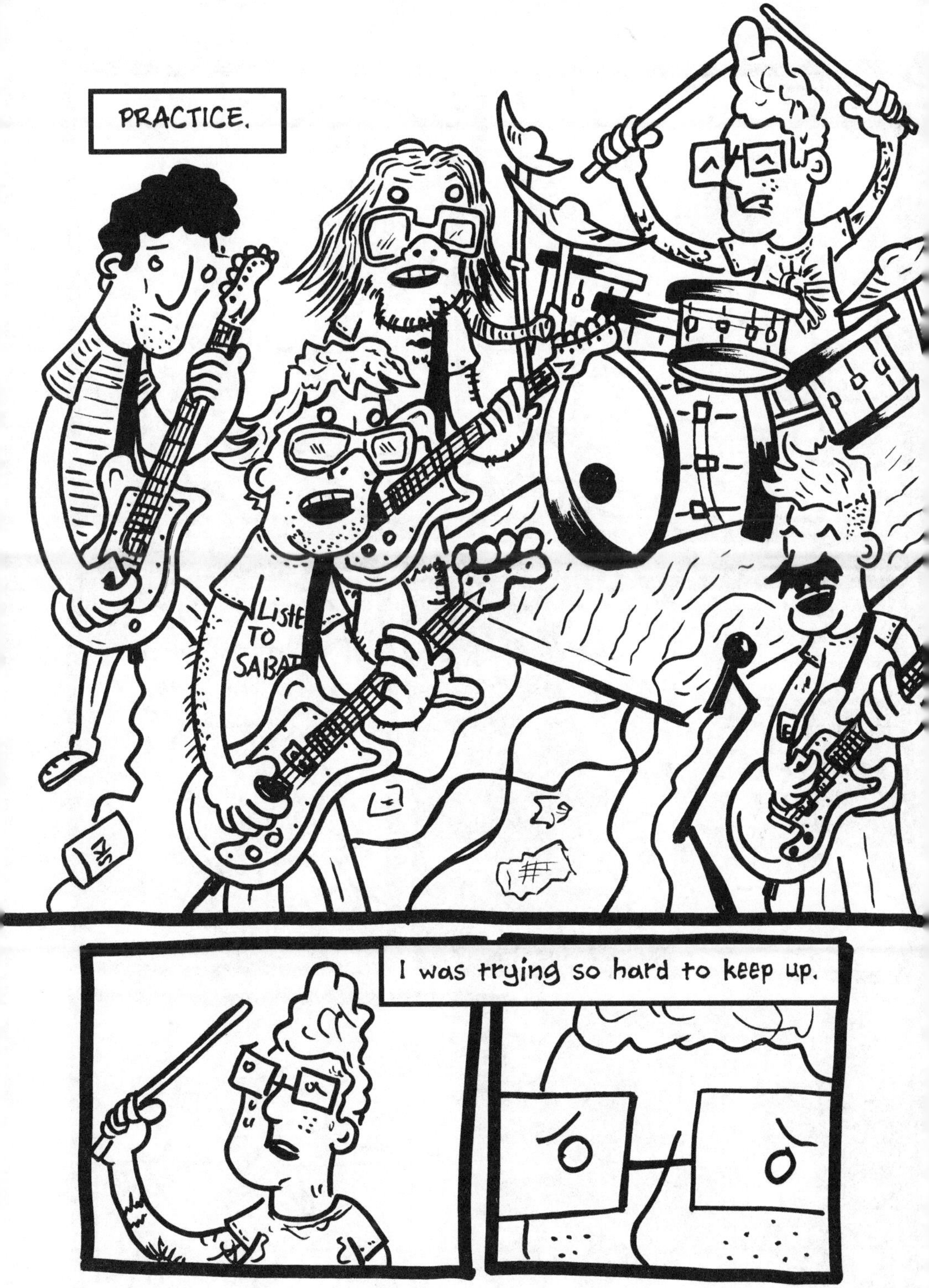
PRACTICE.
LISTE
TO
SABAT
I was trying so hard to keep up.

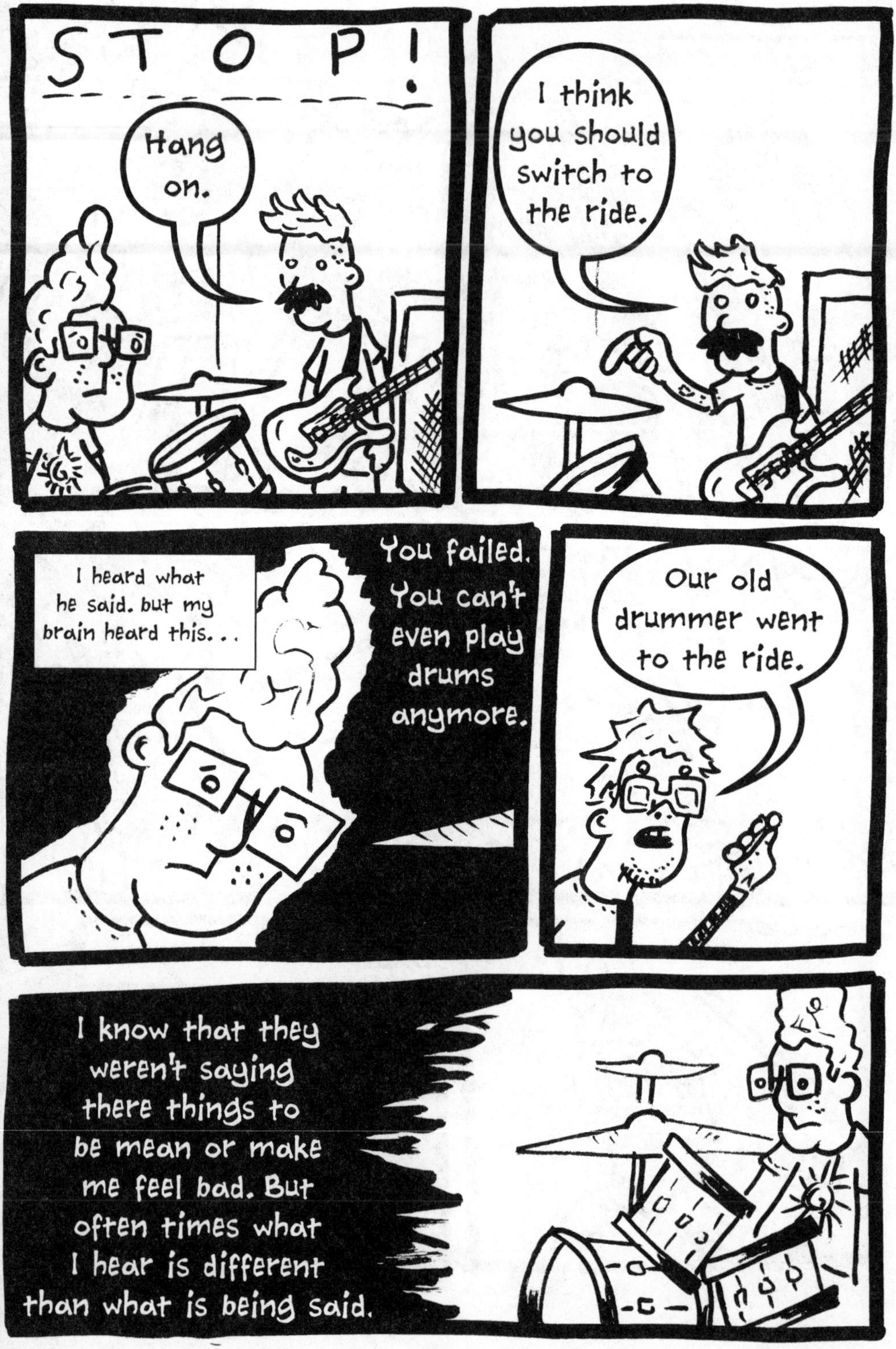
STOP!
Hang on.
I think you should switch to the ride.
I heard what he said. but my brain heard this. . .
You failed. You can't even play drums anymore.
Our old drummer went to the ride.
I know that they weren't saying there things to be mean or make me feel bad. But often times what I hear is different than what is being said.

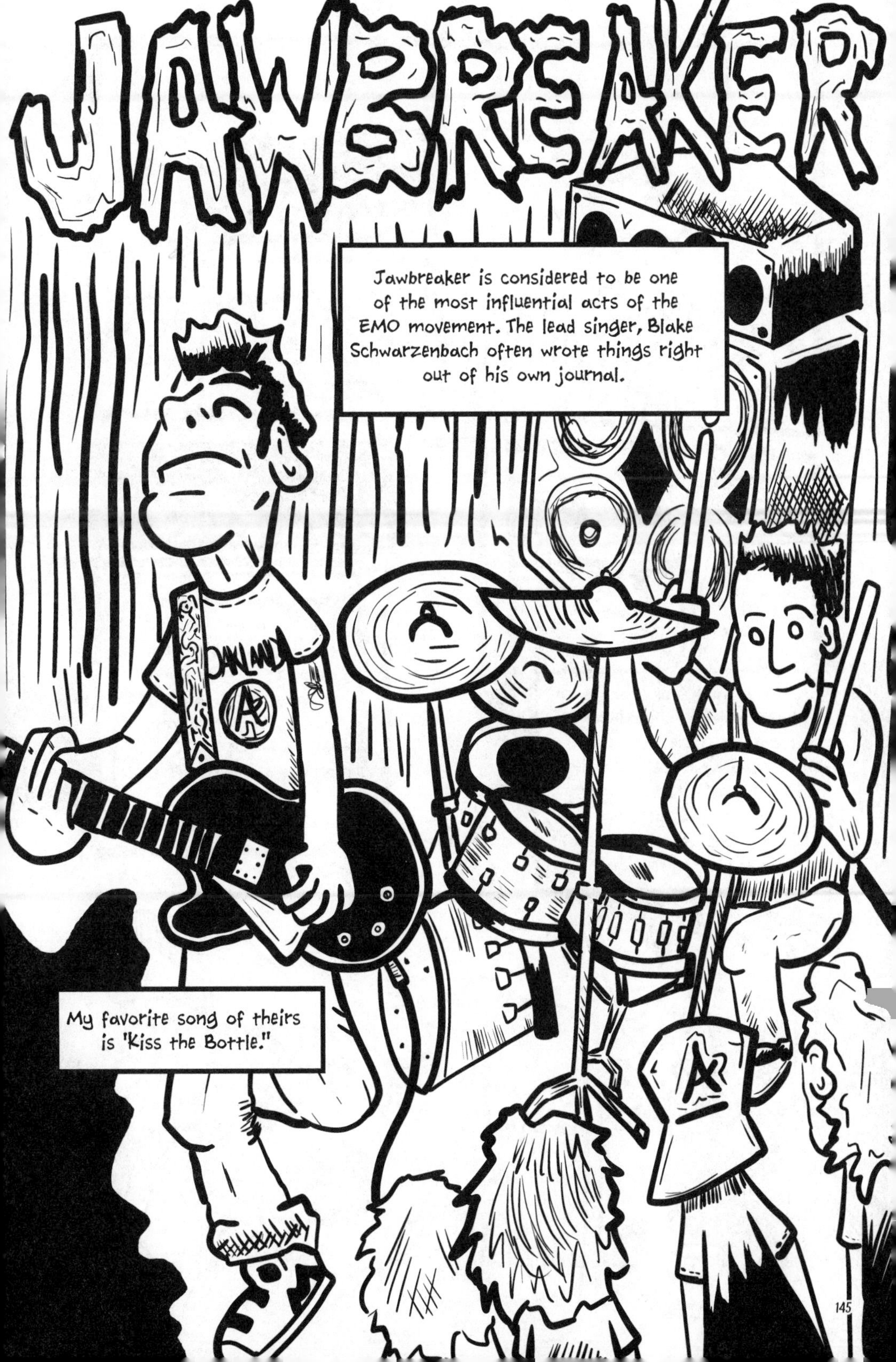
JAWBREAKER
Jawbreaker is considered to be one of the most influential acts of the EMO movement. The lead singer, Blake Schwarzenbach often wrote things right out of his own journal.
OAKLAND
My favorite song of theirs is "Kiss the Bottle."

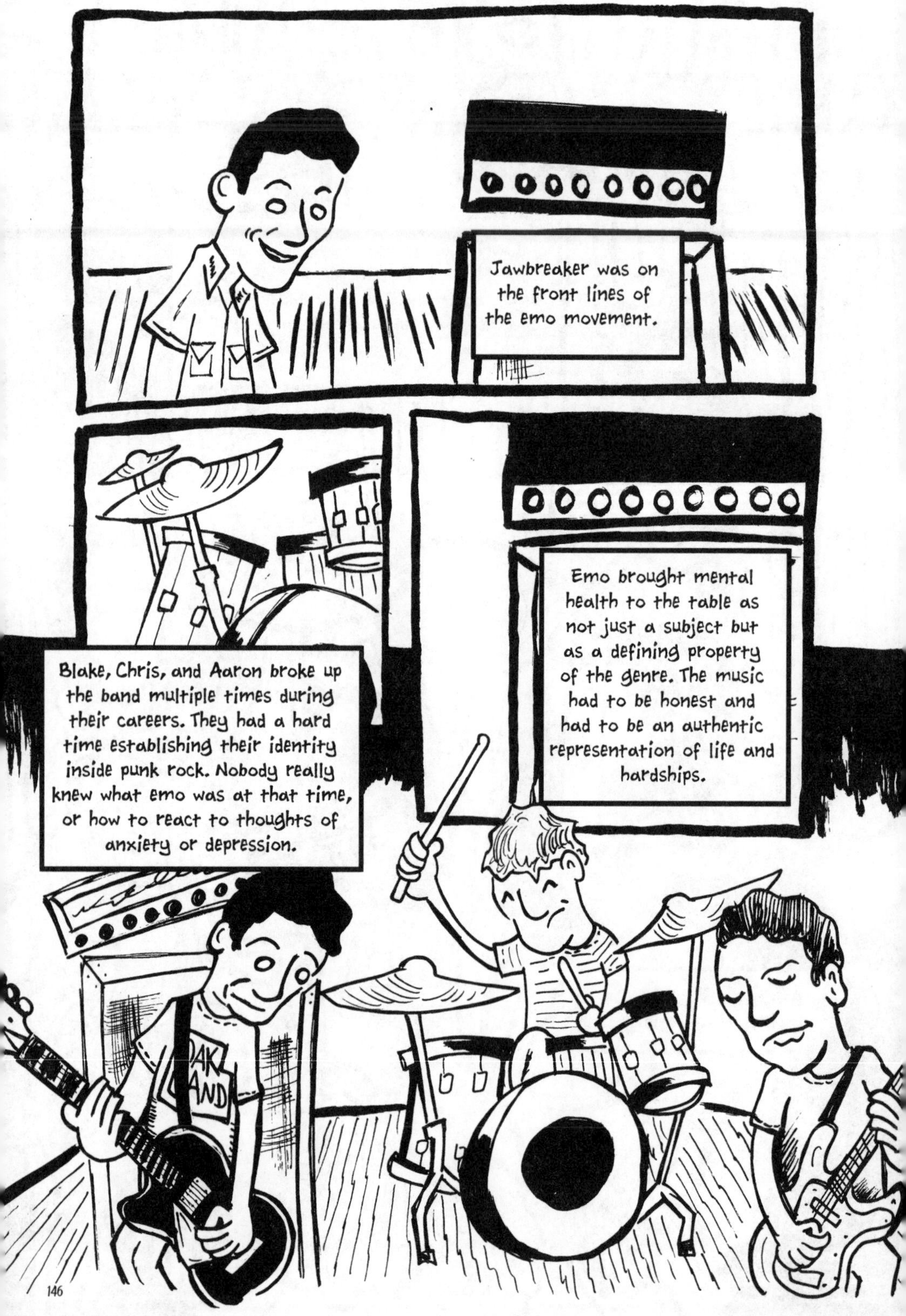
Jawbreaker was on the front lines of the emo movement.
Blake, Chris, and Aaron broke up the band multiple times during their careers. They had a hard time establishing their identity inside punk rock. Nobody really knew what emo was at that time, or how to react to thoughts of anxiety or depression.
Emo brought mental health to the table as not just a subject but as a defining property of the genre. The music had to be honest and had to be an authentic representation of life and hardships.
OAK LAND

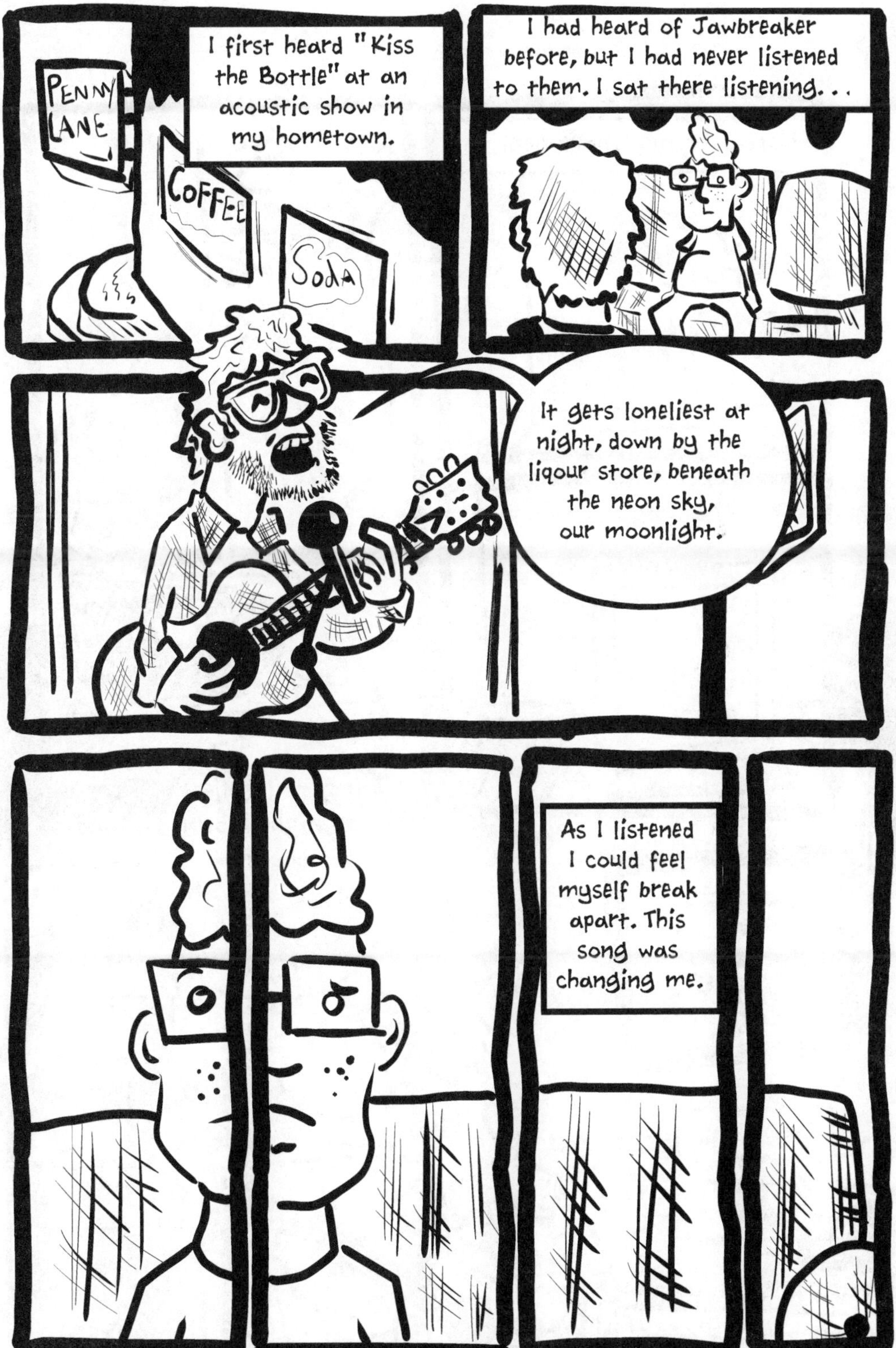
PENNY LANE
I first heard "Kiss the Bottle" at an acoustic show in my hometown.
COFFEE
Soda
I had heard of Jawbreaker before, but I had never listened to them. I sat there listening. . .
It gets loneliest at night, down by the liqour store, beneath the neon sky, our moonlight.
As I listened I could feel myself break apart. This song was changing me.

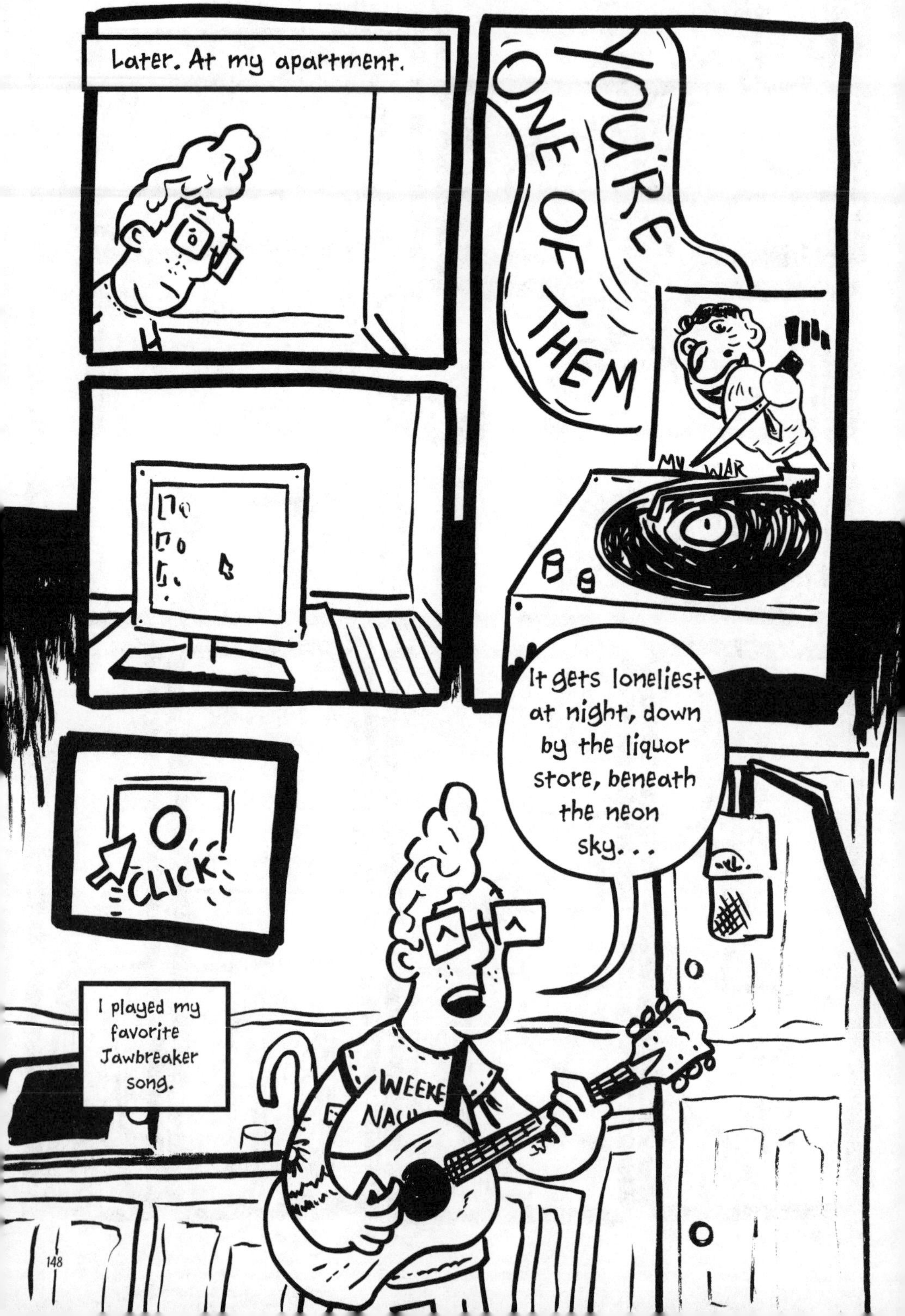
Later. At my apartment.
YOU'RE ONE OF THEM
MY WAR
CLICK
It gets loneliest at night, down by the liquor store, beneath the neon sky...
I played my favorite Jawbreaker song.
WEEKE NAC

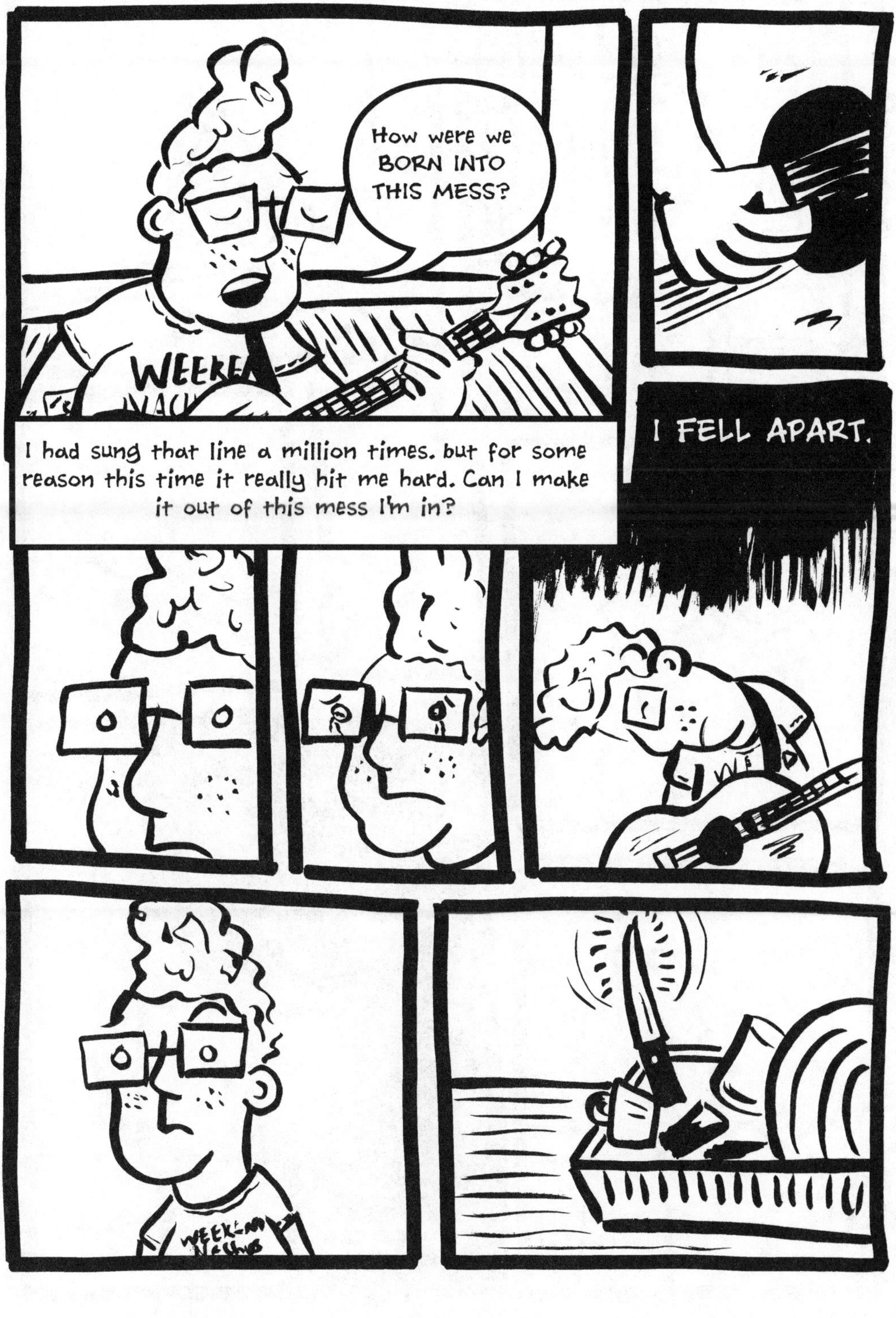
How were we BORN INTO THIS MESS?
I had sung that line a million times. but for some reason this time it really hit me hard. Can I make it out of this mess I'm in?
I FELL APART.

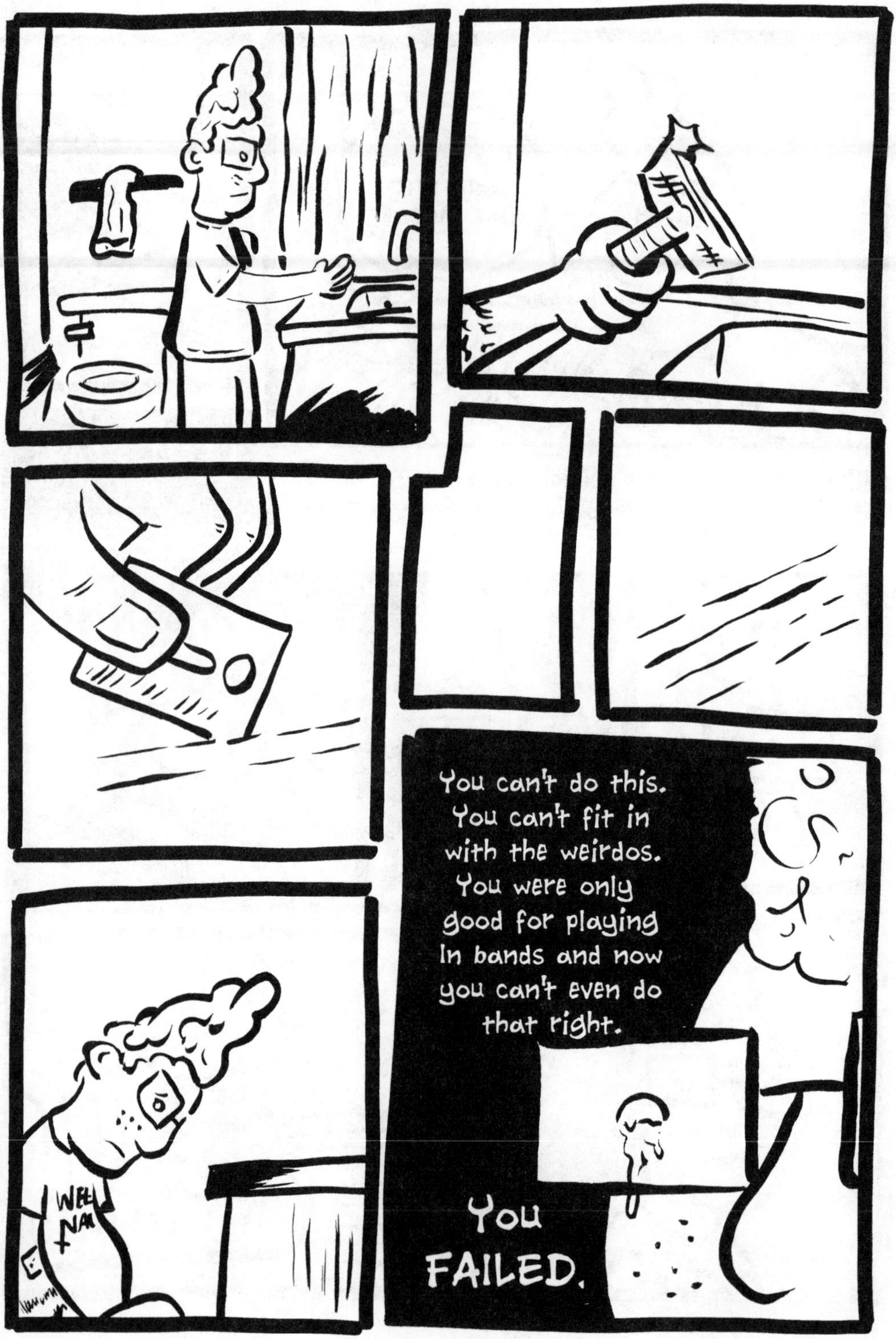
You can't do this. You can't fit in with the weirdos. You were only good for playing In bands and now you can't even do that right.
You FAILED.

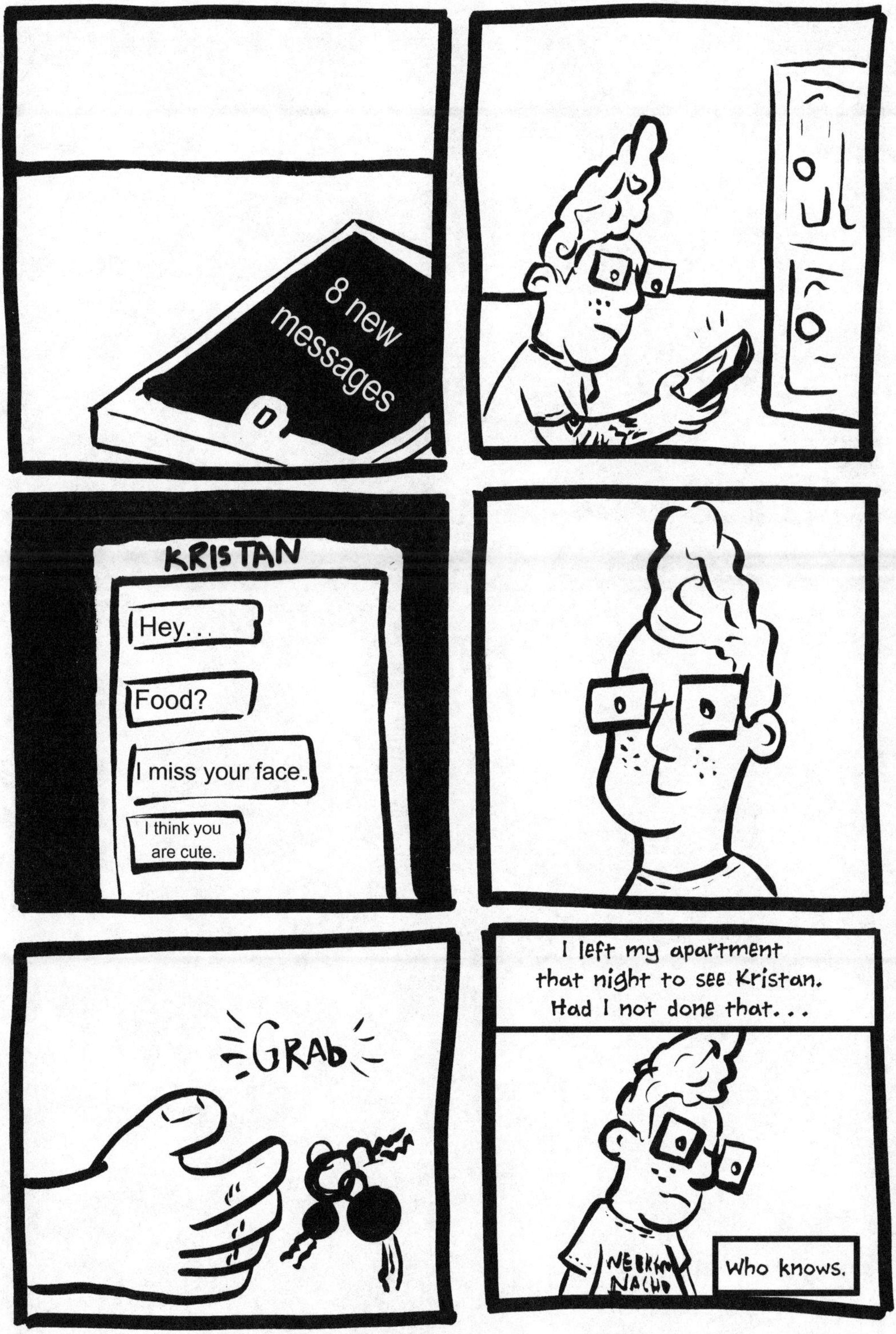

8 new messages
KRISTAN
Hey...
Food?
I miss your face.
I think you are cute.
GRAB
I left my apartment that night to see Kristan. Had I not done that...
Who knows.

Part 5

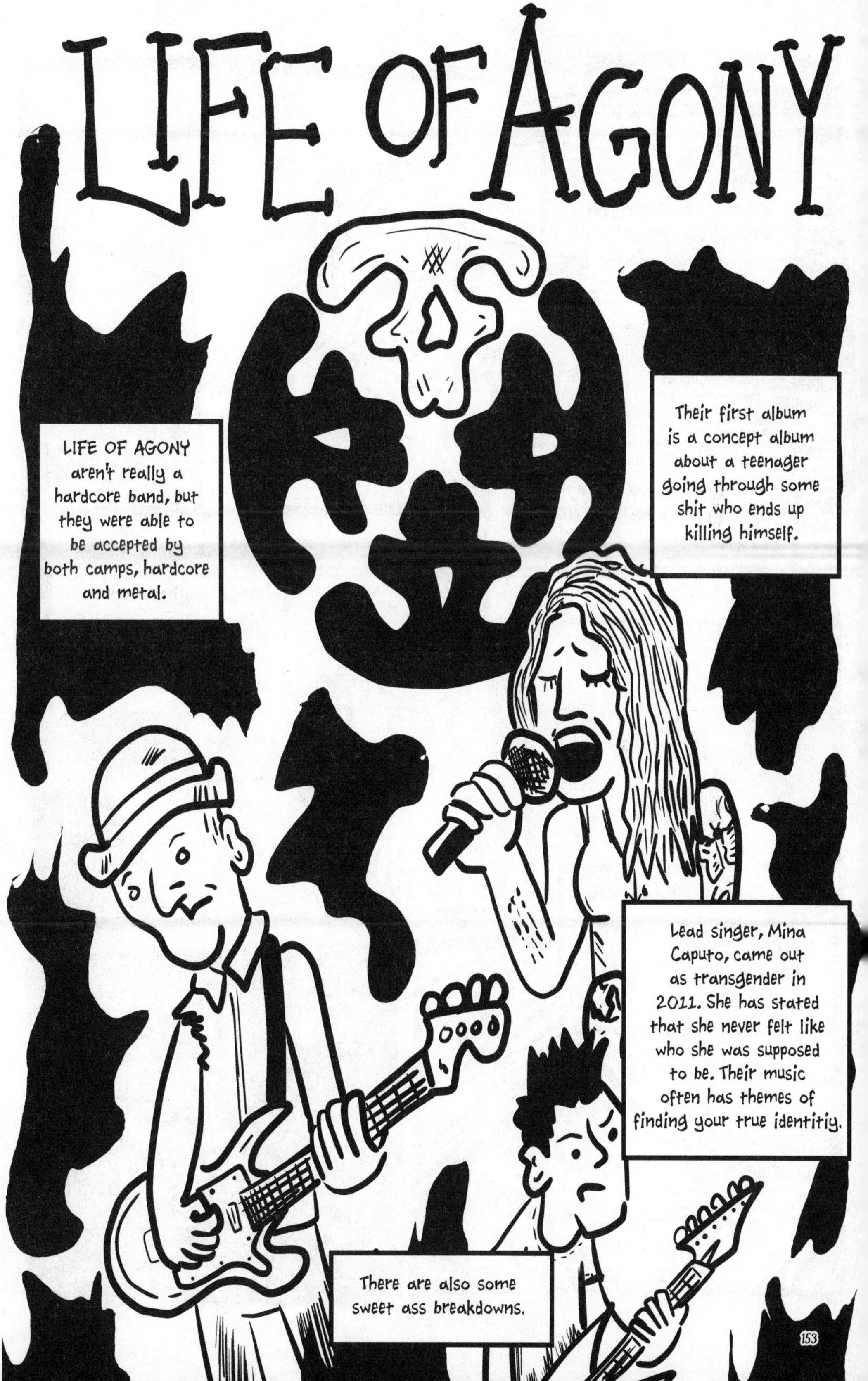
LIFE OF AGONY
LIFE OF AGONY aren't really a hardcore band, but they were able to be accepted by both camps, hardcore and metal.
Their first album is a concept album about a teenager going through some shit who ends up killing himself.
Lead singer, Mina Caputo, came out as transgender in 2011. She has stated that she never felt like who she was supposed to be. Their music often has themes of finding your true identitiy.
There are also some sweet ass breakdowns.

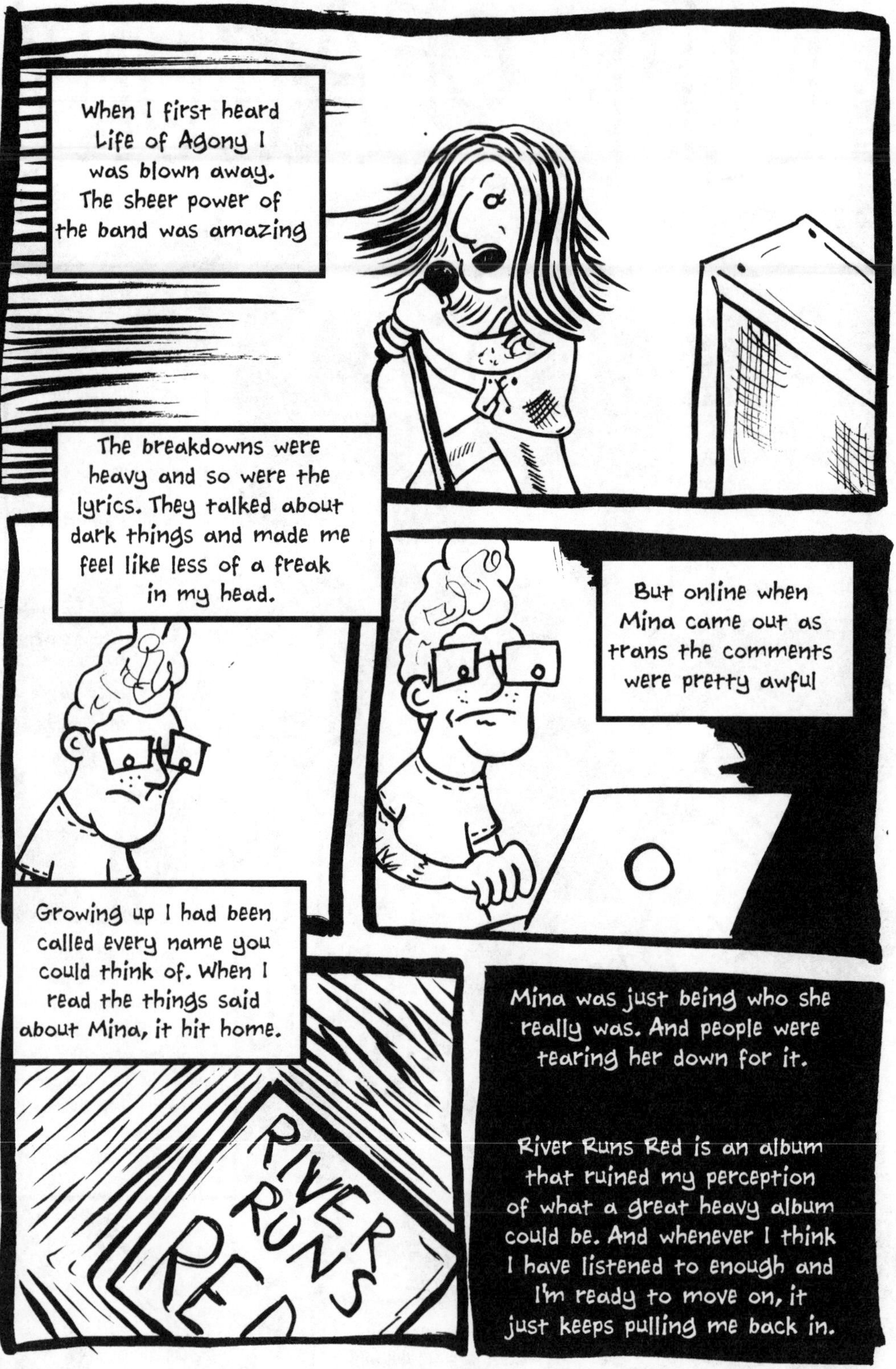
When I first heard Life of Agony I was blown away. The sheer power of the band was amazing
The breakdowns were heavy and so were the lyrics. They talked about dark things and made me feel like less of a freak in my head.
But online when Mina came out as trans the comments were pretty awful
Growing up I had been called every name you could think of. When I read the things said about Mina, it hit home.
RIVER RUNS RED
Mina was just being who she really was. And people were tearing her down for it.
River Runs Red is an album that ruined my perception of what a great heavy album could be. And whenever I think I have listened to enough and I'm ready to move on, it just keeps pulling me back in.

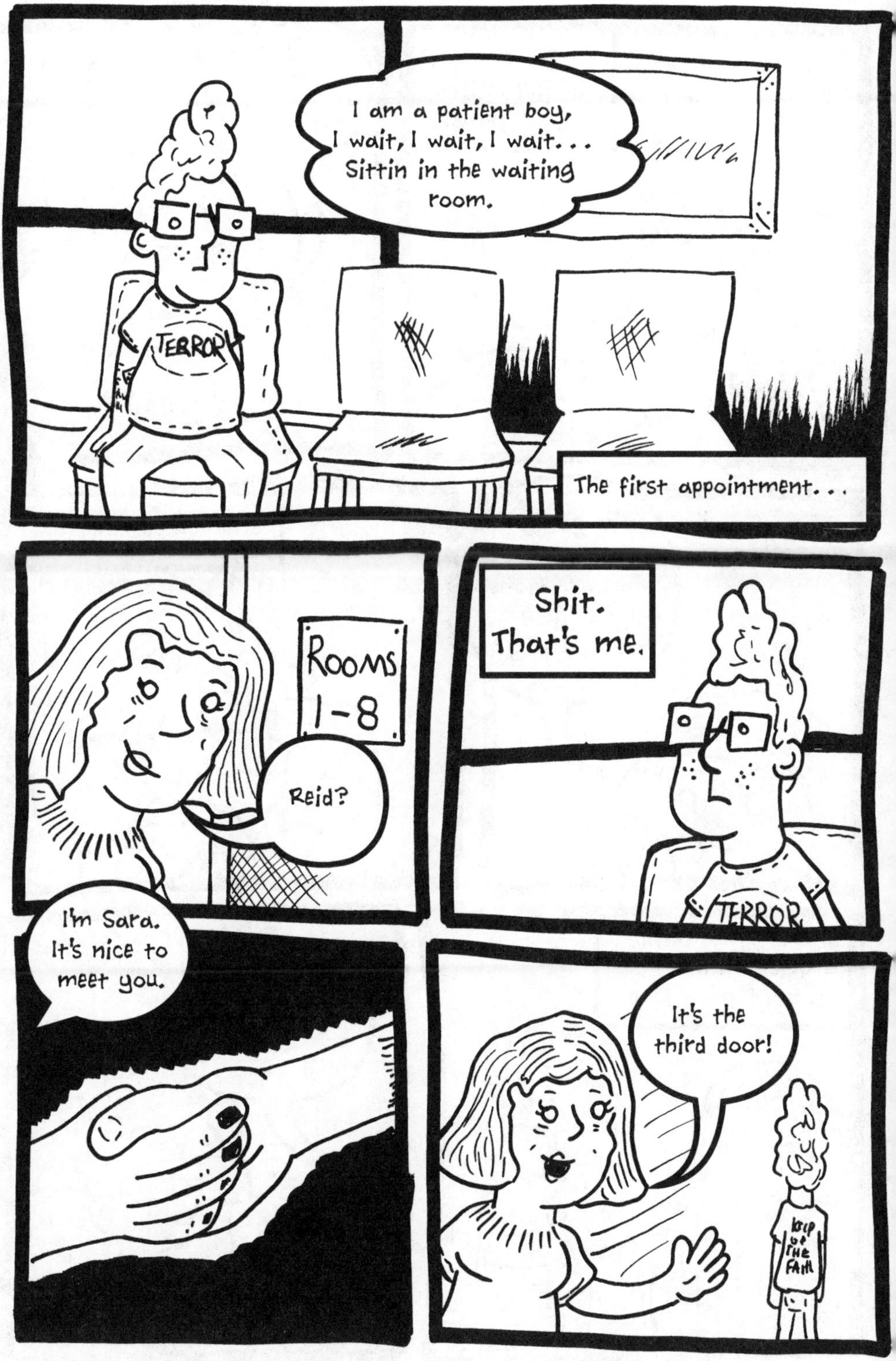
I am a patient boy, I wait, I wait, I wait... Sittin in the waiting room.
TERROR
The first appointment...
Rooms 1-8
Reid?
Shit. That's me.
TERROR
I'm Sara. It's nice to meet you.
It's the third door!

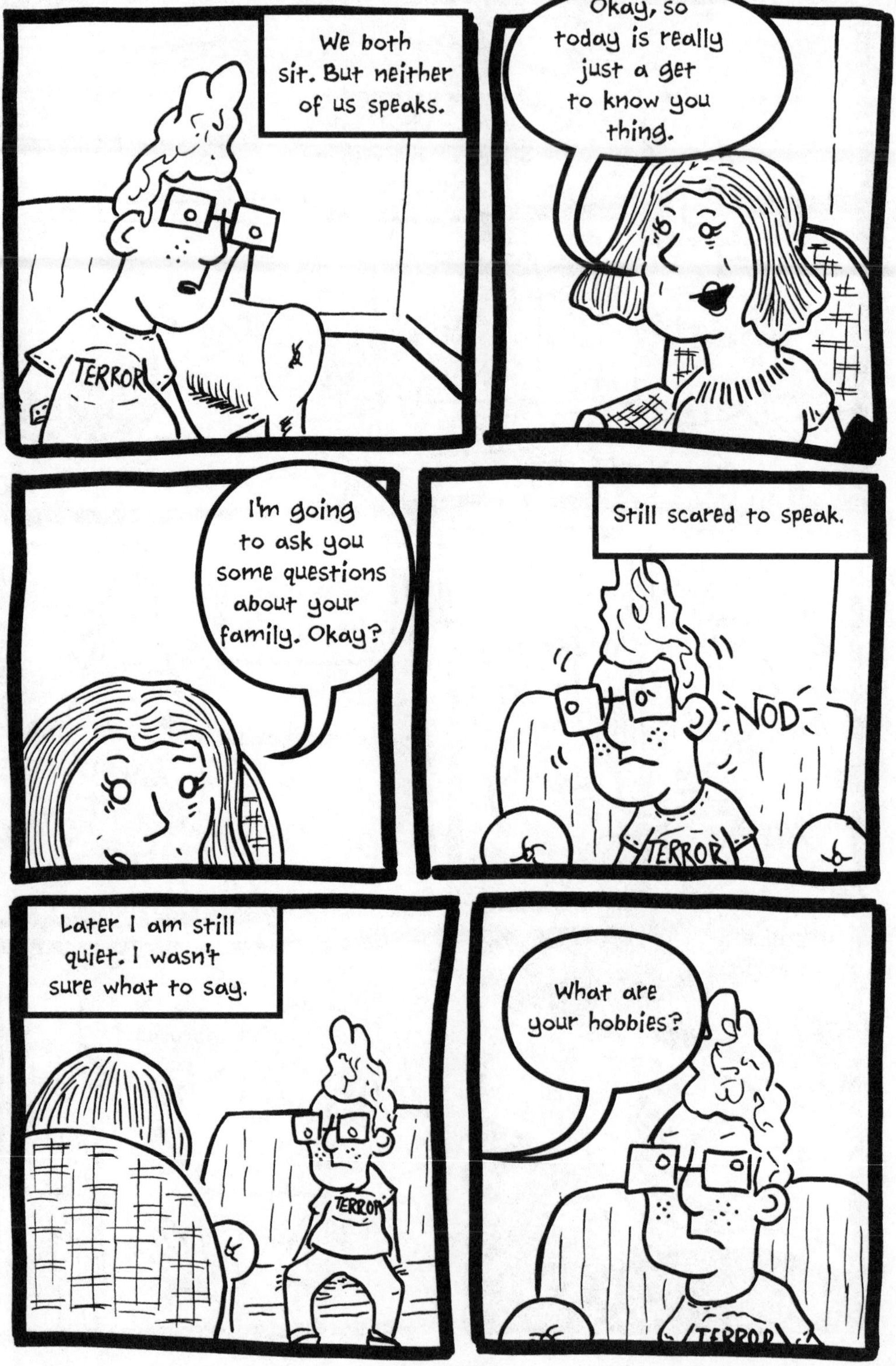

We both sit. But neither of us speaks.
TERROR
Okay, so today is really just a get to know you thing.
I'm going to ask you some questions about your family. Okay?
Still scared to speak.
NOD
TERROR
Later I am still quiet. I wasn't sure what to say.
TERROR
What are your hobbies?
TERROR

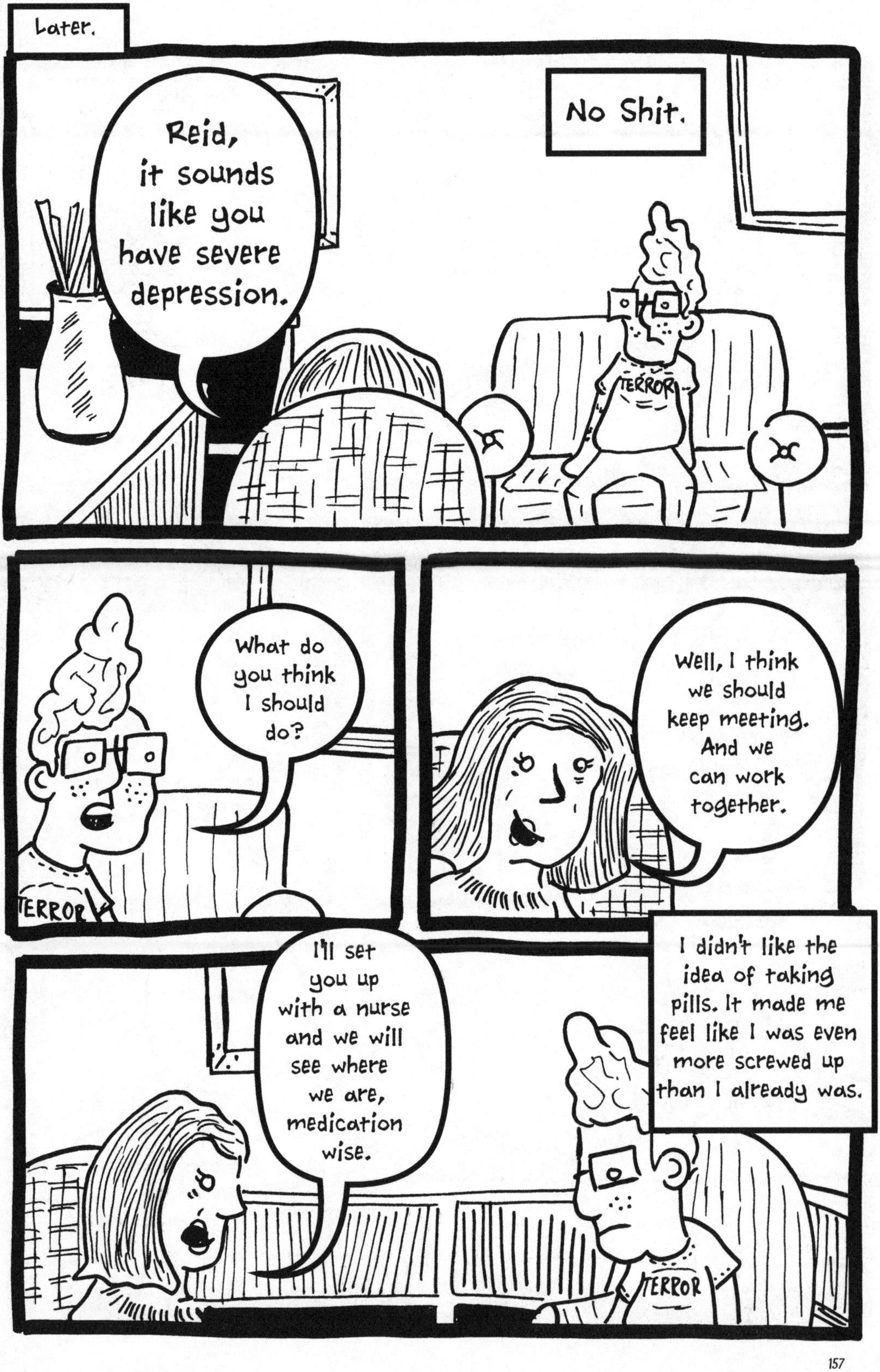
Later.
Reid, it sounds like you have severe depression.
No Shit.
TERROR
What do you think I should do?
TERROR
Well, I think we should keep meeting. And we can work together.
I'll set you up with a nurse and we will see where we are, medication wise.
I didn't like the idea of taking pills. It made me feel like I was even more screwed up than I already was.
TERROR

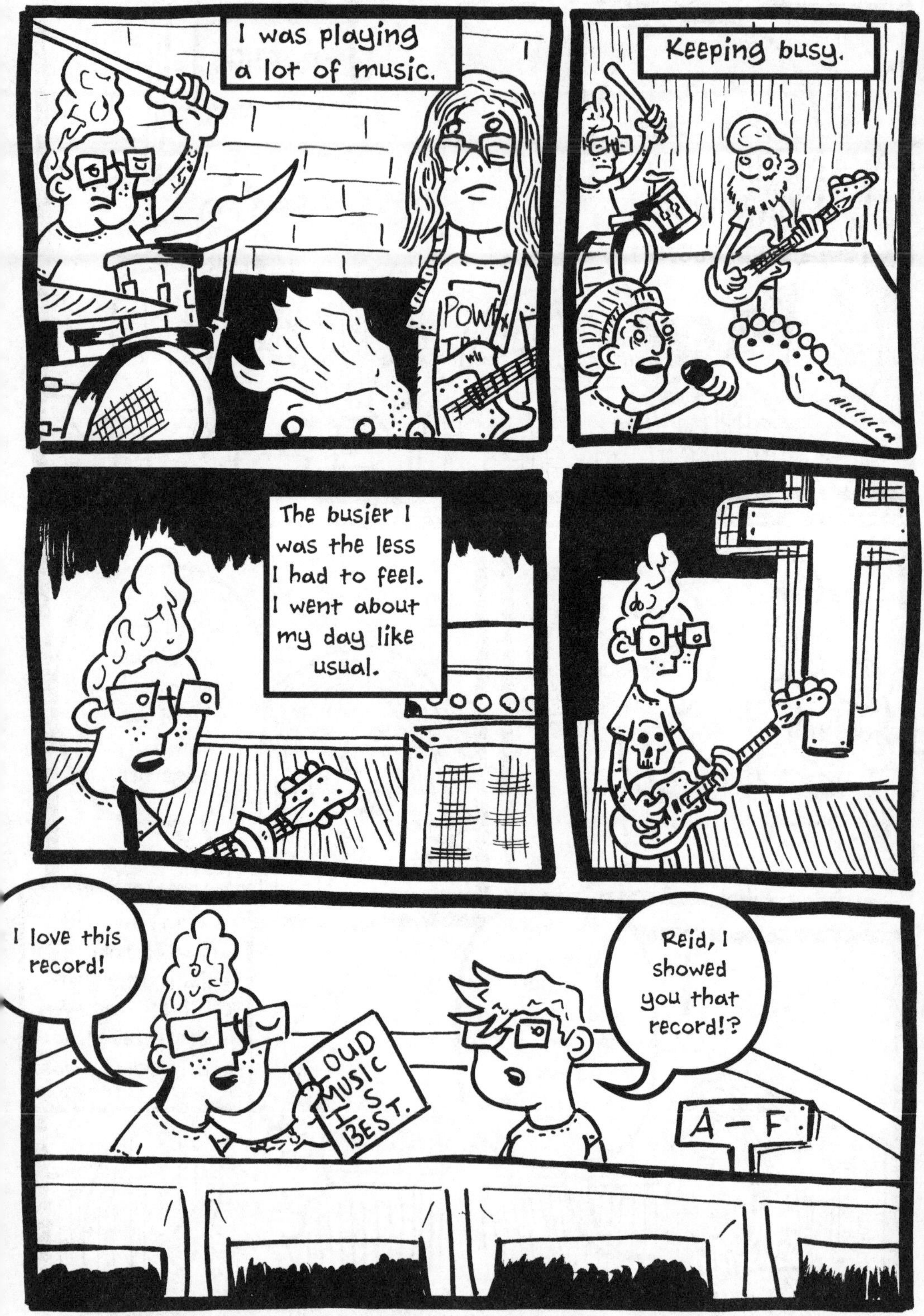
I was playing a lot of music.
Keeping busy.
The busier I was the less I had to feel. I went about my day like usual.
I love this record!
OUD MUSIC IS BEST.
Reid, I showed you that record!?
A–F

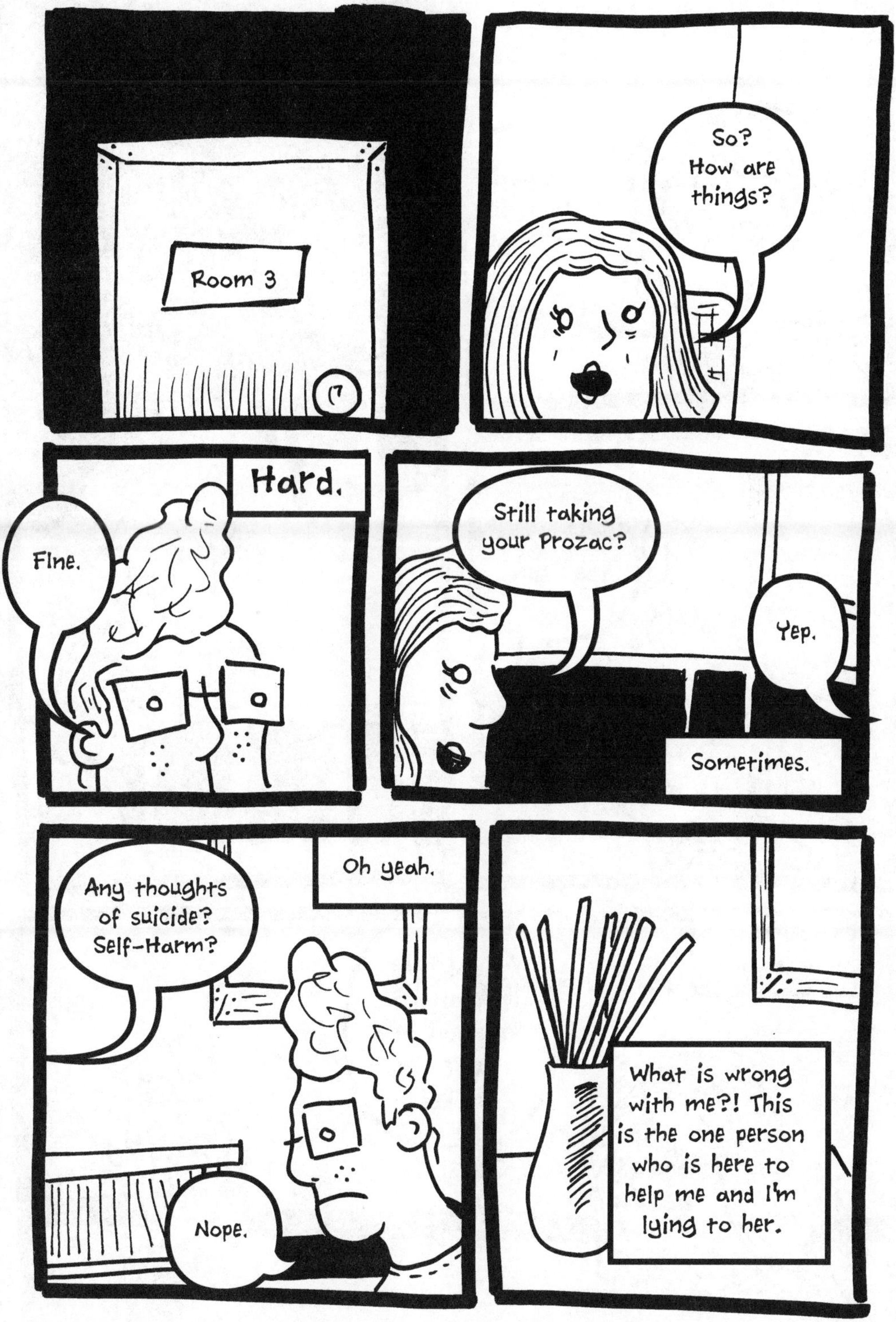
Room 3
So? How are things?
Hard.
Fine.
Still taking your Prozac?
Yep.
Sometimes.
Any thoughts of suicide? Self-Harm?
Oh yeah.
Nope.
What is wrong with me?! This is the one person who is here to help me and I'm lying to her.

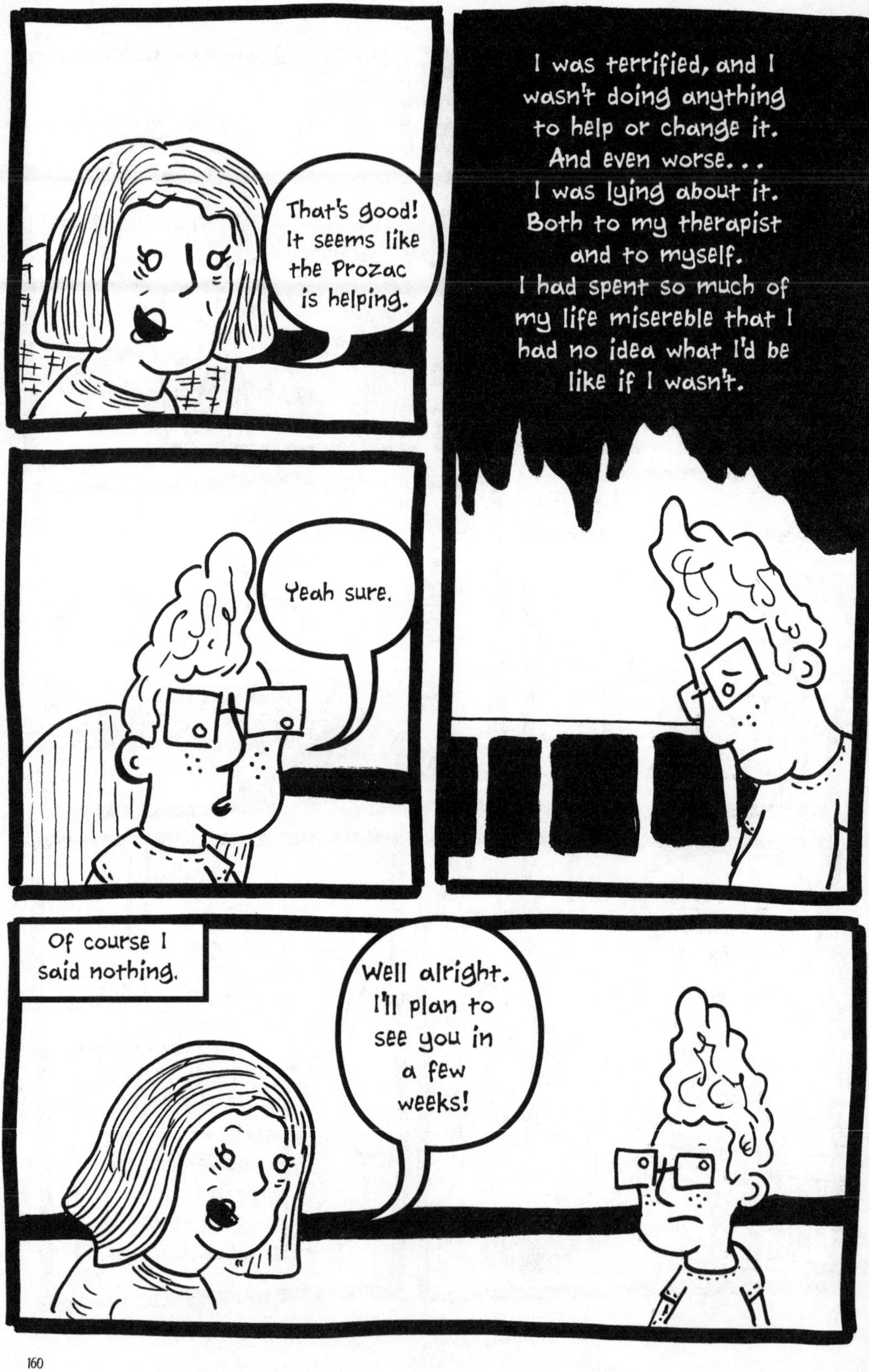
That's good! It seems like the Prozac is helping.
I was terrified, and I wasn't doing anything to help or change it. And even worse... I was lying about it. Both to my therapist and to myself. I had spent so much of my life misereble that I had no idea what I'd be like if I wasn't.
Yeah sure.
Of course I said nothing.
Well alright. I'll plan to see you in a few weeks!

MINOR THREAT

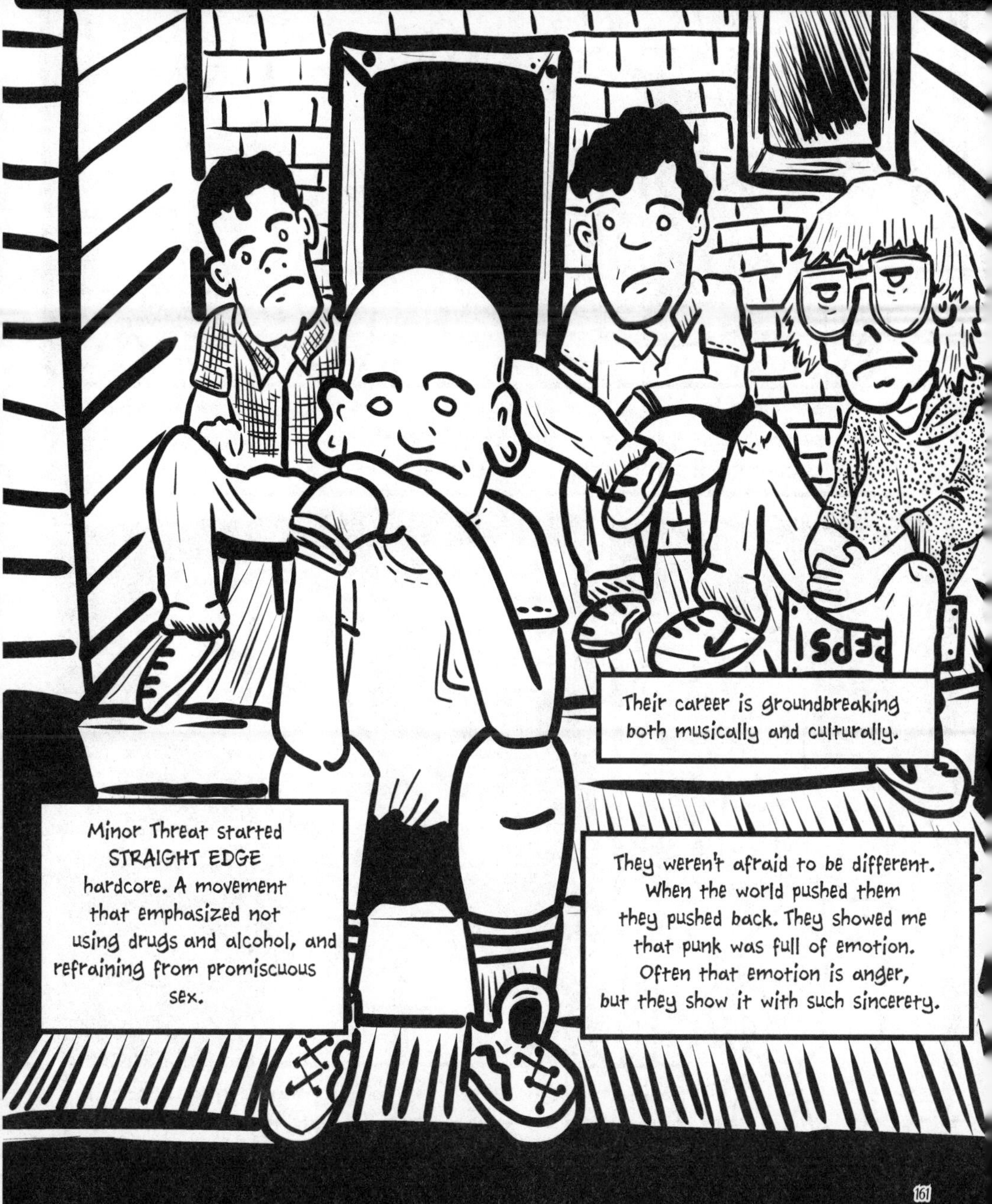
Their career is groundbreaking both musically and culturally.
Minor Threat started STRAIGHT EDGE hardcore. A movement that emphasized not using drugs and alcohol, and refraining from promiscuous sex.
They weren't afraid to be different. When the world pushed them they pushed back. They showed me that punk was full of emotion. Often that emotion is anger, but they show it with such sincerety.

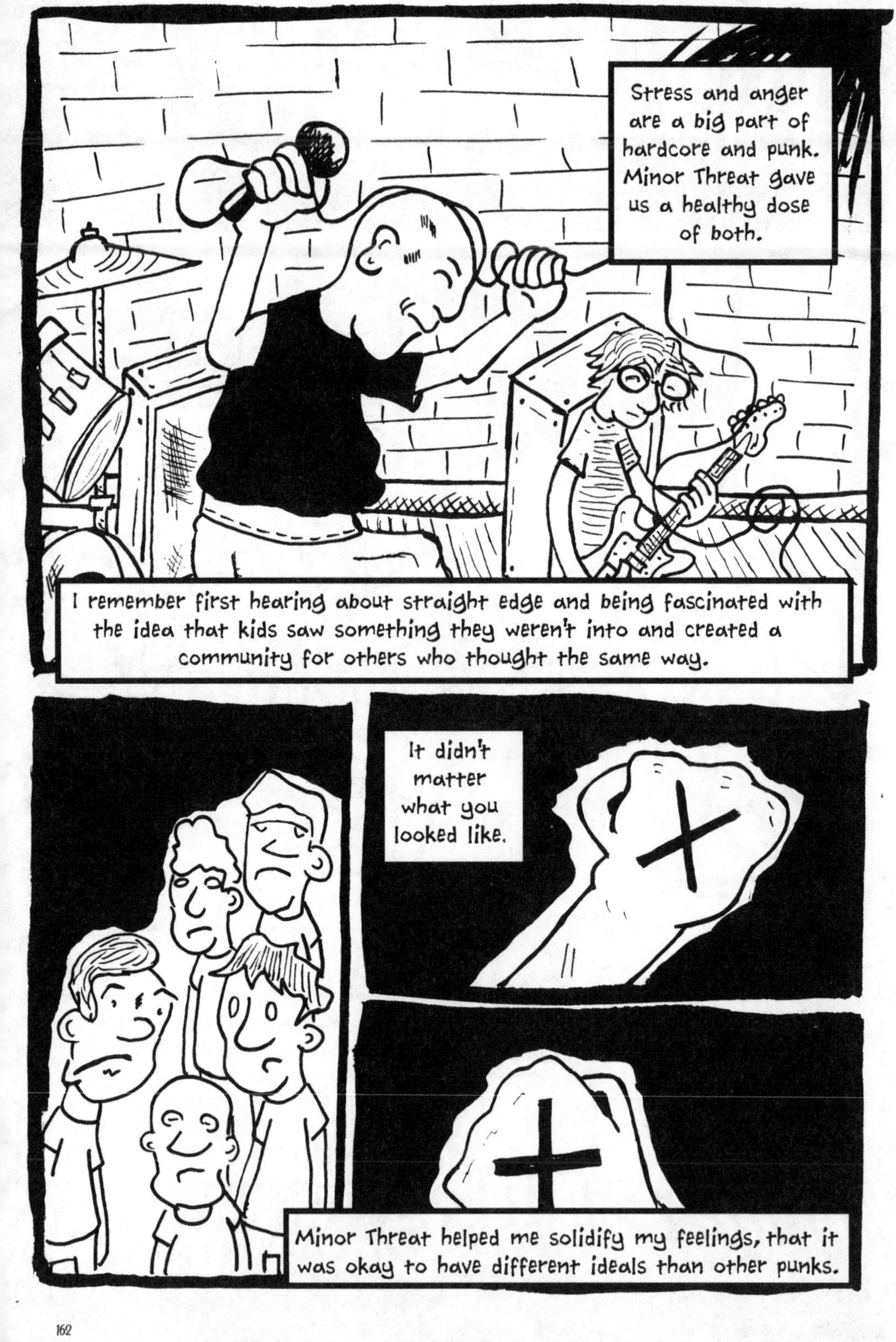
Stress and anger are a big part of hardcore and punk. Minor Threat gave us a healthy dose of both.
I remember first hearing about straight edge and being fascinated with the idea that kids saw something they weren't into and created a community for others who thought the same way.
It didn't matter what you looked like.
Minor Threat helped me solidify my feelings, that it was okay to have different ideals than other punks.

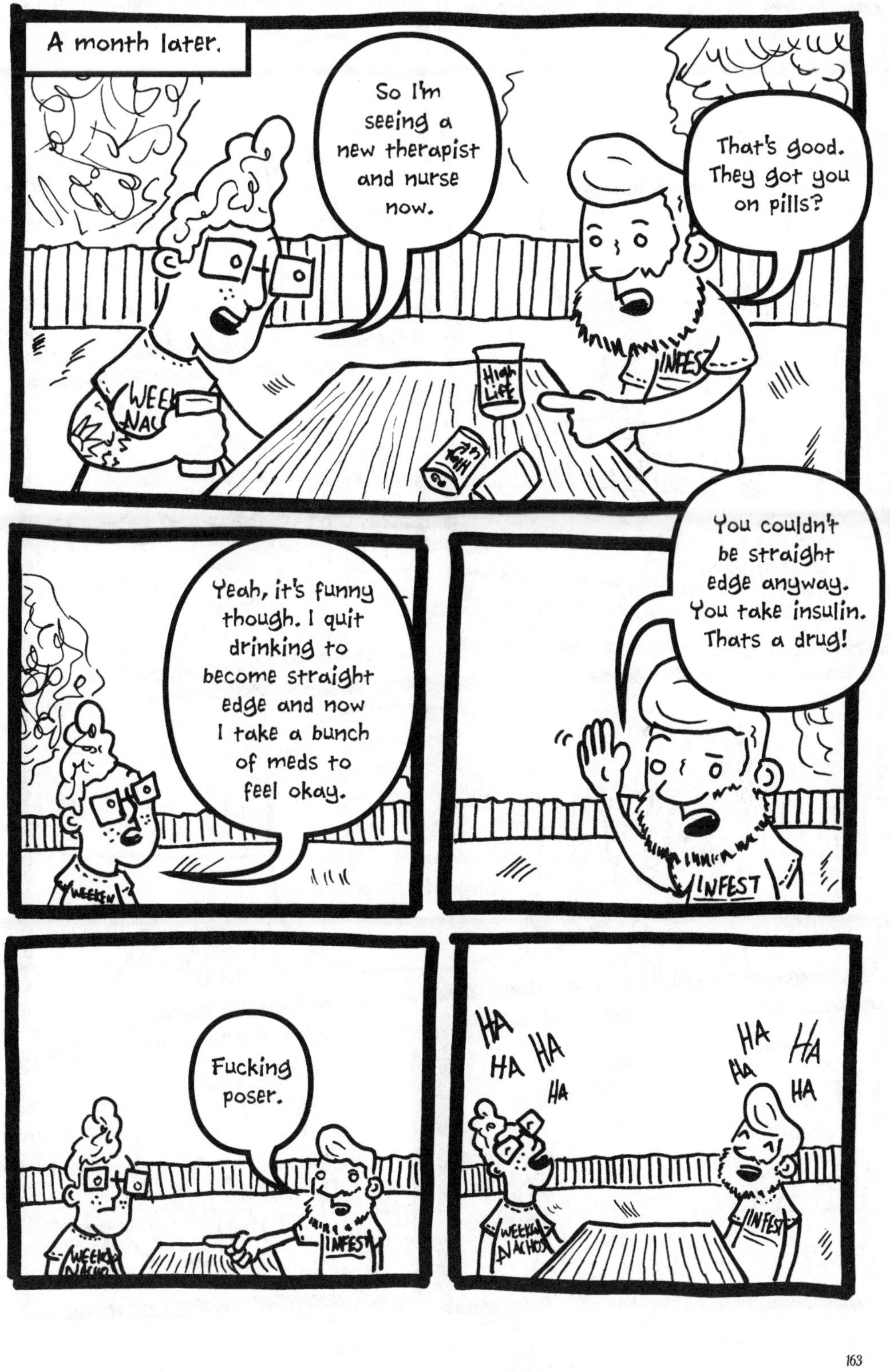
A month later.
So I'm seeing a new therapist and nurse now.
That's good. They got you on pills?
High Life
INFEST
Yeah, it's funny though. I quit drinking to become straight edge and now I take a bunch of meds to feel okay.
You couldn't be straight edge anyway. You take insulin. Thats a drug!
INFEST
Fucking poser.
INFEST
HA HA HA HA
HA HA HA HA
INFEST

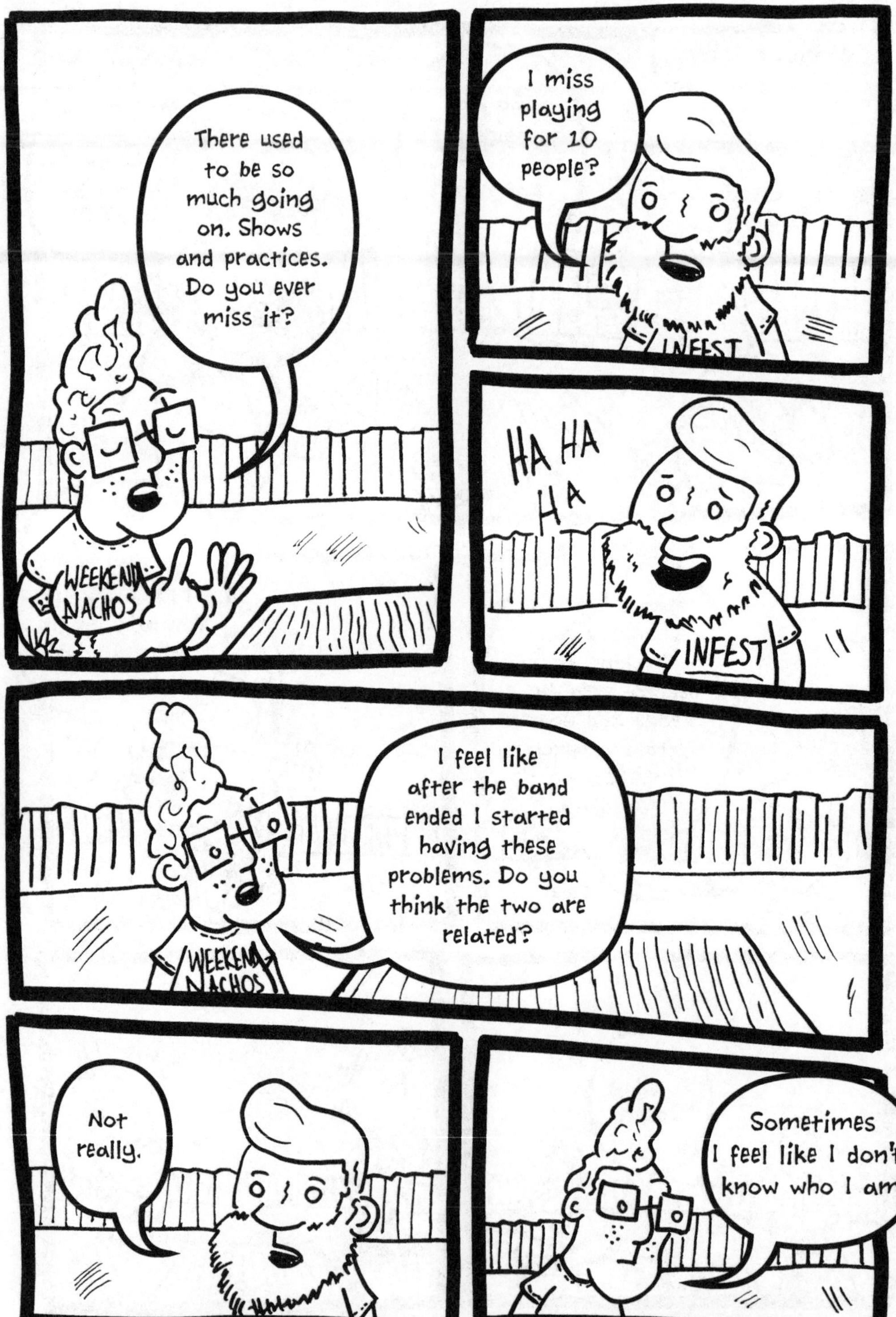
There used to be so much going on. Shows and practices. Do you ever miss it?
WEEKEND NACHOS
I miss playing for 10 people?
INFEST
HA HA HA
INFEST
I feel like after the band ended I started having these problems. Do you think the two are related?
WEEKEND NACHOS
Not really.
Sometimes I feel like I don't know who I am.

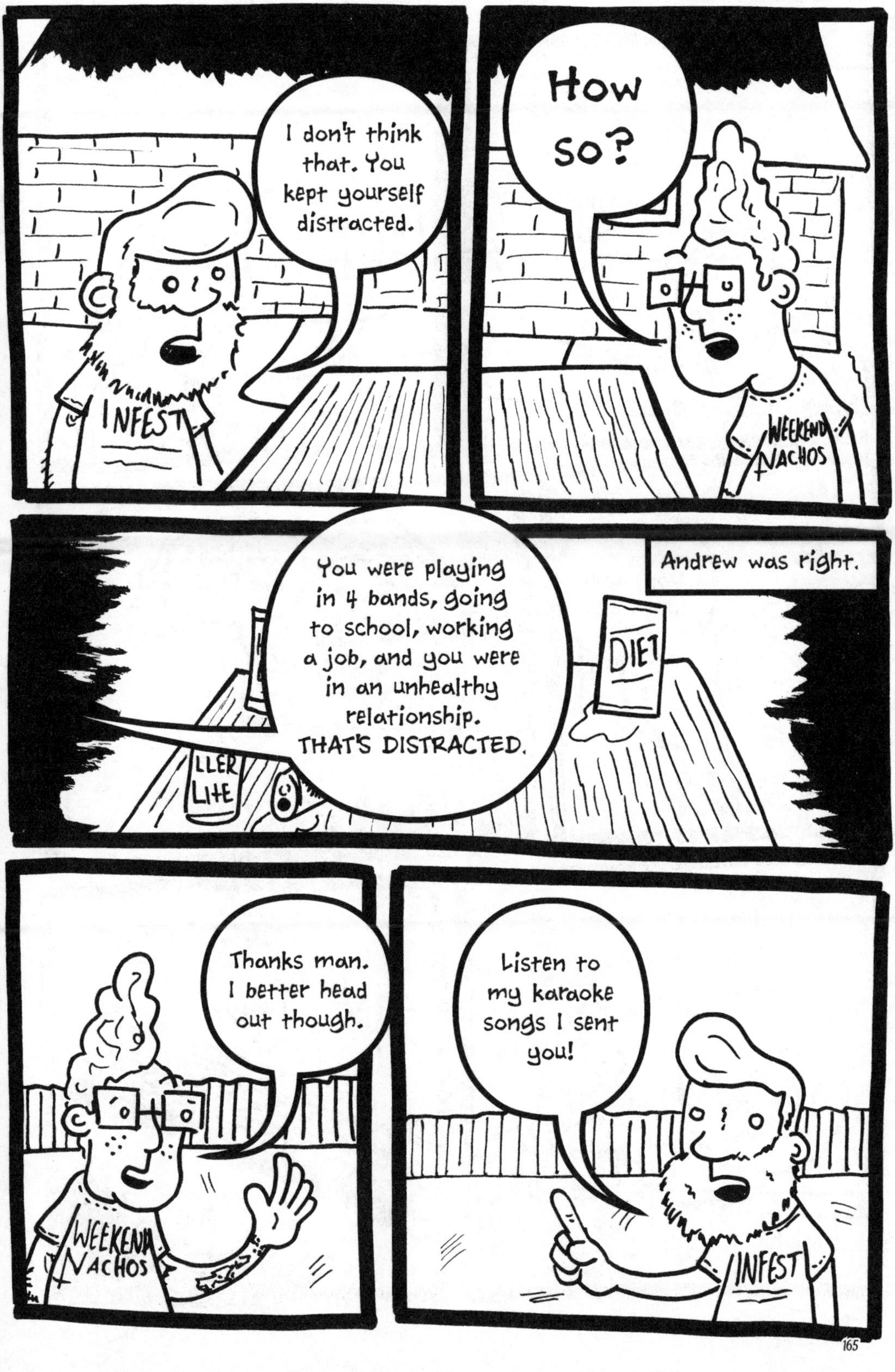
I don't think that. You kept yourself distracted.
INFEST
How so?
WEEKEND NACHOS
You were playing in 4 bands, going to school, working a job, and you were in an unhealthy relationship. THAT'S DISTRACTED.
Andrew was right.
DIET
LLER LITE
Thanks man. I better head out though.
WEEKEND NACHOS
Listen to my karaoke songs I sent you!
INFEST

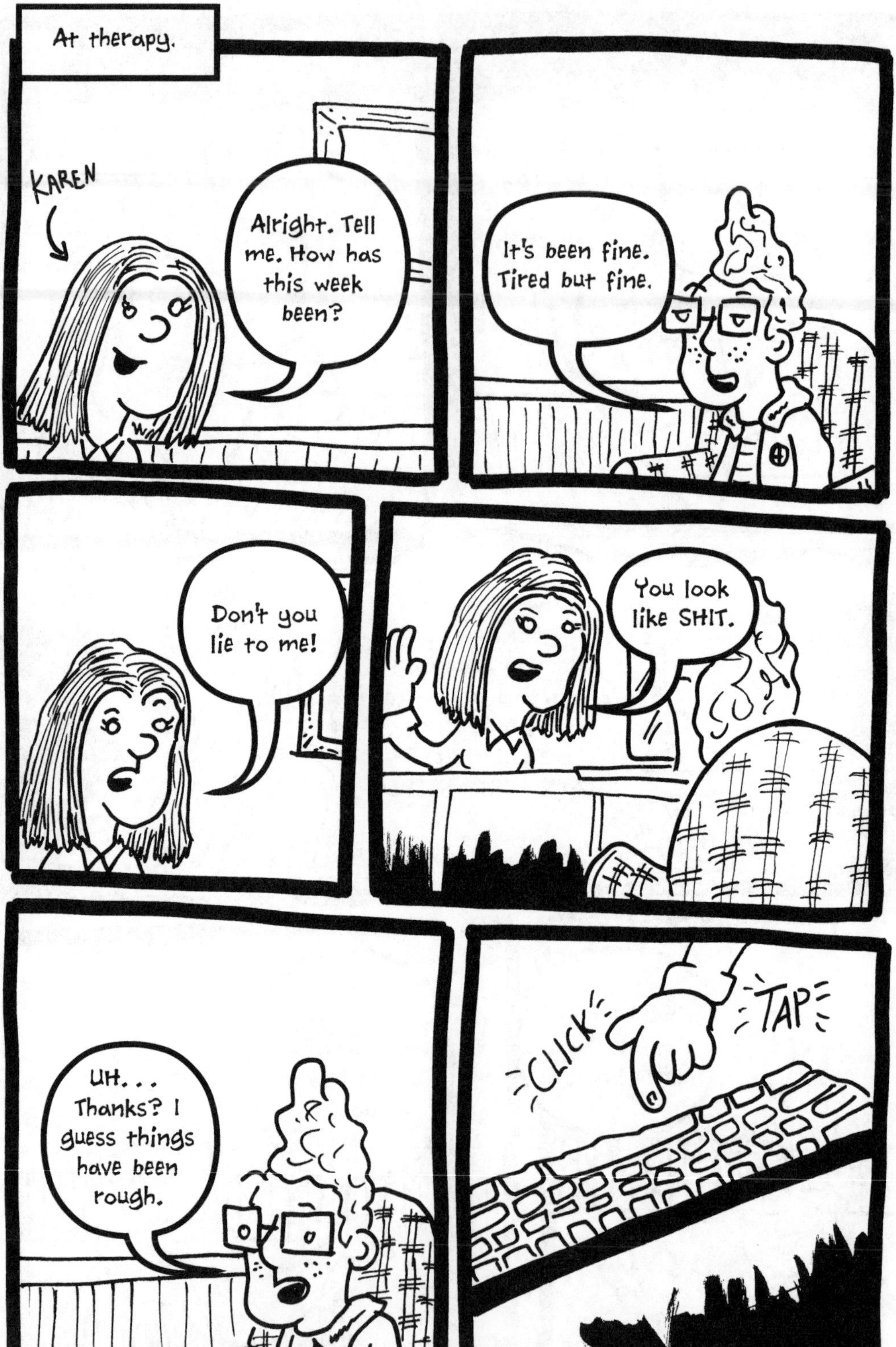
At therapy.
KAREN
Alright. Tell me. How has this week been?
It's been fine. Tired but fine.
Don't you lie to me!
You look like SHIT.
UH... Thanks? I guess things have been rough.
CLICK
TAP

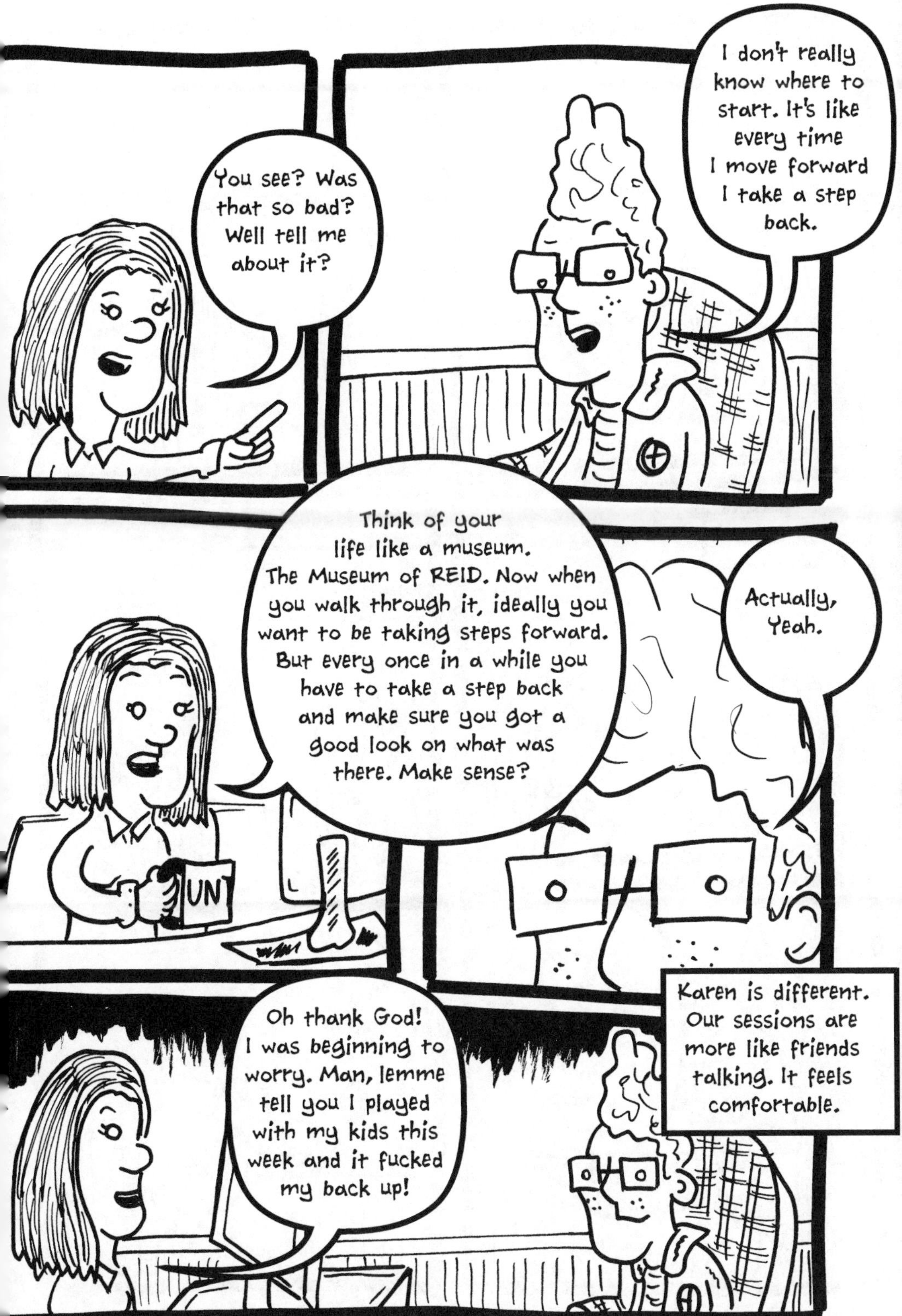
You see? Was that so bad? Well tell me about it?
I don't really know where to start. It's like every time I move forward I take a step back.
Think of your life like a museum. The Museum of REID. Now when you walk through it, ideally you want to be taking steps forward. But every once in a while you have to take a step back and make sure you got a good look on what was there. Make sense?
Actually, Yeah.
UN
Karen is different. Our sessions are more like friends talking. It feels comfortable.
Oh thank God! I was beginning to worry. Man, lemme tell you I played with my kids this week and it fucked my back up!

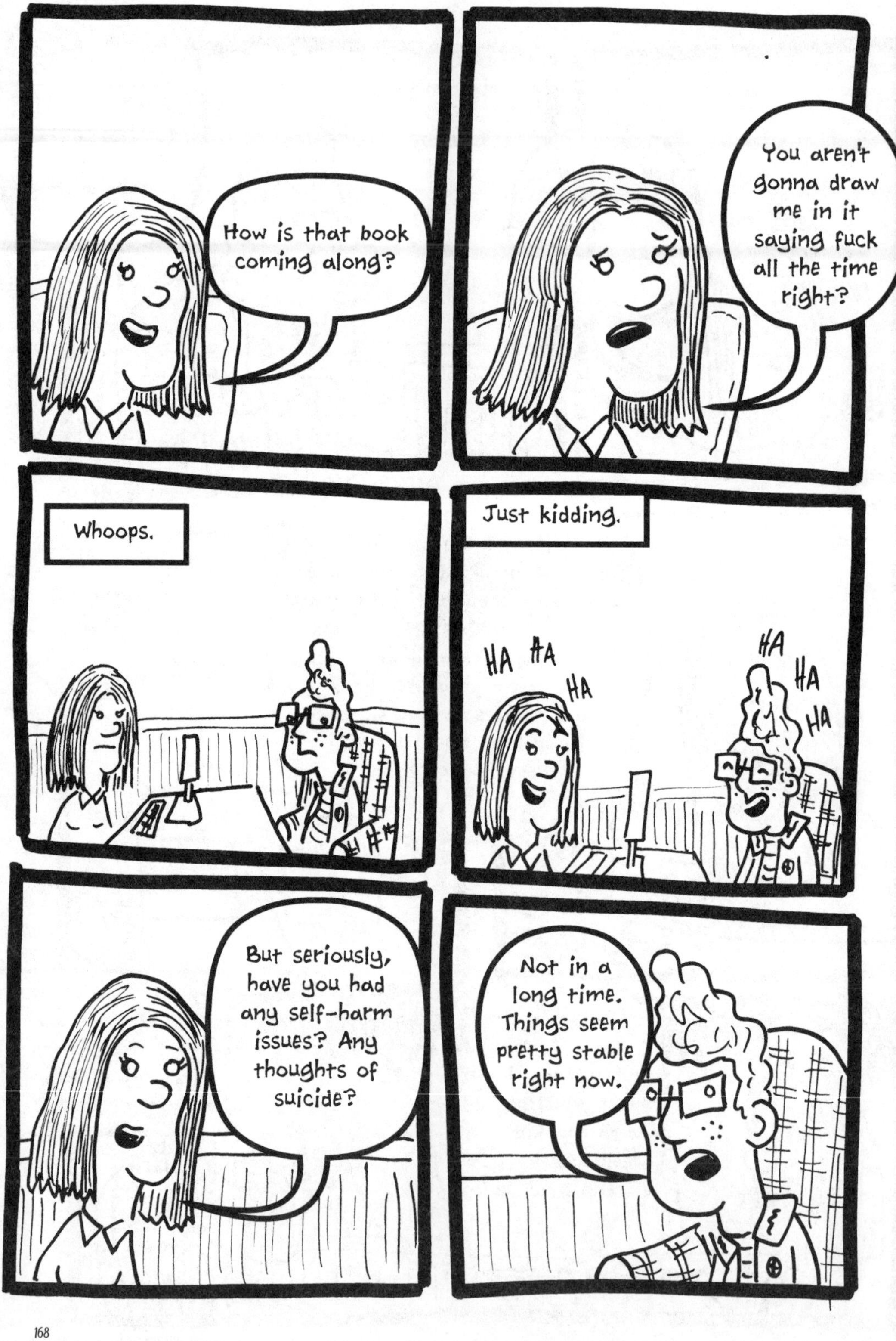
How is that book coming along?
You aren't gonna draw me in it saying fuck all the time right?
Whoops.
Just kidding.
HA HA HA
HA HA HA
But seriously, have you had any self-harm issues? Any thoughts of suicide?
Not in a long time. Things seem pretty stable right now.

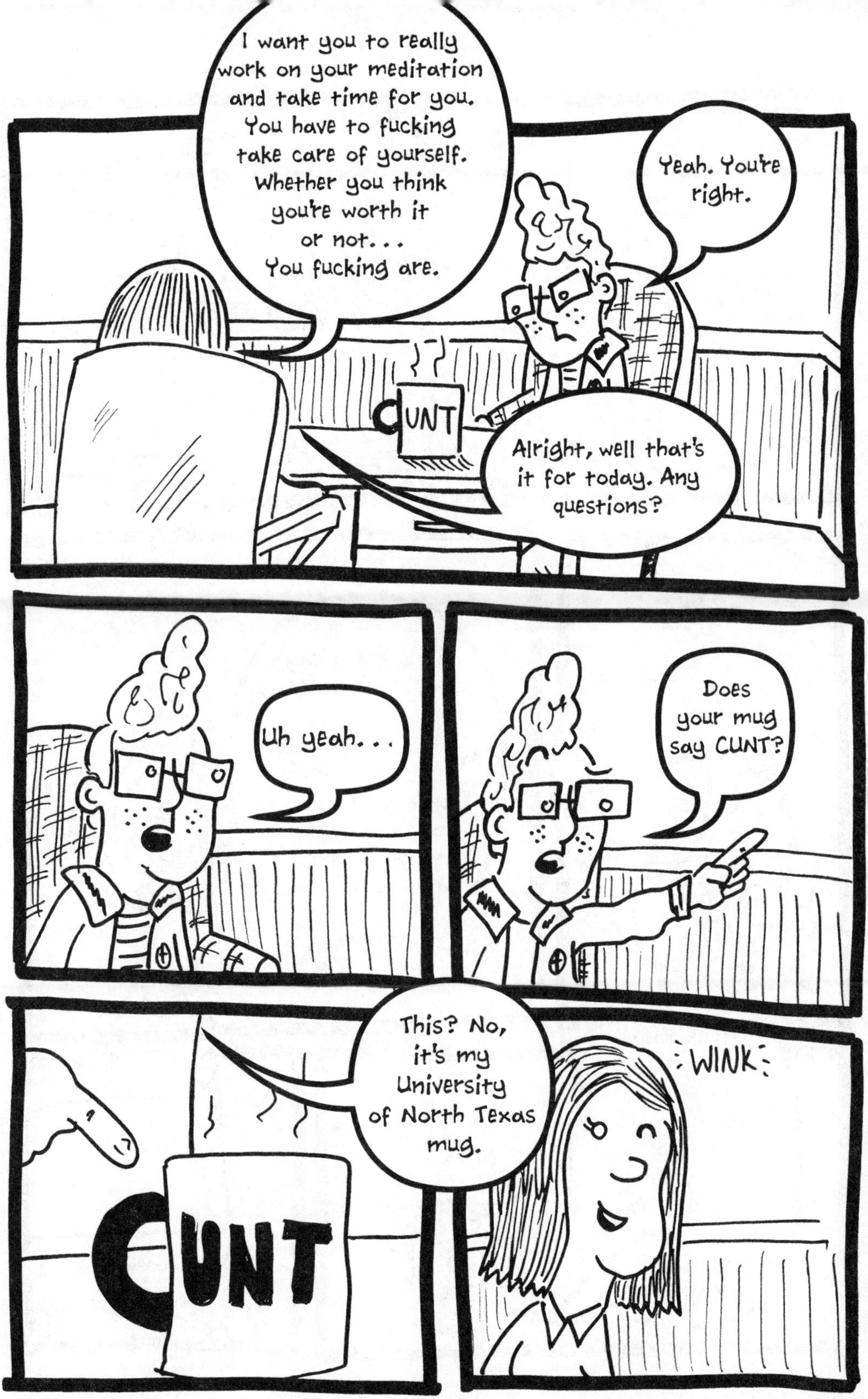
I want you to really work on your meditation and take time for you. You have to fucking take care of yourself. Whether you think you're worth it or not... You fucking are.
Yeah. You're right.
CUNT
Alright, well that's it for today. Any questions?
Uh yeah...
Does your mug say CUNT?
This? No, it's my University of North Texas mug.
WINK
CUNT

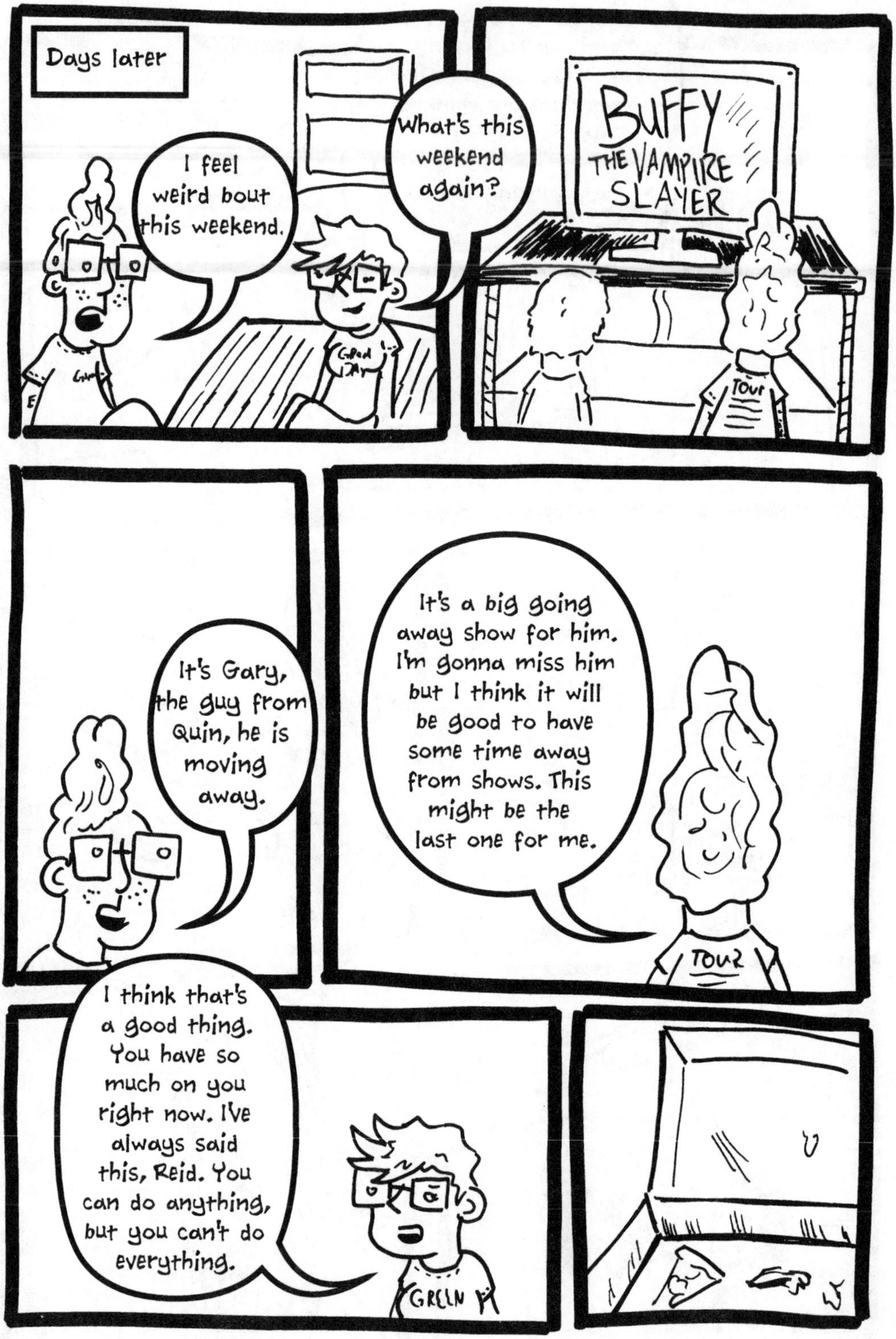
Days later
I feel weird bout this weekend.
What's this weekend again?
BUFFY THE VAMPIRE SLAYER
It's Gary, the guy from Quin, he is moving away.
It's a big going away show for him. I'm gonna miss him but I think it will be good to have some time away from shows. This might be the last one for me.
I think that's a good thing. You have so much on you right now. I've always said this, Reid. You can do anything, but you can't do everything.

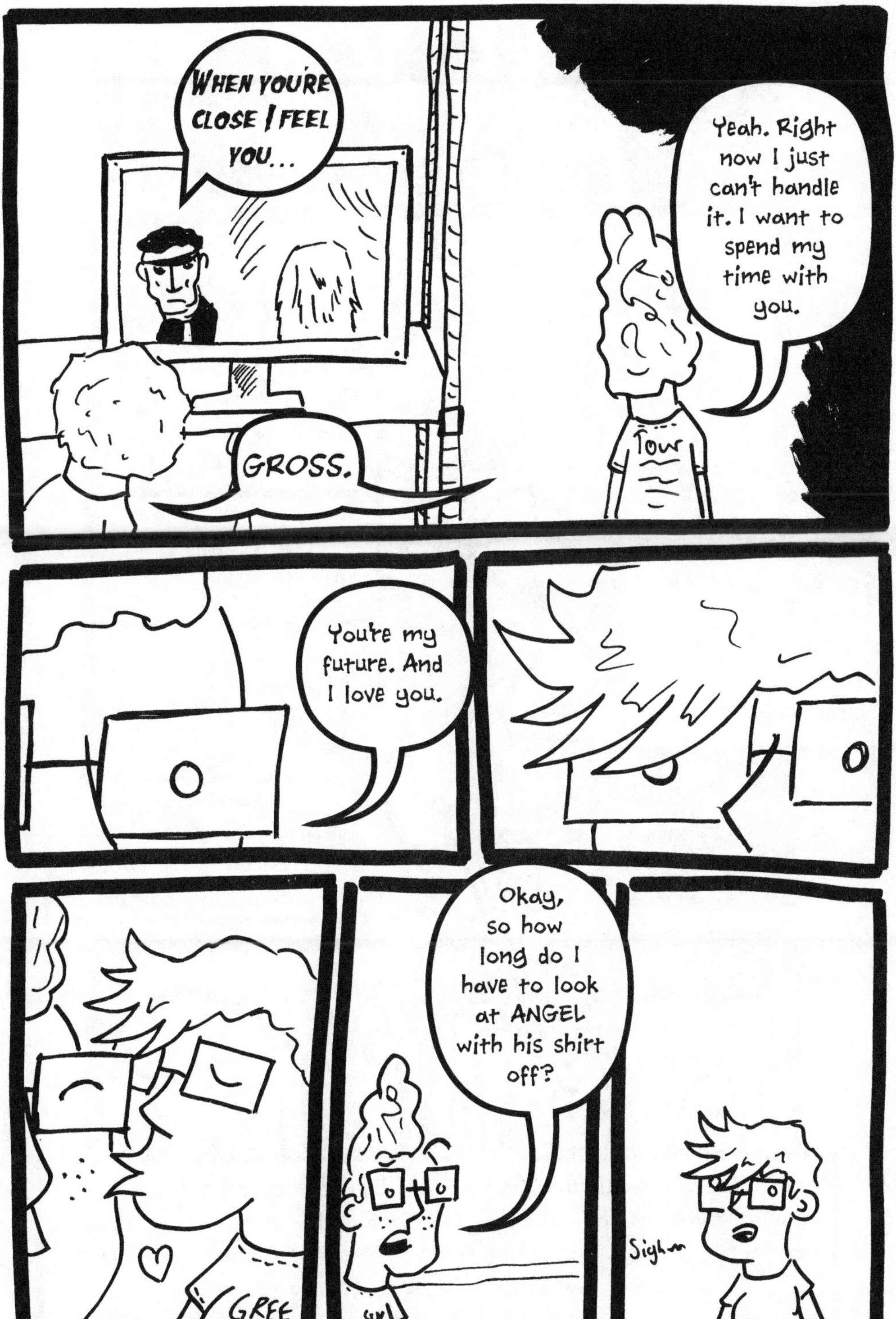
WHEN YOU'RE CLOSE I FEEL YOU...
GROSS.
Yeah. Right now I just can't handle it. I want to spend my time with you.
Tour
You're my future. And I love you.
GREE
Okay, so how long do I have to look at ANGEL with his shirt off?
Sigh

HÜSKER DÜ

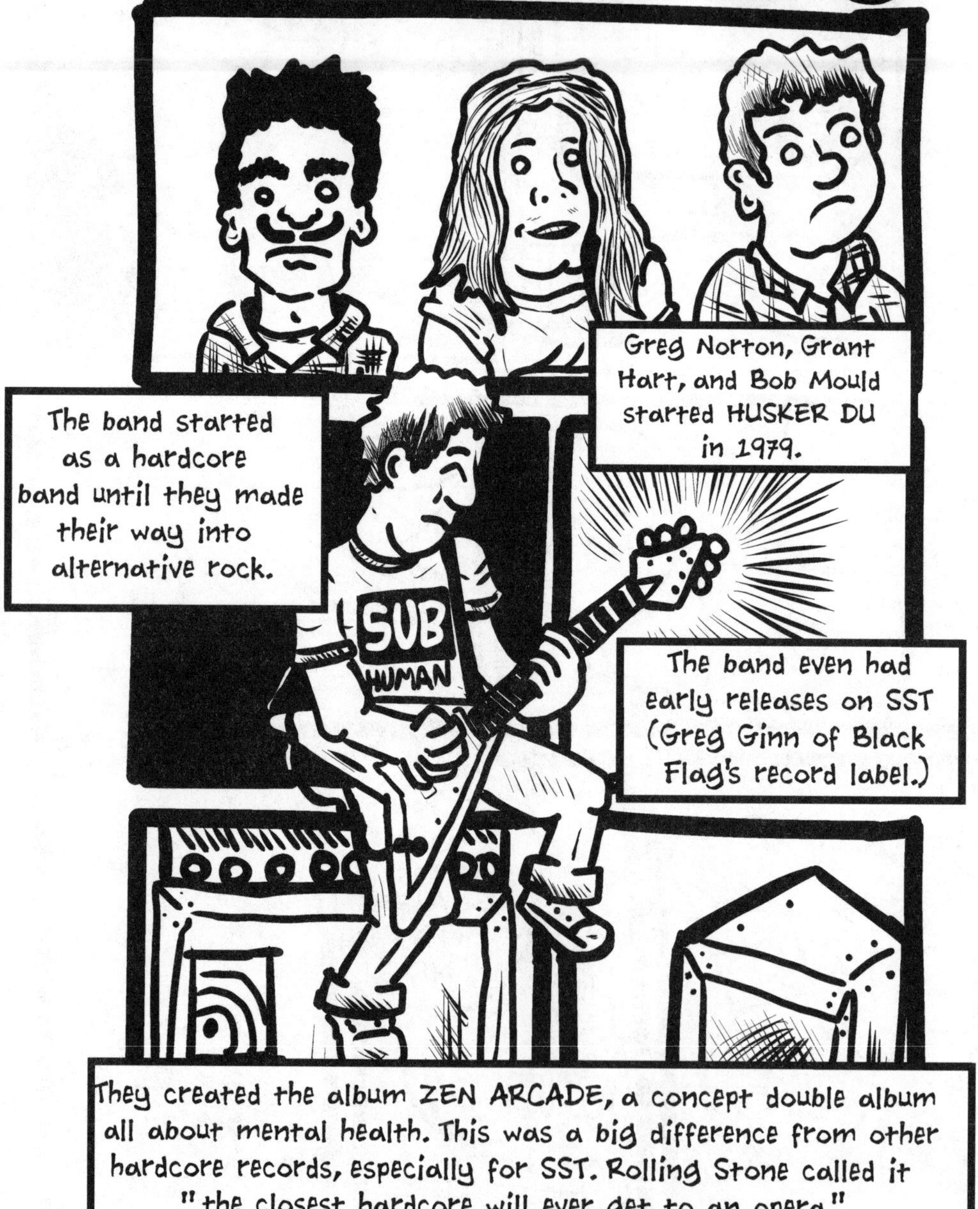
Greg Norton, Grant Hart, and Bob Mould started HUSKER DU in 1979.
The band started as a hardcore band until they made their way into alternative rock.
SUB HUMAN
The band even had early releases on SST (Greg Ginn of Black Flag's record label.)
They created the album ZEN ARCADE, a concept double album all about mental health. This was a big difference from other hardcore records, especially for SST. Rolling Stone called it "the closest hardcore will ever get to an opera."

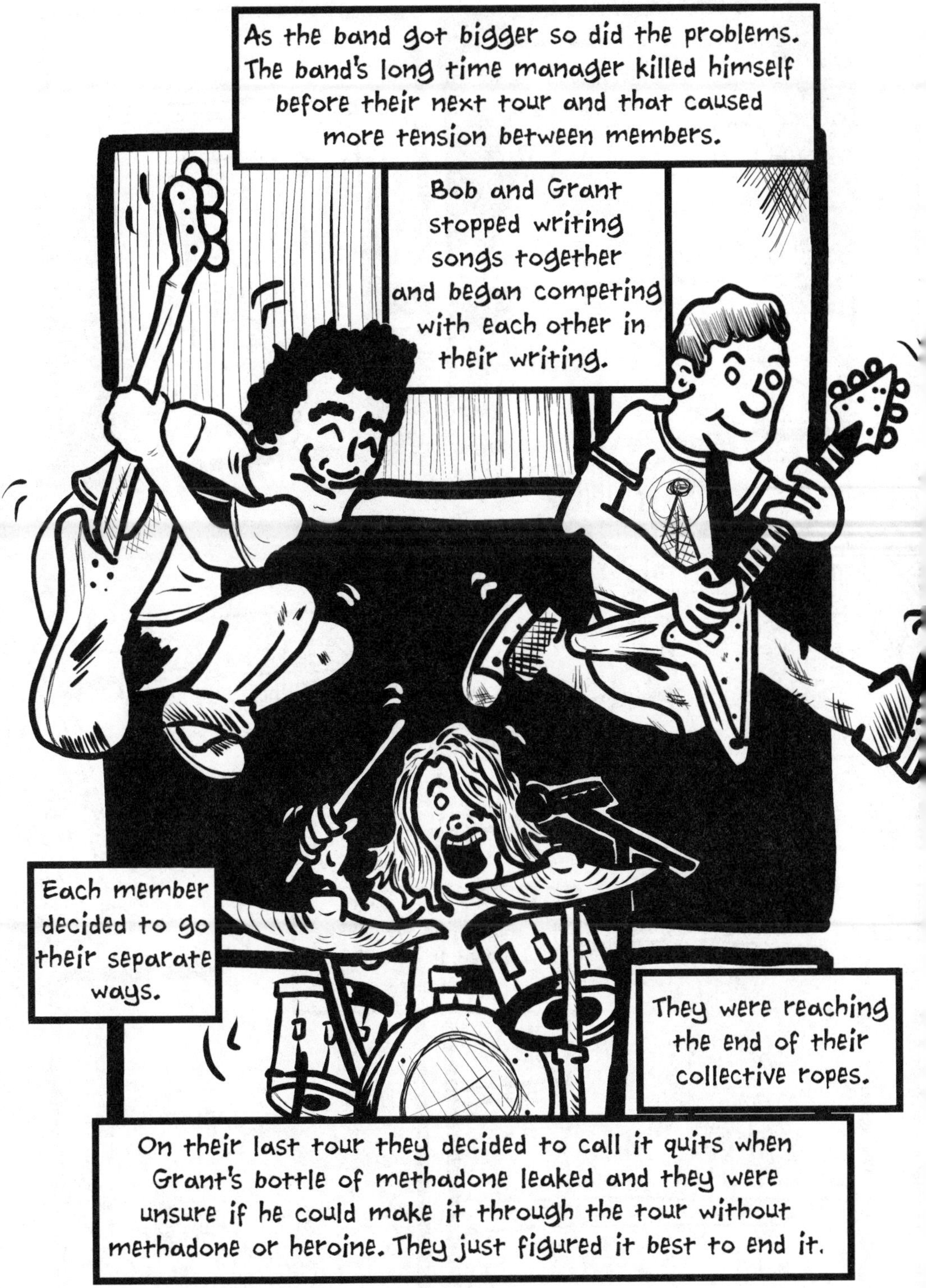
As the band got bigger so did the problems. The band's long time manager killed himself before their next tour and that caused more tension between members.
Bob and Grant stopped writing songs together and began competing with each other in their writing.
Each member decided to go their separate ways.
They were reaching the end of their collective ropes.
On their last tour they decided to call it quits when Grant's bottle of methadone leaked and they were unsure if he could make it through the tour without methadone or heroine. They just figured it best to end it.

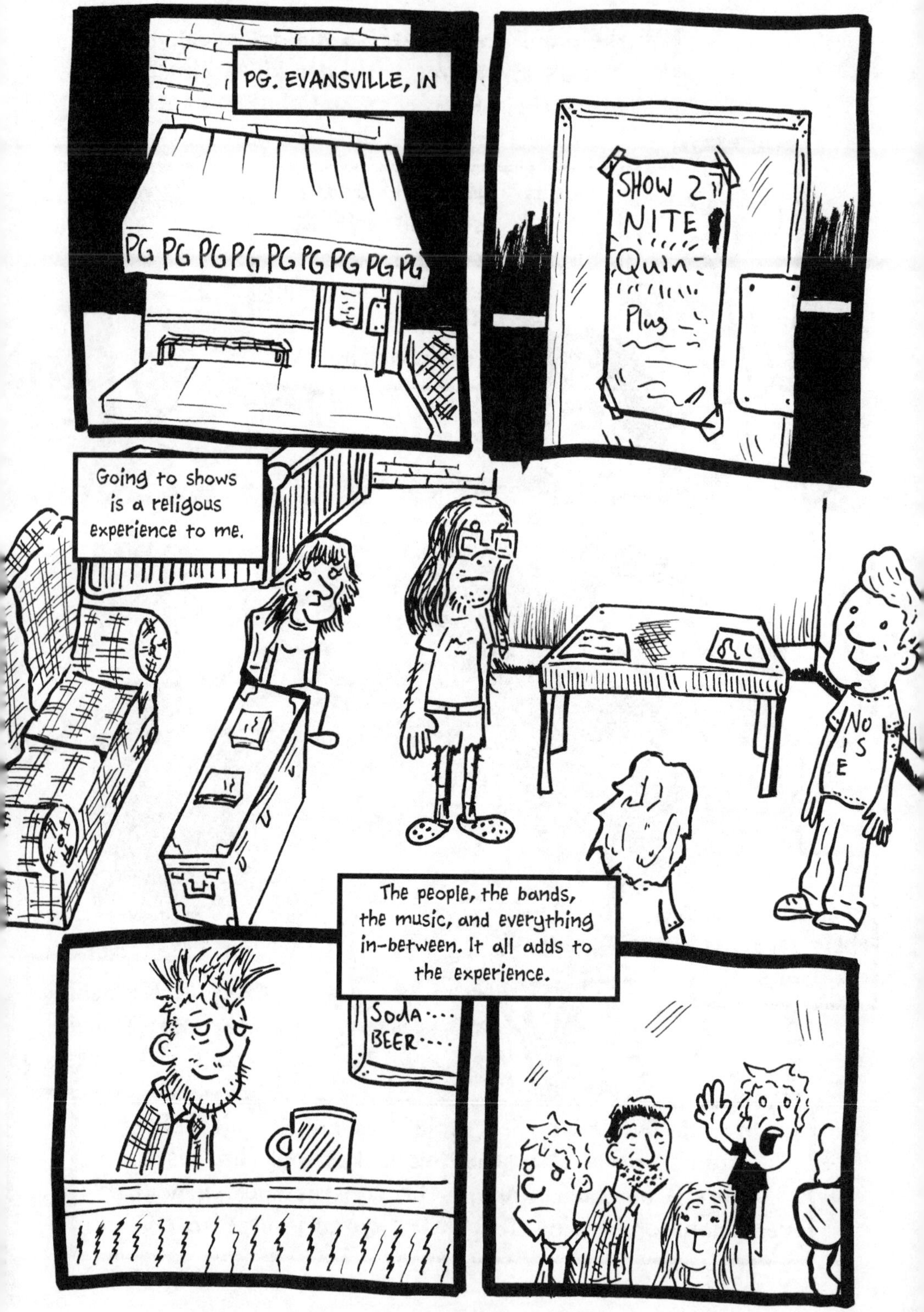
PG. EVANSVILLE, IN
PG PG PG PG PG PG PG PG PG
SHOW 2 NITE Quin Plug
Going to shows is a religous experience to me.
NOISE
The people, the bands, the music, and everything in-between. It all adds to the experience.
Soda....
BEER....

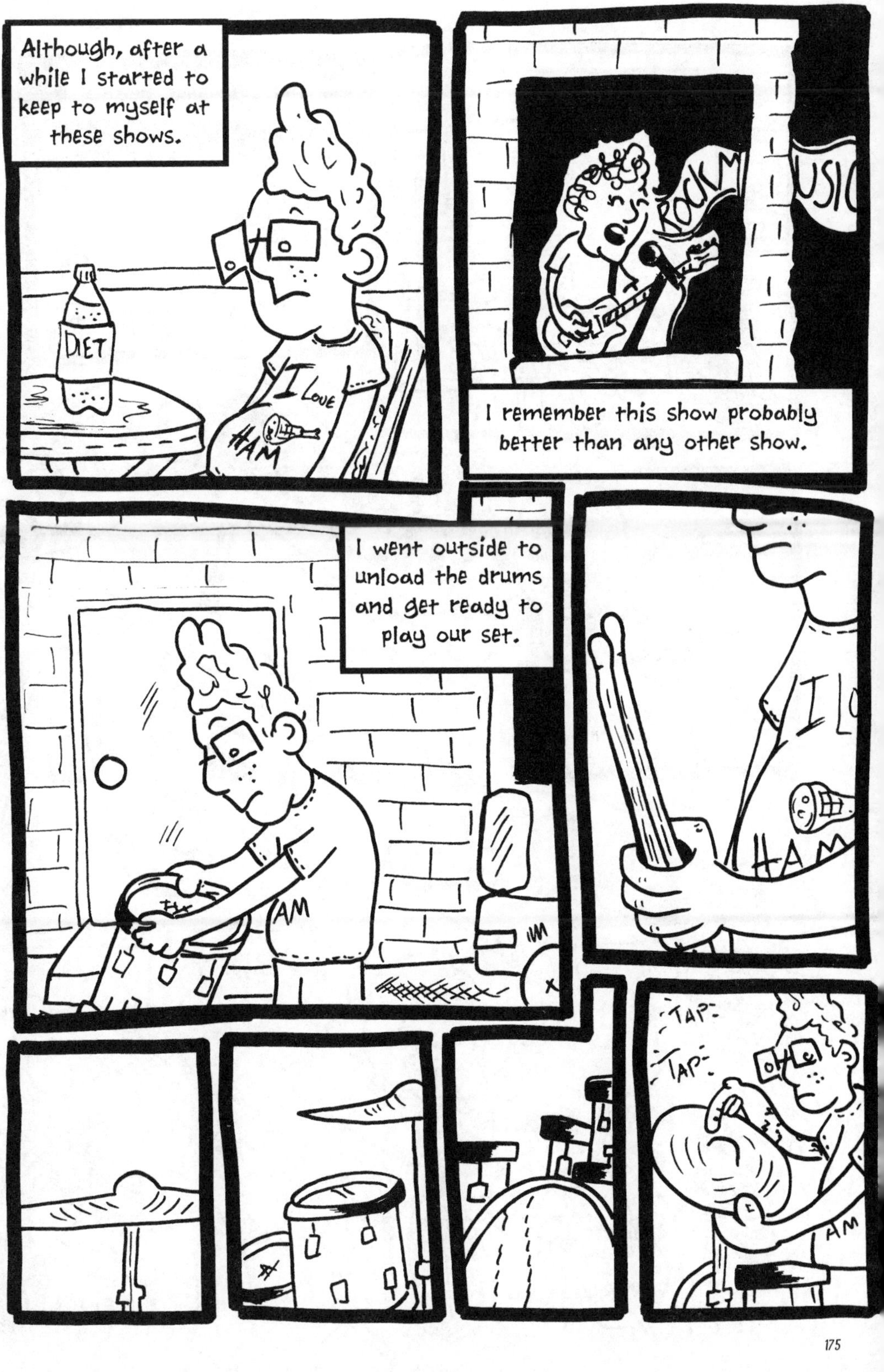

Although, after a while I started to keep to myself at these shows.
DIET
I LOVE HAM
ROCK M
USIC
I remember this show probably better than any other show.
I went outside to unload the drums and get ready to play our set.
AM
I LO
HAM
TAP
TAP
AM

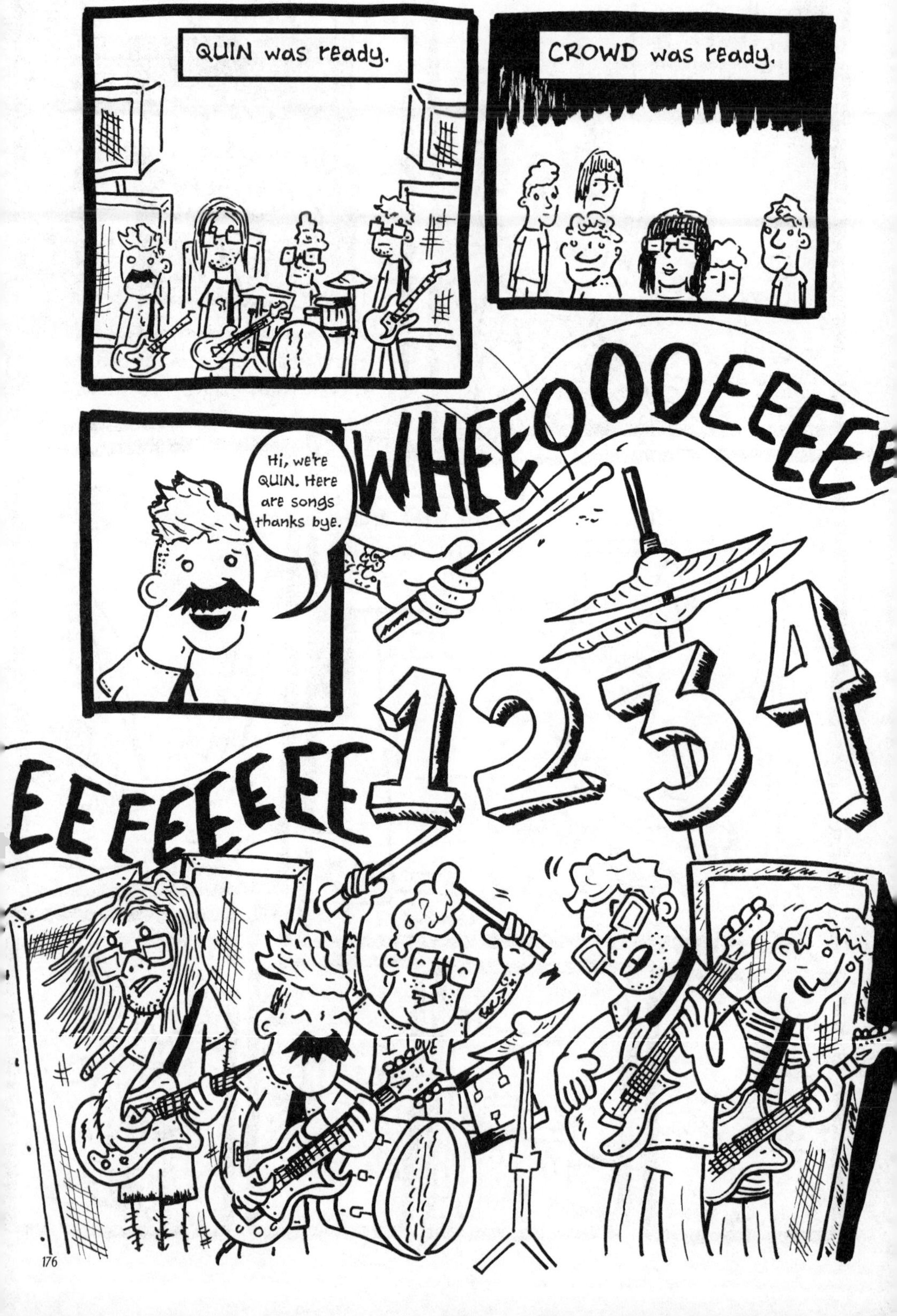
QUIN was ready.
CROWD was ready.
Hi, we're QUIN. Here are songs thanks bye.
WHEEOODEEEEE
EEEEEEEE
1234
I LOVE

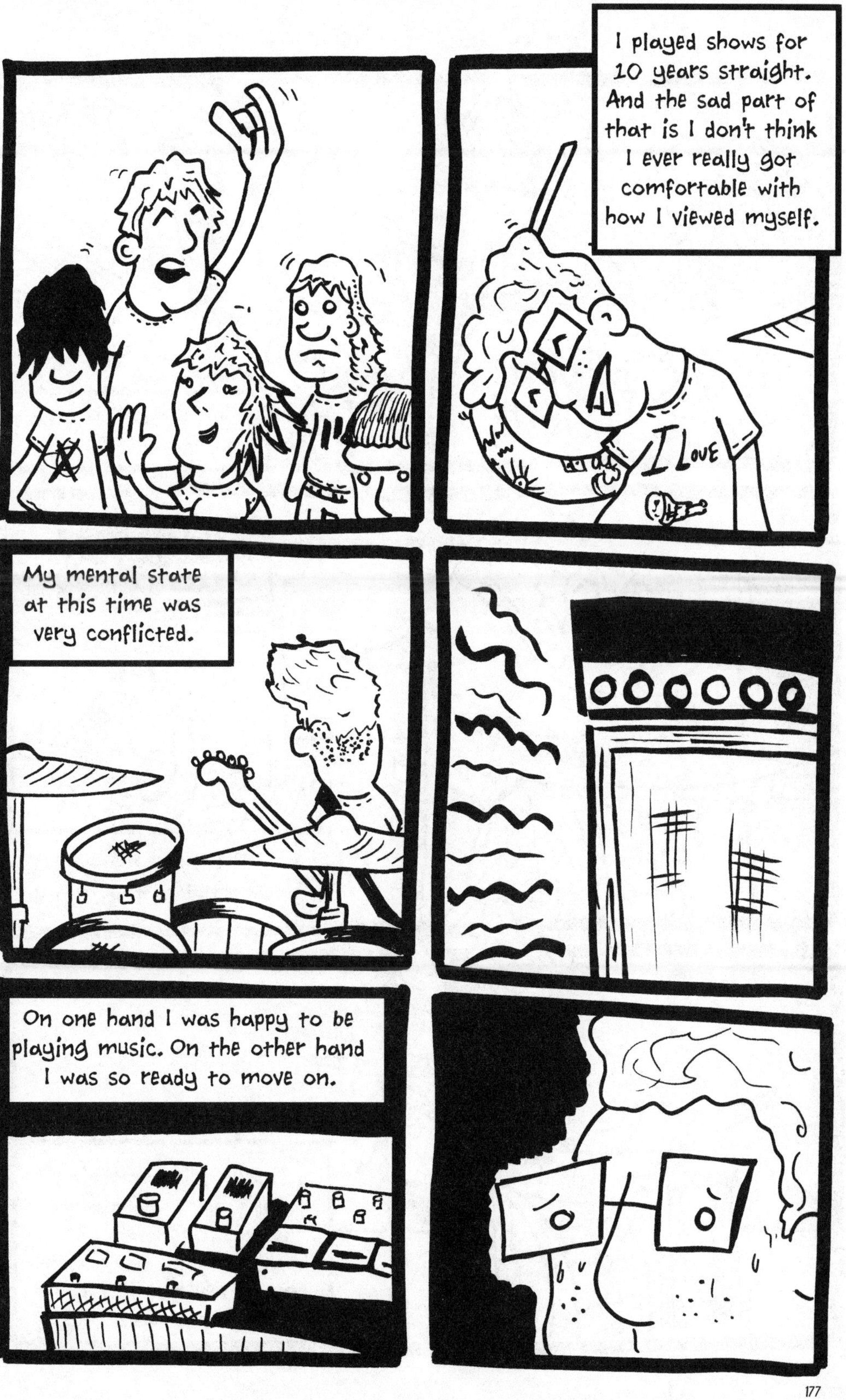
I played shows for 10 years straight. And the sad part of that is I don't think I ever really got comfortable with how I viewed myself.
I LOVE
My mental state at this time was very conflicted.
On one hand I was happy to be playing music. On the other hand I was so ready to move on.

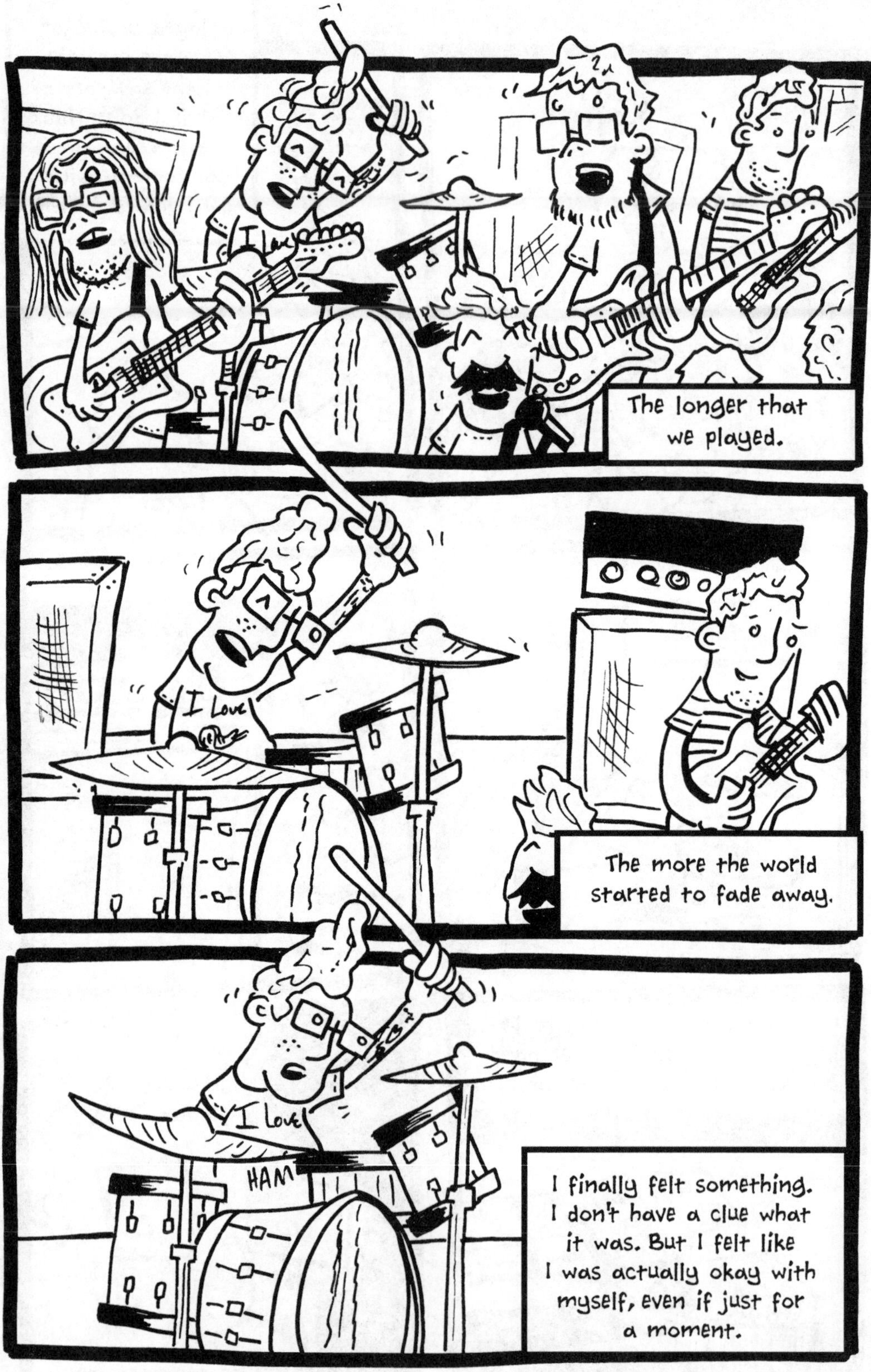
The longer that we played.
I Love
The more the world started to fade away.
I Love
HAM
I finally felt something. I don't have a clue what it was. But I felt like I was actually okay with myself, even if just for a moment.

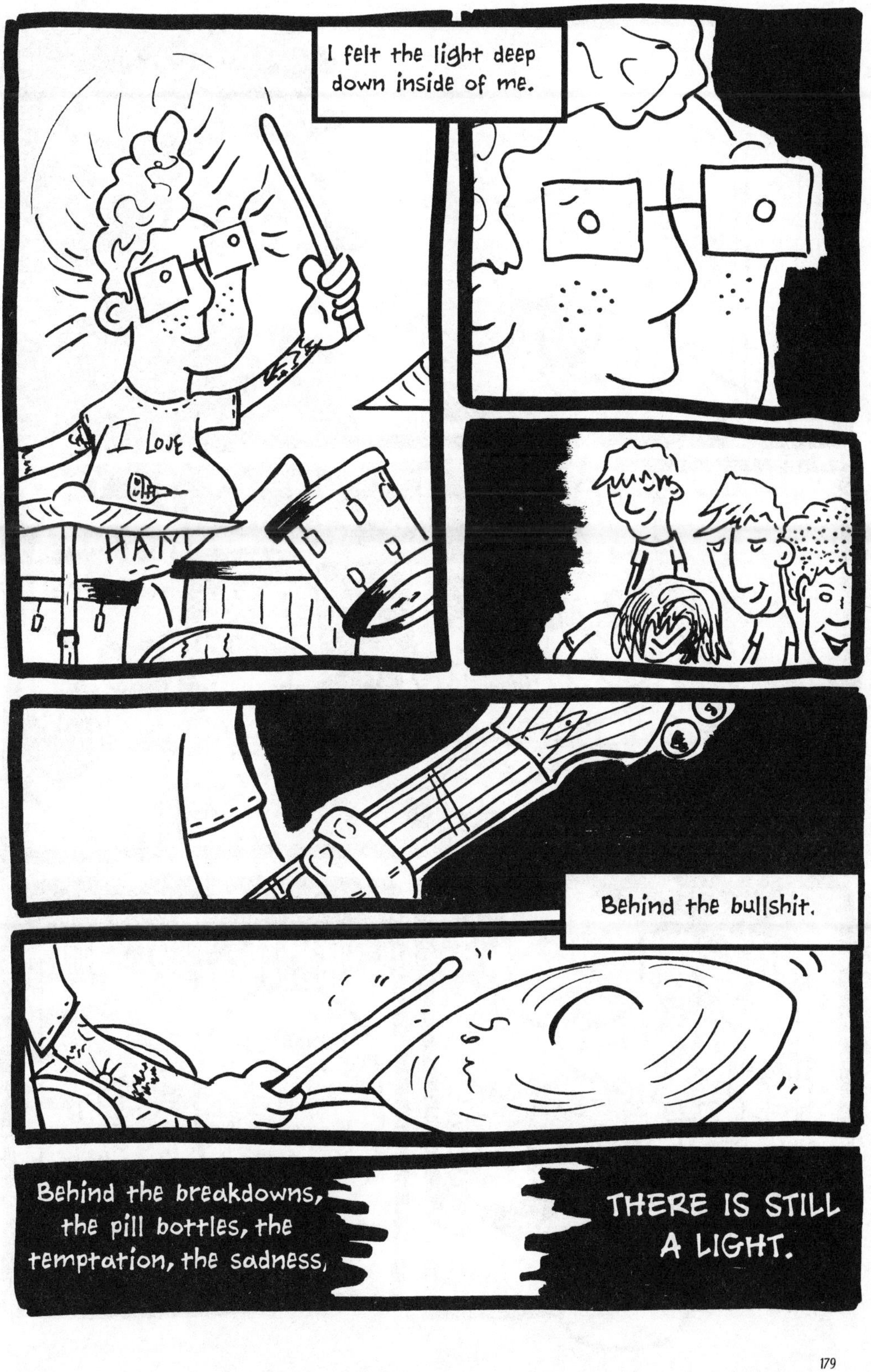
I felt the light deep down inside of me.
I LOVE
HAM
Behind the bullshit.
Behind the breakdowns, the pill bottles, the temptation, the sadness,
THERE IS STILL A LIGHT.

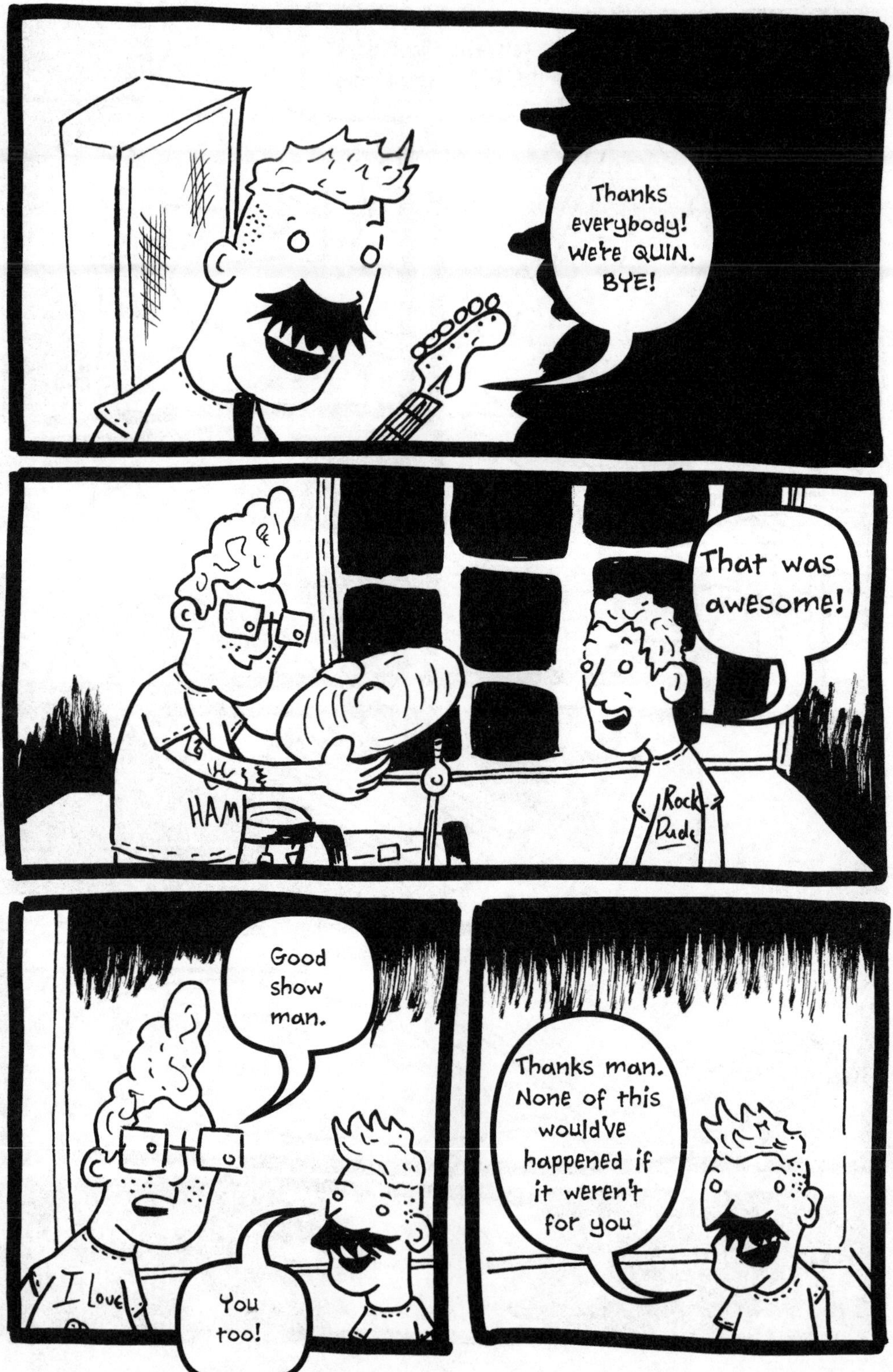
Thanks everybody! We're QUIN. BYE!
That was awesome!
HAM
Rock Dude
Good show man.
I Love
You too!
Thanks man. None of this would've happened if it weren't for you

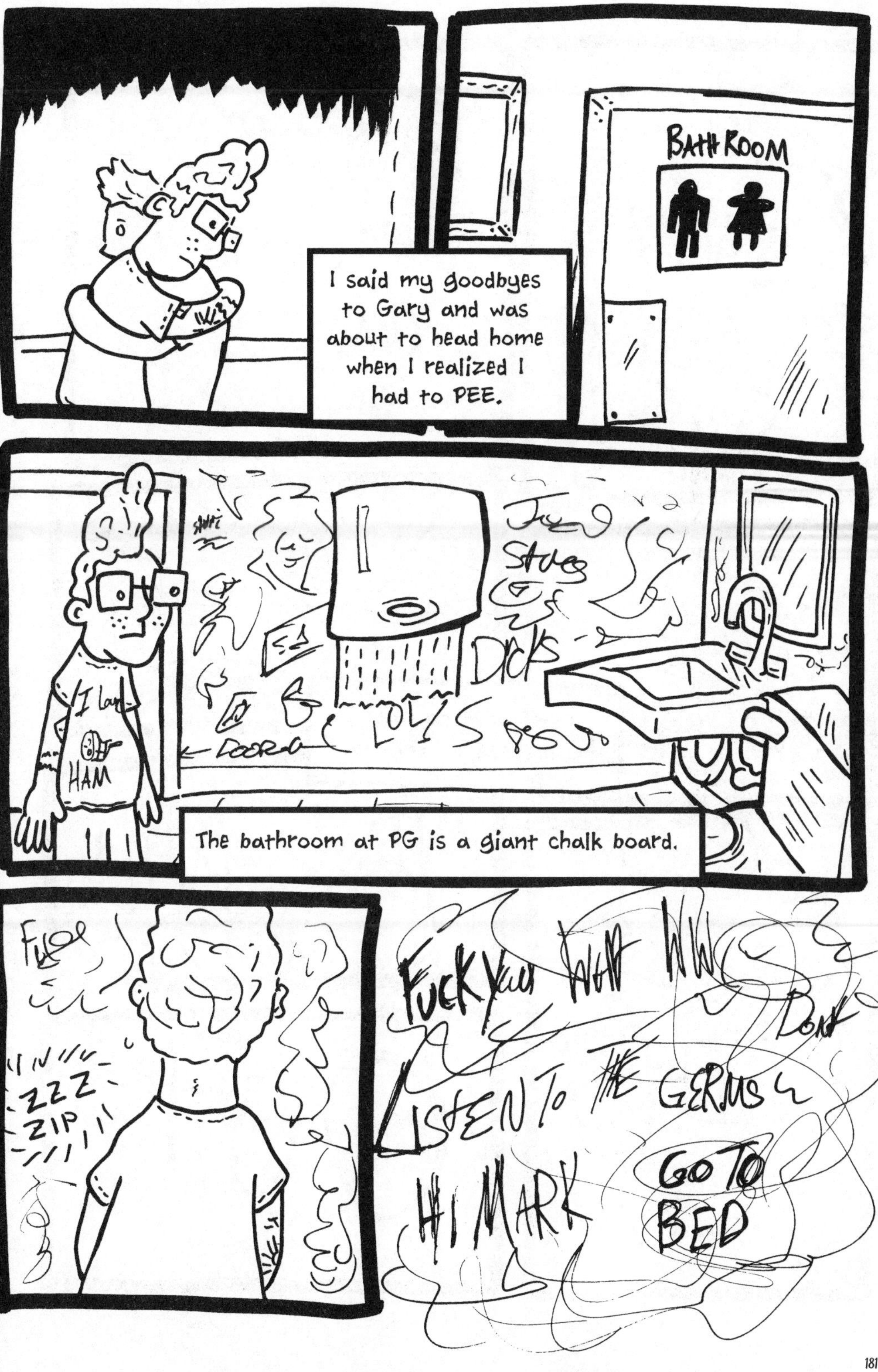
BATHROOM
I said my goodbyes to Gary and was about to head home when I realized I had to PEE.
DICKS
LOL
HAM
The bathroom at PG is a giant chalk board.
ZZZ ZIP
FUCK YOU
DON'T LISTEN TO THE GERMS
HI MARK
GO TO BED

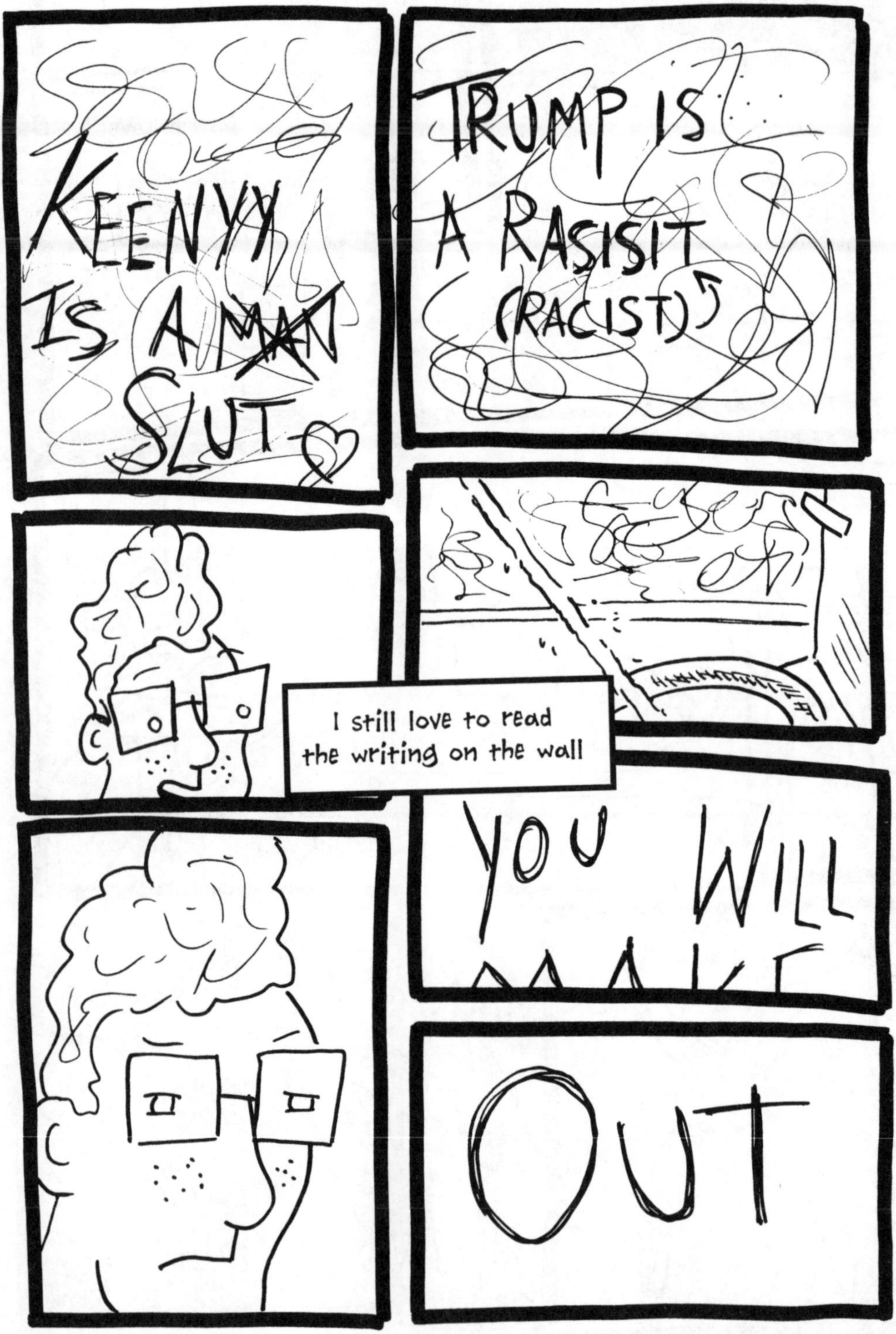
KEENYY
IS A MAN
SLUT
TRUMP IS
A RASISIT
(RACIST)
I still love to read
the writing on the wall
YOU WILL
OUT

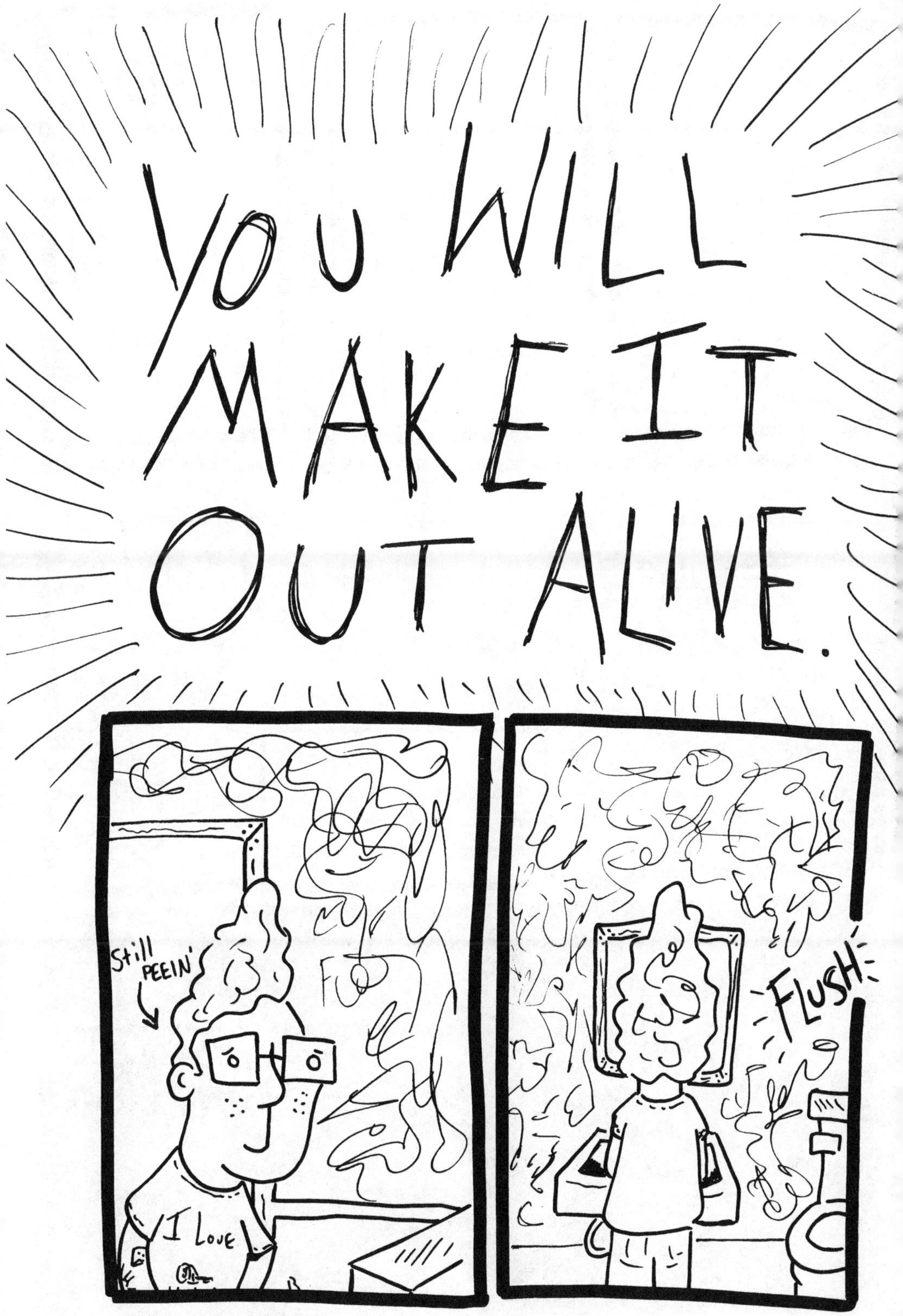
YOU WILL MAKE IT OUT ALIVE.
Still PEEIN'
I Love
FLUSH

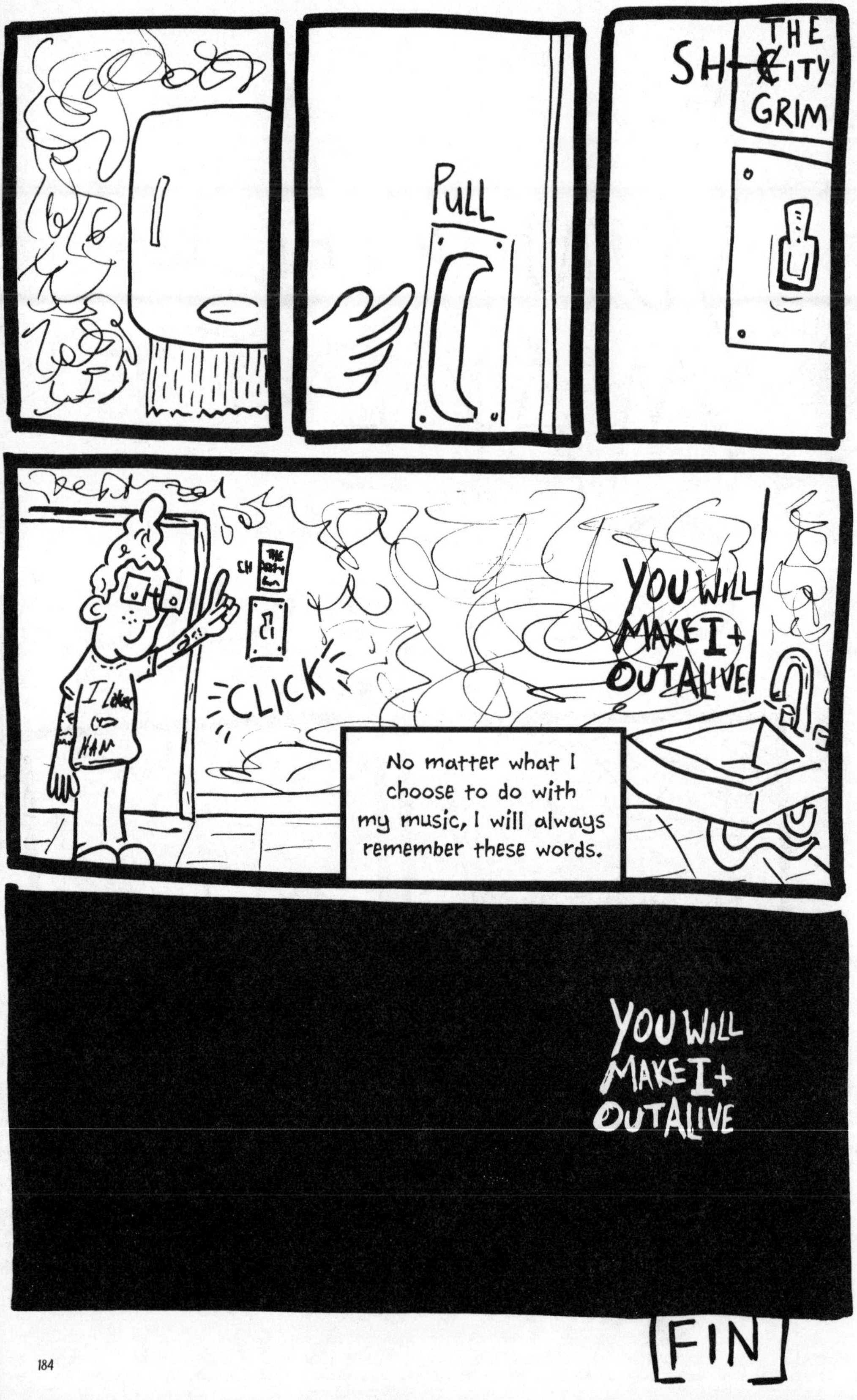
PULL
SH THE CITY GRIM
CLICK
YOU WILL MAKE IT OUT ALIVE
No matter what I choose to do with my music, I will always remember these words.
YOU WILL MAKE IT OUT ALIVE
FIN

Epilogue

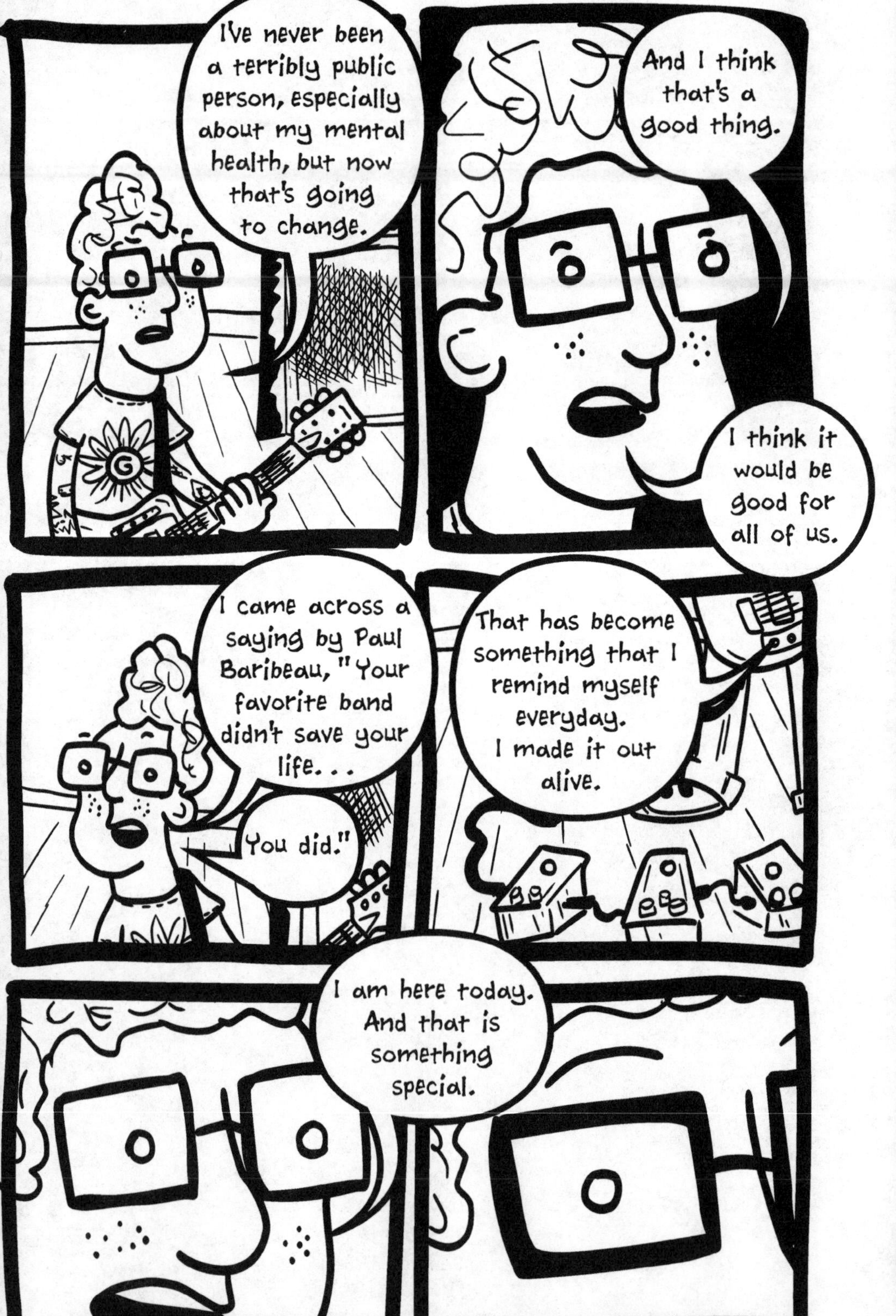
I've never been a terribly public person, especially about my mental health, but now that's going to change.
And I think that's a good thing.
I think it would be good for all of us.
I came across a saying by Paul Baribeau, "Your favorite band didn't save your life...
You did."
That has become something that I remind myself everyday. I made it out alive.
I am here today. And that is something special.

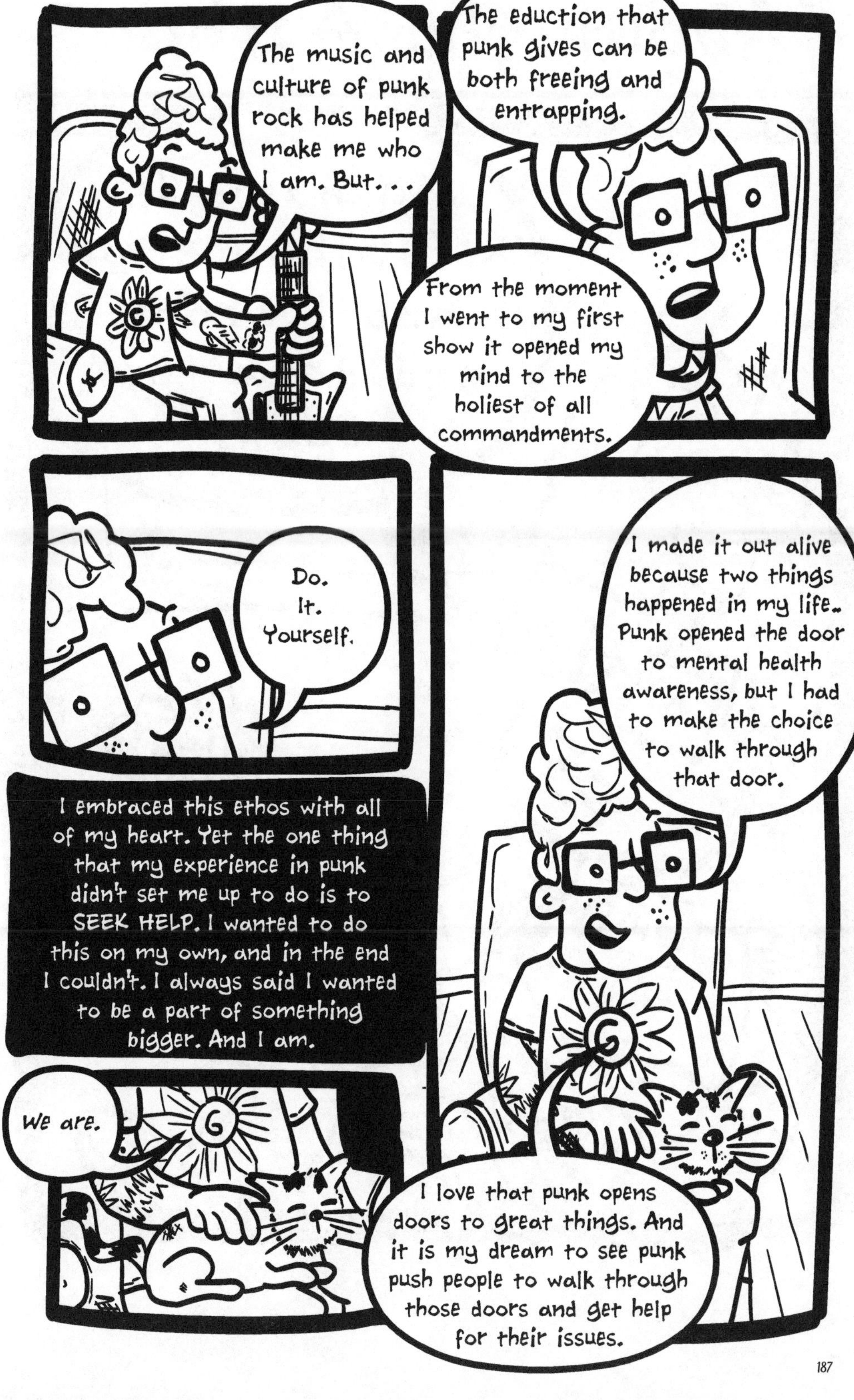
The music and culture of punk rock has helped make me who I am. But. . .
The eduction that punk gives can be both freeing and entrapping.
From the moment I went to my first show it opened my mind to the holiest of all commandments.
Do. It. Yourself.
I embraced this ethos with all of my heart. Yet the one thing that my experience in punk didn't set me up to do is to SEEK HELP. I wanted to do this on my own, and in the end I couldn't. I always said I wanted to be a part of something bigger. And I am.
We are.
I made it out alive because two things happened in my life. Punk opened the door to mental health awareness, but I had to make the choice to walk through that door.
I love that punk opens doors to great things. And it is my dream to see punk push people to walk through those doors and get help for their issues.

About the Author

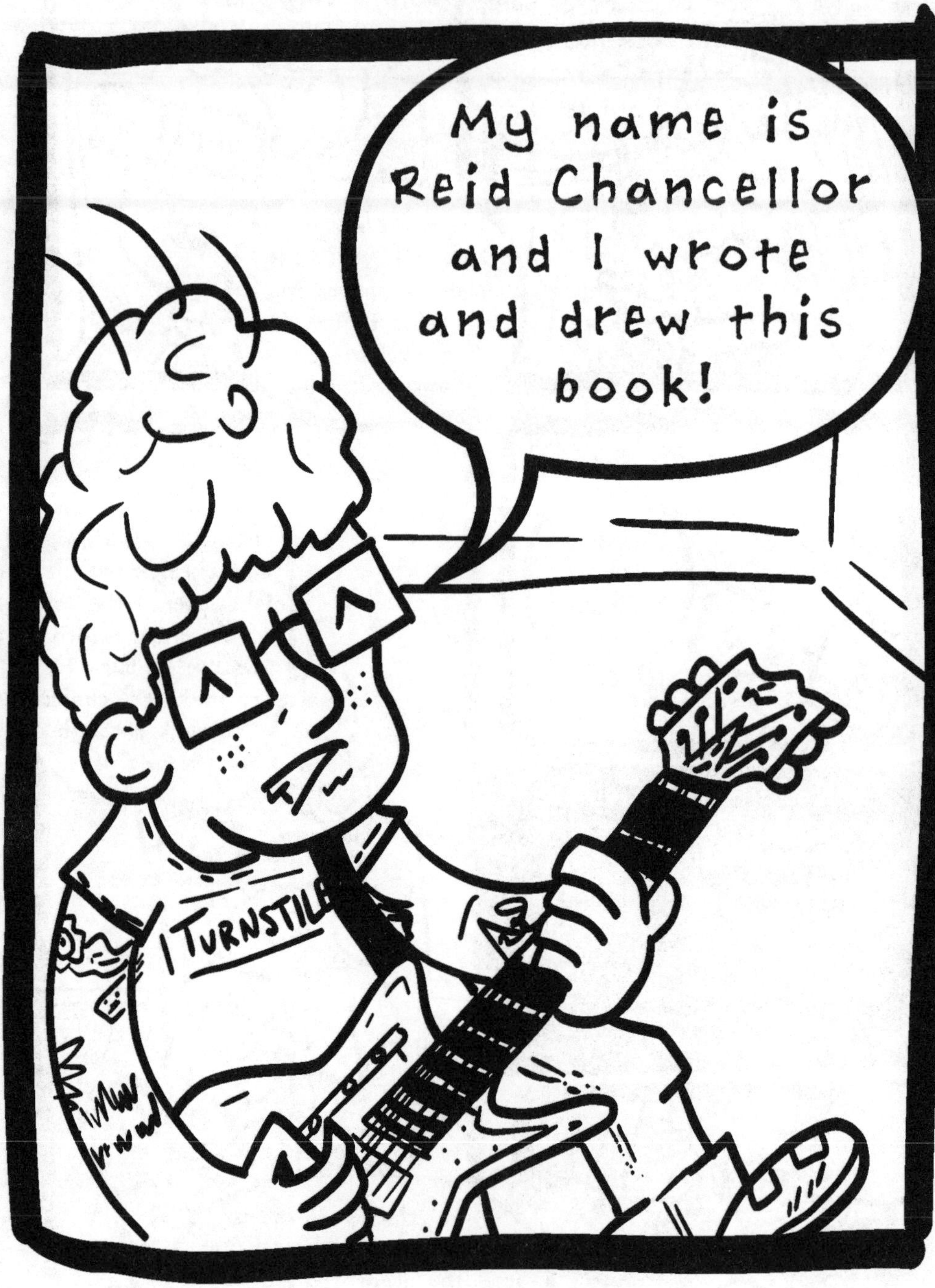
My name is Reid Chancellor and I wrote and drew this book!
TURNSTILE

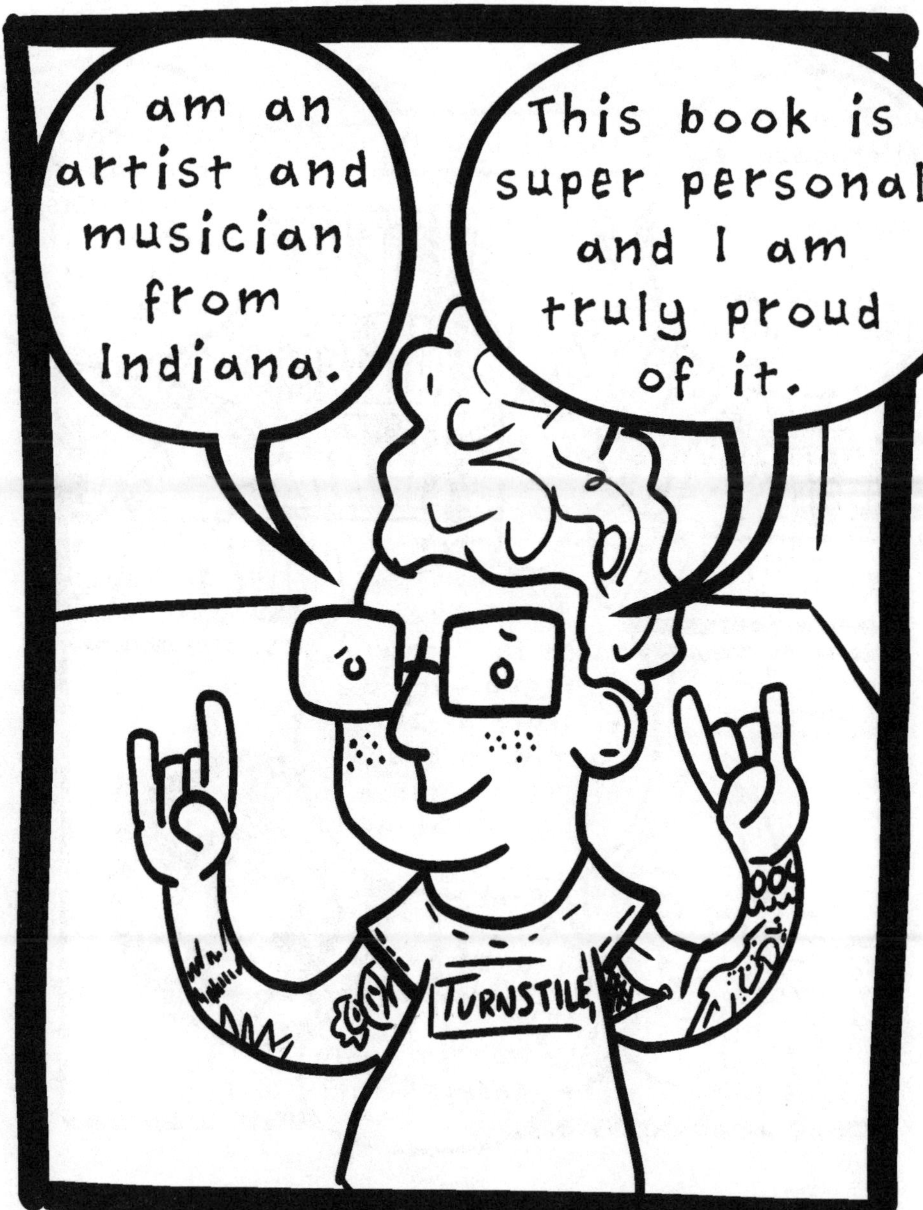
I am an artist and musician from Indiana.
This book is super personal and I am truly proud of it.
TURNSTILE

About the Publisher

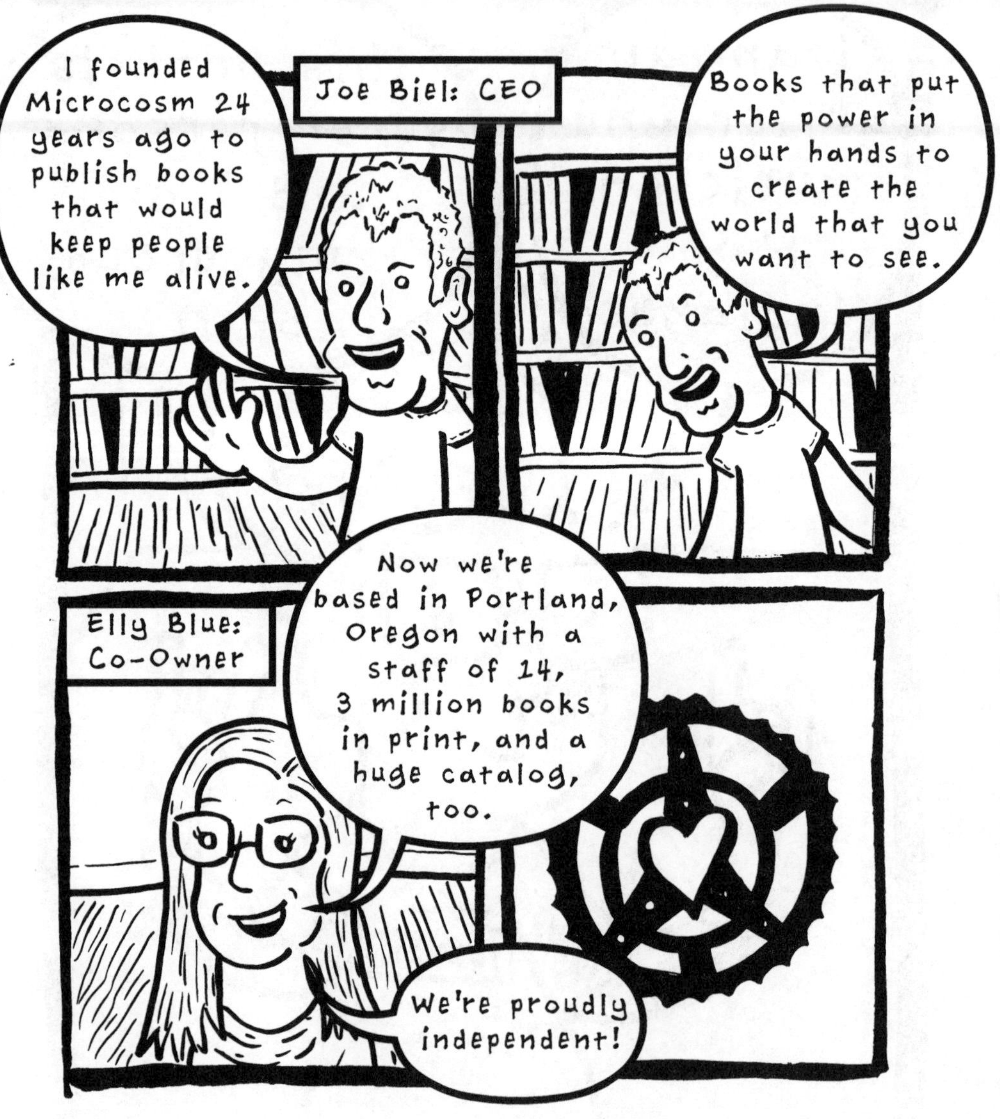
Joe Biel: CEO
I founded Microcosm 24 years ago to publish books that would keep people like me alive.
Books that put the power in your hands to create the world that you want to see.
Elly Blue: Co-Owner
Now we're based in Portland, Oregon with a staff of 14, 3 million books in print, and a huge catalog, too.
We're proudly independent!

MICROCOSM · PUBLISHING

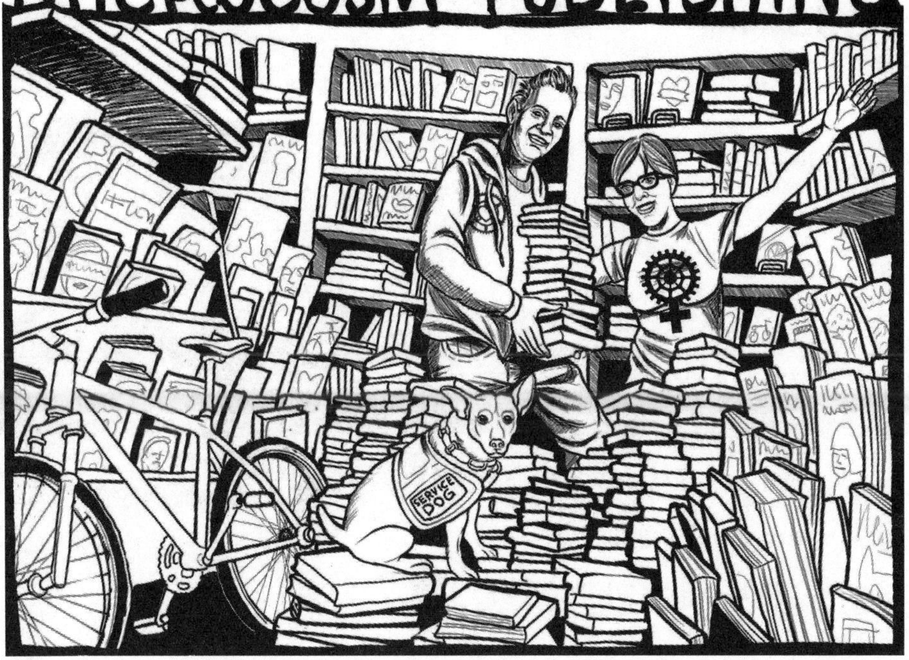
SERVICE DOG

Microcosm Publishing is Portland's most diversified publishing house and distributor with a focus on the colorful, authentic, and empowering. Our books and zines have put your power in your hands since 1996, equipping readers to make positive changes in your life and in the world around you. Microcosm emphasizes skill-building, showing hidden histories, and fostering creativity through challenging conventional publishing wisdom. What was once a distro and record label has become among the oldest independent publishing houses in Portland, OR. In a world that has inched to the right for 80 years, we are carving out a place in the center with DIY skills, food, bicycling, gender, self-care, and social justice.

SUBSCRIBE TO EVERYTHING WE PUBLISH!

Do you love what Microcosm publishes?

Do you want us to publish more great stuff?

Would you like to receive each new title as it's published?

Subscribe as a BFF to our new titles and we'll mail them all to you as they are released!

$13-30/mo, pay what you can afford!

microcosmpublishing.com/bff

...AND HELP US GROW YOUR SMALL WORLD!

...and check out our other fine works of comics journalism and tools to save your life: